The Creative Training Idea Book

Inspired Tips and Techniques
for Engaging and Effective Learning

The Creative Training Idea Book

Inspired Tips and Techniques for Engaging and Effective Learning

ROBERT W. LUCAS

Illustrated by Michael O'Hora

AMACOM

American Management Association

New York • Atlanta • Brussels • Buenos Aires • Chicago • London • Mexico City
San Francisco • Shanghai • Tokyo • Toronto • Washington, D. C.

Special discounts on bulk quantities of AMACOM books are available to corporations, professional associations, and other organizations. For details, contact Special Sales Department, AMACOM, a division of American Management Association, 1601 Broadway, New York, NY 10019.
Tel.: 212-903-8316. Fax: 212-903-8083.
Web site: www. amacombooks.org

This publication is designed to provide accurate and authoritative information in regard to the subject matter covered. It is sold with the understanding that the publisher is not engaged in rendering legal, accounting, or other professional service. If legal advice or other expert assistance is required, the services of a competent professional person should be sought.

Library of Congress Cataloging-in-Publication Data

Lucas, Robert W.
The creative training idea book : inspired tips and techniques for
engaging and effective learning / Robert W. Lucas.
p. cm.
Includes bibliographical references (p.   ) and index.
ISBN 0-8144-7465-9
   1. Employees—Training of.   2. Employee training personnel—Training
of.   3. Supervisors—Training of.   I. Title.

HF5549.5.T7 L755 2003
658.3'124—dc21   2002014950

Printing number
10 9 8 7 6 5 4 3 2 1

Acknowledgments

Dedication to training has been an intricate part of nearly two thirds of my life. During that time I have had some wonderful mentors and friends, have learned much, and have attempted to give back to the profession. This book is a compilation of many of the ideas gathered during my career. It is made possible through the generous conscious and unconscious contributions of many human resource development professionals and others who have worked on this project.

I am grateful to all the people whose training techniques I have imitated, modified, and added to my toolbox over the years. Specifically, I express my thanks to the following people for their contribution to my learning:

Mary Broad and Lenn Millbower—for taking the time to read this book and provide input

Jacquie Flynn—the editor for this book who has offered guidance and patience as we worked through the difficult processes related to titling the book, fine tuning content, and bringing the final product to fruition.

Sylvia Foy—who, as the Director of Training at the AAA National office in Orlando, Florida, gave me the support and coaching needed to succeed, the latitude to experiment and grow, the wisdom to accept me as I am, and the friendship that endures to this day

Janice Mehagher—a former editor from the American Management Association who worked to make this book project a reality

Leon Met—a mentor, former boss, friend, and all-around smart guy

Bob Pike—who, as an internationally known trainer and author, has helped set the tone for creative training throughout the industry and inspired thousands of trainers

Ed Scannell and John Newstrom—whose collective creative genius launched a concept of books on experiential training activities that has been imitated endlessly in today's market, but never exceeded. A special thanks to Ed for reviewing this book and providing thoughts

Steve Tanzer—a mentor, visionary, partner, and good friend who continues to offer wisdom and support in my writing ventures

Finally, and most importantly, I must thank my wonderful wife (MJ) and my mother (Rosie) for their love, support, and tolerance as I sifted through the mounds of research material and books, which have covered our dining room table for months. Also, my "brother" Dave, my son Mike, and daughter Brittney and their families for their subtle understanding as I spent excessive hours focused on such long-term projects as this book, often at their expense.

My only concession and hope is that each reader will extract valuable ideas from this book that will make them successful in sharing information and skills with many others, so that they too can grow and feel the intrinsic satisfaction of seeing a goal attained.

Contents

Preface

For almost three decades, I have been involved in training adults in many different environments. I started as a U.S. Marine Corps drill instructor in the early 1970s, with the approach that there was just one way to train. That way was autocratic, rigid, and left little room for individualism or creativity. Since then, I have come a long way in my thinking, just as many of you likely have since you started your training and presentation careers. Having worked in profit, not for profit, nonprofit, government, and volunteer organizations, and as a consultant to many major companies and organizations, I have been able to see and try many strategies for training adults. Some approaches have been more effective than others.

When I look back on the environment of the military classroom, I certainly understand the theory and reason behind what we did based on the need to train people to respond to orders unquestioningly. I also recognize the need NOT to try a similar approach with today's participants and in a business environment.

My awareness of the need to change and do things differently in the learning environment brings me to the purpose and intent of *The Creative Training Idea Book*. For many years, I have researched and practiced new and innovative techniques and strategies that can capture and hold participant attention while enhancing learning. I have come full circle since my days of military directives and lectures. Today, I attempt to incorporate a more open, participant-centric approach to learning. Through application of brain-based learning concepts, which employ a variety of elements such as color, sound, images, aromas, activity, and music, I strive to tap into various levels of brain activity. My purpose in doing so is to induce and expand learning and assist in retention of ideas, information, and concepts. In writing this book, I want to share the best practices that I have experienced and used.

The need for changing thinking about how adults learn and should be trained is necessary because the world of business is different today. Program attendees are better educated, more diverse, and more exposed to the world than they have ever been. They also have a lot of creative ideas to offer based on their personal observations and experiences. Failure to recognize these factors, and act on them appropriately when interacting with your learners in a training environment, can result in failure of programs and apathy among trainees and their supervisors.

Today, organizations have embraced the concept of learning organizations. Billions of dollars are being spent annually to qualify employees to compete better in a global market. Technology is readily available and being used in training at an escalating pace, with e-learning being the catch phrase for the early part of the twenty-first century. All of this requires the trainer, facilitator, and presenter of the new millennium to stretch his or her imagination and look for innovative ways to engage and challenge learners. This requires thinking "outside the box" when designing training programs and materials and pulling on knowledge that trainees already possess to make their learning experience much more fulfilling and FUN!

That's where *The Creative Training Idea Book* can help. By providing a comprehensive resource of research on learning, creative tips, techniques, and sources for obtaining innovative and inexpensive items to add pizzazz to any training program, I hope to spark your imagination. I also intend to provide you with a valuable tool for future reference in your efforts to create the best possible learning environment and experience for your audiences.

As I developed this book, every attempt was made to identify the originator of all referenced activities and content. Because trainers regularly modify and pass along information and activities, the origins of some material may not have been possible to ascertain. For material included that was not properly credited, I apologize and thank you for your creativity in developing it. If you contact me, we will make appropriate corrections in future editions.

Enjoy reading *The Creative Training Idea Book*; if you have questions or additional tips and ideas you would like to share, please contact me at:

Creative Presentation Resources, Inc.
P.O. Box 180487
Casselberry, FL 32718-0487
EMAIL: blucas@presentationresources.net
(407)695-5535
www.presentationresources.net

Happy Training!

Bob Lucas

Bob Lucas

The Creative Training Idea Book

Inspired Tips and Techniques
for Engaging and Effective Learning

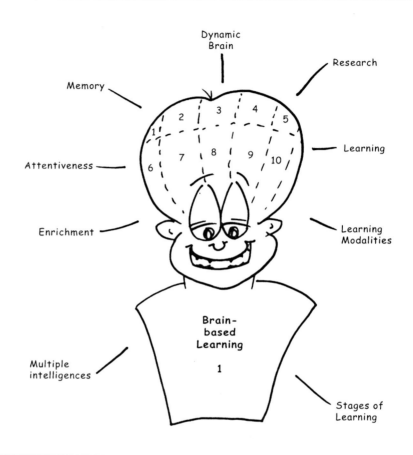

Brain-Based Learning

The human brain: a spring board from which we can leap into the magical world of genius."
Dilip Makurjea
Superbrain

Learning Objectives

At the end of this chapter, and when applying the concepts covered, you will be able to:

- Describe the theory of brain-based learning and how it impacts the training experience.

- Use knowledge of brain functioning to design programs and environments that will stimulate participants.

- Apply recent brain research findings to your training programs to enhance learning.

- Recognize the elements of learning.

- Create training programs focused on multiple levels of intelligence and the different learning styles possessed by participants.

- Assist learner retention of information by developing program content and delivery methodologies to reinforce memory.

Brain-based or brain-compatible learning theory focuses on concepts that create an opportunity in which attainment and retention of information are maximized. These concepts incorporate the latest research on the brain and encourage application of findings to training and educational learning environments. In this chapter you will explore how the brain functions in an effort to better recognize ways to develop creative approaches to training adults and to use props, activities, and incentives offered throughout the rest of the book.

A key to the successful application of brain-based learning theory precepts is for everyone involved in the learning process (program designers, managers, trainers/educators, and learners) first to understand the structure of the brain and how it works. They must then identify personal strengths and areas for improvement related to the theoretical concepts and modify approaches to learning accordingly. They must also consciously focus on learner needs and learning styles to ensure that program format and delivery are effective.

According to brain-based theory, learning is an active process in which challenges, ambiguity, and situations encouraging creativity are presented through use of accelerated learning strategies such as those covered in this book. Everything from the environment to personal actions impacts learners. Participants are prompted to think outside the box when examining information and issues. Problem-solving, questioning, ongoing interaction, and feedback are important elements in the absorption process, and are used freely. Learners are also provided with many opportunities to make associations with knowledge and skills that they already possess while forming new thinking patterns and making additional connections. These connections are strengthened by the use of analogies, simulations, metaphors, jokes, stories, examples, and various interactive techniques.

In brain-based learning environments, materials and instruction must be learner centered and delivered in a manner that is fun, meaningful, and personally enriching. It must also provide opportunities for participants to have time to process what they experience so that they can make mental connections and master content. In doing so, learners can increase personal comprehension and better grasp meaning and potential opportunities for application.

To ensure you are adequately addressing true participant needs when creating program content, take the time to do an advance assessment of what participants already know related to your intended session topic(s). You can accomplish this by mailing a questionnaire to participants and their supervisors a couple of weeks before the scheduled training. You can also conduct face-to-face or telephone interviews, hold focus groups involving those who will be attending and/or their supervisors, or visit work sites to observe on-the-job behavior of participants related to the program topic. Take the information gained into account as you design program content.

If advance assessment is not possible, write closed-ended questions regarding program content on flip chart paper and post these on the training room wall. Have participants respond to the questions as they enter the room. You can also pass out 3 × 5 cards or blank paper and have them respond to questions that are either collected or discussed in small groups and then offered to the entire class. These techniques and more are discussed in greater detail in later chapters of this book.

> ### BRIGHT IDEA
> ## Facilitator Preparation
> To understand and apply **concepts** of brain-based learning to training and education programs **effectively,** you must be aware of what research has found and how it impacts learning. **Explore** brain-based or brain-compatible learning on the Internet. Also, attend **conferences** and workshops and read books and articles on the topic, such as those **listed** in the Resources for Trainers section in the appendices.

● THE DYNAMIC BRAIN

Although it is impossible to condense everything that scientists and researchers know about the human brain and learning into a single chapter, several important concepts pertinent to understanding the brain, learning, and memory are highlighted in these pages.

Recent decades have brought forth an exciting era of neuroscientific (life science that deals with anatomy, physiology, and biology of nerves related to behavior and learning) and cognitive research (related to factual data and knowledge) into the composition of the brain and how it functions. This brain-based or brain-compatible learning research has uncovered a wealth of insight into how the human brain develops, thinks, learns, and retains information. From the research, we have learned much about the physiological structure of the brain, what impacts brain development, and ways that learner motivation can be influenced. Researchers regularly explore the role of such factors as gender, age, body rhythms, emotions, and environment in shaping our reactions to stimuli and thinking.

Research also indicates that the human brain is a wonderfully complex organ that continues to grow, evolve, and learn as a person ages. "Perhaps the most potent feature of the brain is the

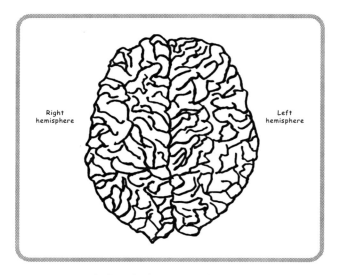

FIGURE 1-1. Brain hemispheres (cerebrum)

capacity to function on many levels and in many ways simultaneously. Thoughts, emotions, imagination, predisposition, and physiology operate concurrently and interactively as the entire system interact with and exchanges information with its environment."[1] The exciting part, related to research findings, is that trainers and educators have an ongoing opportunity to influence that growth in learners.

The brain is composed of three major structures: the cerebrum, the cerebellum, and the brain stem. The largest part of the human brain **(cerebrum)** is covered and protected by a thin layer called the cerebral **cortex** or **neocortex**. This thin layer of nerve cells constitutes about 70 percent of the nervous system and serves to gather and decipher patterns received into the brain by identifying relationships between objects, data, and other stimuli. Further, the **cerebrum** is divided into a left and a right hemisphere (see **Figure 1-1**) and made up of four areas called **lobes—frontal, temporal, parietal,** and **occipital** (see **Figure 1-2**). Each lobe is responsible for a different function.

The **frontal lobe** is located around the forehead and is responsible for such things as problem-solving, creative thinking, planning and organizing, judgment, and will power. The **temporal lobes** are located on both the left and right sides of the head. They are tasked with such functions as processing sounds, language meaning, and some memory. The **parietal lobe** is found on the top rear area of the brain and receives and processes higher sensory data received, as well as assists in processing language input. The **occipital lobe** is located in the back middle section of the brain and has primary responsibility for vision. Some scientists believe that there is also a fifth area imbedded in the midbrain called the **limbic system.** The limbic system includes the **thalamus, hypothalamus, hippocampus,** and **amygdala** (see **Figure 1-3**). It accounts for 20 percent of brain volume. Scientists believe that this area is responsible for, among other things, body regulation, emotions, attention, sleep, hormone production, sexuality, and smell.

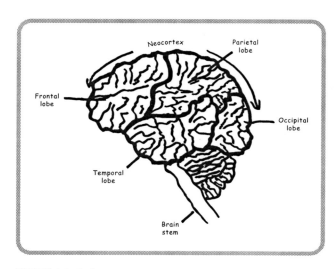

FIGURE 1-2. Lobes

Because of the brain's ability to multi-task or process many pieces of stimuli simultaneously on different levels, you should remember that using a traditional structured or linear approach to training can be a learning disaster. "Even though it seems that we think sequentially—one thought after another—this illusion is far from the reality of our brain's true operating system. Biologically, physically, intellectually, and emotionally, we are doing many things at the same time. In fact, the brain cannot do less than multi-process![2]" Applying a delivery strategy that involves a step-by-step presentation of ideas or concepts can lead to learners becoming disengaged, bored, and seeing the time spent in the session as wasted. This latter reaction can lead to lost support for future training from participants and their managers.

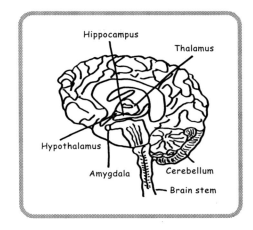

FIGURE 1-3. Limbic system

Because of the brain's complex nature, presenting information through a variety of activities, mediums, and senses increases the likelihood of comprehension and action by learners. As an example of the success of such a multipronged approach to training, consider how learning takes place in children. They are down in the dirt exploring, playing, and using their hands, eyes, and minds to absorb information through various modalities. They play with toys, actual items, and in the absence of these, create their own tools for learning creativity (e.g., toy swords, guns, and cars made from sticks and various other materials for boys and dresses, shoes, and dolls made from cloth, boxes, or stuffed cushioned material for girls). Similarly, adults can rekindle this learning excitement and metamorphic experience if you provide a learning environment focused on multiple levels of the brain, and that sparks excitement, adventure, challenge, and fun.

PUTTING YOUR BRAIN TO WORK: ACTIVITY

Think of the types of programs that you conduct. In what ways are you currently addressing the brain-based needs of your participants? What else could you do based on what you read in the preceding?

_____

_____

_____

_____

_____

Table 1-1. Quick Brain Facts

Based on research, scientists have found the following about the average human brain:

Contains approximately 100 billion neurons or nerve cells.

Average width is 140 mm.

Average length is 167 mm.

Average height is 93 mm.

Average weight is approxmately 3 pounds.

Covered by a thin layer of nerve cells called the cortex or neocortex.

Continues to grow and evolve in various ways throughout a person's life.

Made up of four lobes:
Frontal focuses on processes such as decision-making, creativity, judgment, and planning.
Temporal focuses on functions such as hearing, language, memory, and sensory associations.
Parietal focuses on functions related to short-term memory, language usage, and higher sensory processes.
Occipital focuses on receipt and processing of visual input.

Possibly has a fifth area called the *limbic system* imbedded in the midbrain that controls functions such as sleep, attention, body regulation, smell, hormone production, and sexuality. Has two hemispheres:
Left: focuses on analytical functions.
Right: addresses abstract, ambiguous, and creative functions.

BRIGHT IDEA

Expanding Learner Horizons

To involve learners actively, and to tie into concepts of broadbased research, take participants on a learning excursion to a local mall to allow them to become immersed in their own discovery. Depending on your program topic, assign tasks such as observing, gathering information, creating a journal, or interviewing or surveying people they encounter. Follow observations with discussions, reports, and/or formal classroom presentations to challenge various parts of the brain, and to address a variety of learning modalities. For technical courses, have participants visit local companies, manufacturers, or technical institutes for on-site observation, research, or information gathering. When possible, allow them to touch and use actual equipment or simulators.

Excursions can lend an aire of reality because participants can begin to relate real-world experiences and information to classroom learning.

● NEW PERSPECTIVES FROM BRAIN RESEARCH

Only recently have scientists made great inroads into understanding the human brain. Over the centuries, bits and pieces of information have surfaced; yet there is much more to discover. For example, in the 1950s Dr. Paul MacLean, of the Laboratory for Brain Evolution and Behavior at the National Institute for Mental Health in the United States, proposed the Triune Brain Theory. . . According to McLean's findings ". . . the human brain is, in reality, three brains, each superimposed over the earlier in a pattern of brains within brains."[3] Survival learning is located in the lower brain, emotional learning in the midbrain region, and higher order thinking and learning in the upper brain. According to MacLean's research, the human brain has continued to evolve over millions of years.

At the close of the twentieth century scientists were learning much more about the human brain. Many people therefore refer to the 1990s as the "decade of the brain" because so much was discovered about brain functioning and learning during that period. The biggest lesson learned from research is that we really do not yet know all the facts about the human brain and how it processes information. Scientists have certainly, made tremendous strides in expanding knowledge on how the brain is structured, its capabilities, and how it works; however, they do not have all the answers. One reason is that they have learned that the human brain continues to grow and evolve into adulthood.

That belief was not held prior to the 1970s. At that time, simplistic theories related to such aspects as left and right brain functioning (discovered by Nobel Laureate Dr. Roger Sperry in 1968) were often taken out of context and used to answer many questions related to training and learning (see **Table 1-2**). Even though what we know about left and right brain capacity is still valid, we have learned that many other factors impact learning.

People are essentially "whole-brained," with each hemisphere interacting and processing information. Although each person has a preference related to which hemisphere is activated by certain stimuli, learning is not restricted to only one side of the brain. Both hemispheres work in tandem. For example, a musician uses the right side of his or her brain to create or visualize music played on an instrument (whole concept), and the left side to follow the sequence of notes and to determine what movements are needed to create a pattern in a song (specific parts). Thus, the whole brain coordinates activities necessary to recall and play a musical piece.

Much of what scientists are currently finding is attributable to major advances in technology. Brain scanning mehtods such as magnetic resonance imaging (MRI) and position emission tomography (PET) literally open the brain's functions for visual observation. With such instruments, electrical and radio waves can be used to track and record activity as the brain observes; recalls or stores information; reacts to smells, sounds, and visual stimuli; or reacts to emotional input. Pictures can be taken as a person's brain reacts to stimuli and the brain "fires" or shows activity in different areas. Such observations help better determine the types of functions that occur in various

Table 1-2. Typical Left and Right Brain Functioning

Left Brain (Sequential [parts] processing)	Right Brain (Random [whole] processing)
Analytical	Intuitive
Verbal/language	Visualizes
Logical	Spatial
Sequential/linear processing	Spontaneous
Temporal	Holistic (learns whole/then parts)
Mathematical functions	Nonverbal processes
Prefers structure/predictability	External focus
Internal focus	Prefers to see/experience
Reasoning	Dreams
Judgments	Sees similarities
Deals with one thing at a time	Integrates multiple inputs

parts of the brain. They also offer insights for trainers and educators into better strategies to help provide information and reinforce assimilation in the brain.

The mind is not a vessel to be filled but a fire to be ignited.
—*Plutarch*
Greek biographer and essayist

PUTTING YOUR BRAIN TO WORK: ACTIVITY

What are some things you have heard about how brain functioning impacts training? _____

_____

How have you applied, or seen, brain-based concepts applied in training programs? _____

_____

In the instances in which you have seen or experienced brain-based concepts, what were the results?

_____

_____

Table 1-3. Top 10 Ways to Turn on Your SUPERBRAIN

Throughout this book you will read about the brain and its functioning, as well as its impact on learning. The following models summarizes and expands many concepts about the brain. It was written by Mark Conyers of Brainsmart in Winter Park, Florida. He studies and educates on the brain and how learning occurs.

Seeing is believing and learning. Ninety percent of learning is visual. Our eyes register 36,000 visual impressions per hour. Eighty-five percent of the brain is wired for visual processing. The retina accounts for 40% of all nerves connected to the brain. Color and movement boost learning.

Unconscious learning is 99% of the process. At any one time, we focus on seven to nine bits of information consciously. Only 1% of brain cells do conscious processing. Nonverbal cues and positive suggestion are critical to success. Eighty-two percent of classroom communication is nonverbal.

Preferred learning styles include visual, auditory, and kinesthetic modes. There are at least eight intelligences: verbal linguistic, interpersonal, intrapersonal, mathematical–logical, musical–rhythmic, spatial, bodily kinesthetic, and naturalist. The new question is not how smart I am, but how am I smart?

Emotional states bind learning. Peak learning happens in peak states when the brain is in high challenge and low stress. During stress/threat, blood can move away from frontal lobes, thereby reducing the ability to think clearly or recall information.

Rhythm. Music allows us to encode information effortlessly. The brain naturally works in 90-minute cycles. Brain Gym can balance the brain. Listening to Mozart may boost memory and thinking. Music at 60 beats per minute may maximize retention.

Brain sex. The male brain is great at hunting (video games, throwing things at other things), and tight focus. The female brain is great for seeing, listening, memorizing, reading, nonverbal cues, and articulating emotion. Build on strengths. Viva la difference!

Recall. The brain is able to retain the equivalent of 500 *Encyclopedia Britannica*. Recall is best achieved when it is accessed in the state that it was stored; when multiple search engines are used, when knowledge is organized as a pattern, SUPERBRAIN; and when it is embedded in context. Also, information must be meaningful, and meaning is in the mind of the learner. The first, last, and most outstanding items are remembered most often.

Novelty, curiosity, and relevance to immediate survival boost attention. Notice how talk shows and news headlines exploit these techniques. Use movement and stand in different locations to boost attention in the classroom. Add relevant spin to your material to hook and keep attention. Leave plenty of time for reflection and integration of new material.

Imagination is more important than intelligence, as Albert Einstein suggested. Visualizing success, as well as writing down goals, are critical steps. The 3% of Yale students who had clear written goals had, 20 years later, 97% of the wealth. Optimism is primarily a left-brain activity. Depression is primarily a right-brain activity.

Nutrition is crucial to effective learning. The brain's super fuel is oxygen. Its next most important need is water; dehydration lowers learner performance. Protein helps boost memory and attention. Carbohydrates tend to promote release of the relaxant serotonin (hence drowsiness after lunch). Fruit is an excellent source of energy that requires minimal digestion. The brain needs high-quality omega 3 and omega 6 essential fatty acids.

Reprinted With Permission. Conyers, M., http//www.brainsmart.com/superbr.html

Focusing on the Brain

Because of the coordinated activity within different regions of the brain, learning can be enhanced through a multilevel approach to training. To do this ensure that programs, support materials, and environments offer adequate stimulation. Incorporate a variety of auditory and visual aids (e.g., handouts with colored covers, graphics and bullet points, background music at 60 beats per minute played during certain activities, and inspirational quotes or posters tied to program content in a variety of colors posted on walls). Also, allow learners many opportunities to discuss and process information individually and in small groups.

● HOW LEARNING OCCURS

The term **learning** is often misused when related to the training of adults and the education of children. True adult learning environments focus on the participant and not the facilitator. After all, it is the learner whose behavior, knowledge, skills, or attitude is expected to change. This is often a major difference in the approach used by teachers and trainers in helping participants to learn. Educators often function as change agents who present information to students in an attempt to create a basis for future learning, as children have limited experience or knowledge and have not developed systems to learn. On the other hand, adults have many experiences from which they can draw ideas, information, and knowledge that builds on whatever they are currently experiencing in a learning environment. Assuming that someone has no learning disorder or disability, learning, and the speed at which someone learns, is impacted primarily by four important factors: an individual's age, prior experience, motivation to learn, and intelligence.

Neuroscientists who study anatomy, chemistry, physiology, and molecular biology of the nervous system continue to make amazing discoveries about the brain and how it learns. For example, they have found that proper development of a child's brain depends on continuous interaction with elements of the external environment. Similarly, adult attention, learning, knowledge, skill development, and memory are impacted significantly by the learning environment. This is why so much attention is necessary when you create your learning environments. All aspects must be considered, including such things as the amount of light in a room, wall color, temperature, furniture arrangement, appearance, your appearance and posture, smells, nutrition, sounds, and activities that will be used (see Chapter 7).

There are many ways in which humans receive information and other stimuli, and ultimately how they learn from what is encountered. Each person's needs and approach to learning are unique. For that reason, you need to recognize the importance of varying the techniques and strategies you use in providing information and concepts. Also, you should be aware of the findings of Malcolm S. Knowles. Author of *The Adult Learner: A Neglected Species* and several other books on the topic; Knowles did much research into how adult and children learn and process information differently and developed a series of adult learning principles. Like others, Knowles used the term **andragogy** (adult learning), derived from a variation of the term that is believed to have originally appeared in Germany in 1833 (andragogik), to differentiate it from the concept of **pedagogy** (youth learning) that is prevalent in school systems in the United States. **Table 1-4** shows some of the ways in which the two approaches differ.

For centuries, educators and trainers have used a model of teaching that puts information into a neatly packaged format. A step-by-step, outline approach is common in many school systems and training programs following this format. Unfortunately, research continues to find that the human brain does not naturally process information that way. In fact, studies show that learners (especially adults) need to understand the big picture to recognize the value of each piece of information they encounter. Learners also need time to make connections between information received and knowledge already possessed personally. From time to time, they may even need to have you help them make these connections by pointing out key elements and relationships and discussing how application of content can be useful. In addition, learners should not be pressured during learning or simply prepared to regurgitate information on timed tests without fully comprehending the material.

The ultimate goal of any learning experience should be mastery of material and concepts to a level at which behavior change can be affected and performance improved, and the learner can constructively recall and effectively apply what he or she learned in appropriate situations.

Although learning is a complex process, and one not completely understood by scientists, we do know what happens when people learn. Learners basically extract some type of meaning from all stimuli that they encounter. It is important to understand this because what you or other trainers do, or fail to do, will definitely impact learner success. Simply put, stimuli are anything with which the brain comes into contact through the five senses (sight, hearing, touch, taste, and smell). The input might be information, a smell, a feeling, an emotional exchange, or an image that causes the brain to "turn on" to process what was experienced. If the stimulus is something related to an earlier learning experience (e.g., a review of concepts covered in a training session on the previous day), the brain accepts the input into its neural pathways via nerve cells called **neurons.** It then compares the new material to memorized concepts and reinforces the image imprinted there. If a stimulus is encountered for the first time, electrical energy is produced that converts the input to nerve impulses. These signals travel to various areas of the brain where they are sorted, processed, and/or stored for later recall. When the brain encounters input a number of times, it begins to process it more efficiently because the "roadmap" is already in the neural system. This is why it is so important for you to build in regular **interim reviews** (quick activities designed to reinforce key concepts) throughout a training session. At least every 10–15 minutes, try to inject a quick, fun rehash of material, or give your learners time to process what was gained.

Table 1-4. Youth Learning vs. Adult Learning

Pedagogy (Child)	Andragogy (Adult)
Label of "students" is common.	Label of "participants" is standard.
Participants are directed to attend.	Participants attend voluntarily.
Based on grade achievement.	"Competency or mastery-based."
Dependent style of learning.	Independent (self-directed) learning style.
Learning skills often low.	Learning ability relatively high but may decline with age.
Motivation to learn is often low.	Various motivations exist (e.g., knowledge, money, job enhancement, self-development).
Expect to be told what to do.	Expect a voice in the learning process.
Participants expect all answers to be given.	Expect to answer questions partially from experience.
Participants provide little feedback.	Participant feedback is vital to the success of training.
Displays of immaturity are common (e.g., shooting rubber bands).	Maturity level is normally high.
Accept delayed application (someday they will use the information presented).	Want to see immediate benefit of learning (e.g. understand the big picture).
Past experiences are limited.	Past experiences are common, varied, and impact learning.
Long-term student goals usually lacking.	Specific long-term participant goals set.
Learning is authority based (teacher to student format).	Interactive-based (exchange between facilitator and learner).
Learning is content-centered.	Learning is problem-centered.
Activities are in "I talk/you listen."	Activities are of experiential format.
Senses of sight and hearing are primary target to channel learning.	Multiple senses are often targeted.
Correlation or application of theory usually not discussed with students.	Applications of theory are discussed with participants and action plans used.
Traditional classroom of rows of desks are used.	Various configurations are used based on scheduled activities.
Objectives or goals usually are not outlined to students.	Objectives or goals are given to participants at the beginning of a program.
Evaluation is done by the instructor.	Evaluation is shared by facilitator and participants.

PUTTING YOUR BRAIN TO WORK: ACTIVITY

What are some creative ways in which you or others have provided a review of program concepts during a training session? _____

_____

How have such reviews been effective in reinforcing the learning? _____

_____

BRIGHT IDEA

Guiding Participant Learning

Start all training experiences with an overview of session objectives that describe what participants will be able to know or do differently at the end of the program (the big picture). Make the learning interactive and as the program content is presented, ensure that you link each piece together with transition phrases to help learners mentally follow the flow from one area to the next. Also, ensure that time to review what has been covered is built in at points throughout the session (**interim reviews**). At the end of the session, display the program objectives one more time and ask participants what they experienced related to each, as well as how they intend to apply what was learned. Finally, have each person complete a written action plan with specific dates for accomplishment of next steps in applying what was learned.

● LEARNING MODALITIES

The complex organ that we call the brain uses its hundred billion plus cells to process information and images in many ways and on different levels. For example, in any given hour of consciousness, the brain collects, analyzes, and stores thousands of visual cues. As part of this vast data assimilation, comprehension, and translation into action, learners use different approaches or modalities in gaining input. Most people have a preferred and a secondary modality for learning. These preferences are often called **learning styles** and involve receiving information through *auditory* (hearing), *visual* (seeing), or *kinesthetic* (physically experiencing or emotionally sensing) means.

Simply stated, learning modalities or styles are differing approaches that people use to learn. It is important for you to recognize your own preferred style as well as to be able to recognize that of others. If you are not aware of your preferred modality, you may unconsciously design and deliver information in a format with which you are comfortable, but that ignores the learning preferences of others. In such instances, you might ignore the learning needs of a portion of your learners and ultimately cause a breakdown in their learning cycle. To prevent this from occurring, and to determine your preferred learning style(s), complete **Figure 1-4**. Before doing so, you may even want to first make blank copies of the survey to give to your learners later. This can help identify what they prefer and ensure that you are building training that is truly effective and that learners will accept.

Learning Modalities in Action

There are many strategies available to address participant learning modalities once they have been identified. To help decide what approaches to take in delivering information, use the following indicators to help identify the learning styles of your participants. Look for clusters of signals (several combined) rather than just taking one indicator as being definitive of style preference. Also, keep in mind that each learner brings a unique combination of experiences, needs, and learning modality preferences to the activity; therefore, these are simply common indicators and should not be taken as absolutes. It is always better to ask participants for their input or needs rather than to assume what these are.

Auditory Learners

Easily distracted by people and things around them as well as by actions being processed in their minds.

Often talk to themselves when reviewing information, problem solving, or making decisions.

Often read out loud (their lips move).

Gain the most value from information gathered in verbal lectures or presentations, small group discussions, and in listening to audiotapes or others.

Extract emotional meaning and intent from vocal nuances, such as rate of speech (words spoken per minute), inflection or pitch (high/low), voice tone, volume (loudness/softness), voice quality (pleasant/unpleasant), and articulation or enunciation of words (clearly pronouncing words without cutting off endings or slurring).

Often able to recall conversations, jokes, and stories and to attribute them to the right person.

Typically benefit from learning activities involving verbal interaction. Math, spelling, and writing may be difficult.

Can sometimes be identified by their verbal statements:
I hear what you are saying.

It sounds to me as if . . .

What you are saying is music to my ears.

Take a few minutes to read each of the following statements. In the Preferred Behavior column, place a check (✓) in the space by each statement that is most like you. Once you have selected all statements, look at the instructions at the end of the survey in order to determine your preferred style(s).

Style category	Preferred behavior	
_____	1. _____	Like to touch or handle things when looking at them.
_____	2. _____	Spell well.
_____	3. _____	Like to listen to books on tape.
_____	4. _____	Enjoy reading books.
_____	5. _____	Verbal directions alone confuse me.
_____	6. _____	Enjoy background music while working on a project or an activity.
_____	7. _____	Would rather spend time discussing a topic than reading about it.
_____	8. _____	Prefer use of colors and colored paper on handouts.
_____	9. _____	Enjoy writing.
_____	10. _____	Often talk to myself.
_____	11. _____	Like working with my hands.
_____	12. _____	Good athlete.
_____	13. _____	Enjoy jigsaw puzzles.
_____	14. _____	Have a lot of nervous energy (e.g., manipulating objects or change in pockets, tapping pencils, etc.).
_____	15. _____	Remember jokes, stories, and conversations.
_____	16. _____	Collect things.
_____	17. _____	Comprehend information better if reading aloud.
_____	18. _____	Can read maps well.
_____	19. _____	Doodle or draw pictures.
_____	20. _____	Use finger as pointer when reading.
_____	21. _____	Like games, role plays, and simulation activities.
_____	22. _____	Use rhymes and jingles to remember things.
_____	23. _____	Get meaning from someone's body language and facial expressions.
_____	24. _____	Good at locating things or places.
_____	25. _____	Take a lot of notes during a lecture.
_____	26. _____	Easily interprets and understands messages received orally.
_____	27. _____	Follow written instructions well.
_____	28. _____	Talk rapidly and use hands to communicate.
_____	29. _____	Like to take things apart and put them together.
_____	30. _____	Enjoy talking to others on the telephone.

TOTAL No. 1   A _____   V _____   K _____

After rating all statements, go back and place an A (Auditory), V (Visual), or K (Kinesthetic) in the Style Category column before the appropriate statements, based on the following:

A = Nos. 3, 7, 9, 10, 15, 17, 20, 22, 26, and 30

V = Nos. 2, 4, 5, 8, 13, 18, 19, 23, 25, and 27

K = Nos. 1, 6, 11, 12, 14, 16, 21, 24, 28, and 29

Finally, count the number of checks next to statements, by Style Categories, and put those totals by the appropriate on the **Total** line. For example, if the total number of checks next to statements labeled "A" was 5, you'd put a 5 next to the "A" on the **Total** line. You'd do likewise for totals next to "V" and "K."

The letter with the highest total next to it is your primary learning modality or style, while the second highest score indicates your backup or secondary preference. If you have equally rated styles, you likely shift between them depending on the situation and learning function in which you are involved.

FIGURE 1-4. Learning modality self-assessment

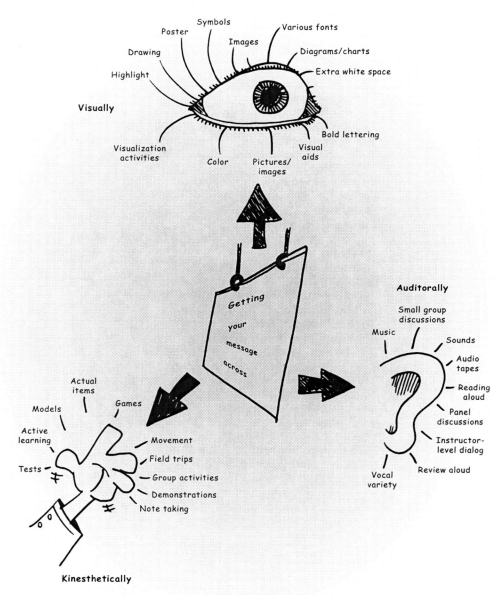

MINDMAP 1. Getting Your Message Across

If I'm hearing you correctly . . .

Sounds like a good idea . . .

It sounds like you are saying . . .

It's clear as a bell.

To help meet the needs of your auditory learners, prepare sessions that include many opportunities for verbal exchange on small and large group levels. Incorporate a variety of aural stimulation, such as instructor-led discussion, music, debates, panel discussions, **role plays,** interactive CD-ROM, reading text aloud, use of tape recorders, or demonstrations involving verbal explanations.

Visual Learners

Gain understanding from stimuli received through their eyes and envisioned in their minds.

Extract interpersonal message meaning by observing a person's body language, facial expressions, gestures, and dress.

Prone to daydreaming or imagining.

Visualize concepts of theory and content received through patterns or pictures in their mind.

Often sit in a location where their view is unobstructed (e.g., front of the room).

Are often good spellers.

Learn best from visual stimulus (e.g., slides, transparencies, handouts, flip charts, posters, or videos).

In general, take many notes to reinforce what they experience and for reference later.

Have a subconscious, emotional reaction to color and light.

Often have trouble following verbal instructions or directions.

Can sometimes be identified by their verbal statements:

I see what you are saying.

I get the picture.

I believe I see what you mean.

The picture is clear to me.

I see your point.

I have a good picture of the situation now.

As I see it . . .

That conjures up images for me.

I can see light at the end of the tunnel.

To ensure that you have provided the needed stimulus for your visual participants, create training programs that offer a potpourri of visual stimuli. Include brightly colored papers, markers, and posters with content that ties to the session topic and previous concepts that learners have experienced. This allows mental images to connect and provides reinforcement of key program elements. Offer quotes, stories, analogies, and examples that are relative to points made in the session and that provide mental images for learners. Use cartoons, graphics, and caricatures on handouts, flip charts, and other visual aids. If you use multimedia presentations, include animation and color. Add video segments that will supplement program content and discussions. Also include visualization activities in which participants are asked to envision how certain situations would appear if they applied content discussed in the session. For example, have them imagine how customer service would improve if they applied effective listening skills learned during a program on interpersonal communication. Then, have learners discuss their ideas in small groups to exchange thoughts and capture them on flip charts for large group discussion and action.

Kinesthetic/Tactile Learners

Gather information and gain maximum understanding by being involved in an activity or by performing a task.

Learn best through explaining, exploring, manipulating, and assembling or disassembling ideas or objects.

May become bored or fidgety during lectures and periods of inactivity.

Extract meaning and comprehension through touching, doing, and interacting.

Prefer physical face-to-face input.

Typically enjoy activity but often leave a mess when working on projects.

Are mentally stimulated by movement (theirs and others).

Interpersonal communication often punctuated by strong gesturing and enthusiastic vocal quality.

Can sometimes be identified by their verbal statements:
    I'm moved by what you said.
    I think I have a handle on what you mean.
    I can't quite grasp your point.
    Let's pick the problem apart and see what we are dealing with.
    Let's jump in and get started.
    It feels to me as if . . .
    Let me handle this.
    I've got a grip on what you are saying.
    Let's do it . . .

To help ensure that you have addressed the needs of your kinesthetic participants, design programs and activities in which movement is a regular part of the learning. Have people physically move to other locations at various points for discussions, or use demonstrations, field trips, games, simulations, stretching, or energizers. Encourage role playing, in-basket, or other similar activities in which learners have to handle things, interact, or move. Have actual items available for touching or exploration when possible. When actual items are not available, try to use mockups (models that look like the real object), simulators, or other substitutes.

BRIGHT IDEA
Appealing to Modalities

Provide brightly colored manipulative toys, such as sponge balls or Koosh® balls, plastic or metal spring toys (e.g., Slinky®), foam rubber squish toys in shapes related to the topic (e.g., a telephone for customer service or telephone skills, a computer for technical training, or a brain for creativity or problem-solving), or various colored shape markers (Crayola® makes these) on participant tables. Tell participants at the beginning of the session that they are free to quietly play with or manipulate the items if they would like to. You might even build in icebreaker, review, or energizer activities that includes the toys. Through use of such toys you can allow learners to personally exercise their minds; add a little levity and relaxation; and, if you see many people manipulating items at the same time, the message might be that they are ready to move on or take a break. This type of approach to training incorporates two of the three learning modalities.

I hear; I forget
I see; I remember
I do; I understand
　　—Chinese Proverb

● STAGES OF LEARNING

For learning to truly occur, a phased process is often helpful. The process that follows moves through five stages or phases. In it, participants are alerted to the learning experience in which they are about to take part. They are then led along a preplanned path for transferring knowledge, skills, or attitudes back to the workplace or other venue.

Stage 1: Preparing for Learning

In the first phase of the learning process, you must condition participants for learning. This is typically done through icebreakers or activities tied to the training program content and by providing behavioral objectives or goals. In this introductory phase you provide a foundation of information and switch learner's brains onto the topic to be addressed. By doing so, you increase the likelihood that they will quickly recognize, absorb, and process new information or stimuli. Further, by providing a verbal, visual, and kinesthetic push, then identifying how the new information connects to what they already know, you can assist in bridging with memory.

Stage 2: Stimulating Learning

This phase of the learning process provides handouts, **job aids,** or other visual material to supplement verbal messages. Such materials allow participants to access information from their own learning style (visual, auditory, or kinesthetic). To supplement such input, you can use associated visual aids to make points, reinforce concepts, or provide alternative methods of information delivery, for example, colorful posters, transparencies or computer-generated slides, or flip charted information.

Stage 3: Expansion

Once information has been delivered to the brain via one or more of the elements in Phase 2, connections are started. As a facilitator, you can help create these bonds by conducting interim reviews throughout a session. During such reinforcements, you help mold and stabilize the learning through repetition and by helping learners see relationships. Such activities aid in increasing the depth of learner understanding while helping prepare for Phase 4.

Stage 4: Memorization

It is during this phase that neural connections are made in the brain to help ensure that a learner can subsequently access or recall information and concepts learned. You can increase the effectiveness of this phase by teaching and using a variety of *mnemonic* or memory techniques. These strategies help learners later access the information acquired so that they can ultimately apply the learning.

Stage 5: Implementation of Learning

In the final phase of learning, knowledge or skills gathered during the training are recalled and put into practice. If a learner is not able to perform tasks or recall information learned successfully, then there was a potential breakdown in the learning process and a review may be required.

To test the success of this phase, have participants demonstrate knowledge or skills through tests, practical application, by teaching others as you observe, or through other means in which they actively apply what was learned.

PUTTING YOUR BRAIN TO WORK: ACTIVITY

Think about a program that you present often.

What are some specific activities or strategies that you can apply for each of the five Stages of Learning that you just read about?

Stage 1: Preparing to Learn _____

_____

Stage 2: Stimulating Learning _____

_____

Stage 3: Expansion _____

_____

Stage 4: Memorization _____

_____

Stage 5: Implementation of Learning _____

_____

INTERIM REVIEW ACTIVITY

To get used to the idea of conducting Interim Reviews in your sessions, Interim Reviews have been inserted into the chapters of this book. Take a few minutes to check your comprehension of material experienced thus far, just as you might have your session participants do.

Take out a piece of paper and write down as many of the key terms and concepts that you have read about up to this point. Take 3 or 4 minutes to do this. Once completed, compare your content against various section headings and the bolded vocabulary words found throughout this chapter thus far. If you forgot some, go back through the chapter to review before moving on.

● MULTIPLE INTELLIGENCES

According to research conducted by Harvard Professor of Education Howard Gardner, human intelligence encompasses a broad scope of at least eight intelligences. This is contrary to the belief held for years that people had one way of learning, and that intelligence could be measured only by quantifiable tests. The Intelligence Quotient (IQ) developed in Paris by psychologist Alfred Binet and used for so many purposes is just one result of the latter belief.

Much of the known cognitive research, such as that of Jean Piaget, viewed human thinking as directed toward scientific thinking. The ability of a person to solve problems through logical processes and succinctly describe findings was previously a primary measure of intelligence. With the 1983 publication of Gardner's research findings on multiple intelligences (MI), much of this view began to change.

Originally, seven intelligences were identified, then Gardner added an eighth—naturalist intelligence (see **Table 1-5**). This latter intelligence historically helped humans survive by allowing identification of edible plants. Today, this intelligence assists in interactions with one's surroundings and in understanding the role that each element of the surroundings plays in daily activities of life (e.g., in learning—recognizing subtle differences between a variety of similar items).

One significant point made by Gardner related to the intelligences is that they are independent and that rarely does a person show high performance in more than one area.

Table 1-5. Gardner's Eight Intelligences

Linguistic intelligence is the ability to read, write, and communicate effectively in a variety of ways.

Logical–mathematical intelligence involves the ability to reason, calculate, think in a logical manner, and process information.

Spatial intelligence provides the ability to think in pictures and to visualize a conclusion or result.

Bodily kinesthetic intelligence gives the ability to solve problems or manipulate items using one's own body or parts of the body.

Musical–rhythmic intelligence allows someone to create or compose music and to understand, interpret, and appreciate it.

Interpersonal intelligence is crucial for understanding others, their emotions, traits, and abilities and how best to interact with people.

Intrapersonal intelligence provides the ability to form accurate perceptions about oneself and use the knowledge to effectively function throughout life.

Naturalist intelligence gives the ability to observe, understand, and classify patterns in nature.

All eight of these intelligences are equally important according to researcher Howard Gardner in *Multiple Intelligences: The Theory in Practice*, p. 8.

MINDMAP 2. Eight Multiple Intelligences

> **BRIGHT IDEA**
>
> ## Addressing Multiple Intelligences
>
> To leverage Gardner's research, and help increase participant learning and retention, build course content that is flexible in format and that uses an approach that builds on learner strengths and knowledge. If you include a variety of stimuli and regularly vary your delivery approach, participants will have more opportunity to address their own specific learning needs. This will also assist in increasing attention and interest, and with the assimilation of course material. Such an approach also ties into the concepts of **andragogy** (adult learning) proposed by Malcolm Knowles and others.

● ENRICHMENT OF THE LEARNING ENVIRONMENT

Presentation of content, concepts, and ideas is not the only thing that causes learning to occur. Researchers have found that the way in which participants perceive their environment can have a significant impact on how material is received, processed, and retained.

A number of elements can assist in gaining attention and helping to stimulate the learning process; some of these include light, sound, movement, nutrition, color, aromas, plants, and activities. All of these are explored in greater depth in Chapter 7.

To create a stimulating learning environment that helps involve and interest participants, try the following:

Use lively, upbeat music as participants enter and during breaks (see Chapter 7).

Use creative openers, including such things as exciting stories, jokes, startling statements or facts, and props (e.g., clown noses, whistles, or toys)(see Chapter 6).

Get participants immediately involved with an icebreaker activity tied to the program content (see Chapter 6).

Have a notable guest introduce you and/or the session, for example, your CEO, a famous author, local celebrity from radio or television, or recognized business professional (see Chapter 6).

Have participants stand and do something such as a *cross-lateral activity* (see Chapter 8).

Challenge participant knowledge by posing a question relevant to session content and then have participants develop group answers as they network (see Chapter 8).

Preposition colorful posters throughout the room with quotes, questions, facts, and other content-related material (see Chapter 7).

BRIGHT IDEA

Enriching the Environment

When planning training programs, you need to take into consideration how your environment will be set up. Ensure comfortable conditions by setting the temperature at around 72° F; arranging chairs and tables in configurations that allow interaction (e.g., U-shape, round, or rectangular patterns; having adequate lighting throughout the room; providing a variety of color on walls, handouts, and visual aids; having appropriate music available; and providing nutritional options (e.g., water, cookies, fresh fruit, soft drinks, decaffeinated and regular coffee and tea) (see Chapter 5).

● ATTENTIVENESS

There are a number of key points during your sessions in which it is crucial for you to gain attention. Some of these include the opening, and when introducing an activity or providing directions, presenting key concepts, eliciting participant input or feedback, and closing your presentation. Various research studies have examined how learners focus on stimuli and subsequently process what was obtained. Based on this research, you must not only quickly gain, but also hold attention, if you hope to be successful in transferring information and having learning occur. In addition, researchers have determined that the average person typically remembers the first and last thing he or she experiences in a session. For that reason, your opening needs to be dynamic, interactive, and have impact. You should also end on a high note (e.g., interactive review using games, competition, or group activities that focus on program concepts). Other options for gaining and holding attention include quotes by famous people that relate to program content, humorous video clips (e.g., Muppets; see Resources for Trainers in appendices), and post-tests following your session, in the form of crossword or word search puzzles that contain key program terms and concepts.

The average learner attention span is 15–20 minutes, depending on age, gender, and background. This is demonstrated in everyday life through the way that marketers place advertisements on television approximately every 15 minutes during a program. Because learners, especially those in the United States and Canada, have been conditioned by television through years of watching such cycles, they often have difficulty staying on task for longer periods of time in other situations (e.g., classroom training). The speed and pace of life activities and technology have also influenced learner behavior.

> **BRIGHT IDEA**
>
> ## Increasing Attentiveness
>
> When facilitating a learning experience or information exchange, build in periods of at least 2–5 minutes every 15–20 minutes for participants to discuss, process information, physically move, review material, or otherwise break their mental routine. This helps participants stay alert and focused.

Factors Inhibiting Attention

As a facilitator, you must compete with many things for the attention of your participants. Although little research has been done on why people become distracted, the following are more common in a classroom.

• **Inadequate time to focus or act on information** during a session is a big issue for many people. Keep in mind that the brain does not process input in a linear fashion and needs time to make appropriate connections when new material is received. Some participants need more time than others to grasp concepts or complete tasks. Your failure to allow enough time when giving instructions or for activities can be very frustrating and ultimately lead some participants to give up or shut down during a training session. This can often occur when you begin to present information at a rapid pace while participants attempt to take notes.

Because a lecture is probably the least effective means of imparting information in the first place, people can become bored and their minds may wander while you move on in such instances. Therefore, try to use other strategies for information delivery that involves learners.

Loss of focus can also occur when there are multiple things competing for your participants' attention. For example, think of times when you were using a flip chart or overhead projector to present key points and someone asked a question or you stopped to discuss something in detail. If you left the projector light on or a flip chart page related to another topic visible, your participants' attention was likely torn between the powerful visual images and focusing on you.

• **External distracters** can draw the attention of participants away from you or a training aid being used to present information. Examples include side conversations between participants in the room; open windows, blinds, or doors that allow participants to view or hear people or events outside; or your appearance and body language. Any of these can cause a loss of focus and ultimately lead to a breakdown in understanding and learning if participants miss a key point of information.

An example of a distracter is movement. Even though movement can attract attention and aid your presentation, it can also cause problems. For example, assume you are facilitating in a classroom that has windows. Outside, someone is mowing grass. As the person walks back and forth with the mower, many participants will likely fix their attention on that person. Why would that occur? Is it because they have never seen someone mow grass before? Are they checking to ensure the grass is being properly cut? These are unlikely possibilities. They are attracted by the movement. This is one of the reasons that you should consider room arrangements and program design when planning your sessions. When possible, select a room in which participants face away from windows and open doors to avoid distractions from people passing by.

• **Low learner motivation** can be caused by many factors over which you may have no control. These might include participants being told that they have to attend training that they do not feel they need or understand, a workplace environment in which learning and implementation of new strategies is not supported, or participants not having learned how to learn. The latter may be a result of poor training in the past or low curiosity or drive on the part of your learners. Advance preparation for training will help prevent and overcome these types of scenarios. This can be accomplished through sending out pre-work to raise learner expectations; contacting supervisors to encourage their involvement in the transfer of training process; and creating a learning environment that is stimulating and incorporates a variety of techniques, props, and strategies to address learner needs.

• **Too much input** on your part or that of other facilitators. As you read earlier, the brain is conditioned to focus for only short periods of time before it tunes out. When too much information is presented, or there are long periods of participant inactivity, distraction can occur. One solution to this problem is to change media, activities, information flow, and the pace of the session on a regular basis. Think of situations in which you have become bored during a training program or presentation. What caused the boredom? Once you have identified these causes, work to avoid them in your own sessions.

Helping Learners Focus

In today's hectic world there are many factors that impede attention or the ability of learners to concentrate. The average participant often packs more into his or her work-day than can effectively be managed. The result is that the mind is in overdrive trying to plan, organize, process, and keep up with everything.

Technology alone can create many distractions as participants try to stay abreast of latest trends and updates and understand how to use all the available features of different sophisticated equipment (e.g., computers, handheld personal planners, cell phones, cars, VCR and DVD players, microwave ovens, satellite/cable television, and computerized toys). Add to this a steadily increasing number of personal commitments, such as family, professional organizations, and religious or social functions, and you have the basis of much mental distraction when someone attends one of your training programs. It is no wonder that you have a major challenge in engaging and maintaining interest in the classroom.

Even though the detractors listed earlier are significant, the problem of distraction is nothing new. Even before the development of technology, episodes of lost focus impacted people's level of concentration. Such distractions are sometimes caused by lack of mental stimulation or a desire to be somewhere or doing something else. One legend tells of how former U.S. President Franklin Delano Roosevelt responded to boredom and distraction at an official State function receiving line.

Supposedly, at some point, he recognized that people moving through the line were not really focusing as introductions were being made and were just going through the motions of listening. To prove his hypothesis, as people came up to him and greeted, "Good evening Mr. President. How are you this evening?," he replied with a smile, "Good evening. I'm fine. I've just killed my mother. She's upstairs in the bedroom." No one reacted to his comment. One person even replied, "That's wonderful. Have a good evening, sir." If the President of the United States could not command attention in a face-to-face setting, you can imagine your challenge in a group situation in which some people do not want to be there.

Because the brain is conditioned to move on to other focuses when the average human attention span is exceeded, it is crucial that you consciously help learners stay focused. If you fail to do so, or if other stimuli distract your participants, there could be a breakdown in the learning cycle. This fact is justification for providing a mental break during your sessions and for using techniques described throughout this book.

Another way to help participants focus is to use movement, novelty, curiosity, and fun activities. Something as simple as moving to different locations in the room throughout your presentation can help stimulate interest. By repositioning yourself, and using planned gestures during a session, you can attract attention toward yourself and build rapport by closing the distance between you and participants in various parts of the room. You can also use learner movement to hold attention by regularly repositioning people to participate in activities during a session. This stimulates their interest, energizes them, and provides opportunities to network with a variety of different people, which can encourage idea and information exchange.

If you do decide to have people move, keep in mind that, because of disabilities that may not be known to you or others, some people intentionally position themselves in specific locations when they arrive in order to help their own learning. For example, someone with a sight impairment may sit directly under a light source, someone with a hearing impairment may sit near the front of the room to better hear what you have to say, or someone with a mobility impairment may take a position near the exit or refreshments and restroom. Because of these possibilities, if you move people around, you may want to allow them the option of returning to their original place if they desire to do so at the end of an activity.

To assist in identifying ways to gain and hold participant attention, try doing a quick check of planned program activities. Ask yourself the questions in **Table 1-6,** then ensure that you build responses to them into your program as necessary.

Controlling Mental Side Trips

Because the human brain loses focus periodically, it is perfectly normal for participants to daydream or to take mental side trips away from your training. As a facilitator, your challenge is to recognize this fact and work to identify and minimize the number of

Table 1-6. Attention Planning

What generally attracts attention during a session?

What techniques generate the most topic discussion?

What types of questions garner the most useful responses?

What type of activities result in maximum participant involvement?

How information is best presented so that it will be attained, remembered, and ultimately used?

What activities do participants seem to enjoy most?

How are participants most challenged to solve problems?

What rewards do participants seem to enjoy?

these. You want to help participants instead convert this down time into productive processing periods. Some techniques for helping participants remain focused include the following.

Originality should be used in the design of your program materials, content, delivery, and environment. Approach training from the perspective that participants will regularly receive an "Ah ha!" on content and application of what is learned if they are presented with opportunities to receive and process information based on their own training needs and modalities.

Differentiation of your materials and approach from that of others, or from what participants already know, can stimulate learning. You can accomplish this by verbally explaining differences, demonstrating or "walking the talk," allowing learners to participate in activities in which they come to this realization on their own, or by taking a contrary approach. For example, instead of stating points obviously (e.g., "Five steps to effective attention getting," try something like, "Getting your participant's attention without them even realizing it").

Involvement of participants by stimulating emotions, such as excitement, fun, stress, curiosity, anticipation, or surprise is an excellent way to enhance learning. This can be accomplished through the use of various strategies and approaches built into your program content and delivery format. For example, instead of having participants simply state their names and organizations as an introduction, create a stimulating **icebreaker activity** (see Chapter 7).

Risk aversion that comes from anxiety or fear of the unknown should be alleviated. Establish early in your session that the environment can be considered safe and that participants should feel free to challenge, question, or voice opinions. Also, be certain that you outline session objectives and what will be covered, along with the schedule of events, so that participants know what to expect and have a sense of personal control.

In addition, part of giving participants a feeling of safety is assure them through your words and actions that they will not be ridiculed or singled out for criticism.

Empowerment of participants is crucial in getting their buy-in. You can accomplish this early in your introduction by communicating your expectations of participants and the session and eliciting their expectations. Flip chart what participants offer or provide handouts to make them visual, such as a **Training Agreement** (see Tools for Trainers in the appendices). Refer to these expectations throughout the session as necessary and appropriate.

During the program, you can further empower participants by encouraging feedback and positively acknowledging points made. This ties to the Principle of Adult Learning that each attendee has valuable knowledge and experiences to share and on which you can build.

Facilitator attentiveness to signs of participant disinterest or distraction. Skilled trainers and educators have learned to master the art of reading participants' nonverbal signals. Such activities as doodling (drawing pictures), checking personal calendars or other items unrelated to course content, looking elsewhere, side conversations, manipulating toys that have been placed on tables, or similar actions are typical signs that you have lost a participant's attention.

Creation of a feeling of personal ownership of program content and process is important. This can be accomplished by designing activities in which participants actively get involved in the exchange of information and in problem-solving, for example, use of question-and-answer sessions and small group discussions in which several participants have been assigned roles as group leader/spokesperson and notetaker/scribe. You might also ask people to form pairs and give them a time limit in which they must identify ideas, solutions, suggestions, or whatever you indicate to present to the other participant groups.

BRIGHT IDEA

Gaining and Holding Participant Attention

To gain participant attention, learn some basic magic or card tricks to help arouse curiosity. In selecting what you will do, figure a way to connect your activity to the content or topic of your session. For example, a card trick in which participants have to anonymously select a card that you later find in the deck could be tied to creativity, problem-solving, observation skills, decision-making, and many other aspects of learning. You could accomplish this by stressing discovery.

To hold attention throughout your programs, include plenty of activities in which participants process information learned every 15–20 minutes. This can be accomplished through small group discussions, journal writing, role play practices, partner activities, action planning sheets, mindmapping, or problem-solving using concepts learned.

How have you seen learners exhibit attention loss in sessions? _____

_____

What ways can you think of to engage learner attention regularly throughout your sessions?

_____

_____

> *We are wasting valuable learning time by having students sit*
> *too much. While standing, even if it's just for a few moments,*
> *your focus is stronger.*
> —Eric Jensen
> *The Learning Brain*

● THE MARVEL OF MEMORY

Learning and memory are closely related and the terms are often used in association with each other. Learning refers to the acquisition and encoding of information, whereas memory relates to the storage and retrieval of that information.

The ability to recall information accurately is often envied by others. One story tells of how the ancient Greeks revered people with powerful memories to the point that they worked very hard to devise techniques for enhancing memory. They created a series of **mnemonics** or memory tools to assist in recalling information, some of which are still used today.

Retention Tips

All the tools in the world, however, will not help participants to retain information if you fail to assist them and to remember that for most adults, information received must be:

Meaningful and something that learners perceive as valuable or useful. When presenting such information it is helpful to put it into a format or structure that aids in retention and allows participants to connect it to previously received information. The use of **analogies** and **metaphors** can assist in this effort, as can short interim reviews done periodically.

Given individually or one item at a time without any simultaneous distractions. For example, if you are presenting a key point for discussion on a flip chart or dry erase board, turn off your PowerPoint or overhead projector images.

Presented effectively and in a manner that allows time for participants to focus on and grasp the concepts. They should have ample time to process what was received and then be able to take notes or ask questions as they feel necessary. Slowing your rate of speech and reducing the numbers of points presented in a session can assist in accomplishing this.

Reviewed and tied to previously learned concepts every 15–20 minutes in order to cement them into memory and enhance understanding of the overall scheme of the concept or material.

Like other brain-based research, the study of memory has led to some significant advances into understanding how the human mind works. In particular, scientists have discovered that memory is not a single function, nor does it occur in only one area of the brain. Instead, memory is a dynamic process that reconstructs various pieces of information stored in different areas of the brain each time someone encounters new items, then attempts to make sense of the material. One key finding that you can immediately apply in your training programs is that pictures have more impact on memory than words alone. Images have a stronger impact than written or spoken words even when pictures and words are combined.[4] I have therefore incorporated a variety of cartoons and other visual images throughout this book to reinforce what you read. You can do likewise in your handouts.

There are some important implications of memory research. First, participants will often recall words or information that is implied rather than actually presented. For example, if in a brain-based learning environment you were to give a series of terms such as fun, excitement, music, color, table glitter, toys, and props, then later ask someone to describe the environment of a brain-based learning program, he or she might likely include a phrase such as "party atmosphere." This is because the brain is an active unit that continually stores and recalls information and material. It may well associate the items you listed with a festive or party scenario.

New external input is typically intermingled with existing memories that are similar. The result is often incorrect memory recall. This phenomenon often occurs at crime or accident scenes, which is why law enforcement officers interview all available witnesses in order to identify common story elements. This collective memory can help them get a more realistic picture of what actually happened, as the officer did not witness the event personally.

Due to the mental distortion that can occur in a training session, it is important that you deliver material to as many senses (e.g., sight, hearing, taste, touch, and smell) as possible (see **Table 1-7**). In addition, you should periodically clarify and verify understanding, then review material from time to time to help solidify concepts in the minds of your participants.

The second implication of memory research is that participants benefit more when related events or items are grouped or presented in logical sequence, for example, step 1, 2, 3 versus step 3, 1, 2. This is important because when unsequenced information is delivered, the brain pauses and attempts to categorize or associate what is received in order to facilitate recall. When you introduce an item or make a point that relates to something presented much earlier in the program and is not associated with your current sequence of material, you can actually cause learning to stop. This is because distracted participants will attempt to sequence internally and compare items in their minds

> ## Table 1-7. Active Learning
>
> On average, people remember:
> - 20% of what they read
> - 30% of what they hear
> - 40% of what they see
> - 50% of what they say
> - 60% of what they do
> - 90% of what they see, hear, say, and do
>
> **Source:** Rose, C., and Nicholl, M.J., *Accelerated Learning for the 21st Century.*

so as to make sense of them. While they do so, you likely continue to introduce additional information, which they miss because they are distracted or mentally busy doing something else.

BRIGHT IDEA
Organizing for the Brain

When presenting related items or showing pictures, make sure that they are grouped and sequenced to maximize the brain's ability to assimilate and store what it experiences. You can do this by distributing them according to a theme, by numbering them sequentially, and by using the Chunking technique for memory enhancement that you will read about later in this chapter.

Stages of Memory

For information to be accurately recalled it must be effectively received or encoded, stored through review or practice, and used or retrieved by associating it with something familiar or a cue.

Encoding the information correctly when it is received is a crucial step in ultimately remembering and recalling it later. For example, think of times when you were introduced to someone and were unable to recall the name a few minutes later. Often in such instances there is mental interference that prevents you from effectively receiving the name in the first place. A common reason for this is that instead of listening as the person tells you the name, you are mentally busy examining his or her appearance and trying to give your own name at the same time.

Storage or strengthening must occur shortly after information is received in order to reinforce what was originally received. In the example of meeting someone, it is helpful to repeat immediately and later use the person's name as you talk with him or her. This allows you to process it mentally as you recall the name and to hear it as you say it back to the person. The more you do this, the greater the chance that you will retain the name. Similarly, in a classroom, ask participants to stop periodically after 15–20 minutes to review and process material received. Have them verbally exchange or repeat what they have heard in an activity.

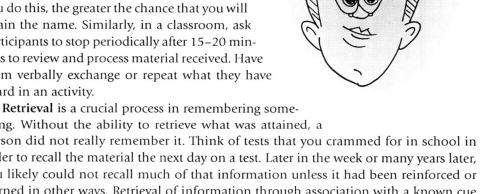

Retrieval is a crucial process in remembering something. Without the ability to retrieve what was attained, a person did not really remember it. Think of tests that you crammed for in school in order to recall the material the next day on a test. Later in the week or many years later, you likely could not recall much of that information unless it had been reinforced or learned in other ways. Retrieval of information through association with a known cue is often helpful in reinforcing a mental image. There are many memory tools to assist in doing this, some of which are covered later in this section.

Categories of Memory

Beginning in the 1980s researchers started to realize that people are often influenced by earlier experiences without consciously being aware of the fact that they are remembering something. As a result of this revelation, scientists typically group retrieval into two categories: implicit and explicit memory.

Implicit Memory

This category of memory refers to a person retrieving information from his or her subconscious mind without trying to do so. For example, think of times when you were writing something and a word that you do not regularly use popped into your head. You may not have recalled the exact definition, but knew the word was correct for the context in which you were using it. Similarly, when applying grammar rules to written material, most people familiar with the rules of the English language can appropriately apply them, but cannot explain why the usage is correct. They might say, when questioned, "I don't know, it just sounds right."

Explicit Memory

Explicit memory relates to the intentional recall of information or events. In general, someone can recall material and episodes that he or she has experienced and remembered. For example, if participants are involved in a multiple-day training program in which subsequent skills and information are built on those presented on the previous day, you might test their recall at the beginning of the second day through some sort of quiz or review.

There are generally two types of memory tests for explicit memory: recognition and recall.

Recognition tests involve having participants review a list of facts, information, or material in an effort to select those that they have seen before or to single out a particular item. From a training perspective, true–false and multiple-choice tests fall into this type.

Recall tests require participants to retrieve information without the benefit of clues or hints. This type of test might be a free recall format in which participants are given a series of numbers, letters, words, or events and asked to recall them in any order. If you asked them to recall in the order originally presented, you are using an ordered or serial recall test, and if you give cues to assist recall you are using a cued recall test. An example of the latter type would be to present a list of items and then ask which applies to a specific item or issue.

Types of Memory

Like many other facets of human functioning, there are a variety of different types of memory. Understanding these can assist you in building a training program that takes a multifaceted approach to stimulating learner memory.

Sensory memory, sometimes referred to as sensory register, is the first aspect of memorization. All incoming stimuli come through the five senses and are held there long enough (milliseconds) to recognize and either pass it along to working memory or discard it. This is one reason for developing activities and delivering information that focuses on all the different intelligences that you read about earlier.

Short-term memory or working memory refers to the ability to retain limited amounts of information for a brief period of time (some researchers say from 5 to 30 seconds). To retain information in short-term memory indefinitely requires repeating the information; otherwise one forgets it. To illustrate how this works, think of times when you were trying to remember a telephone number you looked up in the telephone directory. As long as you continued to repeat the number to yourself en route to dialling that number, you likely accurately recalled it. However, if someone or something momentarily distracted you by interrupting your repetition of the number, you probably forgot and had to look the number up again. Likewise, if you provide information to participants that you want them to act on without giving them an uninterrupted opportunity to focus on the information, they will likely be unsuccessful in recalling it.

In 1956, American psychologist George Miller reviewed many experiments on memory span and determined that the average person can recall up to seven bits or chunks of information, plus or minus two, from short-term memory. The plus or minus came from the fact that studies were inconsistent in their findings. Subsequent studies have found that working memory capability increases as children grow older, and decreases as people age. The latter is especially true in cases of brain disease, such as Alzheimer's disease. The fact that decreased memory occurs with age is also significant when you are designing programs, as many people in the workforce today are **baby boomers** who grow older each year. To address their needs, and that of others, build in a variety of activities that provide time to process and repeat information.

Long-term memory refers to the storage of large amounts of information, procedures, events, and other memories for indefinite periods of time. The result is that when participants recall earlier material learned years before, childhood experiences, workplace examples from throughout their career or any other similar details, they are pulling from long-term memory.

Scientists differ in their perspectives on how memories arrive in long-term memory. Many believe that information first goes to short-term memory where it is processed and forwarded on to long-term memory based on the significance of the information or event. Other researchers believe that functioning of short-term and long-term memory is parallel rather than sequential. According to the latter theory, therefore, information received can be simultaneously processed by both short-term and long-term memory.

From a classroom perspective, the value of long-term memory is that you can design training information, activities, and environments that build on previous information and experiences possessed by participants in order to strengthen current knowledge and skills and add new ones to those already in existence.

Helping the Brain Remember

Many strategies, ranging from simple to complex, have been developed to assist people remember names, information, and experiences. Although many of these techniques must be self-learned, there are some that you and other facilitators can build into your training delivery strategy to facilitate better retention. Some of the more common techniques follow.

Chunking

To help retain information (e.g., list of items needed from the supermarket, phone number, facts, and figures) try chunking items into smaller groups of seven, plus or minus two. This procedure is effectively used in many instances each day. Think about commonly encountered information and how you use it throughout your life:

Phone numbers with area code (_ _ _)_ _ _-_ _ _ _ (ten numbers chunked into three groups)

Social security number _ _ _-_ _-_ _ _ _ (nine numbers chunked into three groups)

U.S. Military service number for personnel prior to the Viet Nam era _ _ _ _ _ _ _ _ (seven or eight numbers)

License plate numbers (up to seven numbers or letters, often with a space between some of them)

Postal zip codes in the United States _ _ _ _ _ - _ _ _ _ (nine numbers chunked into two groups)

The Seven Habits of Highly Effective People

The Seven Deadly Sins

The Brady Bunch television family (mom, dad, and six children)

The characters of *Gilligan's Island* on television (seven people—Gilligan, Skipper, Professor, Mr. & Mrs. Howell, Ginger, and Mary Ann)

Snow White and the Seven Dwarfs

Seven Wonders of the World

Acronyms

By turning key points of a presentation into an acronym using only the first letter of each word or phrase, you can help ensure that your participants get and retain them. This technique was likely used to help you learn much of the information you were exposed to in school. Whenever possible, use familiar acronyms to help participants remember complex terms, titles, or elements in your sessions. The following are examples of well known acronyms:

NATO: North American Treaty Organization

NASA: National Aeronautics and Space Administration

USA: United States of America

NFL: National Football League

Acrostics are formed by taking the first letter of the words in a series and creating another familiar word with them. For example, HOMES—The Great Lakes (Heron, Ontario, Michigan, Erie, and Superior). You can use this technique to create words from lists of steps, phases, or elements in a process or system.

Rhymes

Developing phrases or words that sound similar or organizing into a little song-like process can also help retention of information. For example, in order to remember which way to turn your clock when daylight savings time begins and ends, you may have learned, "Spring forward; Fall back." To remember how many days are in each month—"Thirty days hath September, April, June and November, all others have thirty one, except February with twenty-eight, and twenty-nine in leap year."

As energizers and an interim review, many facilitators have participants develop short rhymes, rap songs, or other tunes based on the key concepts of the program. Often participants are asked to use the musical tempos from well known children's songs such as "Old McDonald," or a popular song heard on the radio.

BRIGHT IDEA

Aiding Participant Memory

When presenting new material to participants, try one or more of the following techniques to help ease their recall.

Use strong transition phrases that help them link one concept to the next. For example, "Now that we have discussed how point A can assist in creating an effective learning environment, let's look at how point B can allow participants more involvement in such an environment."

Make sure you point out the AVARFM (Added Value And Results For Me) so that participants understand the personal value of learning and retaining the concepts being offered.

Use a variety of Interim Reviews every 15–20 minutes to help reinforce key points. For example, have participants take out a sheet of paper, write down five key points that they have experienced, then share them within a group of three to four other participants. Any key points they missed are likely to be offered by someone else, thus reinforcing what they heard originally.

Have participants create a rhyme, song, or acronym using key concepts they have learned.

Have participants create a drawing of someone using or demonstrating key concepts learned.

Have each participants write down one key point learned, then form small groups and have participants reteach the point to their peers in their own words. Encourage group members to add anything that is left out about points being presented.

PUTTING YOUR BRAIN TO WORK: ACTIVITY

What strategies do you use to help you retain information? _____

_____

Who do you know that has a good memory and whom might be able to share their retention tips with you?

_____

_____

APPLYING WHAT YOU LEARNED
Strategies for Stimulating the Brain

1. In what ways can you use research findings about the human brain to enhance your own training programs? _____

_____

2. How can understanding the differences in the way adults and children learn aid in providing a more valuable learning experience for your participants? _____

_____

_____

3. What can you do to address the different learning modalities of participants?

_____

_____

4. What will you do to ensure that you address each of the five stages of learning?

_____

_____

5. Based on the Gardner's concepts of eight intelligences, what strategies can you build into your programs to stimulate learning in each intelligence area? _____

_____

_____

6. How can you enrich your learning environments? _____

_____

_____

7. Based on the concepts of brain-based learning that you read, what techniques can you use in your next session to help gain and hold attention? _____

_____

8. What types of memory devices can you use to encourage retention of material that you present in your sessions? _____

_____

ENDNOTES

[1]Caine, R., and Caine, G., *Mind/Brain Learning Principles,* http://www.newhorizons.org/ofc_21cl.caine.html.

[2]Jensen, E., *Unleashing the Awesome Power of Your Brain,* The Brain Store, San Diego, CA, 2000, p. 4.

[3]Hermann, N., *The Creative Brain,* The Ned Hermann Group, Lake Lure, NC, 1994, p. 31.

[4]Committee on Learning Research and Educational Practice, *How People Learn: Brain, Mind, Experience, & School,* National Academy Press, Washington, DC, 2000, p. 124.

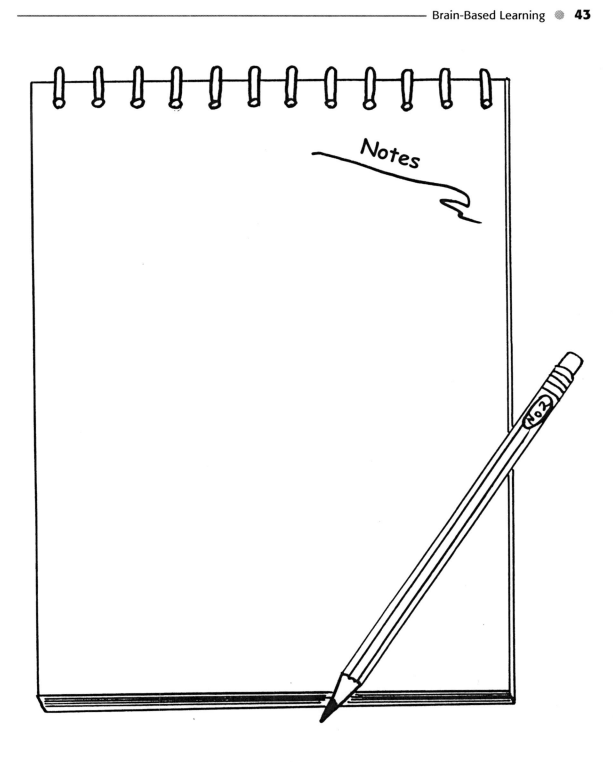

Notes

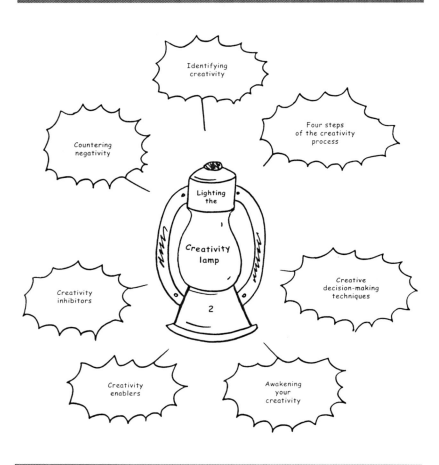

Identifying
creativity

Four steps
of the creativity
process

Countering
negativity

Lighting
the

Creativity
lamp

2

Creativity
inhibitors

Creative
decision-making
techniques

Creativity
enablers

Awakening
your
creativity

Lighting the Creativity Lamp

Creativity involves breaking out of established patterns in order to look at things in a different way.
  —Edward de Bono
  Creative Thinker

Learning Objectves

At the end of this chapter, and when applying concepts covered, you will be able to:

- Recognize different forms of creativity.

- Describe the four steps of the creativity process.

- Develop and use a variety of creative problem-solving techniques in training.

- Modify current training practices to enhance learning outcomes.

- Decide which personal paradigms are stifling creatively and work toward changing them.

- Apply a variety of creativity enablers to training in order to help learners expand their creative thinking ability.

- Find and eliminate personal and organizational creativity inhibitors.

Creativity is a state of mind. For you to be adept at training others in a challenging and successful manner takes thought on your part and sometimes requires thinking outside the box or from a different perspective. Taking such an approach can separate you from the average trainer who follows a standard format and rarely makes changes to his or her content or delivery style.

The ability to be creative is not innate, but rather is a skill that can be learned and improved upon through the use of various systems and strategies. There are certainly facets of the brain at work influencing the approach that you and your participants use as you strive to develop answers or solutions to issues. As you read in Chapter 1, however, creativity is not simply a right-brain function, as was once believed. It is a whole brain process in which creative ideas are the result of many factors. Creativity also requires competency in the areas of **divergent** (generating a quantity of diverse ideas) and **convergent** (selecting the most appropriate idea) **thinking.**

From a creativity standpoint, the average person exhibits a variety of innovative ideas and talents throughout any given day without sometimes labeling such behavior as creative. For example, whenever someone offers a different perspective to a point you or someone else makes, in a training session, he or she is creatively looking at an alternative. In addition, when participants brainstorm potential issues and solutions to problems, they are being creative. Likewise, when someone begins to daydream and starts doodling on a piece of paper, he or she is creating.

Luckily, true creativity can come from a childlike approach to training. Children often are unaware that something cannot be done because they have not previously attempted it. The challenge for many children, who later recall early experiences as they grow older, is that teachers, parents, and other adults teach them not to be creative, by requiring them to "color within the lines," "speak when spoken to," "shut up and listen," and in a variety of other ways.

Adults can regress to that childlike simplicity by experimenting and thinking freely. Too often creativity is limited by a person's attitude or motivation. For example, participants can actually inhibit their own potential creativity by making statements similar to the following:

I'm just not a creative person.

I never have any good ideas.

I don't have time to be creative.

I don't know where to get creative ideas.

I don't know how people come up with all their creative ideas.

Of all those statements, the one that is probably closest to the truth is that they do not know how to come up with creative ideas. That is what you will read about in this chapter. Creativity is more about strategy and technique than ability. By using tools such as those covered in this chapter, you will be able to add a spark to your own creativity and that of your participants.

PUTTING YOUR BRAIN TO WORK: ACTIVITY

To get a better idea of strategies that you can use to increase your own creativity and that of your learners, answer the following questions. You might also want to ask others to respond to the questions and compile their responses.

What are some of the general characteristics of people whom you consider to be creative (e.g., good organizers or problem solvers)? _____

_____

What creative techniques do you use or know of that can increase the number of answers or options identified during problem-solving or in addressing an issue (e.g., brainstorming)? _____

_____

_____

● IDENTIFYING CREATIVITY

Many trainers and facilitators often face a challenge in identifying and implementing new training techniques and strategies. They either do not expend the effort or do not know how to examine things from differing perspectives—to think outside the box. Tradition and status quo often dictate their training design and delivery efforts. They approach the learning environment with the same tools, content, activities, and techniques each time they conduct a session, usually because of their comfort level with the normal way of doing things. It also does not require much thought or any additional design, planning, or rehearsal time. For whatever reason, approaching training in this manner can lead to complacency or boredom on the part of the trainer. Ultimately, there is also a disservice to participants who experience delivery of a program by a less than enthusiastic leader.

You can increase your own effectiveness by remaining committed continually to improving your content and enhancing your delivery style. Simply by taking the time to evaluate the format and content of your sessions periodically you can add a spark. Something as simple as using a different icebreaker activity or using random techniques for identifying small group leaders and scribes (see Chapter 6) can energize you and your group.

To get to a point where you are not afraid to use creative approaches in your training, you must first learn what creativity is. Creativity in training essentially involves looking at program topics, content, and delivery objectively, then searching for alternative ways to present key elements and, if necessary, modify them or your approach to them.

> ### BRIGHT IDEA
> ### Adding a Spark to Training
> To increase your creativity quotient, make a promise to yourself that each time you prepare a session, you will change at least one activity and the way that you will identify and group leaders and volunteers. This will cause you to think and add variety for you and will also potentially engage participants.

A conclusion is the place where you got tired of thinking.
—Martin H. Fischer

It is important to remember that creativity is a process by which you identify new ideas. You do so most effectively by examining each element from various perspectives. This can be accomplished using any of the strategies found in this chapter, or through use of similar ones. To better understand how the creativity process works, look at a road map. Find any two major cities that are geographically located near one another. Note that there is likely a main highway (similar to a program objective) that connects the two cities, however, there are probably many smaller roads (strategies or techniques) that branch and ultimately lead from one city to the other. To apply this **metaphor** to your training, select any program that you currently design and deliver. Next, on a sheet of paper, list as many alternative techniques and activities for accomplishing session objectives as you can. Now, take a "side road" by selecting any alternative from your list to substitute for one that you currently use. The result will be that your session objectives will be met while you take a different route or add variety and creativity to your training.

PUTTING YOUR BRAIN TO WORK: ACTIVITY

To practice viewing items from a different perspective, take a look at **Figure 2-1.** Take a few minutes and attempt to determine how many squares there are in the image.

How many did you find? The solution is in the Tools for Trainers section of the appendices. If you are like most people, you started with the obvious ones. However, to find all of them, you had to go deeper into the image, as if you were peeling back an onion. When you did, you likely started making larger combinations of boxes to form more squares.

Similar to many of the issues that you and your participants encounter in your training, this figure illustrates the value of not making assumptions or approaching a situation from the "normal" perspective. This latter concept is a key element in creative thinking and in your ability to add pizzazz to your training sessions.

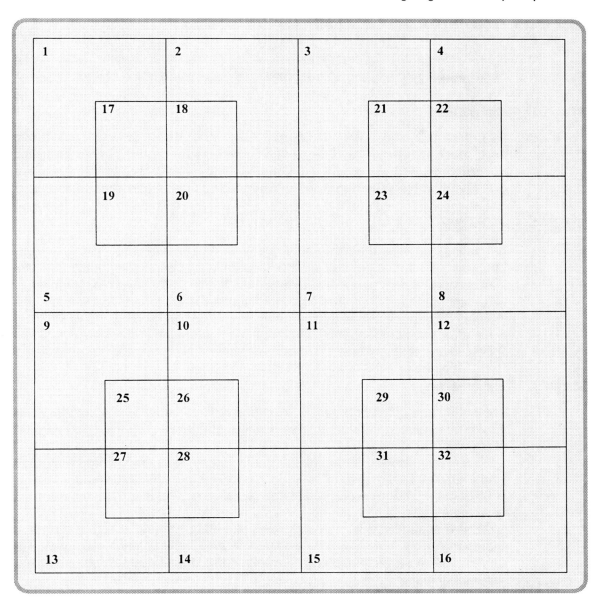

FIGURE 2-1. How many squares do you see? (Answers on page 415.)

● FOUR STEPS OF THE CREATIVITY PROCESS

A well known model for creativity was described by researcher Graham Wallas.[5] In his model, Wallas described four key stages or steps through which creativity is accomplished.

Stage 1: Preparation

In the first stage of creativity it is important that you accurately define the problem or issue (e.g., who, what, when, how, why), then gather as much supporting information as possible through research. In addition, you must establish the criteria for verifying that your solution or decision is appropriate and will truly address your needs.

Stage 2: Incubation

As you read in Chapter 1, you must allow your brain time to process information received. This could take minutes, weeks, or years. It can help to get away from the issue or program you are working on and going to do other things. By stepping away from the situation, you allow your brain to compare and contrast alternatives related to needs. This is similar to reading or discussing something prior to going to bed and then reexamining it the next morning. Your subconscious brain will often continue to process throughout the night and you will arrive at a solution once reintroduced to the material the next day.

Stage 3: Illumination

In the third stage of creativity, you actually arrive at that "Ah ha!" point where the pieces fall together in your mind and your creative light bulb goes on. This may occur as a flash or after contemplating the issue as a whole.

To understand this revelation period, think of times when you had been working to solve a problem for days and suddenly in the middle of the night, while taking a shower, or while doing something else, you realize the solution. Your brain had never stopped working on the issue.

To experience the "Ah ha!" feeling, take a few minutes to look at **Figure 2-2**. Try to figure out what it is you are looking at without looking at the Solution underneath. Was it easy or difficult to see? What made it so? How does this revelation apply to concepts of creative training?

Stage 4: Verification

In the final stage of Wallas' creativity model you actually take steps to determine if the solution or answer in Stage 3 will really meet the criteria set in Stage 1 and will resolve the issue. With a training program, you can often determine this during a delivery rehearsal. If one of your criteria in Stage 1 was selecting an alternative activity to allow participants to practice a skill within a specified time frame, and your practice demonstrated it did, then the need is potentially satisfied.

FIGURE 2-2. What is it?

SOLUTION = IDEA

● CREATIVE DECISION-MAKING TECHNIQUES

Although you cannot get inside the heads of your participants and come up with creative ideas for them, you can help ignite their creative spark by using various strategies to encourage participants to think and examine issues and problems from different perspectives. Doing so can often stimulate thoughts in the minds of your learners while encouraging active involvement during training. By teaching and using creative problem-solving techniques such as the Squares activity regularly, you can encourage involvement and participant application of concepts learned while keeping your own mind actively engaged.

Some of the additional common training approaches for teaching creative thinking and finding solutions include the following.

Graphic Organizers

Visual representations of information can be very useful for organizing and arranging key elements of any issue, concept, or item. They are especially helpful in reinforcing learning and increasing memory for visual learners. The introductory page for each chapter of this book shows how simple such a device might be. It replaces what could be a lengthy linear chapter outline. This is important because, as you remember from Chapter 1, the brain does not easily process information presented in a linear fashion.

Mindmapping

Sometimes referred to as an idea map, mindmapping is a widely used type of graphic organizer, developed by Tony Buzan for visually displaying information and ideas related to a central theme or topic such as the one for the content of this chapter (see **Figure 2-3**).

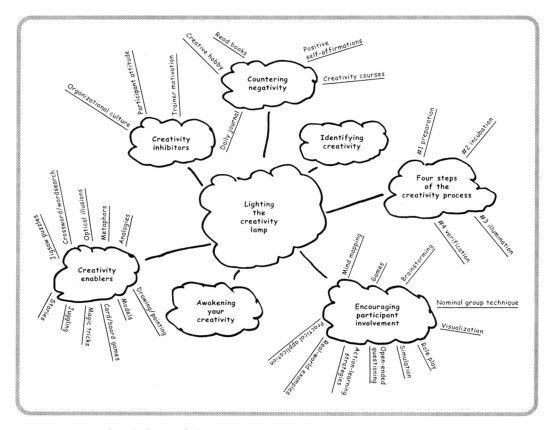

FIGURE 2-3. Sample mindmap of Chapter 2

See Books in Resources for Trainers in the appendices section for resources on the topic). A mindmap is created by placing the central theme or topic in the middle of a page or on a flip chart sheet, enclosing it in a circle or other shape, then branching or other key trigger words in all directions away from the central word. This free-flowing picture of ideas can help create additional thoughts and better mirrors the way the brain processes information. Many people (visual learners) also add graphic images along with various topic headings or concepts to reinforce the points.

Games

Games are structured experiential activities that include learner interaction, some degree of competitiveness, a set of rules or guidelines, designated time frames, and a specific outcome (e.g., winners and losers). If the right game is selected, such events are effective for encouraging participants to think and challenge. If your goal is to encourage teamwork within a larger unit, then other activities that do not result in only one or two winners may be more suitable.

Brainstorming

In brainstorming, participants form groups of approximately six to eight individuals to address a given topic or issue. They shout out any idea they have related to the issue while someone captures all ideas on a sheet of flip chart paper for later discussion and prioritization. (See Tools for Trainers in the appendices for Sample Brainstorming Guidelines). Competition, time constraints, and specific desired outcomes and rewards are typically built into the design of the activity.

Nominal Group Technique

With this process, small groups of six to eight participants are given a written question or issue and a sheet of paper and a pencil. They are asked to individually list as many ideas or solutions to the issue as they can think of without talking. Five to ten minutes is normally given to accomplish this.

Following the time expiration, each person offers one idea from his or her paper in turn. Someone records these ideas, and once a list is developed, all participants in the group discuss the ideas to clarify or add to them. Participants then vote or rank-order the ideas from best or most important to worst or least important. This voting can be done individually and then announced as the votes are added for each issue on the flip chart, or through some creative means (e.g., provide three different colored markers or three different colored dot stickers to each participant who uses them to vote, in turn, for the issues on the flip chart). The items are then tallied and prioritized based on number of votes each received.

Visualization

Using participants' past experiences, this is a powerful technique for helping understand how program content relates to them. During visualization, participants are asked to close their eyes, relax, and recall an event in their lives (e.g., think of a time when you were dealing with an irate customer on the telephone who was yelling and cursing at you). As they think, you ask them questions designed to create reflection and problem-solving (e.g., What caused the person to be irate? How did you feel when he or she was yelling at you? Was there anything you said or did that increased his or her anger? How did you handle the situation? Was there any strategy that you used that was either effective or ineffective? What was it?). Have participants open their eyes and ask, "How do you feel about that incident today?" Have them again close their eyes and again think about the incident. The second time, tell them to think about the program concepts learned and ask, "Applying what you know now, how would you handle that situation differently? What would you do or say that incorporates what you have experienced in the training session?

If you have the time or desire, you could also continue such an activity by having participants close their eyes after they visualize their own feelings and try to visualize from the customer's perspective (e.g., Why was he upset?, How did he feel about the way he was being treated?, and so on).

Visualization activities are an excellent way to allow participants to examine an issue to which they can directly relate and apply what they have learned. It also allows learners to get in touch with their own feelings about an event and better see it from someone else's point of view.

Role Play

Role play is an interactive technique for allowing participants to be involved in acting out real-life situations. Such activities provide a safe way for participants to practice skills such as communication, feedback, questioning, and problem-solving learned and get feedback on their performance from you and their peers in a safe, risk-free environment. The challenge is often getting people to take the practices seriously or to actively participate.

The key to overcoming such hesitancy is for you to effectively design the activity, building in real-world objectives, then to communicate expectations and potential learning outcomes to participants before they begin. Also, at the end of the role play, you must effectively debrief the activity by having the individuals practicing tell what they did well, what they could have improved upon, and how they would do it differently if they could repeat the process. Once the practicing learner has shared thoughts, repeat the same debriefing process with those with whom they interacted and any observers before offering your own feedback and observations.

Some questions to ask each participant following a role play include:

What did the role players do well?

What did the role players do that was ineffective?

If they could do the scenario over, what should they do differently?

If participants do not know each other well, it is often better to postpone role plays until later in a session or on subsequent meeting days when trust and relationships have been better established. This often leads to more realistic practice sessions.

Simulation

Simulations provide a reality-based activity in which participants have a chance to experience some real-world event or function. The activity is based on some actual process or situation. For example, an assembly line format might be used to teach the importance of having an effective workflow, communication within work teams, decision-making, quality improvement time and resource management, and effective supervision or team work. Simulations are typically fast moving, timed, use props (e.g., simulated or actual equipment or workplace items), and require you or someone else to coordinate activities closely and to debrief the activity in order to bring out learning points once it ends. They differ from role plays that typically have two or more people interacting in a dialog.

Open-Ended Questions

Many people have difficulty getting the information they need because they do not know how to ask questions effectively. The key to encouraging participant involvement and getting responses that are meaningful and appropriate is to ask well-phrased open-ended questions. Such questions usually begin with words such as *What, When, How, Why,* and *To what extent,* and challenge or encourage thinking. You will read more about this technique in Chapter 9.

Action Learning Strategies

Any technique that actively engages the minds of your participants or gets them physically involved can lead to increased learning. Whether they participate individually or in small groups, learners can figure out how to modify existing processes or practices, systems, ideas, or techniques in order to develop new variations simply by becoming engaged in the learning. Many of the training strategies outlined throughout this book in which participants move or interact fall into the action learning category (see Books in Resources for Trainers in the appendices).

Real-World Examples

Providing specific experiences and events that mirror those faced by participants is an excellent way to cause reflection and help learners see the relationship between what they already know and what is being presented.

Practical Application

Whenever you can build in opportunities for participants to interact and work toward solving real-world issues (e.g., role play, self-assessment, action planning, or group discussion) you can potentially increase learning and understanding. By giving participants classroom time to deal with workplace issues, you can often help them to feel better about the training experience and to walk away with some practical tools that they can immediately apply. The latter usually leads to a better appreciation of the training, higher evaluation ratings, and more management support for future training initiatives.

You cannot teach a man anything. You can only help him discover it within himself.
  —*Galileo Galilei*
  Italian astronomer

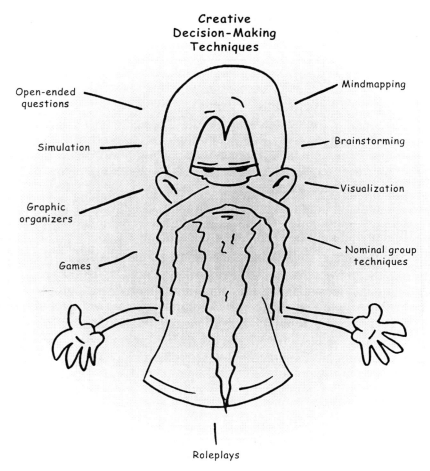

MINDMAP 1. Creative Decision-Making Techniques

INTERIM REVIEW

Take a mental break to challenge your creative brain and review some of the key terms experienced in this chapter thus far by completing **Figure 2-4.** You can also use a similar technique as an Interim Review in any of your training sessions by creating Word Match puzzles with key terms of the program and distributing to participants. Give them a copy of the puzzle and encourage looking in any notes or handouts as needed to find answers. They can work individually or as teams and should be given a time frame for completing (e.g., 5 minutes). Those getting the most correct terms within the time allotted can be rewarded. You can then review key concepts and discuss any additional information related to the topic that they should know.

LIGHTING THE CREATIVITY LAMP

Analogy ____	A. To dissect ideas logically
Brainstorming ____	B. Stage 1 of Creativity Process
Convergent ____	C. Stage 2 of Creativity Process
Divergent ____	D. Creator of Mind Mapping process
Enablers ____	E. Use string, scarves, cards and money
Illumination ____	F. Reality Oriented Performance Experiential System
Illusions ____	G. Stage 4 of Creativity Process
Incubation ____	H. Conversations held with oneself
Inhibitors ____	I. Figure of speech referring one concept to another
Magic Tricks ____	J. The way a person views the world
Metaphor ____	K. Process for structured idea gathering
Mindmap ____	L. Pictures that distort perception
Paradigm ____	M. Allows acting out real-life issues
Preparation ____	N. Technique for making ideas visual
Role Play ____	O. Factors blocking creativity
ROPES ____	P. Stage 3 of Creativity Process
Self-talk ____	Q. Strategies to assist thinking outside the box
Tony Buzan ____	R. Generating large numbers of ideas
Verification ____	S. Relating one thing to something similar

FIGURE 2-4. Word match puzzle. Match the terms to the correct letter of its definition. (Answers on page 417.)

● AWAKENING YOUR CREATIVITY

Being effective at generating creative ideas requires examination of personal **paradigms.** For example, if you are a person who takes a more pessimistic view of the world (e.g., the glass is half empty) versus an optimistic perspective (e.g., the glass is half full), your creativity could be overshadowed. The first step to enhanced creativity is to recognize and believe that you are a creative person.

Next, you must seek out and welcome opportunities to exercise your creativity (e.g., participate on committees or projects that require creative planning and problem-solving; volunteer to deliver programs in which you can experiment with creative training techniques—Junior Achievement, religious groups, nonprofit organizations, or professional groups). It is important to keep an open mind and use a variety of techniques for generating alternatives and creative ideas. You can also participate in activities that cause you to exercise your brain, such as board games or puzzles. Another way of enhancing your creativity is to participate personally in (and use with your own participants) interactive training techniques in which participants individually or collectively work together to solve problems (e.g., **Reality Oriented Performance Experiential System [ROPES], storyboarding,** and **simulations**).

● CREATIVITY ENABLERS

To enhance your creativity, or to get participants thinking outside the box, get back to the basics by keeping in mind that we learn adult behaviors as children. Take time out of your schedule to reconnect with your inner child in order to rekindle the creativity flame. If you have children, raid their toy box or closet. If not, take an idea excursion to a local toy or hobby store and just wander. Pick up toys and really look at them. Check their features and how they operate. Think of what metaphors you can create to tie into your training topics or how you can integrate them into activities or use them as rewards in training. Select items that might cause you or learners to think, plan, organize, develop, experiment, or strategize.

The key in making your selections, and in generating creative ideas, is to have fun. People who have fun and enjoy what they do are typically more satisfied and productive. Just as children learn as they play and have fun, so too can adults (after all, they already know how because they learned the skill as children). Learning does not have to be somber or boring. Some specific strategies for encouraging creativity and fun follow.

BRIGHT IDEA

Challenging Participant Creativity

To help rekindle the creative enthusiasm of childhood in your participants, build a variety of activities early in your session. Start their creative juices going by presenting a challenge in which small groups of learners work together to solve trivia questions. Relate the questions and problem-solving process they use to your program topic. You can purchase decks of cards that offer a variety of such challenges (see Creative Presentation Resources, Inc., in Resources for Trainers in the appendices).

Drawing or Painting

Art can assist participants visualize abstract ideas or concepts. In your training, pass out markers, large crayons, or finger paint along with sheets of newsprint (flip chart paper). Ask participants to create team logos that visually show their group values or any other characteristics that you designate. Encourage them to loosen up and have fun. Stress that artistic ability is not being measured. As a review activity, you could use a similar exercise in which groups or individuals create an image showing people demonstrating key concepts covered in the program.

PUTTING YOUR BRAIN TO WORK: ACTIVITY

What are some ways in which you use art, or have seen it used in training programs? _____

_____

_____

In what programs currently taught could you begin using art to stimulate creativity? _____

_____

How can you use art in one of the classes you have identified (be specific)? _____

_____

_____

Models

Creating structures with building blocks or Legos® can help foster such skills as communication, teamwork, problem-solving, decision-making, resource and time management, and strategic planning. Create a simple model of a building, wall, or structure that will be copied by small groups of participants. Explain to learners that they have a specified time period to replicate your model, which is displayed on a table in the front of the room. Their re-creations must be exact replicas and they cannot remove your model to their work area(s). Designate a single person in each group to be the team leader or whatever title you prefer (see Chapter 6). That person is the only one who can travel to the front table to examine the model. The leader must then return to his or her group to communicate details and what must be done to copy the model exactly. Allow the leaders to view your model as often as they like. Give no other instructions to them other than that they should work at designated tables, think outside the box, and have fun. At the end of the designated time, debrief the activity. Ask questions such as, "What worked?," "What did not work?," and "What could they have done differently?" Many times, group leaders will not ask questions, make drawings of the model, move their table closer to the model so others can view from a distance, or otherwise creatively try to accomplish their task because you did not tell them to do so. They assume that if it is something they can do, you would tell them. This is a common mistake that people make in the workplace. Instead of asking questions, they make assumptions based on their past experiences. Stress this in your debrief as you encourage future creative thinking.

You can add a festive or competitive edge to the activity by offering prizes or having a small celebration upon completion.

PUTTING YOUR BRAIN TO WORK: ACTIVITY

How can models be effective in encouraging creativity in your training? _____

_____

In what way can you incorporate models into your current programs? _____

_____

What rewards might be used to celebrate successes following a modeling activity? _____

_____

Playing Card and Board Games

Training sessions are an excellent venue for the use of playing card and board games to introduce key concepts, conduct interim and final reviews, and provide a break from lecture or other facilitator led learning events. A number of companies have created residual materials in the form of card and board games to be used in team competitions that are based on familiar television game shows (e.g., Concentration®, Family Feud®, Jeopardy®, and Wheel of Fortune®). These companies (see Resources for Trainers in the appendices) offer light tables, game boards, and other items to reduce the amount of production that you have to do in order to incorporate the games into your training. Of course, if you are handy with a hammer and nails, or have an engineering department in your organization, you can build your own props from scrap materials that are lying around. All it takes is time and some creativity on your part.

Games are wonderful ways to relax learners while giving them a chance to review and remember topic concepts. They also help in strengthening creative and mental processes. Monopoly®, chess, checkers, pick up sticks, Chinese checkers, Throw 'n Go Jenga®, Scrabble®, bridge, or similar games can help develop and enhance skills, such as problem-solving, decision-making, strategic planning, and interpersonal communication.

You can use or modify many popular games to address virtually any topic. For example, if you supervise new employee orientation for your organization, you can create an end of the day review of material covered by creating a variation of Jeopardy® in which game board headings are key areas covered in your material (e.g., Employee Benefits, Policies and Procedures, Organizational History or structure, Products and Services, and so on). Divide participants into teams, rather than having individual contestants, and have them line up behind one of three different colored lights on a light table that you create or buy. As the game show host or hostess, you ask the questions and coordinate the game just as it is done on television. Once one category is selected and the answer either given or missed, the first three contestants move to the end of the line and the next three come up. You can add more fun and realism by dressing in a tuxedo or evening gown, rewarding participants with small gifts with the organizational logo on them, and using the actual Jeopardy® theme song (see Chapter 5 for information about using copyrighted music in training). Using a game format adds fun and reinforces what can sometimes be a boring day and topic.

BRIGHT IDEA
Using a Game to Review

Here is another example of how a game might be incorporated into your program to review material at the end of the session. Use Scrabble® or a similar word game as a basis for reinforcing program concepts. Form groups of six to eight participants and give each a Scrabble® game set, flip chart, and markers. Designate a timekeeper, leader/scribe (see Chapter 6). Set a 30-minute time limit and tell the groups to begin playing using the standard rules except that they may only use terms related to the session content. Have the leader/ scribe watch the time and record each term identified on the flip chart (position flip charts so that one group cannot see another's responses). Each person within a group has up to 1 minute to either form a word or pass to the next player. After 30 minutes, call time and have each group display its list as someone in that group explains the term in relation to what was covered during the session. You can add competition and fun by rewarding the group with the most correct terms. Disqualify any incorrect terms or items that were not covered in the session and add key concepts missed. If you desire, you can reward any really creative ideas related to the topic even though they were not part of material covered.

What programs do you currently present that could benefit from the use of a board or card game?

_____

_____

How can games be incorporated into your programs to add excitement while reinforcing content?

_____

_____

What card games can you think of that you might adapt and adopt for your training? _____

_____

What board games can you think of to add pizzazz to your sessions? _____

_____

Magic Tricks

Using money, cards, scarves, string, ribbon, or a variety of other items in magic tricks are excellent ways to attract attention and help sharpen mental skills for you and your learners. There are hundreds of books teaching simple magic tricks that can be used in training sessions (see Creative Presentation Resources in the Resources for Trainers in the appendices). Magic takes participants back to their childhood where they were often spellbound at magic shows trying to figure out how the tricks were done. For a few dollars and a couple hours of invested time you can perfect simple tricks and activities that will mesmerize learners as you gain and hold their attention, then tie the activity into session concepts.

Think of your current training programs.

Which training programs need more attention getting activities? _____

_____

What types of magic tricks can you think of to open your training sessions? _____

_____

How can you tie such tricks into program content to increase learning and retention? _____

_____

Juggling

While juggling appears to be complicated, it is relatively easy to learn and master with practice. It is also entertaining, stimulating, and fun to watch. Although you may not want to start with chain saws, you can easily incorporate juggling into your sessions as an attention gainer and as a mental break for participants. Probably the easiest and most physically draining form of juggling uses silk scarves. Since these float slowly back toward the ground, they are easy to master and teach. The technique can be learned from any basic juggling book (see Creative Presentation Resources, Inc. in Resources for Trainers in the appendices). The technique energizes while teaching hand–eye coordination, concentration, mental alertness, and creativity. Juggling can be used as an individual or group activity in which pairs of participants practice to enhance teamwork and communication. They can coach one another, then provide feedback as they learn the skill. You can even add the element of competition [e.g., the person(s) who can keep juggling longest without making a mistake].

PUTTING YOUR BRAIN TO WORK: ACTIVITY

In what ways can you incorporate juggling into your training programs?_____

_____

How do you envision juggling being tied into program content?_____

_____

_____

Jigsaw Puzzles

Most people learn to put jigsaw puzzles together as children. They can often recall spending hours trying to assemble the odd shaped pieces to form a picture just like the one on the box. The challenge and feeling of satisfaction after completing the puzzle (especially when there were 500 or more pieces) is exhilarating and provides a feeling of accomplishment. Similarly, you can help participants recall those youthful feelings by incorporating jigsaw puzzles into your programs. Jigsaws can be used to introduce objectives or key concepts, as an interim review, as a teambuilding activity, at the end of a program for review, and in a number of other ways.

There are several ways to create a customized jigsaw puzzle to use in a session. Many art and craft stores sell blank white jigsaw puzzles that have coated surfaces onto which you can write or draw terms, objectives, or images. You can create one for each participant, pass them out in small paper bags, and have participants try to assemble them in a timed activity during your introduction or later as a review.

Another option for team activities is to purchase small children's puzzle (18–25 pieces is usually plenty; otherwise, an activity becomes too time consuming) at any hobby, toy, or similar retail store. Create a list of key session terms or other information on your computer, print multiple copies (on different colored paper), and then cut them to the shapes of the puzzle pieces. Paste these cutouts to the face or back of the puzzle you purchased. When you are ready for an activity, pass out the puzzles and have participants work in small groups to solve the puzzle, thus revealing key terms that they then discuss within their group or as a class. A variation of this activity is to create a number of puzzles with differing content on the pieces. You will need one puzzle for each small group that you have. Put each puzzle into a small paper bag; however, take two pieces from each puzzle to mix into another team's bag. Each team will then have pieces belonging to another team. Do not tell teams of the missing pieces. Specify a time limit, then tell participants that their goal is to complete their puzzle using whatever means they need to. Someone will eventually realize what is going on and will start checking with other groups. This type of activity encourages creativity, thinking out of the box, communication, negotiation, time management, and a number of other skills.

Crossword and Word Search Puzzles

These types of puzzles are nonthreatening, fun ways to conduct a pre- or post-session test without causing test anxiety. They can also be used a session interim, such as in this chapter, and final reviews. During a session, you might use one of these puzzles to introduce key concepts or objectives that will be discussed during the session by having the clues for the puzzle mirror those key concepts.

To create crossword or word search puzzles, you can either purchase computer software that will make up a puzzle along with an answer key from terms that you input (see Crossword Puzzle Software in the Resources for Trainers in the appendices) or you can manually create them with pen and paper. As participants complete the puzzles, they naturally reflect on what was learned and recognize the terms, thus reinforcing the learning and aiding memory.

To get creative ideas for other types of puzzles such as word match that you might create or use, visit teacher supply stores or bookstores in your area, or log onto the Internet to search under the heading puzzles or to check online booksellers (see Resources for Trainers in the appendices). These companies sell books and magazines with puzzles and activities for use by children and in schools that can be modified for adult learning environments. You can also visit local libraries and search their shelves.

PUTTING YOUR BRAIN TO WORK: ACTIVITY

How can you begin using crossword and word search puzzles in you programs? _____

_____

What types of puzzles do you believe will work best for your training topics? Why? _____

_____

What value can your learners gain from using puzzles? _____

Optical Illusions

People are fascinated by things that are not what they seem. Optical illusions are wonderfully creative tools for emphasizing that first impressions are not always correct. They can also be used to grab or regain attention as an energizing activity throughout the day. You can include them in your sessions by making transparencies of several illusions. To do so, have participants take out paper and pencil, project the images on the screen for 10 seconds, and have learners write down what they see. After going through a few of the illusions, go back and project them one at a time and ask, "What did you see?" It amazes people how many different perceptions there were about the same material. The point that you can then make is that each learner is unique with different experiences and perspectives, and each can serve as a resource to another in training and in the workplace. **Figures 2–5 through 2-10** offer some sample illusions. More can be obtained from books or on the Internet by typing in Optical Illusions.

FIGURE 2-6. What do you see?

POSSIBLE SOLUTION: Can be seen as a face looking left or as the scripted word liar running vertically down the page.

FIGURE 2-5. What do you see?

POSSIBLE SOLUTION: Elephant or elephant with extra legs

FIGURE 2-7. What do you see?

POSSIBLE SOLUTION: Can be seen as a saxophone player or a woman facing the viewer.

FIGURE 2-8. What do you see?

POSSIBLE SOLUTION: Can be seen as an Eskimo with back towards the viewer or an Indian facing left.

FIGURE 2-9. What do you see?

POSSIBLE SOLUTION: Bird with lady in its beak or big fish with a canoe and a man in its mouth.

FIGURE 2-10. What do you see?

POSSIBLE SOLUTION: Can be seen as an Old Woman if viewed one way, if flipped upside down, can be viewed as a young princess.

PUTTING YOUR BRAIN TO WORK: ACTIVITY

How can optical illusions add creativity to your training sessions? _____

_____

To which learner modality do you think optical illusions would most appeal? Why? _____

_____

How can you ensure that optical illusions will appeal and add value for all three learning modalities?

_____

_____

Stories

Sharing personal experiences and other types of stories based on events that will interest participants and relate to a session topic is an excellent, proven method for gaining attention and helping learners understand relationships between what is being offered and the real world. When designing your programs, use tales about successful people and events from within your organization, industry, or other sources. Explain how concepts being presented are used successfully in the workplace by others. Doing so will likely generate more interest and buy-in from your participants. For example, Walt Disney World employees in Orlando, Florida, have gained international recognition for the excellent manner in which they relate actual Disney experiences to new employees in their orientation program, *Traditions*.

By relating personal experiences and sharing information based on actual events or situations, you can also help your learners to better grasp key points and ultimately translate them into personal action.

BRIGHT IDEA

Finding Stories

Take some time in the next couple of weeks to gather organizational and personal stories that can be used in the classroom. Elicit examples of what works and does not work from others in your organization. Start a file or log of the stories you collect along with the name and contact information of the contributor, in case you later need to reference them or ask additional clarifying questions. Once you have a good number of tales, organize them by their relationship to various program topics that you conduct, then start building them into program design.

PUTTING YOUR BRAIN TO WORK: ACTIVITY

What types of events or experiences can you think of that would make good stories for use in your sessions? _____

_____

What are some potential sources of stories that you might tap within your organization? _____

_____

Metaphors

By using a **metaphor** or figure of speech that is used to explain or illustrate points you are making, you can help learners visualize key concepts. An important thing to remember is that their successful understanding is dependent on whether your learners have a base of knowledge related to your example. A sample metaphor that might be used during a training program might be, *high as a kite*. This metaphor could be used to explain interest rates in a financial class, the impact that drugs have on someone in a drug prevention class, or the emotional level that a participant might experience on coming to an understanding of a difficult point during a training program.

PUTTING YOUR BRAIN TO WORK: ACTIVITY

How have you seen metaphors used in the past? _____

_____

What was the result? _____

_____

List some metaphors that you can use to relate to program topics that you present. _____

_____

_____

Analogies

Comparisons of different things that share similarities are known as **analogies.** Using an analogy typically involves sharing information that participants can relate to something they already know. For example, in a train-the-trainer session in which the importance of setting behavioral-based learning objectives is discussed, the analogy might be made to Christopher Columbus' trip to the Americas in 1492. Before using it or any other analogy, however, it is important that you ask if everyone is familiar with Columbus' exploits. In a multicultural world, you should make no assumptions.

Assuming that everyone is familiar with the story, you can then explain that the use of learning objectives is important to help participants know where they are going in the session, to gauge progress, and to evaluate end of program achievement of the objectives. The analogy is that without objectives, programs end up like the trip Columbus took:

When Columbus started out on his journey to the new world, he was not sure where he was going. (relates to where they are going for a session)

When he arrived in America, he was not sure where he was. (relates to gauging progress)

When he returned home, he was not sure where he had been. (relates to program achievement)

PUTTING YOUR BRAIN TO WORK: ACTIVITY

What program concepts do you present that lend themselves to analogies? _____

_____

What kinds of analogies can you think of that will appeal to a large range of participants (e.g., industry, pets, cars, or hobbies)? _____

_____

What do you perceive to be the biggest challenge in using analogies in your training? _____

_____

How can you overcome these challenges? _____

_____

An idea is nothing more nor less than a new combination of old elements.
—James Webb Young
Author

BRIGHT IDEA
Creativity Resources

To learn more about creative thinking and techniques for developing creative problem-solving skills, do an Internet and library search for the following creative thinkers and authors:

Jordan Ayan   Doug Hall

Edward de Bono   James M. Higgins

Tony Buzan   Bryan W. Mattimore

Jack Foster   Michael Michalko

Richard Forbes   Roger von Oech

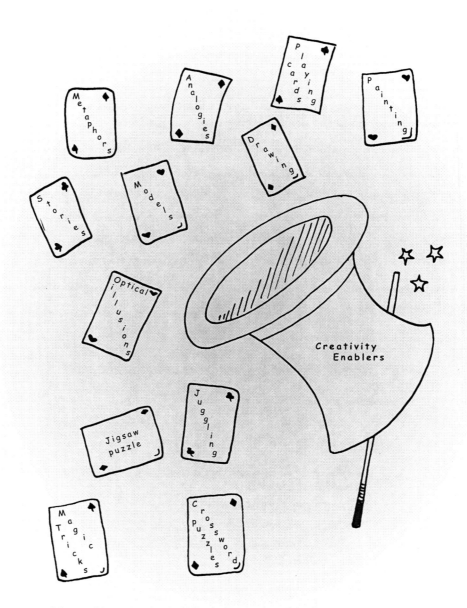

MINDMAP 2. Creativity Enablers

● CREATIVITY INHIBITORS

Although there are likely an unlimited number of strategies for encouraging creativity, there are also factors that can block your creativity and that of your learners. By identifying and dealing with such factors in advance, you can potentially reduce or eliminate them in your sessions. Some typical creativity inhibitors include the following (see also Table 2-1).

Organizational Culture

The organizational environment in which you work or train can either spark or extinguish your creative lamp and that of your learners. If your supervisor or organization effectively plans and welcomes change and new ideas, you are more likely to experiment with program format and the way you approach learning. Likewise, participants are more likely to become excited and actively involved in brainstorming ideas and

Table 2-1. Trainer Characteristics

Creative Trainers	*Average Trainers*
Model creativity.	Make excuses for not being creative.
Continually search for creative alternatives.	Accept status quo.
Encourage participant involvement.	Stifle involvement.
Celebrate creative thinking.	Discourage creative thinking.
Make time for creativity.	Use limited time as an excuse.
Partner with participants through activity.	Control participant thinking and activity.
Interact.	Lecture.
Have a broad range of knowledge and interests.	Are narrow minded.
Seek new knowledge and skills.	Are satisfied meeting minimum standards.

solutions to organizational issues. This is often the result of their belief that there is opportunity for implementation and reward of such efforts. On the other hand, if there is an atmosphere of strict control where supervisors or others dictate content and delivery style, then creativity is usually limited.

Another potentially inhibiting factor within the organizational culture is the percentage of left- and right-brain thinkers. As you read in Chapter 1, people with right-brain dominance often tend to think more about the bigger picture and are more abstract in their thinking whereas left-brain dominance often leads to focus on specifics and minutia. For that reason, organizations that traditionally have a large number of linear thinkers (e.g., accounting, some associations, certain government agencies, legal firms, and some types of technical companies) may be more prone to follow existing guidelines or maintain the status quo. Although creativity does exist within such organizations, and predominantly left-brain thinkers are capable of creative thinking, their efforts are often directed at activities and processes that satisfy an issue or need that arises rather than an unstructured attempt to spontaneously redesign training or other system. When such attitudes carry over into your training sessions, participants may be hesitant to think outside the box unless given specific directions or promised individual rewards.

Speaking of rewards, although they can encourage creativity (e.g., during brainstorming), they can also limit it. For example, if you provide small incentives for participant responses or to the first person to offer and idea in your sessions, you may encourage participation. If such rewards are not fairly and equitably distributed to many people, however, the impact might be negative and counterproductive (see Chapter 10).

PUTTING YOUR BRAIN TO WORK: ACTIVITY

What are you currently doing in your organization or client organizations to ensure that training is a fluid function where learning and exploration is encouraged? _____

_____

What else could you do to encourage a creative learning environment? _____

_____

Who can you enlist to assist you in increasing the creativity quotient in the organization and how will you go about doing so? _____

_____

Participant Attitude

Another factor potentially inhibiting creativity is the attitude that each participant brings to the training environment. If your participants arrive excited about their impending learning opportunity, they are more likely to become actively involved. On the other hand, if participants are forced to attend training, or have not been adequately briefed on expected outcomes or how they will benefit from the training, their perspective of the training may be grim. For participants to embrace training, they have to see the value in terms of personal gain (e.g., how it will help them do their job in a more effective and efficient manner). They must also believe that their supervisor and organization support the training initiative and will allow them to apply what is learned and reward appropriately as a result of improved performance. These things failing, participant attitude will likely be poor and there will be creativity disconnect.

BRIGHT IDEA

Opening the Creativity Door

If you want participants to be creative, use activities that leave the "how to" up to them. Provide tools and instructions on what they are to accomplish; however, do not set expressed goals or objectives. Let them determine outcomes and explain their end results.

Another alternative is to explain the activity and then jointly set objectives and outcomes that they will work toward with learners. If you set goals and objectives for them, you will likely end up with standard or cookie cutter results.

PUTTING YOUR BRAIN TO WORK: ACTIVITY

In what ways can you encourage participant involvement and creativity in training? _____

_____

What strategies can you use to prepare your participants for a creative learning experience before they arrive? _____

_____

Who can you enlist to assist you in increasing the creativity quotient in the organization and how will you go about doing so? _____

_____

> *A conclusion is the place where you got tired of thinking.*
> *—Martin H. Fischer*

Trainer Motivation

A third creativity inhibiting factor relates to your own motivation and desire to be creative. Whether you consider yourself to be creative and having the desire to be so can increase or decrease training and participant effectiveness. Too often, trainers stifle their own creativity and fail to try new ideas or techniques because they fear failure. Rather than attempt a new activity or approach to training (e.g., a magic trick, telling a joke, wearing a funny prop during their introduction, or otherwise experimenting), many trainers stick to the tried and true strategies that they and others have used for some time. In their mind, even average program evaluation is better than running the risk of trying something new and being less successful. Some of the reluctance might result from inexperience, while other aspects might relate to fear of the unknown or criticism, lack of confidence, or simple complacency. Whatever the logic, you are likely doing yourself, your participants, and your organization a grave disservice if you allow similar reasons to impede your own creativity initiatives.

● COUNTERING NEGATIVITY

To help you overcome any potential reluctance to experiment and be creative in your approach to training, try the following.

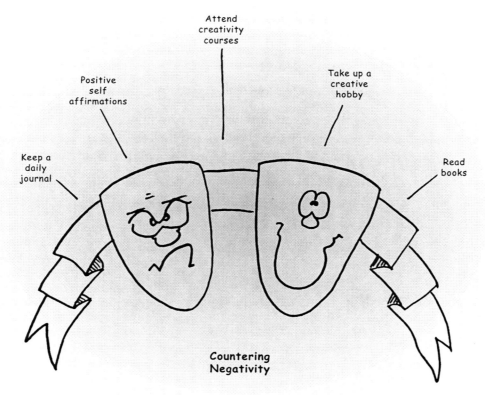

MINDMAP 3. Countering Negativity

Provide Positive Self-Affirmations

Negative **self-talk** can lead to decreased self-respect and lowered confidence. It can also ultimately lead to decreased personal effectiveness. To counter such possible negative results, give yourself some positive strokes throughout your day (e.g., "I am a creative person," "I can do a better job by being creative," or " My ideas are valuable").

Attend Creativity Courses

Identify and participate in training sessions that address creative training techniques and/or in which the facilitator models such strategies. Make notes of approaches that you like and can modify for your own sessions. In your training adapt what you learned to your own style and situation in order to add new dimensions to your delivery.

Read Books

There are many books (see Resources for Trainers in the appendices) on creativity, creative training techniques and strategies, creative thinking, and creative problem-solving. Build a library of these books and use them to stimulate your own creative processes regularly. If you borrow an activity or material from a book, ensure that you appropriately site the copyright owner to prevent claims of copyright infringement that can discredit you and your organization professionally.

Take Up a Creative Hobby

You often gain ideas for training through creativity in other areas. For example, if you started cartooning as a hobby, you could easily adapt the skill to develop material for your participant training materials, classes, and visual aids. Working crossword puzzles or reading mystery novels can also challenge and stimulate your brain.

Keep a Daily Journal

You likely get creative ideas at various times during the day related to how you can improve training materials or content. Have a pad and pen nearby (e.g., next to your bed, in your car, or on your desk) so that you can capture such ideas or thoughts. These provide a visual record when you have time to go back to review them and begin blending them into your programs or training strategies.

The key to effective creativity is to be willing to take a chance, try something new and do things that have a direct correlation to your sessions. Letting past experience and beliefs stand in the way of using new strategies or techniques is not helping you or your learners.

APPLYING WHAT YOU LEARNED
Strategies for Lighting Your Creativity Lamp

1. What are some ways that your personal creativity can help increase training effectiveness?

_____

_____

2. How can you use the four steps in the creativity process to improve the level of creativity among your learners? _____

_____

3. Which of the creative problem-solving techniques from this chapter can you immediately start applying in your training sessions? _____

_____

4. In what ways can you change the way you currently deliver training to incorporate more of the ideas that you read about in this chapter?_____

_____

5. Based on what you have read in this chapter, what personal and organizational paradigms do you plan to reexamine?_____

_____

6. How can the enhancers listed in this chapter assist you in expanding your creative thinking?

_____

_____

7. What are some of the organizational inhibitors currently preventing creative thinking in your organization and how can you help eliminate them? _____

_____

ENDNOTES

[5]Wallas, G., *The Art of Thought,* Harcourt Brace Jovanovich, New York, 1926.

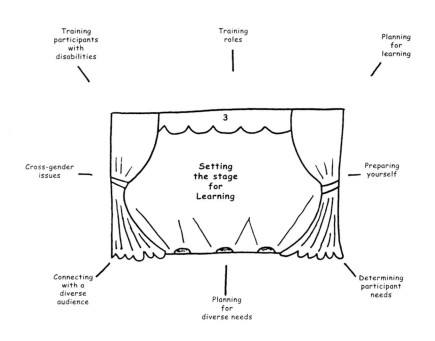

Training
participants
with
disabilities

Training
roles

Planning
for
learning

Cross-gender
issues

3

Setting
the stage
for
Learning

Preparing
yourself

Connecting
with a
diverse
audience

Planning
for
diverse needs

Determining
participant
needs

Setting the Stage for Learning

I never teach my pupils; I only provide conditions in which they can learn.

—Albert Einstein
Physicist

Learning Objectives

At the end of this chapter, and when applying concepts covered, you will be able to:

● Effectively determine techniques for discovering participant training needs before, during, and after a session.

● Present yourself in a professional, positive manner.

● Prepare to address the learning needs of participants with disabilities.

● Address the needs of participants from other cultures.

● Recognize the learning differences between men and women and the need to adapt to the needs of both groups.

It is a mistake to think that your participants know how to learn effectively and understand the learning process. Many trainers nonetheless make this assumption every day. The result is that participants likely arrive for a training session with no clear understanding of what their role is or what you will provide. To help eliminate stress, confusion, and potentially a learning failure, you would be wise to consider ways to prepare participants for their learning experience.

I have found that when I put more effort into planning and preparation, there has been greater success and satisfaction for my learners and me. The most important factor to remember is your learners. Everything you do in training should be learner centered and focused on ensuring that a transfer of knowledge has occurred so that participants can use what they received in real-world situations. In this chapter, you will explore some of the techniques and strategies that have worked for me in training various types of learners over the past three decades. Many are adapted or adopted from other trainers who may be smarter and more talented than I, but the important thing is that they work.

● TRAINING ROLES

An important first step in creating a situation in which learning will be successful is to determine the roles that you and your participants will assume. This requires a bit of forethought on your part and a flexible attitude, as you are partnering with your learners. Often, they will arrive for training with past experiences or preconceived ideas that require you to modify your planned agenda.

One technique that I use for programs that last a day or more is to place a copy of a **Training Agreement** or contract (see Tools for Trainers section in the Appendices) at each learner's location prior to his or her arrival. As part of my introductory remarks, I focus on the agreement and ask for learners' input and comments and elicit any additions. Any further roles identified are listed and posted on flip chart paper as a reminder. By raising the issue of roles and expectations early in the session, you can help focus the learners' attention and potentially better encourage participation throughout the day.

BRIGHT IDEA
Identifying Expectations

In addition to using a training agreement, you can use an icebreaker activity in which participants are given a 3 × 5 index card and asked to write down one expectation that they have of the session (e.g., content, delivery style, format, schedule or whatever they are interested in). Have them then form small groups, select a leader and scribe, list each expectation on a piece of flip chart paper, and then discuss how they can individually play a role in ensuring that each expectation is met. After 10–15 minutes, have the group leader present his or her group's list to other groups and share ideas on how they will assist the session's success.

Using the 3 × 5 approach can help draw out expectations from people who are either shy or who often do not share openly when simply asked, "What are your expectations?" It also helps learners become involved early and prompts them to take ownership for the success of the session.

PUTTING YOUR BRAIN TO WORK: ACTIVITY

What roles other than those listed on the sample training agreement can you think of that you play in training? _____

_____

What other roles do your participants typically play? _____

_____

How can you better ensure that you and your participants succeed in fulfilling your roles? _____

_____

_____

There is no guarantee of reaching a goal at a certain time, but
there is a guarantee of never attaining goals that are never set.
  –David McNally
  Even Eagles Need a Push

◉ PLANNING FOR LEARNING

As in many other aspects of life, the prime element for ensuring the success of your training involves planning. You cannot overplan for a session because there are so many variables that can impact participant learning. No matter how many times you have presented a specific topic, I encourage you to use a checklist similar to the sample found in the Tools for Trainers section of the appendices (Presentation Pre-Session Planning Checklist) each time you schedule a program. Modify it to meet your needs.

PUTTING YOUR BRAIN TO WORK: ACTIVITY

Think about the way you currently plan for your sessions.

What do you do to plan and track activities for each session? _____

_____

Have there been times when you failed to plan and realized during the session that you forgot something? If so, what challenges did that create for you and/or your participants? _____

_____

_____

What can you do in the future to ensure that you are ready for your sessions prior to the arrival of participants? _____

_____

● PREPARING YOURSELF

A difficult concept for some trainers and facilitators to grasp is that they are not the center of attention or the reason participants attend a program. It is the message and the learning that results from their presence that is the crucial element; you and all trainers are simply the catalyst or change agent for learning. Granted, some facilitators or trainers are more effective than others owing to their "stage presence," style, communication ability, knowledge, and experience. If you put on too good of a show by using too many bells, whistles, and fancy equipment, however, you can actually distract and detract from comprehension of the message.

To prevent a negative learning experience from occurring, there are a number of personal areas that require advance attention.

Clothing

I have heard that within the first 30 seconds, participants form an impression of you that can last a lifetime, no matter what you subsequently do. Coupled with the research you read about in Chapter 1 related to attention span, this should certainly be reason enough to focus on your appearance. What you wear and how you look is a very important part of setting the learning environment for your participants. The old adage, "You never get a second chance to make a good first impression" is certainly true.

The standard advice for professional trainers and facilitators for years has been to wear good quality clothing and dress equal to or one level above audience members. Make sure that your clothing is clean, well tailored, and freshly pressed. Also, keep jewelry low-key and minimal. What complicates this concept is that many organizations now have casual days or dress down days in which employees wear all combinations of clothing. This can certainly mean frustration and confusion for you. Often your dress will be dictated by organizational culture, whether you are internal (working for an organization) or external (consultant or contract trainer), the dress of participants, and the topic and location of training. For example, if you are conducting ROPES training in an outdoor environment, you may wear shorts and a collared sports shirt versus a suit or dress in the corporate setting. Luckily, there are books (see Resources for Trainers in the appendices) and websites[6] with valuable information on dressing in a casual and changing world.

A guideline that I normally follow is that I overdress and remove things, as appropriate. For example, if my audience is in business casual, I typically wear a suit or sports jacket and slacks. During my opening remarks, I encourage participants to get comfortable and I do the same. For example, I might take off my jacket and possibly my tie. Often, I will do this in a lighthearted manner. I might say something during opening remarks about how I want them to feel comfortable and encourage them by saying something like, "Do whatever you need to do to be comfortable. If you want to take your shoes off, go ahead as long as your neighbors do not complain." I might also comment that "I usually wear a jacket to a session so that you will know that I own a jacket and trousers that match." At that point, I approach a random participant and say, "Can I get an independent verification. Do these trousers and jacket match?" Once he or she says yes, I say, "Good, now that I've accomplished my purpose, I'm going to get rid of it and I encourage you to do likewise if you feel like it." Such an approach can get the message across about a relaxed environment, reduces possible tension, and shows that I do not take myself too seriously, thus making me seem more approachable.

General Clothing Guidelines for Women

Women typically wear conservative (one color) dresses or skirt suits when doing formal presentations, or to groups to whom they are new and trying to gain credibility. In some organizational cultures, pants suits can be substituted.
For less formal occasions, a professional looking multicolored dress with jacket usually suffices. The jacket can later be removed, if desired.

General Clothing Guidelines for Men

Men can often wear dark suits with white shirts for formal presentations or when they want a dramatic impact. Likewise, the same clothing is worn when trying to establish credibility with a group. For less formal occasions, when groups know the presenter, or when his reputation is known, a nice sport jacket, slacks, and colored, button-collar shirt usually work well.

While we are talking about clothing, do not forget the importance of well-maintained, freshly polished shoes. Also, if your clothes have belt loops, wear a high-quality belt that matches your shoes.

Color

Another aspect to remember related to clothing is color. Psychology experts who have studied the impact of color have reported the following[7]:

Men and women from upper class backgrounds are attracted to blue-based red tones, including burgundy. Interestingly, the color burgundy creates feelings of uneasiness and distrust in lower-class people because of its richness. Consider the fact that burgundy has been the color of choice of many royals throughout history.

Dark greens (Lincoln and forest) are also upper-income colors that send a message of classiness, status, and high price. Remember the rash of forest green vehicles that hit the U.S. market in the late 1990s and positive consumer response to them?

Blue-green tones are best for attracting the attention of both sexes; however, some experts find that many men often view women who wear these colors as "easy," in the same way they might a prostitute. Even so, research shows that women like the color on other women and react positively to those wearing it.

Brown on men tends to elicit distrust, however, the same is not true when worn by women.[8]

Grooming

As with dress, much has changed over the years for men and women related to personal grooming and styling. It is still usually safer to stay more mainstream in your grooming habits. Eccentricities in the length, shape, and color of your hair; makeup that stands out; glittery nail polish; or facial hair that is extreme (or in some organizational cultures, facial hair at all) can all detract from your message and should be avoided.

PUTTING YOUR BRAIN TO WORK: ACTIVITY

Think of instances in which the clothing or grooming of a presenter or trainer distracted you from receiving his or her message.

What aspect about him or her was distracting? _____

_____

_____

How can you use his or her mistake to ensure that you present a professional image each time you step in front of your participants? _____

_____

_____

● DETERMINING PARTICIPANT NEEDS

Asking your participants what they want or need is one way of ensuring that you truly provide information and tools that add value for them. Ideally, such information gathering should occur prior to the design of your program in order to incorporate material that is needed by participants. If this is not feasible, then obtain the information as quickly as possible before or at the beginning of a session.

Pre-Session Needs Assessment

There are a variety of ways to gather information related to participant needs prior to your session. The best choices are face-to-face or over the telephone, which allow for follow-up questioning and clarification of information.

One-on-One Interviews

If at all possible, meet with or talk to all participants on the telephone prior to a scheduled session. Also, contact their supervisors, managers, team members, and if possible, their customers to get a broader perspective of needs. Talking to others helps give you insights into areas that those people see as performance needs. This is helpful because participants often do not recognize or admit to knowledge or skill gaps witnessed by those around them. Such interviews should be conducted before the design and delivery of training when possible.

At the least, I encourage you to speak with participants even when you have been told of needs by supervisors or program sponsors. My experience has been that the latter groups do not always have an accurate picture of the needs of their employees. These people are too often not in daily contact with participants. As a result they only believe they know performance and knowledge gaps, or skills required to do a job.

Focus Groups

Interviewing 6–10 participants at a time in a focus group is an alternative to one-on-one interviews when you have limited time or participant availability. With this format you do lose the intimacy of personal interviews, but you gain opportunities for one participant to piggyback on the ideas of others or to generate additional needs based on something said in the group. There is also an opportunity to validate an issue that surfaces by eliciting the input or ideas of others. Such groups can consist of participants, supervisors, peers, managers, customers, or any combination of those groups.

Surveys

Questionnaires that collect data are effective when time is limited or you have large numbers of people to query. To address the time issue, you should keep your surveys short and focused. Even though closed-ended (e.g., yes/no responses) are easy to tabulate, they often do not give enough valuable information to act upon. For that reason, I use open-ended questions with a few closed-ended ones to gather statistical information (see **Table 3-1**).

The advantage of using surveys is that you can gather large numbers of responses simultaneously and have a written record of actual comments for analysis and future reference. It is a good idea to leave space at the bottom of your questionnaire for general comments or questions related to the program.

When developing your survey, try to involve supervisors of your attendees to get their input and buy-in early in the process. Failure to do so might lead to lost support later.

Walk Around/Observation

If you will be training many members of a team or department, one very helpful technique that I use for determining knowledge and skill needs is to visit their work site and observe behavior. While there, you can get to know participants before the training, as well as ask questions of them. You can also potentially speak to their supervisors and customers. A big advantage of this technique is that you develop rapport and recognition with learners before training.

Table 3-1. Sample Assessment Questions

Here is a list of potential questions to get your interviews, focus groups, or surveys started. Some or all might be appropriate to your situation.

1. Related to the training topic, what would help you better perform your job?

2. What skills do you need to gain or improve to increase workplace effectiveness?

3. From a growth perspective, what do you hope to learn during the training?

4. What knowledge or skills would someone else say that you need to obtain in order to increase your effectiveness?

5. What training techniques do you find to be most effective? Why?

6. What training techniques do you find to be least effective? Why?

7. What is one thing that you hope to learn during the training? (Be specific)

8. What do you hope does not occur during the training?

9. If you were facilitating the program, what would you be sure to include? Why?

10. What can you do to ensure that this program adds value for you and your organization?

Pretests

Using a pretest based on the session topic can help determine current knowledge levels of your participants. They can also help participants recognize what they do not know about a topic. This latter point is important in helping to potentially open their minds to the learning experience. The format of your pretests can be true–false, multiple-choice, fill in the blank, or essay; however, you should limit the length to fewer than 20 questions (fewer than 10, if open-ended essay type questions are used). The reason for this is that many people find that time is a precious commodity and will procrastinate or ignore a complex pretest, or one that is unduly long.

Some people dislike tests or have test anxiety (stress that leads to poor test performance), so I often create pretests in the form of crossword or word search puzzles (similar to the one you experienced in Chapter 2). Such puzzles introduce session concepts and terms while gathering information about learner knowledge in a fun format. They also help subconsciously set their expectation that the upcoming training session will be different and fun, thus raising anticipation. Puzzles are also quick and easy to grade.

One practice that I have found effective when using pretests is to work with the highest level of management possible in distributing the documents. I often request that the CEO or other executive officer send out a memorandum to attendees stressing the importance of the training and directing them to complete and return the pretest. Otherwise, the tests often get put aside and forgotten. Using incentives is also an effective strategy. I sometimes provide small gifts at the beginning of training sessions to participants who returned the pretests. This again raises expectations for the program while rewarding positive behavior. Such action often leads to enhanced participation during the program.

I touch the future; I teach.
—Christa McAuliffe
Teacher/NASA Astronaut

PUTTING YOUR BRAIN TO WORK: ACTIVITY

What other techniques have you used or seen to gather pre-session data? _____

_____

How are such techniques helpful in preparing participants for learning? _____

_____

What drawbacks, if any, can you think of to using pre-session assessments? _____

_____

How can such drawbacks be overcome? _____

_____

In-Class Needs Assessment

If you are unable to contact participants and others to determine learning needs prior to the start of your program, all is not lost. With a bit of advance preparation, you can still gather some important information once participants arrive. Most of the techniques for doing so take little time and can easily be built into your program content and activities.

The following are some of my favorites.

Flip-Charted Questions

Prior to the arrival of my participants, I create six to eight newsprint sheets (flip chart pages) with questions. The key is to use closed-ended type questions (e.g., yes/no or short answer). The way I use these sheets is that at the beginning of the session on Creative Training Skills, I prepare an instruction sheet such as **Figure 3-1** for each participant. This is copied onto colored paper, for visual impact, and given to participants as they arrive. Such a handout prompts learners to immediately get involved in disclosing helpful information. As they are walking around responding to the questions, they are also encouraged to talk and get to know one another. Once they finish, there is a visible record of their responses for all to see. Based on the responses, I modify my comments appropriately and can tie them into my opening remarks. By using such an activity, I am also addressing visual, auditory, and kinesthetic learning modalities.

The following are examples of questions I used in a session on management skills to determine who my audience was and their comfort level on a few issues:

How many years have you managed others?

0–1   2–5   6–10   More

Do you directly supervise others?

Yes   No   Sometimes

At what level do you manage others?

Frontline   Middle   Upper

Are you comfortable with your current supervisory skill level?

Yes   No

3 × 5 Index Cards

A second technique that I use regularly in class is 3 × 5 index cards. I pass these out (see **Figure 3-1**) and have participants write one question, concern, or whatever I desire on them. I then either have the cards deposited in a box by the entrance or into the center of their tables so that I can collect and read while they are otherwise occupied (e.g., going around answering flip-charted questions). These comment cards give me advance notice

IMPORTANT PROGRAM INFORMATION

Please follow these guidelines to assist in the facilitation of this workshop. Thank you.

Bob Lucas—Your Facilitator

- Find a seat where you are most comfortable, yet can fully participate in the program.

- Sit next to someone whom you do not know (Networking is so much FUN!!!).

- Switch your brain to the creative training mode before entering the room.

- Be prepared to share and gain new ideas with your peers.

- Upon entry into the room, go around and respond to each flip-charted question by placing a single vertical mark, where applicable (e.g., "I").

- On the 3×5 card given as you entered the room, please write something you expect from the workshop (i.e., one thing I expect from this workshop is . . .). Deposit the card in the box on the chair by the entrance as you enter the room.

WARNING ◆◆◆ WARNING ◆◆◆ WARNING ◆◆◆ WARNING

Entry into this program could change your views on how to conduct training and give presentations.

People who are. . .

✓ Set in their ways

✓ Unwilling to share their knowledge

✓ Of the belief that learning must always be serious

✓ Reluctant to have FUN

. . . may want to grab some coffee and go for a walk!! ☺☺☺

FIGURE 3-1. Entry handout

of issues and needs directly from learners. I can then either incorporate their feedback into my session or address them in my opening remarks. If expectations are raised that are not part of the program, I list those issues on a flip chart page titled "Important Issues." I also explain that although the items are not planned for the session, they are important (thus, the flip chart page IMPORTANT issues) and will be addressed if time permits. If not, I explain that they may be the basis of future sessions, which will be researched.

An alternative to this approach is to place 3×5 cards on tables before you begin your session. Have each participant take one and write a question, concern, or expectation related to the session and place it back into the center of the table. As you have each person stand to introduce him or herself to the group, ask him or her to select a card randomly and read what is written. You can then capture the issues on a flip chart page for discussion or to address later. Using either of the 3 × 5 formats outlined allows shy people or those who do not think quickly on their feet to add input and have their needs identified and potentially addressed. This is also helpful when employees are in a session with their supervisor and feel uncomfortable surfacing an issue or concern.

Show of Hands

The quickest, yet most helpful, means of gathering information in your sessions is probably achieved by simply asking closed-ended questions and asking participants to raise their hands to indicate response (e.g., "As a facilitator, how many of you have used the show of hands technique to elicit participant input?"). The technique is simple to use if you begin by telling your learners that you're going to ask a question to which they should respond by raising their right hand, as appropriate. Such a questioning technique can be used to gain information about participants, their feelings on an issue, whether they agree or disagree, and many other things.

When using this technique, it is helpful to ask positively phrased or generic questions, such as the earlier example. Asking negative, leading questions can stifle participants' true feelings. An example of the latter type question is, "Don't you think it is important to respond to these types of questions?" Such phrasing can indicate that you have already made a decision on the "correct" answer, but just want participants to agree with you. Some may do so reluctantly, whereas others may simply withdraw and not respond to further questions during the session. They may also form a negative impression about you as a result of feeling manipulated.

Small Group Discussions

Another successful strategy that I like to use is to separate participants into small groups. Once teams are formed, I generally ask each group to select a leader and scribe (see Chapter 6). Once they have done so, give each group flip chart paper and markers to record their ideas and assign topics for which they can brainstorm possible issues or needs. For example, in a skills-based class on handling customers, I might ask, "What type of customer situations do you face regularly that require special skills to handle?" Among other things, this is a great technique for gaining involvement, getting ideas into the open, creating some movement and noise in the room, and causing participants to think outside the box or creatively.

One-on-One Interviews

This is a tried and true technique used by many trainers—so much so that although it works, I encourage you to use it infrequently or be creative in modifying it. I say this because most experienced trainers have either used the technique or experienced it as a participant. Besides, there are thousands of creative alternatives in the profession. With that said, here's how the process works. If people do not know each other well or at all, have them form pairs. Give them 10 minutes to introduce themselves to their partners and to learn three things about the person that they do not already know (e.g., something they are good at, characteristics that they feel make them unique, or workplace skills that add value to the team). At the end of 10 minutes, have each person introduce his or her partner and tell the three things learned about the person. In turn, their partner does the same for them.

This is a good activity to use in orientation, teambuilding, or other situations in which new people or groups are coming together for the first time. In using the activity, you can learn strengths or areas for improvement about participants.

Biographical Introductions

A sixth technique that can be used to learn about participants and their needs is to have them complete a biographical handout similar to **Figure** 3-2. Once everyone fills out a form, have him or her stand, do self-introductions, and read their responses to each statement on the form. As they do, capture the responses to the last statement on a flip chart for comment and referral.

* My name is _____

* I work as _____

* The subject matter of the last five training programs/courses that I have attended are:

    1. _____

    _____

    2. _____

    _____

    3. _____

    _____

    4. _____

    _____

* To expand my professional knowledge/skills, I need the following from today's session:

    _____

    _____

    _____

FIGURE 3-2. Biographical data sheet

Errors using inadequate data are much less than those using no data at all.
—Charles Babbage

PUTTING YOUR BRAIN TO WORK: ACTIVITY

Take a few minutes to reflect on the data gathering strategies you have read about. Think also of other techniques you have used, seen, or experienced for collecting information in the past.

In what other ways can you creatively gain needs data from your participants? _____

_____

_____

BRIGHT IDEA
Engaging Learners

To help learners take ownership for a program's content and recognize the value it can bring, get participants involved early in a session. At the beginning of the session, discuss session objectives. Separate participants into small groups of six to eight people. Select a leader and scribe for each group by giving a small game spinner to each group (get these from board games you own or at hobby, craft, teacher supply stores, or The Trainers Warehouse in the Resources for Trainers section in the appendices). Have each person in a group take turns spinning the dial until a predesignated number, letter, color, or whatever is selected. That person "volunteers" to be the group leader. He or she can then turn to the person on the right or left and select the scribe, who will capture group ideas on a flip chart page. Next, to help identify needs and involve participants in an active learning process, pass out a handout that contains a single sentence question to prompt thinking about the course. You may want to use a variety of questions so that each small group works on different issues. Sample questions might be:

At the end of this session, what new knowledge do you hope to have?

Based on the session objectives, how do you see program content adding value to you, your customers, and your organization?

Why is this program topic important to you, your customers, and your organization?

Allow 5–10 minutes for brainstorming and then have groups present ideas to the rest of their peers for discussion and comment.

Post-Session Needs Assessment

Determining participant needs is not limited to before and during a session. Even though it takes valuable time, it is a good idea to reassess needs following your training to determine if the session was:

Successful in meeting identified needs.

Focused on the right needs.

A catalyst for newly identified deficits or needs. In other words, did participants recognize additional gaps in knowledge, skills, or attitudes as a result of classroom activities and content?

Following a training session, there are a number of ways for determining needs. Some of the more common strategies follow.

End of Session Evaluations

By eliciting feedback from participants at the end of a program, you can sometimes immediately determine changes that should be made in content, format, and delivery. If the evaluation form is well designed, you can also potentially determine additional participant needs that surfaced as a result of their learning experience. For example, they may have not realized a deficit in some area of knowledge until the subject was brought up during training. Chapter 9 provides more specific information on evaluations.

Post-Tests

A good way to gauge new awareness and knowledge is to administer a post-session quiz or test at the conclusion of a program, or to e-mail/mail one to participants within a few days after they return to the workplace. Another option is to have supervisors distribute and collect the tests, then return them to you. This might help ensure a better return rate; assuming that you got supervisor/management buy-in and support prior to training.

If you used a pretest, you should use the same test at the end of the program to compare answers and determine if an improvement in knowledge occurred. Based on the results, you may need to place more emphasis on program topic areas that resulted in the most incorrect questions.

Post-Session Questionnaire

At 30, 60, or 90 days following your session, depending on your organizational culture and other functions, you should send out a questionnaire. The purpose of such a questionnaire is to help determine if the learning "stuck," what has been diminished and needs a review, and to see if knowledge and skills are truly being applied. Like pretests and other communication to participants, it is always a good idea to involve management in the distribution and collection of data. This makes them aware of the process, uses their clout, involves them in the learning process, and potentially gains valuable training support.

There are generally two approaches to using post-session questionnaires. The first is to send them only to participants to elicit their ideas, perspectives, and input related to on-the-job application of what was learned. A more reliable and broad-based approach is to send questionnaires to participants, their supervisors, peers, and, if appropriate and possible, their customers. This strategy usually results in more feedback and a broader perspective from others around the participant. Such insights often help paint a true picture of how the participant is performing since the training compared to pretraining performance. Such an approach can also help identify needed changes in program content and delivery.

On-the-Job Observations

By coordinating with the supervisors of your participants, you may be able to arrange time for on-the-job performance observations. In sitting with or standing behind participants as they work and interact with customers, or by simply walking around and observing, you can get a good sense of how well training concepts are being applied. You are also afforded a crucial opportunity of answering clarifying questions that participants and others have related to training concepts taught. In addition, you can function as an on-site coach and provide performance feedback to participants to help reinforce classroom learning. With what you learn through such observations, you can more effectively revamp program content and objectives. You can also incorporate success stories of how participants improved performance as a result of their training into future learning experiences. If you plan to do the latter, it is important to inform participants and supervisors and get permission first or to omit names and specific details that would lead others to know who you are talking about.

Interviews

Another strategy for gathering future participant training needs is to interview participants and their supervisors, peers, and customers. This strategy can be coupled with the on-the-job observations you read about earlier. To conduct your interview, you can follow a format similar to the pre-session interviews you read about. Your goal is to determine if, and how, participants' knowledge, skills, and attitude have changed since their training.

Customer Feedback

In addition to any information you can glean during interviews with customers, you can also analyze any written feedback they have provided. Many organizations have customers complete counter cards (short feedback forms located on tables, counters, or at point-of-sale locations). They also send out surveys via e-mail or mail. In addition, customers often write to comment, compliment, or complain about service or a specific employee. All of these types of feedback can be invaluable in analyzing how well participants are performing on the job and when determining future training needs for individuals or groups.

Performance Reports

An additional source of needs feedback is employee performance appraisals. By examining and analyzing the reports of session attendees and other employees with similar job descriptions or at similar job grade levels, you can gain a perspective of how well your learners are performing compared to others. You can also potentially identify broader organizational training needs.

In addition to performance appraisals, you should examine organizational performance reports. Documents such as sales and customer service summaries, internal employee satisfaction surveys, and internal and external customer satisfaction surveys offer a wealth of valuable training need information.

Focus Groups

You can also use focus groups, as you did before training. You may want to use the same people from the pretraining groups in order to close the loop on their ideas and opinions. Such people can be helpful in determining how effective their ideas before the session were in meeting training needs. Their feedback can be useful in increasing their knowledge and awareness of the complexities of the training process, providing feedback to them, and potentially in gaining their future training support and involvement.

PUTTING YOUR BRAIN TO WORK: ACTIVITY

Think about post-session follow-up efforts that you have seen used in the past.

What strategies were employed to get feedback and data? _____

_____

Do you think that those initiatives were effective? If so, in what ways? If not, why not? _____

_____

_____

How can you use post-session assessments in the future to improve learning quality in your sessions?

_____

_____

BRIGHT IDEA
Sharing and Learning

Contact other trainers and facilitators you know (possibly through local professional groups such as The American Society for Training and Development; see Resources for Trainers section in the appendices). Brainstorm tools for effectively collecting needs data prior to, during, and following training. Share resources and sample forms with one another. Possibly identify shared resources that can help improve your programs.

INTERIM REVIEW

Celebrating Learning

If you were conducting a training session covering the topics you have read about up until this point, you could use this activity as a form of review and reinforcement at this point in our program.

Keep this activity fast and upbeat.

Have participants stand and find a partner (if you have an odd number of participants, one group may have three people).

Have pairs decide who will be number 1 and number 2 in their team.

Instruct participants that when you say "go" the 1s, in turn, shout out a key idea, concept, or term they have experienced thus far in the session.

Each time someone successfully shouts a term, they are to give each other a "high five" (thumb along forefinger and fingers extended and joined and used to slap the palm of their partner).

Following the "high-five", the 2s shout a key term and the process continues to alternate.

Have them continue shouting out key terms and congratulating each other with high fives until you sound a train whistle or other signal that they should stop (approximately 2 minutes or until most people seem to be running out of ideas).

Once the time is up, show a flip chart or other type of visual with key terms and concepts and ask which ones they did not remember.

Based on key points they forgot, do a quick review of those items to reinforce learning.

Generally, until human beings have the opportunity to learn otherwise, they assume that other people look at the world just as they do, everyone has similar values, and everyone is motivated for the same reasons.
—Sally J. Walton
Cultural Diversity in the Workplace

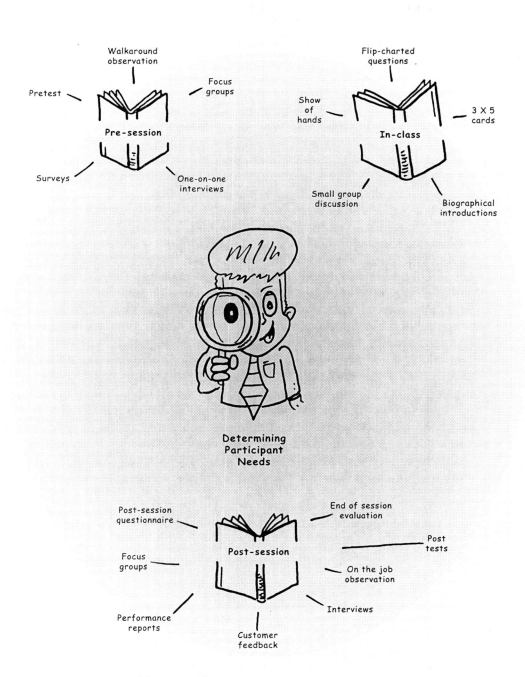

MINDMAP 1. Determining Participant Needs

● PLANNING FOR DIVERSE NEEDS

One training factor that cannot be ignored, if you want to prepare for and influence the learning of others successfully, is the diverse nature of today's learner population. Too many trainers and facilitators overlook this crucial element intentionally or through ignorance. In failing to prepare to address diverse needs, they ignore a major portion of their training audience. I encourage you to learn as much as you can about people, their beliefs, values, and needs before trying to conduct training programs. Do not focus on the obvious, visible elements of race, color, and sex. Instead, explore the subtle elements that make us all unique yet similar. As with the various learning modalities, intelligences, and other brain-based factors that you read about in Chapter 1, the facets of diversity have just as great an impact on learning ability.

To help you, there are an enormous number of advocacy groups, written materials, organizations, websites, and other resources that address various groups of people and their needs. Many of these offer helpful tips that you can incorporate into your programs. Still, do not lose sight of the fact that each learner is unique and has individual needs based on his or her own situation and preferences even though he or she is part of a larger diverse group. For this reason, the best way to find out what learning needs your participants have is to ask them. You can do so by eliciting information (e.g., special learning and/or nutritional needs, language needs, and so forth) on course registration forms or through in-class activities in which people self-disclose information about themselves. If the latter approach is used, give participants a chance to opt out of public disclosure if they desire. Do not pressure or otherwise embarrass anyone.

To get you started in preparation for dealing with a few groups, here are some techniques that I have discovered in reading materials, researching, and in working with various advocacy groups and participants. Keep in mind that these are general suggestions and that you should address the needs of your specific learners as they are identified. Build these strategies into your lesson notes and plan to use them regularly.

● CONNECTING WITH DIVERSE AUDIENCES

The population expansion of the United States and the world continues each day. For the first time in history, in the United States the number of Hispanic entry-level employees in the workforce has surpassed that of other groups. Meanwhile, the number of people living in the United States who were born in other countries grows steadily (see **Table 3-2**). With this growth comes the challenge of people who speak different languages coming together in training. For you and other trainers, the opportunity is to design and deliver programs and materials that will be understood and successful.

Table 3-2. Foreign-Born Population by World Region of Birth (Numbers in Thousands)

World Region of Birth	Total
Total Population	**28,379**
Naturalized citizen	10,622
Not a citizen	17,758
Europe	*4,355*
Naturalized citizen	2,265
Not a citizen	2,090
Asia	*7,246*
Naturalized citizen	3,415
Not a citizen	3,831
Latin America	*14,477*
Naturalized citizen	4,098
Not a citizen	10,379
Other Areas	*2,301*
Naturalized citizen	844
Not a citizen	1,457

From U.S. Census Bureau, Current Population Survey, March 2000 Ethnic and Hispanic Statistics Branch, Population Division, Table 2.6.

The majority of those born in Latin America are from Mexico. Those born in other areas are from Africa, Oceania, Bermuda, and Canada.

General Guidelines

Respect Personal Preferences

Do not assume familiarity by addressing people by their first names until you have established that type of informal environment or relationship. To do this, you can either introduce yourself as people enter a session or, at the beginning of the session, explain that the program will be in a relaxed and informal format. Then, request that participants print the name they prefer to be called on their name tents. Whatever they write should be used. If someone writes Mr., Ms., or Dr. Nyugen, then address him or her as such. Unlike North Americans, who tend to be more informal, people in many cultures covet and respect titles and academic credentials. Failure to recognize and honor this value could cause a learning and relationship breakdown.

Speak Clearly and Slowly

According to various research studies, the average adult in the United States speaks at a rate of about 125–150 words per minute. Someone trying to comprehend and translate your message into his or her own language, or someone with a learning disability, will struggle with that rate. Anything faster may negate effective communication. Speak at a rate slow enough that allows understanding without being insulting.

Speak at a Normal Volume and Tone

Just because someone speaks another language does not make him or her deaf. Yelling or changing tone does nothing to enhance understanding. In fact, it is insulting. Many times, people unconsciously raise their voice in an effort to try to increase comprehension when speaking to someone from another country. This is not an effective tool for communication and will likely offend the participant(s) to whom you are speaking.

Use Open-Ended Questions

If your goal is to gauge understanding and increase communication, try using open-ended (e.g., ones that start with who, what, when, how, why, or to what extent) to encourage participants to voice opinions and increase dialog. Closed-ended questions get little information and may actually allow a person to mask his or her inability to communicate in English. In fact, a question such as "Do you understand?" can be very offensive. Such a question could be interpreted by the person as your believing that he or she is not smart enough to comprehend your message.

Use Nonverbal Cues Cautiously

Many common nonverbal cues or signals are used throughout the world. Unfortunately, their meaning is not always interpreted the same in each country, **culture**, or **subculture**. As a trainer in a global world, you would be wise to learn as much as you can about other cultures and subcultures and the way people within them communicate. Once you have done so, incorporate findings into your training and work to educate others around you (see **Table 3-3** and Resources for Trainers in the appendices for additional information).

Use Verbal Pauses

To allow someone who speaks English as a second language, or someone with a hearing, mental processing, or speech deficit to comprehend and respond to messages, include frequent pauses as you speak. At the end of a sentence or thought, pause, then proceed.

Table 3-3. Nonverbal Cue Meaning

This excerpt from my Glencoe/McGraw-Hill text (2002, pp. 346–347), *Customer Service Skills and Concepts for Success,* provides a few examples of nonverbal gestures or symbols commonly used in the United States, along with their potential meanings in other parts of the world. The following are symbols and gestures commonly used in the United States that have alternate meanings in other parts of the world:

Cue/Gesture/Symbol	Meaning	Country
Beckoning by curling and uncurling index finger[a,b]	Used for calling animals or ladies of the evening	Hong Kong, Australia, Indonesia, Yugoslavia, Malaysia
"V" for Victory sign (palm facing you)[a,b]	Up yours!	England
Sole of foot (pointed toward a person)[a,c]	You are lowly (as sole is lowest part of the body and contacts the dirt)	Thailand, Saudi Arabia, Singapore, Egypt
"Halt" gesture with palm and extended fingers thrust toward someone[a–c]	Go to hell	Greece
Thumb up (fingers curled) indicating okay, good going, or everything is fine[a,c]	The number five Rude gesture Up yours!	Japan Nigeria Australia
Thumb and forefinger forming an "O" meaning okay[a,c]	Zero or worthless Money Rude gesture (symbolizes female genitalia)	France Japan Brazil, Malta, Greece, Tunisia, Turkey, Italy, Paraguay, Russia
Waving goodbye with fingers extended, palm down and moving the fingers up and down toward yourself[a,c]	Come here	Parts of Europe, Myanmar, Colombia, Peru
Using red ink for documents	Symbolizes death; offensive	Parts of Korea, Mexico, and China
Passing things with left hand (especially food)	Socially unacceptable, as this is the "bathroom hand"	India, Pakistan

Sources: [a]Axtell, R.E., *Gestures: The DO's and TABOOs of Body Language Around the World,* John Wiley & Sons, New York, 1991.
[b]Wolfgang, A., *Everybody's Guide to People Watching,* Intercultural Press, Yarmouth, MA, 1995.
[c]Morris, D., *Bodytalk: The Meaning of Human Gestures,* Crown Trade Paperbacks, New York, 1994.

Listen Patiently

Take your time and focus on what the participant is saying and then try to understand the intent of what is being said. You may feel frustration, but imagine what the participant is feeling as others look on.

Use Inclusive Language

When addressing participants or speaking, be aware of your audience demographics. Avoid terminology that could potentially exclude, isolate, or discriminate. For example, instead of using language such as, "You fellows, guys, or gals have found out . . .," try referring to participants generically as, "Many of you have found out . . ." This is a more inclusive approach and not likely to offend.

Avoid Offensive or Discriminatory Jokes or Remarks

Humor often does not easily transcend cultural boundaries. In addition, some people have hidden sensitivities. Jokes or comments that center on race, culture, politics, religion, sexual orientation, height, weight, or other personal characteristics can offend. Each participant has personal preferences and defines social acceptability in different ways based on his or her own value system. Although you do not have to agree with the views of others, you should respect them to maintain credibility and not potentially alienate learners.

Watch Terminology

Just as titles, jokes, and remarks can offend, so too can your words or terms. It is a good idea to avoid words that focus on, or single out, one person. Also avoid words that might demean an individual or group. For example, instead of, "The black participant in the corner," you could say, "The participant in the corner with the blue shirt on." Other terms that some people might find offensive include handicapped or crippled, boy, girl, idiot, ladies and gentlemen, and ma'am. These may conjure up negative stereotypes or project condescension to some participants.

Use Standard English

Technical terms, contractions (e.g., don't, can't, wouldn't), slang (e.g., like, you know, whoopee, rubberneck) or broken English (e.g., sentences that are imperfectly spoken or that fail to follow standard rules of grammar or syntax) can be obstacles to someone who does not speak English well. You would do well to recognize that some participants might understand a language without being able to speak it effectively. Also, some participants may not speak a language (especially in public forums) because they are either self-conscious about their ability, or choose not to. An additional factor to consider is that, unlike Western cultures, some cultures value and use silence as an important aspect of communication. Many Westerners might interpret this to mean that the person does not understand what he or she has been told.

Avoid the Word "No"

Unlike many North Americans, people from some cultures (e.g., parts of Asia) are careful not to offend or cause someone embarrassment or to loose esteem or **face** in the eyes of others. For that reason, some languages do not even have a word for *no*. In some instances people from such cultures might say yes or something such as "That may be difficult or impossible," instead of simply saying no. Being conscious of this cultural variation can help prevent frustration and potential animosity within your learning environment.

Use Care When Giving Constructive Feedback

Any time feedback on performance is given, it should be in a positive, assertive, and friendly manner. This is especially important when dealing with participants from other cultures. If you must make corrections or give constructive feedback, try language that is not directed at the person. You may even want to take responsibility for the error on yourself. For example, if someone fails to correctly perform a task or fill out a form, you might say, "Maybe I wasn't clear about what I wanted you to do." Then, repeat your instructions.

Avoid "Americanized" References

Remember what you read in Chapter 2 about assumptions when using analogies and metaphors. To help reduce the risk of misunderstandings by people who speak English as a second language, use universal language and references. Avoid words, examples, or acronyms that are uniquely American or tied to sports, historical events, or specific aspects of American culture. For example, avoid a comment such as, "I'll need your 'John Hancock' on this form," "If plan A fails, we'll drop back and punt," "Looks like we scored a base hit with that last activity," "Close, but no cigar," or "Win one for the 'Gipper.'" These phrases might be understood by someone acculturated to the American society, but will likely make no sense to others. They will only confuse your participants and do little to enhance comprehension.

Introduce Activities in a Clear, Concise Manner

By breaking tasks into concrete individual steps, providing written as well as clearly communicate verbal guidelines, using short sentences and words and verbal transitions from one point to the next, you increase your chances of success when communicating. In addition, be specific when providing directions and instructions. For example, do not simply gesture to a group of participants and say, "If you are on this side of the room, please pick up your materials and move to that side of the room." Instead, say, "If you are on my left, please pick up your materials and move to the corner on the right side of the room for an activity." If you use language similar to the first example, people who are not paying attention or those with visual impairments may have no idea what you want done. As a result, they may take extra time in accomplishing the task, thus disrupting your schedule and creating a need to repeat directions, or they may simply be too embarrassed to ask and try to figure it out on their own.

Repeat Information When Necessary

If you are asked to repeat something, take your time and do so without appearing irritated or distracted. Remember that people who speak English as a second language and those with certain types of disabilities may not get every word spoken or may not fully comprehend the first time they hear something. This is where written information can also help. If instructions or information is written, refer participants to it as you explain or discuss. Remember that some people from other cultures may read but not speak English well.

Allow Adequate Time for Movement and Task Completion

Each person processes information at a different speed. Also, some people with mental or physical disabilities may not be able to think or react as quickly as others. Build time into your programs to accomplish activities and tasks.

Ensure Written Materials Are Clear

You can ensure message clarity by choosing a font that is large enough to reduce eyestrain (a minimum of 12-point font is standard). Visual aids (e.g., slides, transparencies, and flip chart lettering) should be larger (see Chapter 8).

PUTTING YOUR BRAIN TO WORK: ACTIVITY

What other communication strategies might help include participants who speak English as a second language? _____

_____

What other strategies might aid communication with participants who have a disability? (e.g., hearing, sight, speech, learning) _____

● CROSS-GENDER ISSUES

Much research has been done related to how women and men communicate and process information. Add to this the fact that the roles of women and men differ dramatically between cultures and you have a formula for potential communication breakdown in the classroom. Like any other issue of diversity, you cannot generalize about any group or issue.

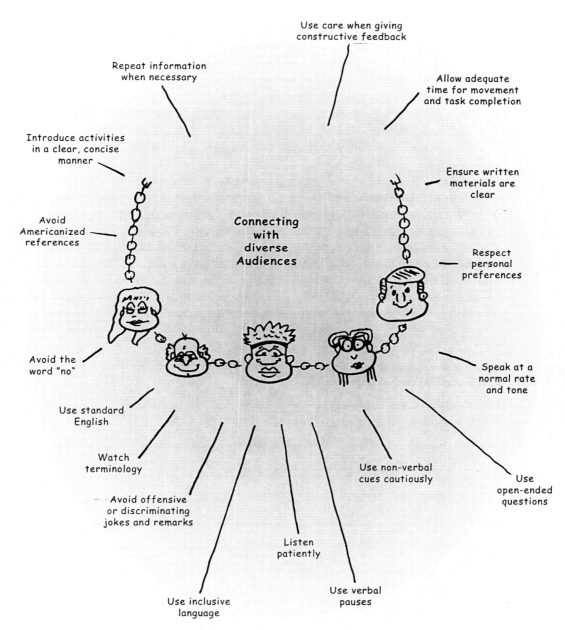

MINDMAP 2. Connecting With Diverse Audiences

Because this topic is far too complex to adequately address in this small section of the book, I encourage you to visit your local library and the Internet to research it in depth. There are also a number of books on the issue of gender communication cited in the Resources for Trainers section of the appendices.

A key gender issue that has surfaced in research is that men and women listen and communicate differently. There is a physiological difference in the structure of the brain in men and women that often leads to women taking in and attempting to process multiple signals and pieces of information while men often filter out background noise or input and focus on one issue. These differences and approaches to communication can sometimes lead to frustration, confusion, and even relationship breakdown.

Deborah Tannen, John Gray, and many others have written numerous books and articles on the way in which men and women listen and communicate. According to Tannen, women often listen for more emotional or rapport type messages, as well as for details. On the other hand, men often want the bottom line and listen for report type of information, such as facts, figures, or specifics. These differences in the classroom add the need for you to provide a variety of information in differing formats to address the needs of all of your participants. For example, you might pass out a fact sheet for the bottom-line people while telling an embellished story that gives background information related to the handout for the detail-oriented people.

PUTTING YOUR BRAIN TO WORK: ACTIVITY

Think of situations in which you were interacting with someone from the opposite gender and you encountered message breakdown.

Did their listening and communication style differ from yours? If so, in what ways? _____

_____

What challenges or complications did these differences create? _____

_____

In retrospect, how did or could you have overcome the challenges? _____

_____

How can you apply lessons learned in that situation to your classroom? _____

_____

Communication does not begin with being understood, but with understanding others.
—W. Steven Brown

● TRAINING PARTICIPANTS WHO HAVE DISABILITIES

Because there are so many different types of disabilities and each person's disability affects him or her in potentially different ways, it is impossible to list all of them here. In addition, many people have nonvisible disabilities that can affect their ability to function as others might and create learning challenges for them (e.g., diabetes, dyslexia, alcoholism, and cancer). Such participants may not always be willing to disclose their disability to others and in some cases have learned consciously to mask them from others for personal reasons. Often this is done because of either embarrassment or the fear of discrimination should their disability become known. At any rate, respect rights and desires of all your participants and attempt to provide a learning environment that is accessible to everyone.

When a disability is disclosed to you, do whatever possible to accommodate the participant(s). The Americans With Disabilities Act of 1990 and other legislation requires you to do so, but more importantly, it is the right thing to do. After all, isn't your role as a trainer to facilitate learning? Beside, with the rising estimate of more than 55 million people with some type of disability in the United States alone, the chances of having at least one disabled participant in your session is very high.

The first step in creating a positive learning environment for people with disabilities is to ensure that your language, that of other trainers and participants, and your learning materials is not offensive or discriminatory. **Table 3-4** offers some possible terminology, although the best approach is not to single out for their disability or any other diversity factor. Instead, simply address people by name or a generic term, such as man or woman, when referring to someone. In addition, avoid the potentially offensive word *handicapped*, as this has an attributed historical connotation from old British language

Table 3-4. Referring to People with Disabilities

Instead of . . .	Use . . .
Handicapped	Disabled or the specific disability
Manuel is confined to a wheelchair.	Manuel uses a wheelchair.
Michele suffers from . . .	Michele has . . .
The deaf and dumb participant	The participant with a hearing and learning disability
Richard is a victim of . . .	Richard has . . .
Jheri is an epileptic.	Jheri has epilepsy.

as referring to a beggar or someone who traditionally was disabled and stood on corners with "cap in hand" soliciting money. Also, if you must refer to someone with a disability, put the person before the disability to indicate that they are important and the disability is only a detail about them.

BRIGHT IDEA

Learning About Disabilities

To help yourself better understand disabilities in order to better prepare to train such learners who might have them take some time to visit the library or log onto the Internet for information on various disabilities. Specifically look for materials and information on ways to create a learning environment that meets the needs of such learners. You can also look in the phone book for agencies that support people with disabilities and even volunteer time to work with such groups. In doing so, your knowledge and empathy will likely increase immensely. Once you gain insights, encourage your organizational management group to support disability sensitivity and diversity training initiatives, which you might facilitate.

General Suggestions for Training People with Disabilities

Along with the preceding suggestions, here are some general things you can do to increase your effectiveness when training learners with disabilities.

Sensitize Trainers

Prior to the start of training, ensure that co-trainers and other assistants are sensitized to disability issues and that they are aware of any need for accommodation within your learner group.

Get the Facts

Before training, elicit information about the disabilities and special needs from participants in order to plan appropriate accommodations.

Never Assume

Instead of thinking that you know the best approach for effectively interacting with someone who has a disability, ask the participant what can be done to help or improve his or her learning experience. Keep in mind that two people with a similar disability may have different needs.

Facilitate Learning

Provide a safe, comfortable, accessible learning environment in which discrimination and exclusion of people with disabilities is not tolerated.

Accommodate Needs

Make whatever accommodations possible when designing materials, classroom setup, activities, and other facets of learning. For example, ensure that doorways are at least 36 inches wide to accommodate wheelchairs and that water fountains, restrooms, elevators, and other facilities structures are accessible.

Pay Close Attention to the Environment

This includes elements such as heating, lighting, noise levels, seating arrangements, and the types of food and refreshments served (see Chapter 5).

Build in Adequate Breaks

Make sure that you plan enough breaks for personal comfort (at least once every 60–90 minutes), even if you just allow getting more refreshments, stretching, and a quick bathroom break for those who need it. As you read in Chapter 1, the mind tends to wander when it focuses on other things.

Provide Opportunities for Small Group Learning

Building small group activities into your session can increase effectiveness for participants who have disabilities, speak English as a second language, or are simply more comfortable in small group settings. Often, such people will become active participants when given such opportunities.

PUTTING YOUR BRAIN TO WORK: ACTIVITY

What other strategies can you think of to help engage and encourage learning for participants with disabilities? _____

_____

Sight Disabilities

Many people have either total or partial sight loss. Sometimes, their impairment can be improved somewhat with corrective lenses or surgery whereas in other instances it cannot. Even so, some people categorized as **legally blind** have limited vision under certain circumstances (e.g., either reduced or bright lighting).

To maximize learning experiences for participants with sight impairments or loss, you should become familiar with the different types of loss and make efforts to accommodate them in your training programs.

Training Strategies for Improved Effectiveness

Determine the level of sight impairment (e.g., loss of some vision or blind).

Prior to training, ask participant(s) what accommodations might increase their learning success.

Ensure that your training environment is free of obstacles and barriers.

Focus on the participant's abilities and be positive about his or her accomplishments.

Position the participant in a location that maximizes his or her abilities. This is typically near the front of the room.

If you have participants move for an activity, allow them the option of returning to their original preferential seating location.

Point out things and areas that the participants need to be aware of (e.g., potential obstacles or hazards, doors, materials, refreshment location, and restroom location).

Use common language and do not be afraid to use words such as "look" or "see."

Speak in a normal tone of voice. The participant cannot see, but he or she is not deaf.

Give details slowly, specifically, and concisely.

If the participant has a working dog, ask permission before attempting to touch or otherwise interact with it. Also, do not forget to build in time to allow the dog to be taken outside occasionally.

If necessary and appropriate, print materials in larger font sizes on white, nonglare type paper.

Allow plenty of time for participants to assimilate information and instructions and to follow through on tasks.

PUTTING YOUR BRAIN TO WORK: ACTIVITY

Think of your own training environment. Then, answer these questions.

What other strategies can you think of that might assist someone with a sight loss to maximize a learning experience? _____

_____

What specific aspects of the learning environment might you have to modify to accommodate a participant with a sight impairment? _____

_____

Hearing Disabilities

Just as with vision impairments, many people have difficulty hearing with one or both ears. In some cases, they do not even acknowledge or recognize their own hearing loss because it has been a gradual process over time.

There are a number of things that you can do to better enhance learning opportunities for participants who have hearing loss.

Training Strategies for Improved Effectiveness

Try to determine the level of impairment prior to training (e.g., mild, intermediate, or total). Also, is it in one or both ears?

Ask the participant what accommodations might increase his or her learning effectiveness.

Focus on the participant's abilities and be positive about his or her accomplishments.

Position the participant in a location that maximizes his or her abilities. Typically this is in the front of the room and near any audiovisual aids you will be using.

If you have participants move for an activity, allow them the option of returning to their original preferential seating location.

If you are going to use audiovisual aids, you may want to inform the participant prior to class so that he or she can adjust hearing aid volume as necessary.

Keep background noise to a minimum if participants are using hearing aids or have only partial hearing. This can distort what they do receive.

If an interpreter is present, position him or her where he or she can effectively see and hear you and where you can see both the participant and the interpreter.

When an interpreter is used, address comments and questions directly to the participant, not the interpreter. Remember that the interpreter is the tool through which the participant communicates. In addition, do not have side conversations with the interpreter in the presence of the participant. Ethically, he or she is bound to share messages received with the participant.

Face participants when speaking.

Speak slowly, clearly, and concisely.

Keep hands and other objects away from your mouth. This includes bushy facial hair that might obscure the lips.

Use facial expressions and gestures freely to emphasize points.

You can use hand and arm gestures to get participants' attention or you can lightly touch them on the shoulder if they are looking away.

Ensure that only one person in the group speaks at a time. This is important if interpreters are used, as they have to capture and translate what is said.

Provide materials and instructions in writing as you communicate verbally.

Use diagrams, charts, posters, clip charts, and other types of graphic and visual images when possible. These help maximize the participant's acquisition of information.

Consider having someone take notes for the participant or give him or her a copy of your leader guide so that he or she can focus on discussion and conversation instead of having to look down.

Repeat any question or comment from other participants to ensure that the hearing impaired participant got it.

When reading certain material is required, allow plenty of time before speaking again. Get the participant's attention before you do start speaking.

PUTTING YOUR BRAIN TO WORK: ACTIVITY

Think of your own training environment. Then, answer these questions.

What other strategies can you think of that might assist someone with a hearing loss to maximize a learning experience? _____

_____

What specific aspects of your program and the learning environment might you have to modify in order to accommodate a participant with a hearing impairment? _____

_____

Mobility Disabilities

Millions of people have various forms of motion (e.g., multiple sclerosis, muscular dystrophy, and cerebral palsy) or mobility impairments (e.g., spinal cord injuries, arthritis, or amputations). Each of these disabilities can create pain and loss of the ability to navigate or move easily or at all. To assist in providing access to participants with these impairments, you should become aware of their causes, symptoms, and strategies for accommodating.

Training Strategies for Improved Effectiveness

Ask the participant what accommodations might increase his or her learning effectiveness.

Focus on the participant's abilities and be positive about his or her accomplishments, not on disabilities.

Allow them to find seating wherever they are most comfortable and can have the maximum mobility (e.g., near exits, restrooms, or aisles).

Design room layouts that afford easy access for assistive devices, such as canes, crutches, wheelchairs, or prosthetics. Typically freestanding chairs or tables that can be moved are best. Classroom, V-shaped/fishbone and theater style seating can limit access and mobility.

Design activities in which participants can interact equally with others. Be careful of requiring excessive relocation within the room or timed events requiring movement.

Post materials on the wall at a height that does not require excessive neck strain to view them.

Allow plenty of time for activity and task completion.

Be careful of competitive activities in which participants must accomplish tasks and be compared to others.

When speaking one-on-one to someone in a wheelchair (e.g., individual coaching, explanation, or discussion) sit at eye level with the participant.

Ensure tabletops are approximately 32–54 inches above floor level with knee space at least 28 inches high, 20 inches deep, and 32 inches wide to accommodate wheelchair access.

PUTTING YOUR BRAIN TO WORK: ACTIVITY

Think of your own training environment. Then, answer these questions.

What other strategies can you think of that might assist someone with a motion or mobility impairment to maximize a learning experience? _____

_____

What specific aspects of your program and the learning environment might you have to modify in order to accommodate a person with a motion or mobility impairment? _____

_____

BRIGHT IDEA
Disability Audit

Do a proactive audit of your training environment before someone with a disability registers for programs. Take a look at the classroom, overall building, and parking area to determine what accommodations have been made for people with disabilities or might be needed (e.g., water coolers lowered for accessibility, restroom stalls, lighting configuration, Braille signage near elevators and other areas, telephones with amplifying devices, and so on). You can find ADA requirements for such accommodations on the Internet by typing in the word "disabilities." Also, identify possible barriers or obstacles and remove them if possible. In addition, think about various seating configurations that are possible in order to maximize accessibility. Work with maintenance and facilities staff and co-workers to modify where appropriate and possible.

PUTTING YOUR BRAIN TO WORK: ACTIVITY

We sometimes have biases that interfere with our interactions with others. Typically, these are based on learned behavior (something we have personally experienced or have been taught by others). By thinking of and bringing your biases to a conscious level, you can better control or eliminate them in dealing with your participants.

Think about qualities or factors related to others that you do not like or prefer to avoid. List these, along with the basis (why you believe them to be true) for each.

BIASES   **BASIS**

_____   _____

_____   _____

_____   _____

_____   _____

_____   _____

_____   _____

APPLYING WHAT YOU LEARNED
Strategies for Lighting Your Creativity Lamp

1. How can you more effectively determine learner needs for your future training sessions?

_____

_____

2. What strategies that you read about related to personal appearance can you apply in your training programs? _____

_____

3. What local resources do you have for learning more about the needs of participants with disabilities?

_____

_____

4. Which strategies for training people from other cultures can you apply immediately in your training sessions? _____

_____

5. How do the differences between the learning behaviors of men and women impact your training?

_____

_____

6. What can you do to address the divergent needs of all your participants that you are not currently doing? _____

_____

ENDNOTES

[6] www.casualpower.com

[7] Walker, M., *The Power of Color: The Art and Science of Making Color Work for You,* Avery Publishing, Garden City Park, NY, 1991, p. 13.

[8] Maysonave, S., *Casual Power: How to Power Up Your Nonverbal Communication and Dress Down for Success,* Bright Books, Austin, TX, 1999, p. 73.

Notes

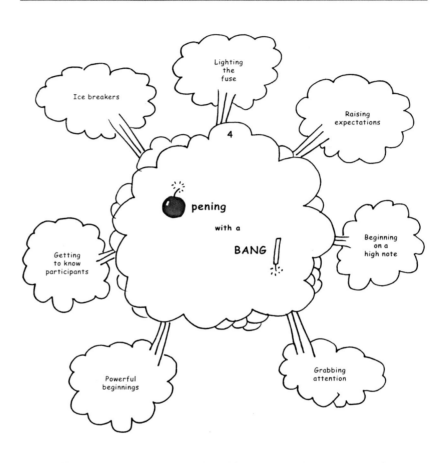

Opening With a Bang

*Where before there was a spectator, let there now be
a participant.*

—J.S. Bruner
Child Talk: Learning to Use Language

Learning Outcomes

At the end of this chapter, and when applying concepts covered, you will be able to:

● Identify creative techniques for making a positive first impression.

● Raise participant expectation levels for training sessions.

● Focus on strategies for starting your sessions on a positive high note.

● Use a variety of powerful techniques to start your sessions.

● Create an environment in which participants self-disclose information useful for increasing training effectiveness.

● Encourage networking in a relaxed atmosphere through creative icebreaker activities.

● LIGHTING THE FUSE

First impressions are often lasting ones. As soon as participants hear of your session, they begin forming opinions about it, and ultimately about you. Based on promotional materials used to communicate session objectives and content narrative about the program, participants begin to anticipate value depending on their actual or perceived needs. This is why the format of such materials should be well thought out and should mirror program content. For example, if you were facilitating a workshop on an Equal Employment Opportunity (EEO) issue, you probably would not want to use caricatures or clown clip art on the flyer. Instead, a business appropriate graphic would be more suitable. You want your message to stand out. Creative fonts, colored paper, and novel approaches to formatting your message can do this.

To get ideas of how to sell your programs and communicate effectively, look at samples of all the promotional material received through the mail. The people who create such brochures and advertising materials are usually well trained in the marketing field. Capitalize on their expertise and knowledge, rather than wasting time trying to re-create a look.

Once participants are in your classroom, your efforts must be focused to grab and hold attention. Engage them in some manner within the first 30–90 seconds. Greet them, assign an activity, ask a question, or do whatever else you feel would get them quickly tuned into the session content because participants immediately start scanning their environment to determine whether it is conducive to learning. Some of the things that they focus on are:

Refreshment availability

Furniture configuration

Room appearance

Temperature

Lighting

Background music

Participants also scrutinize you and their peers to gauge friendliness and receptiveness. Nonverbal signals such as smiling and a relaxed body posture are important. This involves such gestures as arms and legs being uncrossed, leaning forward, and facing someone as he or she speaks. All of these gestures send powerful messages that one is interested in others and what they are saying. Just the way you dress and groom yourself can speak volumes about your attitude toward yourself, participants, and the training (review Chapter 3).

According to Eric Jensen, who has done research and written on brain-based learning, you should "enter a room on the audience's left side and move towards their right to speak."[9] The reason he gives is that the human brain often processes information from a right-ear and attention preference when taking in new data or information. The result is that a more positive first impression is derived from use of the right-brain hemisphere. With this in mind, it becomes obvious that even minute details can work toward creating a favorable image with your participants and should not be overlooked.

PUTTING YOUR BRAIN TO WORK: ACTIVITY

Think of training sessions you have conducted or attended.

What factors made a positive first impression on you and participants? _____

_____

How was participant interest piqued before the session started and/or during the first few minutes?

_____

_____

In what ways can you use the preceding techniques to aid in grabbing attention in your future sessions?

_____

_____

⬤ RAISING EXPECTATIONS

You can begin building participant interest before your session starts. This can assist your in-class performance and accomplishment. It is also helpful because participants who arrive with higher expectations, an anticipation of the learning experience, and an overall positive outlook are more likely to actively participate and ultimately learn more.

Some of the techniques that I use in training to help raise expectations include the following.

Pre-Class Assignments

To help ensure that participants take ownership for some of their own learning, I like to give pre-class assignments. If you decide to do likewise, it is important to ensure that you address the assignment during the session. Otherwise, participants typically resent the time they thus wasted unnecessarily. Depending on the session topic, time allocated for the training, and organizational culture, I sometimes send assignments in the form of a welcome announcement to everyone who registers. These assignments might be something related to the session topic that learners have to look up on the Internet. It might also be something that they must do associated with the learning. For example, in a recent class on interpersonal communication, I asked participants to identify someone they knew whom they believed to be an excellent communicator. They were then told to create a list of 8–10 open-ended questions and conduct an interview of that person. They were asked specifically to learn how the interviewee learned his or her communication skills, and to obtain suggestions from the person that would help the participant in improving his or her own communication ability.

Once the class started, I formed small groups and asked participants to share what they had learned and to develop a common list of characteristics and strengths. They also compiled suggestions for improvement. Both lists were then shared among groups and discussed in class.

Activities such as this help with self-discovery while actually encouraging participants to practice skills in advance. For example, after my class discussed their lists, I pointed out that they too had used interpersonal skills such as feedback, questioning, listening, and nonverbal communication during their interviews and again during the small group activity. The experience is more powerful when learners come to such revelations on their own.

Interactive Announcements

To stimulate interest and registration in programs, I often send out flyer announcements that typically include a series of questions based on the program topic. I challenge potential registrants to answer the questions based on their current knowledge level. Elsewhere on the flyer, either on the reverse or upside down at the bottom, I provide the correct responses so that they can check the accuracy of their answers. I then suggest that if they missed questions or want additional knowledge on the subject areas, they should attend the session. This call to action is based on potential interest stirred in learning more about the program topic while increasing their own knowledge and abilities. An alternative approach that I sometimes use is to leave the answers off the flyer. Instead, I state that the answers to the questions and much more will be addressed in the training session. In my opening remarks at the session I share the answers to the questions.

A variation of the flyer is to use e-mail announcements with creative attachments like crossword or word search puzzles with key session terms or concepts used as their basis.

Teasers

A second technique that I use to stimulate interest and curiosity is one that is often used by marketing professionals to introduce a new product or service. Prior to the actual promotion announcement for a program, I send out a series of teaser announcements through interoffice mail or e-mail. I use either brightly colored paper or graphics, or departmental or organizational letterhead. Each of these pieces often only state a known problem or issue (e.g., "Revenue is down here at ABC Corporation," " Diversity is an issue that we deal with everyday," "Customers want better service") along with a statement suggesting that the training can help (e.g., "We have a solution") (see **Figure 4-1**). The day after the final teaser goes out, I send a promotional flyer or e-mail that starts with all the previously communicated teaser issues in bold letters followed by the session information (see **Figure** 4-2). This format connects the previous teaser correspondence to the program announcement.

Revenue is down here at ABC Corporation.

We have a solution!

FIGURE 4-1. Teaser announcement 1

Agendas

Like many other training tools, an agenda is valuable in announcing your intended session outcomes or goals. By creating a listing of topic areas to be addressed during your session you can paint a visual picture of the program format and content for yourself and participants. At the same time, you can raise the level of anticipation that learners have about what will be covered.

When developing an agenda, you may want to leave times off of participant copies rather than locking yourself into specified time slots. This allows you to adjust time spent on sections of material and activities as necessary. Otherwise, someone in the group is likely to watch the clock to ensure that you are on schedule. This can distract him or her from learning and will likely result in a negative comment on program evaluations concerning your ability to facilitate effectively. One strategy related to time is to let participants know up front that times for each activity and topic are flexible based

---

Revenue is down here at ABC Corporation.

Diversity is an issue we deal with everyday.

Customers want better service

Here is the solution:

Realigning Workplace Strategies: Tools for Increased Profitability

May 21, 2002: 9:00 a.m.–5:00 p.m.

In this program, you will learn:

1. . . .

2. . . .

3. . . .

Since the founding of ABC Corporation, we have worked to increase market share while becoming known as. . . . .

Registration: To register for this fast-paced, informative program, contact Terry Shelton at extension 7399. Seats are limited, so hurry.

FIGURE 4-2. Sample announcement

on their needs and discussion. Doing this shows concern for them while allowing you to adapt content and flow as needed during the session.

Articles

As you read professional literature, newspapers, and periodicals, be on the lookout for articles about trends or issues related to program topics. Save these and send them out to people who register for your sessions with a brief note suggesting that the issues covered in the material, and others, will be addressed during training (assuming that they will). This approach can help tie training to organizational and real-world issues.

Jigsaw Puzzles

As you read in the last chapter, jigsaw puzzles are excellent vehicles for accomplishing a variety of training objectives. To add a little creative twist to training in which there are fewer than 25 attendees, I like to use puzzles in opening team activities. To do so, I create two identical jigsaw puzzles from a printed sheet containing program objectives, a quote, or startling fact related to the session content (see **Figure** 4-3). On the reverse side of the printed sheet, I copy a jigsaw format (see **Figure** 4-4). At that point, I have a two-sided copy with information on one side and the jigsaw piece format on the back.

I cut the puzzles into pieces and place each puzzle in its own large manila envelope. Before doing that, I randomly take two sections from each team's puzzle, mix them, and then insert two pieces in with each team's puzzle pieces so that they potentially have incomplete puzzles. After giving each team a puzzle and selecting group leaders, I stress teamwork throughout the day and tell them they have 10 minutes to assemble their puzzles to discover the program objectives. I do not tell them about the mixed pieces. At some point someone usually figures out that another team has their pieces and goes off to exchange. The team whose members assemble their page first wins a prize.

An alternative is to make two poster-sized copies (approximately 27 × 34 inches) of the jigsaw content so that it covers a flip chart easel. This can be done with the enlarger (poster maker) machines that many organizations or print shops have. Once this is done, you can draw lines to form various shapes (as in **Figure** 4-4) on the back before cutting the puzzle into pieces. I then number the pieces of both puzzles identically on the back, starting with one and running through the number of pieces I have. This allows me later to identify missing pieces if someone does not show up for the session or forgets to bring his or her piece. I can then replace the missing numbered piece from my duplicate puzzle. Next, I cut both poster puzzles (keeping each one separate) to create two sets of large individual puzzle pieces.

As learners register for the program, each participant gets one piece from one of the puzzles, along with a program announcement or other important session information. In the announcement I inform participants that there will be a drawing and that the number on the back of their piece is their entry (another use for the numbers if you desire). I also state that the piece will be used for an activity so they should bring it to the session. When I use the numbers on the pieces for a prize drawing, I generally randomly select a number and write it on a flip chart. After they arrive, I announce the winning number and award a prize prior to the assembly of the puzzle.

In class, following the drawing, I have participants approach a flip chart page that I have sprayed with repositionable artist's adhesive or photo mount (available at most art, craft, and hobby stores, or see Resources for Trainers in the appendices) so that the pieces will stick without the use of tape, yet can be repositioned as needed. Each person places his or her piece of the jigsaw puzzle on the page, then returns to be seated. Ultimately, the entire puzzle is assembled to reveal the program objectives, quote, or whatever I used as content for the puzzle. I then ask the last person placing a piece to read what the puzzle says to the group. I then reward everyone and have them give a round of applause for their accomplishment. Thus, I have engaged participants early in the program, added a bit of pizzazz, revealed program objectives or otherwise introduced pertinent information, and set the expectation that the session will be fun and that they can earn rewards for active involvement.

Here's how to make your own puzzles:

Select and put the text you will use (e.g., session objectives, quote, or other information) on a standard 8.5 × 11 inch piece of paper.

Have two large poster-size images made of the text.

Create your puzzle pieces on the reverse side of one of the sheets by randomly drawing lines in various shapes (see **Figure** 4-4).

Place the poster sheets one behind the other with the lined pieces visible and trace them onto the second puzzle content page.

Numerically, identically label puzzle pieces by placing like numbers on each piece of both puzzles.

Use scissors to cut out the pieces of both puzzles (keep the two puzzles separated).

A mind stretched by a new idea never returns to its original dimensions.
    —*Oliver Wendell Holmes*

Card Games

Similar to the jigsaw puzzle idea, you can use card games as a basis for participant involvement. To do this use a standard deck of playing cards with four suits (hearts, clubs, spades, and diamonds). Form small groups of four to eight participants. Based on the total number of participants, select a run of cards from each suit (e.g., for a class of 20 or groups of five participants each, you need something like 9, 10, jack, queen,

(text continues on page 128)

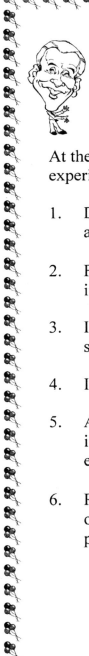

WORKSHOP OBJECTIVES

At the end of this workshop, you will be able to use techniques experienced to:

1. Design creative program openers that will grab participant attention and help set the stage for learning.

2. Facilitate training programs and presentations that can help induce behavior change and are FUN.

3. Identify, make, or obtain inexpensive materials that add spark to your training programs and presentations.

4. Increase interaction with participants.

5. Assign participants to small groups in a variety of imaginative ways in order to facilitate networking and exchange of ideas.

6. Review program concepts throughout your sessions in order to get an interim check of learning <u>before</u> the program ends.

FIGURE 4-3. Sample jigsaw content

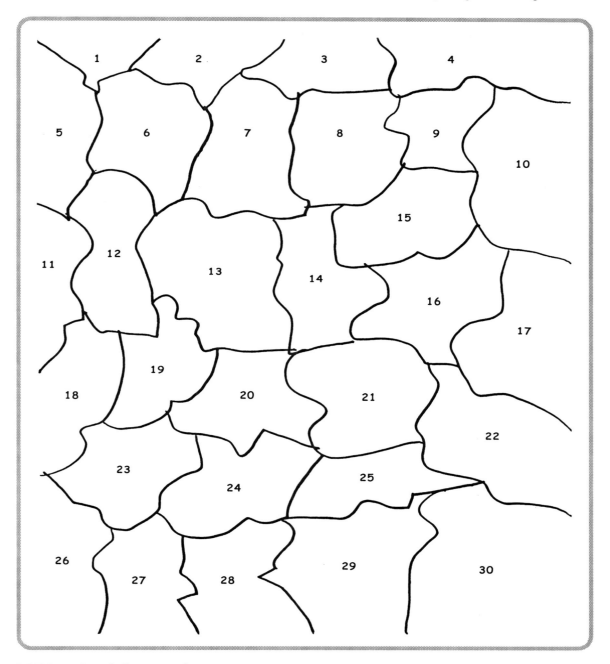

FIGURE 4-4. Sample jigsaw puzzle

and king). Just as with the jigsaw puzzle pieces, randomly send out a card to each participant with instructions to bring it with him or her to the training session. Once everyone arrives, you can immediately group participants by having them assemble according to their suit. The people holding the highest card from each group can be designated as the team leader and any other card you designate, the scribe. Once grouped, have them participate in an in-class needs assessment (see Chapter 3) or icebreaker activity before you begin the session.

Individual Reflection

During introductory remarks, many trainers have participants share one expectation, question, or concern that they have related to the session. Unfortunately, what often occurs is that many participants do not, will not, or cannot think of anything to say on the spot, or they repeat something said earlier. To reduce the chances of this happening, I often give participants an index card or piece of paper and ask them to write their expectations or whatever. I then use the written comments in one of three ways: (1) I have them read what they have written; (2) I have them put all cards/papers into the middle of their table, then one by one, have participants at each table select any one and read what is written; or (3) I have them passed to me and I read them aloud to the group. In any instance, I have someone capture the items on a flip chart page for future reference. These approaches often result in more responses as some people need time to think and visualize, while others are reluctant to say something in front of a large group without preparation and planning. Techniques 2 and 3 allow the authors of comments to remain anonymous. Of course the down side with anonymity is that you cannot follow up and ask for clarification of a comment if no one claims it.

Brainstorming

An alternative to the individual reflection technique is to form small groups that create a list of expectations in a specified timeframe. This approach can be turned into a friendly competition with the team generating the most responses receiving a reward. To increase the effectiveness of any brainstorming, you may want to write and post some brainstorming rules, such as those found in the Tools for Trainers section.

PUTTING YOUR BRAIN TO WORK: ACTIVITY

Pull from personal training experiences in order to enhance the sessions that you facilitate.

When you attend training, what are some typical expectations that you have going into programs?

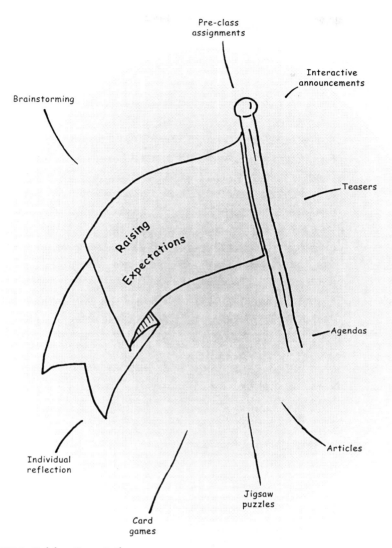

MINDMAP 1. Raising Expectations

How have trainers identified and capitalized on those expectations in the past? _____

_____

In what ways can you apply your experiences related to expectations to your own sessions? _____

_____

_____

BRIGHT IDEA

A Cast of Characters

Use an innovative approach to grouping participants, and then have them use the brainstorming technique to gather expectations. One strategy for grouping is to pass out strips of paper to each participant as he or she arrives. On the strips, write the names of the characters of famous television shows or movies. For example, "Gilligan's Island"—The Professor, Skipper, Gilligan, Mary Ann, Mr. Howell, Mrs. Howell, and Ginger or "Star Wars" (the original)—C-3PO, Chewbacca, R2D2, Princess Leia, Han Solo, Grand Moff Tarkin, Luke Skywalker, Lord Darth Vader, Ben (Obi-wan) Kenobi. Other well known shows are "Family Ties," "The Beverly Hillbillies," "Friends," "Scrooge," "All in the Family," "Married with Children," and "The Jeffersons." Tell participants how many people will be on each team (based on the total number of session attendees). When you are ready to start the activity, have participants wander around the room introducing themselves and looking for other cast members from their show or movie. Once all cast members for each group are assembled, give them an assigned time to brainstorm and flip chart expectations, questions, or issues, then review the lists as a class and discuss.

There is nothing so wasteful as doing with great efficiency that which doesn't have to be done at all.
—Anonymous

● BEGINNING ON A HIGH NOTE

As you saw in previous chapters, your role in setting the proper learning environment is key to training success. The following are some strategies for helping to ensure that an atmosphere exists in which maximum learning can occur.

Be Prepared

Ensure that you have done everything possible to be ready for your session and to receive participants. Try to anticipate every possible contingency and prepare for it. Do this by using a checklist (see Presentation Preplanning Checklist in Tools for Trainers in the appendices) to guarantee that all the materials and equipment needed are present and functioning. If you use an overhead projector, make sure you have a backup projector or that it has dual bulb capability and that both bulbs work. Depending on room and group size, a flip chart also makes a good backup alternative.

If you are using a computer slide show, test it before participants arrive and have an audiovisual technician standing by in case of technical glitches.

Establish the Atmosphere

Another technique for fostering a feeling of unity related to the topic and your participants is to adopt a theme for your session and decorate the room accordingly. For example, if you were facilitating a session related to increasing sales on the telephone you could put telephones around the room at various locations, have colorful posters of flip charts made with dollar signs, and provide small incentives in the shape of telephones (e.g., pencil erasers, squeeze toys, or refrigerator magnets that sound like little phones). You could also start the session with a humorous role play demonstration in which a sales representative and customer have a humorous conversation leading to a huge sale. Following this, you could have teams develop a team identity as outlined previously with a focus on something related to telephone sales.

Part of the atmosphere relates to the roles played by everyone in the room. Some participants may wonder what you expect of them and what they should expect of you. This is easily handled through use of a Training Agreement or Contract that you read about in Chapter 3 (see also Training Agreement in the Tools for Trainers section of the appendices).

Start on Time

Time is a precious commodity for everyone in today's workplace as employees are being asked to do more with less. For that reason, participants should be able to expect that you will start, stay, and end on time. You should respect their investment and that of their organizations related to commitment to training. Besides, starting late sends a potential message of disrespect and lack of professionalism.

Come in with a Bang

Do the unexpected to grab participant attention. Change lighting (e.g., flick lights on and off or if they were dim, raise the brightness as you enter); start with loud, upbeat music; run into the room; wear something outrageous; use whistles, bells, and other noisemakers; or do whatever else you can to startle and wake participants up.

Be Positive

Even if some unforeseen events occur (e.g., handouts did not show up or you run out of them, unplanned additional participants arrive, participants arrive late, or equipment malfunctions) do not dwell on problems or waste time apologizing. Such reactions make you look unprepared and unprofessional, while focusing attention on negative things at a crucial point in your presentation. Besides, if you do not say anything about errors or omissions, your participants will likely never know how since they do not have a copy of your leader's guide, or do not know what you had planned.

Keep Administrivia to a Minimum

Sharing housekeeping details about such things as no smoking; cell phones and beepers off; and location of refreshments, bathrooms, and telephones is important. However, keep the time spent reviewing such information short. You can always list these on a handout or post a flip chart page on the wall, do a quick referral, and move on. Time is precious and you do not want to bore participants and lose their attention with such mundane material.

Use Group Energy

Immediately involve your audience. You can do this by conducting a quick energizer activity (see Chapter 7). You can also engage participants in a quick question-and-answer activity by raising expectations with questions such as "How many of you would like to walk out of here with at least five ideas on how to maximize your own effectiveness?"

A couple of quick standard activities that you can use that involve a bit of humor and some physical movement follow.

The first is to have everyone stand and face you and extend their arms straight out in front of them with palms facing each other. On the count of three, have everyone in unison rapidly bring their hands together and clap five or six times. Once done, casually say, "Thank you. Please be seated. I just wanted to be able to tell everyone back home that I got a standing ovation today." This type of activity gets the blood flowing, raises anticipation and expectations, adds humor, and helps break the ice a bit.

A second movement activity, which ties into the brain-based learning that you read about in Chapter 1, is tied to cross-lateral movement, or movement in which one side of the brain is controlling activity on the opposite side of the body. Cross-lateral activity stimulates different parts of the brain. To accomplish this, have everyone stand and raise their hands as high above their head as possible. Have them shake their hands vigorously for a few seconds, then tell them to lower the left hand but keep the right one up and shake it. After a few seconds, reverse and have the left hand lowered and right one raised, then shaken. Next, have participants reach across behind their necks with the left hand and pat their right shoulder several times (you can add humorous commentary throughout the activity such as "You have all done a good job so far so give yourself a pat on the back"). After a few seconds, have them reverse and pat the left shoulder with the right hand. Have them then reach across the front of their bodies and pat the left hip with the right hand, then the right hip with the left hand. Continue such movements touching different parts of the body with opposite hands for a few minutes to get

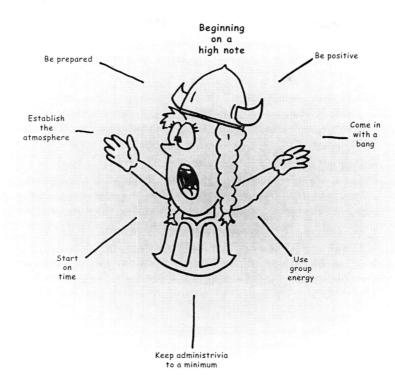

MINDMAP 2. Beginning on a High Note

participants moving and to activate their minds. The latter occurs because learners have to consciously think about which body part to use and how to accomplish the activity given in the instructions. Cross lateral activities can also be used throughout a session when you need a quick energizer after periods of sitting.

Create an institution where people aren't allowed to be curious,
and people won't be curious.
    —*Tom Peters*
    Liberation Management

● **GRABBING ATTENTION**

So much of the success of your training initiatives is dependent on the initial approach you take. Underestimating the need to start off with a powerful introduction could be a serious mistake. By slowly drifting into your topic or unemotionally greeting participants when presenting a session overview, you can lose learner attention. Once this has occurred, you may never be able to fully rekindle a spark of curiosity and interest. To that end, make your opening remarks with enthusiasm. Put power into your words and say them with a vocal quality that uses all your capabilities (e.g., volume, inflection, pitch, and rate). Also, make sure that your nonverbal cues are in congruence or match your vocal messages. For example, if you say, "Good morning," do so with enthusiasm. Say "GOOD MORNING!" energetically and in a loud voice. As you offer the greeting, make sure that you smile, and use open body language and gesturing (e.g., arms extended out and away from your body toward the audience). I will often say "GOOD MORNING!" and if participant response is weak, I'll jokingly say something like, "I know the coffee has not kicked in yet and it's early, but if we start the day off with a low-key approach, it's going to be a long one. Can we try that again . . . GOOD MORNING!" This generally gets a laugh and a stronger refrain because everyone is now tuned into the start of the session. I can then launch into my planned content and activities.

Because of the time issue I mentioned earlier, your participants want to know that every minute spent in training is worth the investment. As such, part of the power from your opening remarks can be derived by explaining the Added Value And Results For Me (AVARFM) to each learner. By telling participants up front the importance of the information they will receive, and stressing its value to them personally, you can increase the likelihood of their buy-in. Put your comments, related to value, in the context of how their knowledge, skills, and attitudes can improve through use of program concepts. Also, stress other value-added elements, such as time savings, increased revenues, decreased expenditures, enhanced service levels, or whatever applies to your group.

INTERIM REVIEW

If you were facilitating a workshop on this chapter's topic you could energize learners while reviewing information covered thus far. This could be done by having participants form two equal lines, one person behind another, facing a wall. Give the first person in each line an inflated balloon that he or she is to put between his or her knees. When you say "GO" the person should quickly run to the wall, slap the wall, and shout out one term, concept, or idea experienced in the session thus far, then return (with the balloon between his or her knees) to the line where he or she passes the balloon to the next person, who repeats the process. Tell participants that they cannot repeat something said by another person. Continue this evolution for a set time limit or until everyone has made a trip to the wall. If someone cannot think of a something to yell on reaching the wall, they slap the wall and yell "Pass." After everyone is done, have everyone give a round of applause and do a quick review and highlight any key areas they missed. You may want to award all participants a piece of candy or small prize.

If you have participants with disabilities (e.g., sight impaired or who use a wheelchair or other mobility device), they can still participate to their level of comfort or with the assistance of others, as they desire. For example, someone in a wheelchair could still place the balloon between his or her knees and go to the wall.

Now, before moving on in this chapter, take a few minutes and write down all the key concepts you can recall, then check for accuracy before proceeding.

● POWERFUL BEGINNINGS

As you have already read, the ways to introduce yourself and a session, and to quickly engage learners, is limited only by your imagination and willingness to think outside the box. There are dozens of books on the market that focus on **icebreaker activities** and creative training strategies (see Books in Resources for Trainers section in the appendices). I encourage you to take the time to locate 10–20 standard opening activities that you can incorporate into your training programs. Doing this will allow flexibility and keep your sessions upbeat and fresh. This is important because while providing a diversity of learning experiences for your participants you will also be guarding against becoming bored yourself. For you to be effective, you have to enjoy what you are doing.

There are many creative ways in which you can gain participant attention to focus their minds on what you are about to say or deliver. The important part is that you should get them tuned in to the session subject before you start discussing objectives, content, or any other pertinent information. Otherwise, some participants will miss portions of your remarks and might distract others as they continue to talk or do other things (see **Table 4-1** for possible attention getting ideas).

Here are seven specific strategies for grabbing the attention of your participants.

Table 4-1. Ideas for Grabbing Attention

Use noisemakers as you enter the room to attract attention (e.g., train whistles, cow bells, party noisemakers, sliding whistles; see Creative Presentation Resources, Inc. in the Resources for Trainers section of the appendices).

Wear props (e.g., clothing, disguise glasses, or clown hair, nose and shoes).

Do magic or card tricks tied to program content in some manner.

Enter with upbeat music (e.g., theme song from the movie "Rocky").

Share startling facts or statements.

Use analogies or metaphors.

Involve participants immediately in an activity.

Share factual trivia, possibly through use in small group competitions.

Create an environment that says excitement (e.g., colorful posters, motivational quotes or sayings on the walls, party glitter on tables and balloons).

Give things away (e.g., enter with music playing and a prop on as you run around the room giving out candy or small noisemakers to participants).

Make 'Em Smile

Each participant has a different threshold of what he or she thinks is humorous. For that reason, it is important that you use a variety of humorous techniques to grab attention and aid understanding. It is also important that you remember what you read in Chapter 3 about humor sometimes failing to cross cultural boundaries.

Your options for humor encompass many possibilities. Jokes, stories, cartoons, nonverbal gestures, actions, and props are just a few of the things that can make people laugh and make a point. The key to their success is for you to "get into" the delivery when you are using them. For example, animated gestures and facial expressions can often enhance the effect of a good joke.

One approach that I use when conducting a session, that I call *Presentation Pizzazz: Adding Impact to Learning,* is to have someone else introduce me while I wait in the rear of the room. While there, I put on a pair of disguise glasses (e.g., Groucho Marx with bushy eyebrows and mustaches, glasses, and large nose). As soon as the introduction is over, I run into the room blowing some type of whistle to attract attention. Once at the front of the room, I conduct a quick needs assessment through the use of either flip-charted or projected questions. The questions I use are closed-ended and often in short or abbreviated format (e.g., What Is Your Name?, Y R U Here?, What do U Hope to Learn?, and What R U Thinking?) and are surrounded by a colorful, creative border (e.g., balloons, clown faces, or other festive images). Without saying a word, I smile and gesture to the written question and then to someone in the group, indicating that they should respond. After a number of responses, I put up the second, then third question, and repeat the process until all questions are answered or until someone says something such as "Are you ever going to speak?" At that point, I remove the glasses, smile, and say, "I was wondering if you wanted me to. Since you do, let's get started . . ". This approach gets laughs and relaxes me and the group. Later in that session, I go back to discuss the opening activity and what it accomplished. Some of the potential accomplishments include the fact that I:

Relieved possible participant tension

Demonstrated that while I take the topic seriously, I do not take myself so

Gained attention

Tied into the program content

Gathered useful information about the group

Helped get to know some participants

A key point to remember about using humor is that you should address it at yourself and not others. Even if you make fun about some physical aspect about yourself (e.g., height, weight, size of a body part, religion, race, sex, or sexual orientation), if offense to others who share those characteristics might result, do not use it. It is better to err on the side of conservatism than to alienate participants.

Another thing to remember is that some people are just not funny or good at telling jokes. If you know this to be true about yourself, find another means to grab attention. Just as the lonely walk back across a dance floor after having someone reject your offer to dance, recovering from a bad joke can be equally painful and difficult. If you fail in your opening attempt to spark interest, you could lose or struggle to gain audience attention. By the way, did you catch that use of analogy in the preceding?

PUTTING YOUR BRAIN TO WORK: ACTIVITY

What humorous techniques do you think are most effective? Why? _____

_____

In what ways have you seen trainers successfully use humor in the past? _____

_____

What are some humorous techniques that you could incorporate into your own training sessions?

_____

_____

Amaze 'Em

Many people are fascinated by the unknown. When confronted with new ideas or information, many participants often revert to a childlike stage of wonderment and awe. You can capitalize on this phenomenon by using demonstrations of magic, science, basic physics, or other little known areas to grab attention and leave them wondering, "How did they do that?"

Two of my favorite techniques for accomplishing amazement follow; however, a visit to a magic, teacher supply, book, Nature, or Discovery store can result in materials on all types of elementary tips and scientific experiments that can be adapted to virtually any environment and topic.

Stepping Through the Paper

This is an activity I saw used years ago by a trainer whose name I unfortunately cannot recall.

To do this demonstration, you will need two 8½ × 11 inch sheets of blank paper (folded either lengthwise or sidewise) and a pair of scissors.

Start your demonstration by holding up one sheet of the paper and asking, "How many of you believe that I can physically pass my body through a piece of paper?" For those who say that they believe, ask them why. Generally it is either because they have seen similar demonstrations or they believe you would not say you can unless you are

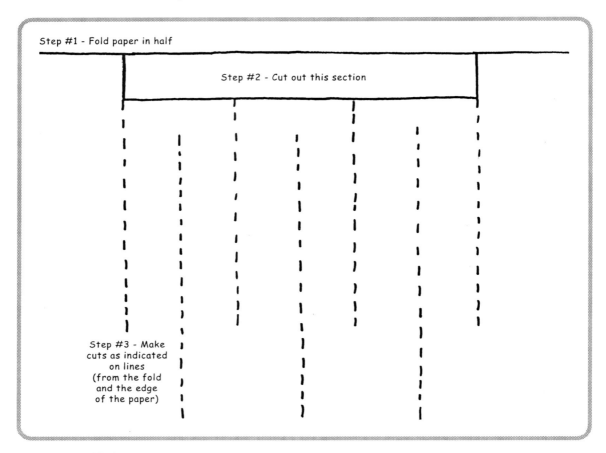

FIGURE 4-5. Folded paper

able to. Next, ask those who said they do not think you can why they believe that. Often, they are either linear thinkers and have difficulty thinking outside the box, or believe that certain things are not possible, in this case, putting one object through another.

Once you have discussed their reasoning, proceed to cut one piece of the paper based on the illustrations in **Figure 4-5.** Once you have made the cuts, open the paper until it forms a large circle, then carefully step into the circle and move it up and over your entire body until you have stepped entirely "through the paper." Discuss how thinking outside the box and looking at things from different perspectives are important skills in today's changing workplace and world. Tie these concepts to your session topic.

Piercing the Balloon

Another amazing demonstration involves inserting a sharp knitting needle through an inflated balloon. To accomplish this, you will need a sharpened 18-inch metal knitting needle, on which the tip has been filed to a sharp point, and several balloons (in case

you accidentally pop one). You will also need a small amount of petroleum jelly or baby oil for coating the tip of the knitting needle.

Just as with the Stepping Through the Paper activity, this one involves thinking outside the box and doing what most people believe is not possible.

To get ready for the demonstration, blow up two rubber latex balloons (the less expensive thin ones work best if you do not fill them to maximum capacity). When you are ready to begin, start with an animated and exaggerated explanation of the laws of physics that make some things impossible. Emphasize how sharp objects typically cause a balloon to burst. You can poke a balloon to make it explode to emphasize the point and also show that these are not trick balloons. Ask for a show of hands of those who believe that you can pass the point of the knitting needle entirely through a balloon. Stress that like many things in the workplace, all sorts of possibilities exist if you have the right knowledge and tools. Proceed to gently insert the point of the needle into the balloon (there is typically a strong point at the end in the area where the rubber has not been stretched). A very slow rotating motion between your fingers as you work the point through the rubber and talk to the group about various elements of creativity and thinking outside the box works best. The key is not to rush or the balloon will pop. Once the point is through the end, guide the needle to the other side and out the opposite side of the balloon, next to where you have blown it up and tied it (again, the rubber is stronger at this point). This feat is possible because the petroleum jelly eases the entrance through the latex. Once completely through the balloon, withdraw the needle to show that it was not a trick balloon. For emphasis prick the balloon with the needle so that it too explodes.

This is a great attention gainer and can be used to lead into a discussion of the value of the session topic for gaining new knowledge and skills.

Shock 'Em

Through a variety of techniques, you can startle or shock your audience while gaining attention and making a key point. Such approaches can often be used to answer, "So what?" for your participants and to give them a reason to listen further.

Some common techniques include the use of quotes, statistics, role-play, graphic images, or facts. For example, did you know that the most used letter in written English is "e" and that "the" is the most commonly used word?[10] What has this got to with this chapter? you ask. Everything. Just as such information can jump start a presentation, by providing startling information that many readers did not likely know, I have possibly informed, piqued interest, and challenged your thinking by using such information. All this was done with a couple of simple facts that you could phrase as a question to introduce a training program.

Graphic images can also be powerful. For example, when I used to teach courses on firearms safety, I would often use graphic photographs of body parts that had been injured through careless handling of weapons. This immediately gave the AVARFM to each participant, who now were focused on the fact that if they failed to listen effectively, they or someone else could be seriously injured or killed.

A third effective technique that I have used in the past is role-play. I used to teach identification techniques to law enforcement officers in a classroom that had a door to the left and right at the front. As I was beginning my introductory remarks, the door to my right would burst open and two people would come running and screaming through the room, then out the opposite door. One person was chasing the other with a large plastic knife raised above his or her head as if trying to catch and cut the other person. As soon as they were gone, I'd say something such as, "Did you see that? What was that all about? Well, let's take advantage of the opportunity. Everyone take out a piece of paper and write down everything you remember about both people." I then had them form small groups and compare descriptions. Typically, their views varied significantly. The learning point was that if they had trouble accurately describing an event, how could they expect less of untrained witnesses at crime and accident scenes to do better? I had them. In that quick activity they experienced a need to be more humble and empathetic when dealing with witnesses. We then proceeded with the class.

You can build similar scenarios involving customer service, employer, employee, peer, or other situations into your own training.

BRIGHT IDEA

Build a Reference Library

To have a variety of handy facts, figures, and other material available for use in training, start collecting trivia, information books, and articles. A great resource is the Internet, as it contains virtually any topic you could want to reference. When designing your training programs, build in this value-added information as opening remarks, team-based trivia competitions, energizers, or as additional information related to the topic.

PUTTING YOUR BRAIN TO WORK: ACTIVITY

What startling strategy do you think works best to capture participant attention? Why? _____

_____

_____

What are some startling techniques that you have used or experienced in the past? _____
_____
_____

Were the strategies you experienced successful or not? Explain? _____
_____
_____

Relate 'Em

In Chapter 3, you read about analogies and other similar techniques that are useful for helping learners relate current knowledge to new material or concepts. Through use of such techniques you can potentially assist participants in recognizing that all of what they are about to experience is not new or foreign to them. This can help relieve anxiety or potential frustrations that can possibly impact learning.

To better recognize the power of relating learners to current knowledge, think of training or education classes in which you felt initially overwhelmed because you did not think you knew anything about the topic (e.g., algebra, math, a foreign language, or science in school, introduction to computers, or a technical skills course). If the instructor was effective, he or she likely tried to help relieve your tension by stressing your ability, and emphasizing how you likely already unconsciously knew some of the basics. For example, in a foreign language class, the instructor may have had you list different ways that you already knew how to say hello in other languages. Many people know several that they have learned through life, but do not consciously realize this fact. Or, you may have been shown a number of English terms derived from foreign base words (e.g., the word attachment is derived from the French word *attaché* meaning one attached to an embassy, or the word educate derived from the Latin word *educo*, meaning to lead forth). By helping you mentally bridge knowledge and learning, you were probably more successful at assimilating information. If, on the other hand, the instructor incorrectly assumed that you knew certain pieces of information, or took a superior approach in which he or she used terminology unfamiliar to you, you likely shut down and gave up. For example, assume that you are an adult learner with no previous computer knowledge or experience who has enrolled in an introductory computer course. After arriving, your instructor says, "Okay, let's get started by booting up your computers. Go ahead and turn on your PC and monitor, then take a look at your desktop." She then proceeds to tell you how exciting and easy computers are to operate, and shares a story of how her 6-year-old son uses his all the time. How do you think you might feel at that point? Now ask yourself if you have made similar assumptions in sessions you have taught. Such comments typically intimidate or frustrate learners and ultimately create an environment where, even it they do not know something, they will not ask out of fear of appearing stupid. After all, if a 6-year old can do it, they should be able to also!

Have you experienced sessions such as the examples offered in this section? Explain what happened.

_____

How did you feel about the instructor? The session? _____

_____

What could have been done differently to reduce any frustrations you and others may have experienced?

_____

Challenge 'Em

One of the fastest ways to get participants immediately thinking about session content is to form small groups and then present an issue or problem related to the session topic. Have members of each group introduce themselves to teammates and brainstorm elements of the problem, causes, effects, or other aspects related to the issue. Following a set time limit, have them present their ideas to the others in the class, then post them on the wall for future use. Refer to these lists as you go through program materials.

This type of activity can be used effectively immediately following an introduction and overview of session objectives.

How is learning stimulated through challenging participant thinking? _____

_____

What are some other ways to challenge participants and get them thinking about your program content?

_____

Communicate with 'Em

By sharing a story or personal experience you can begin to connect and build rapport with participants. The power of this strategy is that in the process of relating your tale, you share events to which participants can often relate and you potentially self-disclose a personal event and demonstrate that you are human and approachable. You also form a psychological bond with participants and encourage them to participate and possibly to share their own experiences.

A story I sometimes share in trainer development workshops relates to an error in judgment on my part as an inexperienced trainer years ago. I was in South Tucson, Arizona. For whatever reason, I decided to pack transparencies for an upcoming class in my airline checked baggage. I assumed that because I'd never lost a bag and was flying in on Saturday for a Monday class, even if the bag were delayed, it would get there by Sunday, but I was wrong. I use the story to illustrate the need for a backup plan. In my case, I was forced to improvise because there were no office supply stores available from which I could buy transparency film on Sunday. I ended up buying several boxes of 1-gallon plastic storage bags at a local supermarket, along with transparency markers found in their school supply aisle, to create handwritten transparencies. After relating my story, I elicit similar training horror stories from participants and normally get many. In doing this, we all learn from one another, participants become actively involved in their own learning, and we bond psychologically through similar experiences.

PUTTING YOUR BRAIN TO WORK: ACTIVITY

Think of a specific topic on which you deliver training (e.g., customer service, supervision, and communication), and then respond to the following questions.

What real-life workplace examples can you think of in which something did not go according to plan (e.g., a customer service situation got out of control) related to the session topic you selected? _____

_____

How was the situation handled or resolved? _____

_____

What might have been done differently? _____

_____

Use your answers as a possible basis for an activity or discussion in your own training programs.

Involve 'Em

Use whatever technique or activity you can think of to get participants interacting quickly. For example, as soon as you have introduced yourself, you can get participants involved by asking them to write down the most important thing they know about the session topic (e.g., in a session on being a successful bank cashier, a comment might be that accuracy on the job is absolutely crucial). Then, as they introduce themselves, have them share their point with others and ask for comments from the group.

PUTTING YOUR BRAIN TO WORK: ACTIVITY

In what other ways can you immediately involve participants in training? _____

_____

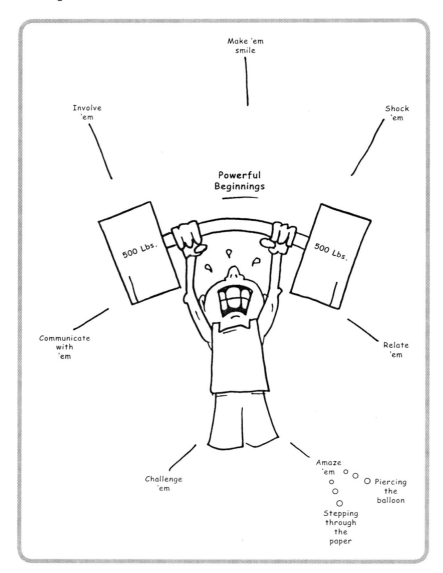

MINDMAP 3. Powerful Beginnings

What do you believe the advantages of such a tactic to be? Why? _____

_____

What are the disadvantages? Why? _____

_____

BRIGHT IDEA

Pique Their Interest

Walk into your session with one of the "arrow through the head" props that are available through many party, novelty, or costume stores. Somehow, incorporate its use into your opening remarks by saying something such as, "Good morning. I apologize if I seem sluggish this morning. For some reason, I woke up with a terrible headache today!"

One can never consent to creep when one feels an impulse to soar.
–Helen Keller

● GETTING TO KNOW PARTICIPANTS

Trust is the basis for all relationships. It is also better gained in a friendly environment.

In my experience, one of the best ways to start a session on a relaxed note, and to set the tone for trust and learning, is to include introductions with your opening remarks. Participants are less likely to disagree with or challenge your comments, and may be more receptive, if they feel that they know you and have psychologically bonded. This **rapport building** can actually begin as participants arrive through the use of the following strategies.

Prepare Biographical Information

By providing brief background information on a handout, you can help establish yourself as an expert (assuming you have experience) while saving precious classroom time. You can still give a brief personal overview, then refer participants to the handout if they want more information about you. Make sure that you include your organization, mailing and e-mail address, and phone numbers on the biography so participants can later follow up with comments or questions.

The handout can be included in participant guides or as a separate sheet of paper and can be used by an organizational representative to introduce you, if necessary. To assist the latter, you may also want to bullet point five or six key accomplishments on a flip chart or projected visual to use during your opening remarks and introduction. This helps the visual learners.

Display a Welcome Message

Either on a flip chart by the entrance or on a projected image, use a *Welcome to . . .* message, accompanied by colorful, creative graphics (e.g., fancy borders, clipart, drawings of flowers, the sun, moon, or stars; geometric symbols, or whatever you think appropriate).

As I travel around the country, I have caricature artists create images of me in different postures along with flip charts, projectors, lecterns, or other training related equipment. I turn these images into transparencies, flip chart pages, or handouts to add a humorous personal touch (see my caricature in **Figure 4-3**).

Greet Participants

Having all your pre-session preparation (e.g., equipment and facilities checks and handouts distributed) done prior to the actual arrival of participants allows you to be available to greet participants at the door as they arrive. As they do so, greet them with a smile and friendly welcome, shake hands, and give any necessary instructions, such as seating, activity assignments, name tag preparation, and refreshment information. By physically making contact with each person and using his or her name, you subconsciously form a psychological bond with them.

Encourage Networking

If you have ever attended a training session in which there was silence as people arrived, because there was no background music or talking and the instructor was busy going through a checklist and ignoring participants, you probably recognize how awkward, sterile, and boring such a setting can be.

To help alleviate the possibility of your sessions feeling this way, get participants involved with one another as soon as possible. You can do this by having a statement on your welcome flip chart or projected visual that humorously states, "It's okay to talk to each other." Another way to accomplish interaction is through an assigned activity. For example, if you have a group of 20 or fewer participants, greet them at the door and hand them a playing card, colored balloon, or strip of colored paper. Tell them to find someone who has a matching item, get to know the person, and determine a strength the person has related to the session topic. During your introductory remarks, have each person do a brief introduction, then tell the strength they found in the room and to whom it belonged. As the strengths are revealed, capture them on a flip chart for later reference and program relationship.

Through such an activity, people get to know each other, silence is broken, and you identify potential resources within the room. You can also determine areas that you do not need to spend much time covering because many people share a strong skill or knowledge area. Using such an approach can encourage networking by stressing that participants should get to know one another during breaks, rather than returning to their offices to check e-mail and voice messages. This latter approach can also help ensure that everyone returns from breaks on time so that you can remain on schedule.

Conduct "I Hope" Exercise

As adults, participants generally arrive at sessions with expectations and needs based on prior experiences. Use their previous encounters to your advantage by having them share one thing that they hope will or will not happen in your session.

One of the ways that I do this in my sessions is to have each participant write down one issue or concern on a piece of paper. For example, "I hope we get regularly scheduled breaks" or "I hope there won't be a lot of lecture." I then have participants find partners, exchange papers, introduce themselves, and share why the issue is important to them. After several minutes, I have everyone retrieve his or her own paper, find a new partner, and repeat the process. Next, I have participants form small groups of four to eight members and have them share what they have written with team members as someone captures all their concerns on a flip chart page for discussion and display. In doing this, I gradually work people into small groups, encourage interaction, and ultimately discover concerns that I might need to address.

You can likely find other variations of this activity to fit your training needs.

Play Background Bingo

A fun way to encourage interaction and introductions and to get people up and moving is to play a variation of the game Bingo. To start, create handouts of a Bingo card similar to **Figure 4-6**. You can use whatever characteristics you prefer on your cards. Give participants a card as they arrive and tell them they have 10 minutes to locate people who fit one of the categories on their card. A participant can sign only one box on another participant's card, as the object is to have them meet as many people as possible while searching for signers.

You can either have participants try to get a line Bingo (all boxes filled in one line either vertically, horizontally, or diagonally) or cover-all Bingo (all boxes on the card filled). Tell participants that the first person filling his or her card should shout Bingo. If they in fact do get their card filled correctly, stop the game, reward the participant, and get started with your session.

PUTTING YOUR BRAIN TO WORK: ACTIVITY

Think of various ways that you have used or seen for getting participants to know one another and to foster a friendly environment early in a session. List those ideas here for future reference when designing your programs.

Has attended a session on this topic before	Knows at least one other person in the room	Has blue eyes	Has long hair	Has gold jewelry on
Has a nickel on him or her	Volunteered to attend this session	Traveled more than 20 miles to get to this session	Has attended college	Is a registered voter
Provides service to internal customers (within his or her own organization)	Is wearing something red	**X**	Is married	Has more than two siblings
Owns a cat	Drives a car less than 5 years old	Is at least 5 ft 8 inches tall	Has a 401K Plan or an IRA	Owns a dog
Loves Italian food	Has been on a cruise	Is a Democrat	Has donated blood in the past 6 months	Is a Republican

FIGURE 4-6. Background Bingo

BRIGHT IDEA

Getting to Really Know Them

As an interactive and fun way to allow participants to get to know one another, bring in an instant or digital camera that allows rapid preparation of photos. Take individual pictures of all participants as they arrive. Once you have photos of everyone, number the pictures consecutively and post them along a wall. Pass out 5 × 8-inch index cards or pieces of paper and ask each person to letter their cards

MINDMAP 4. Getting to Know Participants

A, B, and C, then write down a fact about themselves next to each letter. Two of the facts should be true and one a lie. These should be things that others might not know about them at work. Once everyone has done so, have participants post their list under their photos. Next, give each participant a handout that is numbered consecutively down the left side of the page to correspond with the numbers under the photos (e.g., 1–25). Tell participants they have 15 minutes to review the photos and things each person has written. They are then to select the item that they believe is a lie and list the letter of that item next to that person's number on their handout. After the time has elapsed, have participants do personal introductions, tell what their own three items of information were, and which one is a lie. After all introductions and self-disclosures are done, award a prize to the person having the most correct responses on his or her sheet.

You can tie this activity into any session; however, it really fits well with team-building, interpersonal communication, customer service, and other people skills programs, as you can emphasize that you cannot always tell something about someone just by seeing them or a picture of them.

Imagination rules the world.
—*Napoleon Bonaparte*

◉ ICEBREAKERS

There are literally endless possibilities related to helping participants relax and get to know one another at the beginning of a session. Even if you are conducting a short 1-hour presentation, you should include an icebreaker of 5 minutes to get learners into the right frame of mind.

An icebreaker is typically a structured activity designed to encourage networking, relaxation, and brief introductions. They should be fast paced, upbeat, and fun. They are not necessarily content driven, although connecting to your program theme can be a value-added plus.

Here are some of my favorite icebreakers.

Creating a Team Identity

In sessions in which you will have participants interacting in small groups, you can encourage a team mentality during introductions. To accomplish this, form teams in some creative fashion (see Chapter 6). Have team members get to know one another as they generate a list of characteristics, strengths, or whatever you designate. After they have done so, have each team identify a group name that describes them or that they prefer. This name might be based on the list they have generated. Next, give each team flip chart paper and an assortment of colored markers. Tell participants that they have 15 minutes to create a graphic image that illustrates their team. Encourage them to get creative and think outside the box. Once they have finished, have them put their team name on the picture and post it on the wall. For introductions, have each team member introduce himself or herself and have someone explain the reasoning behind their name and image. You can award prizes to one or all teams, as desired. Later in the session, build in friendly team competitions thorough activities, reviews, and in other ways.

Animal Attraction

This is a creative introductory exercise that uses some fun props. The way I use this activity is to buy some small brown paper bags (candy size) at one of the local Warehouse Clubs (Sam's, BJs, COSTCO, or Price Club) or other businesses that supply retail stores. I then stamp both sides of each bag with a rubber stamp that I had made at an office supply store. The stamp says, "PLEASE DO NOT OPEN UNTIL TOLD." Inside each bag, I place either a flat foam rubber animal face mask or a rubber animal nose (see Creative Presentation Resources in the Resources for Trainers section of the appendices). I then staple the bags closed and put them in the center of participant tables. When I am ready to start the icebreaker activity I tell participants to take a bag, open it, and put on whatever they find inside. I typically put on a mask or nose myself to reduce the inhibitions that some might have of being the first to look silly. Participants are then told to wander around the room and find everyone else who looks like them, form a group to introduce themselves, and exchange whatever information that I designate. You can substitute any prop for variations of this activity (e.g., hats or other party items).

What a Great Place to Be

To get participants into a positive frame of mind related to training attendance, I often help them recognize that there are worse places to be. To accomplish this, I pass out blank pieces of paper and ask each person to think of one task that is waiting for them in their office or at home that they are dreading. I then have them write down the task, crumple the paper up, and toss it to someone else. Participants take turns introducing themselves and reading the task on the page that was received. Next, I show the session objectives and ask participants to think of one way in which they believe that the session content will benefit them and/or their organization and to write the benefit down. Finally, I have each person read the benefit that he or she wrote and stress that instead of being elsewhere doing something they do not want to do, they can stay in class, participate actively, and gain new knowledge or skills that can help make their lives easier and more interesting.

Fantasyland

For this icebreaker, use one of the creative strategies for grouping participants found in Chapter 6. Once small groups are formed and a leader and scribe have been selected for each group, tell participants that they have just been transported to Fantasyland. In that mythical place, they can do anything they like. Have them brainstorm some aspect related to the session topic and the workplace. For example, if they could change anything (e.g., boss, customers, peers, job tasks, or workplace environment) what would the perfect change look like? Once each group has developed a list, have them share with others. Stress that they now have a blueprint for improvement that they can use in their real workplace to effect change. Later in the program, you may want to revisit the lists from this activity and have groups develop an action plan for making changes. This gives a tangible result that they can go back to the workplace with and adds value to the training. You can modify the topic that they address in this icebreaker to focus on any issue you desire or that relates specifically to your program topic. It is a wonderful way for determining what participants think and issues that are important to them.

Who Am I?

There are a couple of variations of this activity that you may want to use to help participants get to know more about one another. In the first version, you can have participants write on an adhesive nametag either four or five bits of information about themselves (e.g., height, eye color, ethnicity, highest year of schooling, or whatever) or hobbies and interests that they have. They should not put their name on the tag. Have them toss all the nametags into a pile. Finally, have each person randomly draw a tag from the pile and search the room for the author. Once found, they should do introductions and get to know one another until told to stop and regroup.

A second variation is to have people write four or five strengths (e.g., good listener, fast reader, good negotiator, works well on teams, or whatever) on a sheet of paper or flip chart paper, then post the page on the wall. Each person has a set period of time, depending on the size of the group, in which to read what is on the sheets and then try to determine to which participant the information applies.

Brain Teasers

These visually stimulating puzzles are great as an introductory individual or small group activity or to use as an energizer throughout training programs. There are many sources for these puzzles; however, you can create your own by taking simple phrases and converting them to vertical, horizontal or diagonal configurations and even adding pictures to substitute for words (see **Figure 4-7**).

Word Search Puzzles

Participants love challenges that are fun. You can add both of these elements to the beginning of your session or at any point throughout the program through use of word search puzzles that use key words or concepts from the training. As you read in earlier chapters, this is an excellent way to introduce key learning elements, assess current knowledge, or reinforce program words and content. The way I use these in my introduction is to have participants either individually or in groups take 5 minutes to try to find all the terms listed at the bottom of the puzzle. Once that has been accomplished, I reward the person or group getting all or most of the terms correct and then review the terms related to how they will be covered in the session. This is an easy and less boring manner to introduce your objectives (see **Figure 4-8,** which is based on key elements of this chapter; answers are in the Tools for Trainers section in the appendices). This sample was created on a crossword software package (see section in the appendices for Word Search puzzle software).

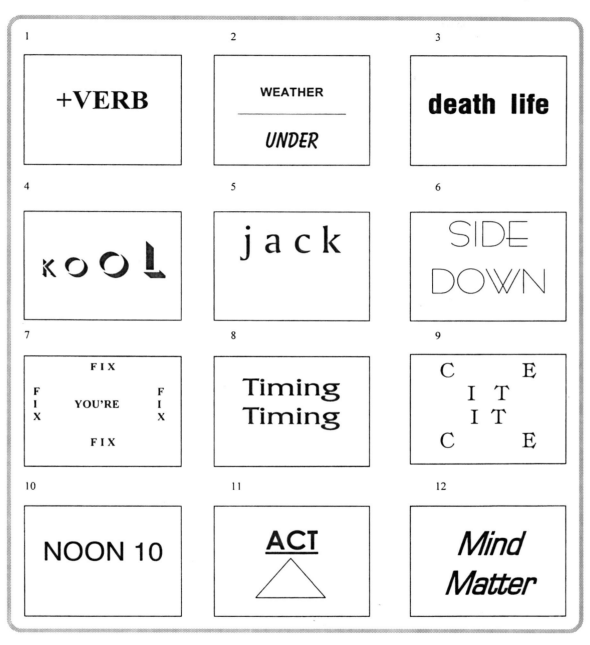

FIGURE 4-7. Brain teaser

ANSWERS TO BRAIN TEASERS ON PAGE 153

1. Adverb
2. Under the weather
3. Life after death
4. A look backwards
5. Highjack
6. Upside down
7. You're in a fix
8. Two timing
9. Excite
10. 10 past noon
11. Balancing act
12. Mind over matter

OPENING WITH A BANG

```
G  N  I  M  R  O  T  S  N  I  A  R  B  S  U
X  D  S  N  O  I  T  C  U  D  O  R  T  N  I
H  H  E  B  T  J  U  F  B  A  L  L  O  O  N
C  S  R  R  B  E  V  L  O  V  N  I  L  I  R
R  N  U  U  E  R  E  H  P  S  O  M  T  A
A  E  T  R  G  N  O  I  T  N  E  T  T  A  P
E  T  A  C  I  N  U  M  M  O  C  L  C  T  P
S  W  C  H  N  J  S  P  O  R  P  W  E  C  O
D  O  I  A  N  I  C  E  B  R  E  A  K  E  R
R  R  R  L  I  G  F  A  C  T  S  V  T  P  T
O  K  A  L  N  S  K  J  E  E  U  A  I  X  L
W  I  C  E  G  A  V  C  R  Z  L  R  I  E  I
D  N  S  N  S  W  W  S  O  E  A  F  U  G  W
S  G  O  G  N  I  B  F  R  H  U  M  O  R  F
I  C  S  E  T  O  U  Q  F  I  S  L  A  Y  K
```

AMAZE
ATMOSPHERE
ATTENTION
AVARFM
BALLOON
BEGINNINGS
BINGO
BRAINSTORMING
CARICATURES
CHALLENGE

COMMUNICATE
EXPECTATIONS
FACTS
HUMOR
ICEBREAKER
INTERIMREVIEW
INTRODUCTIONS
INVOLVE
JIGSAW
NETWORKING

PROPS
QUOTES
RAPPORT
RELATE
SHOCK
TEASERS
WORDSEARCH

FIGURE 4-8. Sample word search: opening with a bang.

Hidden Messages

This final icebreaker is one that you can modify and integrate into virtually any training program opener and also use as an energizer. I found the concept in a book by Karen Anderson[11] a number of years ago. I had seen similar puzzles used in training sessions in the late 1980s but had forgotten about them.

The concept focuses on having people think outside the box to discover a message that is written on a page. Normally, when you tell someone to read across the page to see what is written, he or she looks down at a page expecting to see easily identified words. However, in this activity, the words are written in a long, stretched format and overlaid on top of other words or phrases. The concept challenges people to literally read across the page. Based on a person's visual ability and focal point, he or she can either bring the page up to nose level and scan across the page to read what is written, or some people can actually see the words better by placing the page on a flat surface and stepping back a few feet to see the words. Once the beginning word or phrase is located, the page must be rotated to see remaining ones (see **Figure 4-9**).

I often use this activity in interpersonal communication and coaching classes as a tool for people who find the word/phrase to coach or teach others how to do so.

APPLYING WHAT YOU LEARNED
Strategies for Stimulating the Brain

1. What are some ways that you can make a powerful first impression with your learners?

_____

_____

2. How are you currently raising participant expectations and what can you do differently to be more effective in the future? _____

_____

3. What strategies can you think of to start your sessions on a high note in the future?

_____

_____

4. How can you use the powerful beginnings discussed in this chapter, and others, to create an environment in which learners share and become involved? _____

_____

_____

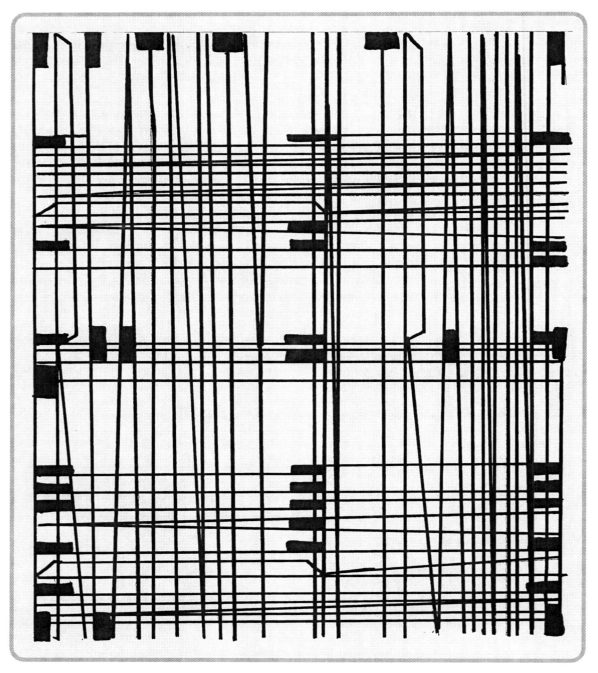

FIGURE 4-9. Hidden message

SOLUTION: Figure = Creativity in Training Increases the Learning

5. Based on the concepts of brain-based learning you have read, what techniques can you use in your next session to help gain and hold attention? _____

_____

6. Which activities that you read about can be used to assist in getting to know your learners better?

_____

_____

ENDNOTES

[9]Jensen, E., *Sizzle and Substance: Presenting with the Brain in Mind,* The Brain Store, San Diego, CA, 1998, p. 63.

[10]Hayward, A. (editor), *The Top 10 of Everything in 1999,* DK Publishing, New York, 1998, p 119.

[11]Anderson, K., *Riddles: Puzzles to Tickle Your Mind,* B & P Publishing, New York, 1994.

Notes

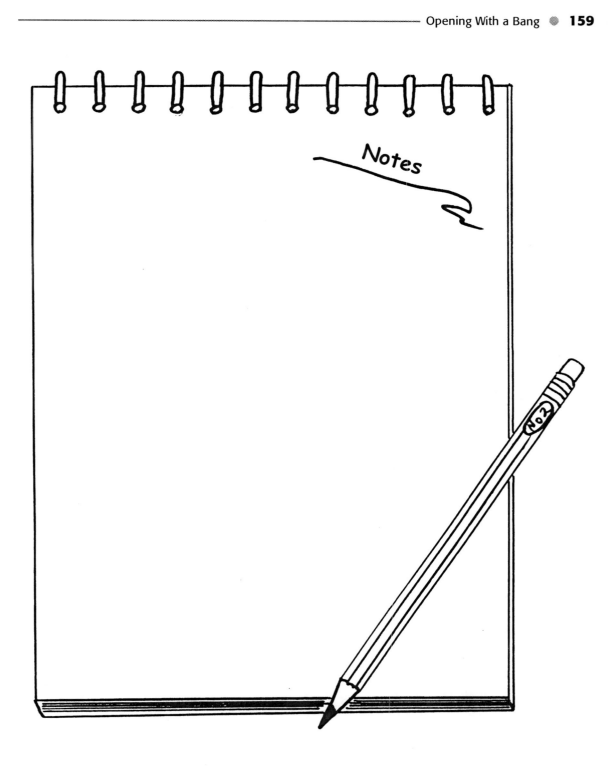

Notes

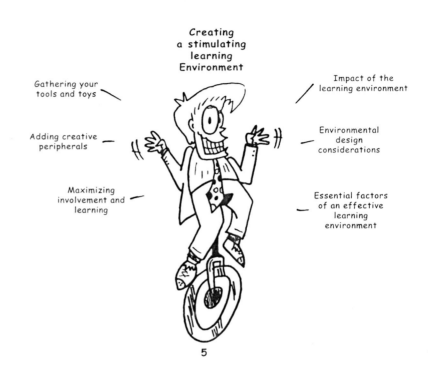

Creating
a stimulating
learning
Environment

Gathering your
tools and toys

Impact of the
learning environment

Adding creative
peripherals

Environmental
design
considerations

Maximizing
involvement and
learning

Essential factors
of an effective
learning
environment

5

Creating a Stimulating Learning Environment

Learning is experience. Everything else is just information.
   —Albert Einstein

Learning Objectives

At the end of this chapter, and when applying concepts covered, you will be able to:

● Recognize the impact that the environment plays learning.

● Incorporate the psychological needs of learners into a training environment to help ensure return on investment.

● Apply various research findings to the design of a learning environment.

● Identify the room layout best suited to your group and planned activities.

What techniques or strategies do you currently use to ensure your learning environment has maximum impact as participants walk into the room? _____

_____

What approaches have you seen others use that you have not, but could incorporate into your environment design? _____

_____

● THE IMPACT OF THE LEARNING ENVIRONMENT

Brain researchers continue to discover the importance of environmental factors on the human brain. To capitalize on their findings, you can design your learning environments in a manner such that participants have maximum access to information. You should also plan activities in which they can best use their five senses to receive and process information. In building your programs, your training environment should complement subject matter as closely as possible. To accomplish this, consider the audience, organizational culture, subject matter, and expected outcomes for the training. With these factors in mind, set out to create a learning utopia in which all the elements of brain-based learning are addressed to your fullest capability. Even if you have only indirect control over the room (e.g., a hotel or conference room) in which training will take place, you can still incorporate many of the ideas outlined throughout this book.

The wonderful thing about being a creative trainer is that through a little innovation, you can procure and use a variety of inexpensive tools to stimulate your sessions. You can also reconfigure seating and, in some cases, lighting, to accommodate better participants and learning needs. Often, for only a small amount of time and money (less than $50 dollars), you can obtain decorations, materials, and props that will add pizzazz to your classroom. In doing so, you will be helping to better attract and hold attention while relaying your thoughts and ideas to learners. The key to enhancing and enriching your learning vestibule is to add variety and novelty while fully engaging learners. Your goal should be to entice, challenge, elicit an emotional response, and stimulate minds to a point at which transfer of training to the workplace is a natural outcome.

Remember what you read about first appearances? To create a good first impression in your training room, you simply have to do some advance planning and preparation. To start with, locate some inspirational quotes by well known people that relate to your topic. Either have a graphics company create an assortment of professional looking posters or produce your own visually stimulating flip charts as discussed in Chapter 8. Use a variety of bright colors, borders, and clip art or other images. Post sayings around the room at eye level to reinforce the program theme. The reason you want to

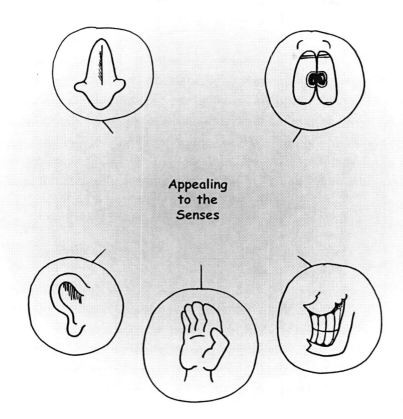

Appealing
to the
Senses

find quotes specific to your topic is that they should change each time you use the room. This keeps participants interested whenever they come to training and also creates a stimulating environment for you. This is especially important if some participants return on multiple days. You will want each day to be fresh and stimulating and to spark a positive emotional reaction. Likewise, if you have a standard training room in your organization, you may want to rotate the location of pictures or images hanging there. Perhaps you can even keep a few extra pictures around for rotating or exchanging images between rooms. These simple changes can generate thought in learners. Relate this to rearranging the furniture in a room of your home to make it look different, or to wearing different clothes each day of the week to project a variety of images. In doing such things, your brain has to go through a conscious effort of cognition and reflection.

Since attention to detail says a lot about you and your ability, use a table setting in a fine restaurant or at a formal dinner as a model for room setup. In such places, everything is exactly placed and each setting is like the one next to it. Taking care of even small details, such as checking for fingerprints on silver and glasses, ensures that a positive first impression is made. That is the impression you should strive for in your training room. Aesthetics, or overall appearance, definitely make a strong mental impact. For that reason, consider the following questions as a checklist and address them before participants arrive for your training programs.

Is the overall appearance from the doorway inviting?

Have you emptied all trashcans and picked up any scraps of paper from the floor?

Have any spills or stains been cleaned from tables and the floor?

Are training aids (e.g., flip charts, projectors, screens, VCR and monitor) properly positioned?

Have tables and chairs been neatly placed? (All chairs should be pushed under tables and in similar locations at each table)

Are any extra chairs or tables neatly positioned against walls or where they will be used later?

Have dry erase or chalkboards, if used, been cleaned and have any pre-session instructions been neatly written on them?

Are handouts, if used, neatly placed so that all are in a similar position for each participant? (This includes name tents, pencils, and markers)

Are your instructor table and materials neatly arranged?

Have refreshments been neatly positioned out of the way (e.g., in the rear of the room)?

Are there plants or flowers on tables or positioned around the room? If so, are they fresh or dust free (if artificial)?

● ENVIRONMENTAL DESIGN CONSIDERATIONS

Psychological Considerations

Many trainers become so focused on their program content and delivery that they often neglect a major component of the learning process—the environment. Studies by educators and cognitive and developmental psychologists stress that trainers and teachers must strive to incorporate basic elements of environmental enhancement if they truly desire to encourage learning and promote the transfer of training to the workplace. Training is typically more cohesive and effective when it is conducted at one location or site. That is, once participants arrive at the training site, they do not have to relocate to another during the training cycle (e.g., travel to several remote locations). A psychological transition is made once participants leave their workplace or other location to travel to the initial training site. Once at the training site, the facility becomes their temporary "home" and they settle in, claim their turf, and become used to their personal space. Should they be required to move again, this psychological equilibrium is disrupted and a state of flux results, making learning more tenuous. This should not be construed to mean that field trips or use of breakout rooms for activities is ineffective, but simply that any movement should be well thought out, planned, and necessary. With respect to breakout rooms, select and organize them with the same care described earlier for primary training rooms.

As you create an environment in which participants can transition from a workplace to a learner mentality, it is helpful to look at a facility from their perspective. Identify objects or elements that will enhance learning and those that might distract or detract from it. Thinking back on what you read in Chapter 1 about how the brain functions and processes information can aid in your assessment and planning.

Return on Investment

Creating an environment in which participants are encouraged and helped to learn requires assessment of the learning atmosphere. To some extent this element of preparation rests with you and your attitude toward the program, delivery, yourself, and participants. All of the information you read in previous chapters pertaining to your preparation and that of learners impacts your success level.

Your training initiatives need to be well organized and designed to foster comprehension on the part of participants. This means that after training, learners should be confident in what they gained and able to apply it to real-life scenarios to demonstrate **return on investment (ROI)** for their time spent in training.

One step in ensuring that training is created to support a valid learning process is to build content and activities around assessed needs as discussed in Chapter 3. The next step is to build in as much reinforcement during training as possible. Finally, add in a variety of stimulating activities and factors that will appeal to the brain through regular use of elements such as light, sound, color, motion, variety, novelty, and contrast. By appealing to as many senses as possible, you are more likely to have a training success story on your hands. Some sample ways to build these factors in are for you to physically change your location in the room throughout your presentation and to use a variety of well-planned gestures as you speak. You can also change media often, pass out handouts or other items for examination during the program, conduct activities in which you play music, dim the lights for introspection, and use a variety of colors in materials and visual aids.

BRIGHT IDEA

Reinforcing the Learning

Conduct activities at various points in your session in which participants have to revisit or rethink program objectives, for example, by forming small groups and giving each group a flip chart page listing one of the session objectives. Have each group review key elements taught to that point in the program and list them in a column on the left side of their page. Next, have them brainstorm real-world applications of what they have learned so that they can start to recognize ROI and how to use information on the job. Similar activities could be done at various points during the program as Interim Reviews and as a closing review activity.

What are you currently doing in training to ensure that the participants understand the return on investment they receive from attending your programs? _____

_____

What else can you do to help learners better appreciate and benefit from strategies and techniques you use to enhance learning? _____

_____

● ESSENTIAL FACTORS OF AN EFFECTIVE LEARNING ENVIRONMENT

Room Size and Shape

Although it is unlikely you will encounter an ideal training room very often, there are some factors to look for in a room and how it is set up. The key is that wherever you conduct your sessions, you should strive to find a facility that best fits the needs of your participants and your planned activities. In selecting a training venue, look for one that is open and spacious, yet sized to fit your group and scheduled activities. You will generally benefit from a room in which the length is not exceeded by its width by more than 40–50 percent. This allows flexibility without an awkward appearance. In addition, try to find a location that has ceilings of 9–10 feet to facilitate light and sound distribution and temperature control. In my experience, a room that allows me and my participants freedom of movement while providing me easy access to learners and support materials throughout the session is a plus. You don't want a room that is overly large or overly small. The former can lead to a perception of being lost in the unused space or that someone did not show up to fill the space. The latter can cause heat, noise, and personal space problems, all of which can negatively impact learners. Similarly, rooms that have an awkward shape (e.g., long and narrow or L-shaped), or that have obstacles such as weight-bearing ceiling posts, create serious training challenges.

The Impact of Color

Color is powerful. Marketing experts have known and used that knowledge for decades. Those who excel in successfully selling products to the public often do so through the use of color. For example, Heath[12] relates how when Tide detergent was created in the

1950s, white (symbolizing cleanliness and purity) was selected for the detergent and bright orange (bold, bright, powerful) was chosen to contrast with the gold (rich, valuable) on the package.

Color can be used to attract participant attention, stimulate the senses, and get learners emotionally involved in your sessions (see **Table 5-1**). Over the years, researchers in various areas of interest have studied how people react to color. When comparing the results of various studies, it becomes obvious that there are differing opinions related

Table 5-1. Emotions Associated with Color

Color	Emotions Stimulated
Red	Stimulates and evokes excitement, passion, power, energy, anger, intensity. Also, can indicate "stop," negativity, financial trouble or shortage.
Yellow	Indicates caution, warmth, mellowness, positive meaning, optimism, and cheerfulness. It can also stimulate thinking and visioning.
Dark blue	Depending on shade, can relax, soothe, indicate maturity, and evoke trust, tranquility, or peace.
Light blue	Cool, youthful, or masculine image can be projected.
Purple	Projects assertiveness or boldness, youthfulness, and contemporary image. Often used as a sign of royalty, richness, spirituality, or power.
Orange	Can indicate high energy or enthusiasm. Emotional and sometimes stimulates positive thinking. Organic image can result.
Brown	An earth tone that creates a feeling of security, wholesomeness, strength, support, and a lack of pretentiousness.
Green	Can remind of nature, productivity, positive image, moving forward or "go," comforting, growth, or financial success or prosperity. Also, can give a feeling of balance.
Gold/silver	Illustrates prestige, status, wealth, elegance, or conservative image.
Pink	Projects a youthful, feminine, or warm image.
White	Typically used to illustrate purity, cleanliness, honesty, wholesomeness; to enhance colors used and provide visual relaxation.
Black	Represents a lack of color. Creates sense of independence, completeness, and solidarity. Often used to indicate financial success, death, seriousness, or heaviness of situation.

Source: Lucas, R.W., *The Big Book of Flip Charts*, McGraw-Hill, New York, 2000, pp. 40–41.

to the impact of color; however, many similarities have been found. For example, lighter, primary colors are preferred over white, gray, black, and brown. According to Howard[13] the following applications of color often seem to work in various environments:

Cafeterias	Purple
Sales rooms	Yellow, orange, and coral
Conference rooms	Red
Offices	Blue with a tinge of red
Production areas	Green
Rooms for overly active children	Pink (tends to calm)
Waiting areas	Green (restful)

In his book, *The Power of Color*, Dr. Morton Walker explores many facets of using color in a variety of settings while citing a multitude of studies done in the field of chromatology (the science of color). Walker states that, "Whether you realize it or not, you probably associate every color with some particular feeling, behavior, lesson, action, experience, environment or event in your personal past."[14] Much of this association also comes from historic or cultural relationships. Think about how certain colors represent social and economic status (e.g., burgundy and gold for royalty in some cultures) whereas others have a particular significance (e.g., white is often associated with purity and weddings in some countries while black is associated with death).

By understanding the impact that color has on the subconscious mind, you can potentially harness its power in designing and using your learning environment, posters, handouts, and other support materials. For example, while cool, darker colors can soothe, calm, and relax, bright, hot and neon colors can stimulate, excite, grab attention, and raise emotions.

BRIGHT IDEA

To better determine which colors have the greatest impact on learning and your participants, why not give a little test. List all the colors shown in Figure 5-1 on a flip chart or writing board and have participants copy them, then write beside them one to three adjectives that they think of related to each color. Use the consensus gained to determine what colors to use for handouts, visual aids, training materials, and peripherals that you will post on the wall in future sessions. Keep in mind that the cultural and age makeup of your group will often influence how they perceive colors. For this reason, you may want to have them indicate gender, place of birth, and age group (e.g., under 20, 21–30, 31–40, 41–50, and 50 plus). You can then implement a demographically focused use of colors.

Learning . . . should be a joy and full of excitement. It is life's greatest adventure; it is an illustrated excursion into the mind of noble and learned men, not a conducted tour through a jail.
—Taylor Caldwell

Wall and Floor Coverings

If you are given any choice of floor coverings, opt for carpeting on all floors because this helps absorb excess sound and cuts down on noise reverberation. Also, avoid bright, floral, or striped patterns, as these can distract participants.

For walls, you have many color and material options. The key is to use colors that are mentally enhancing (light, primary colors). Light blue is one of the most used colors, although it can have a relaxing, soothing effect. This could be a learning challenge, however; if you use many of the ideas in this book related to color, visuals, movement and so on, any soothing effect can be minimized. Whatever colors you select, ensure that they do no contrast with or distract from items you intend to display.

When looking for a surface material, either in construction or selection of a training site, keep in mind that you need one that is functional and facilitates the display of materials. You will need to be able either to tape or pin items to the wall, so check to ensure that this is not a problem. Otherwise, you may find your options during the session limited. In many training facilities cork strips are mounted around the room at a height at which flip chart pages and posters can be pinned during a session.

If your walls will have dry erase boards, ensure that the lighting of the room does not glare off the surface and distract learners.

BRIGHT IDEA
Use Functional Carpeting

Some companies actually make carpeting that has a single large square grid or a board game pattern on it. These are perfect for nonverbal communication team activities in which members of teams must work their way through a secret pathway of boxes without communicating verbally or in writing. Only the facilitator knows the path that they must take and whenever and incorrect box is stepped on, a whistle or other creative noisemaker sounds to let them know to go back and start over. Incentives such as candy and play money make it more fun and can prompt a bit of competition between teams.

Other options include purchasing small rugs that are designed for children's rooms that have designs, such as checkerboards or hopscotch grids, on them. You can incorporate these into your sessions as icebreakers, energizers, review activities, or in whatever creative manner you come up with.

Windows and Doors

As you will read later, the amount and type of light provided in a learning environment can greatly impact learning. For that reason, look for facilities that have an ample number of windows or other light sources. If you have windows, make sure that there are coverings to control the amount of light, glare, and distractions that they cause. Also, consider whether you will open the windows (if possible) to have good exchange of air that can stimulate learners. There is a disadvantage in having windows because you lose valuable wall space for displaying items and training aids. You also have a potential distraction if learners can look out of the windows to the surrounding area.

If at all possible, position the front of your room opposite doors. This prevents learners from being distracted as someone enters or leaves the room. It also prevents distractions as people walk by the door when the door has windows or is left open. You may want to close any doors to reduce outside distractions.

Illumination (Lighting)

The significance of lighting cannot be overlooked when considering your learning environment. Physiologically, the retina of the human eye accounts for 40 percent of all nerve fibers connected to the brain, which may account for the high number of visual learners in any group. This fact points to the need to do whatever possible to stimulate those nerves effectively. By providing natural or effective artificial lighting along with other visual stimuli, you can help improve the chance that learners will be more alert and take in more information.

Light affects the level of alertness a person has by limiting the amount of melatonin produced by the body. This natural substance causes drowsiness. Researchers have found that sunlight, and to some extent certain forms of artificial light, also impact responsiveness and mood, help cure rickets, reduce infections and colds, and can generally lead to better health. Studies on the impact of light in a variety of settings have resulted in some important discoveries related to human performance and physical and mental conditions in humans. Such research has also caused many school systems and organizations to rethink and retool the lighting in classrooms and work areas. For example, one study by a Vermont psychiatrist[15] on the impact of lighting in three elementary schools found that lighting impacted absenteeism. In the experiment, London changed the light bulbs in a number of classrooms from standard to **full-spectrum** (Vitalite) to better simulate sunlight. According to London, when comparing absentee rates before and after the switch it was noted that absenteeism decreased by 65 percent following the change. Reportedly, fluorescent lighting raises the level of a hormone called cortisol in the blood. This substance suppresses the immune system and impacts stress, and increased levels can potentially adversely impact learning.

Even with all the research indicating the importance of light, many organizations have not gotten the word. For example, many conference facilities and training rooms often have lighting that is aesthetically attractive (e.g., chandeliers, recessed lighting, or sconces on the walls), but not functional from a learning perspective. Although such light fixtures may be attractive, they often do little to illuminate the room and to aid vision. In fact, they often detract from the learning experience because of reduced visibility, shadows, and darkened areas of the room.

In an internal report from the Institute for Research in Construction,[16] D. Downing reported that "There is no area of our mental and bodily functioning that the sun does not influence. Our bodies were designed to receive and use it in a wide range of ways. We were not designed to hide from it in houses, offices, factories and schools. Sunshine, reaching us through our eyes and our skin, exercises a subtle control over us from birth to death, from head to tail." Assuming that Downing is correct, we should strive to make our training environments rich in light, either natural or artificial, or a combination of both.

An important point to remember is that all artificial light is not equal. Depending on the type of bulbs used, learners will receive more or less light value. Many artificial bulbs are designed to reproduce a wide spectrum of lighting compared to natural sunlight, which has a 100 rating on the color rendition index (RDI) used to rate various artificial light sources. Higher light ratings equate to a more positive benefit. In comparison to full-spectrum sunlight, incandescent lights emit red and yellow light, but radiate little energy in the blue and green region of the spectrum whereas cool-fluorescent bulbs emit mostly green and yellow bands. The blue-green part of the light spectrum is the most beneficial to humans.

Although it seems clear that lighting can definitely impact learning, the extent of such influence is subject to interpretation. As with any research, there is sometimes inconsistency and lack of experiment control. According to a comprehensive overview of scientific literature on behavior, performance, mental well being, and physiology,[17] there is room to question the direct correlation of the amount of impact of artificial light sources on humans. Still, you may want to do as much as possible to provide adequate lighting for your learning environment. This means reducing or limiting glare and shadows, and reducing eyestrain while allowing ease of vision.

Temperature

Various research studies have found that the optimal temperature for a learning environment ranges between 68 and 72° F or 20–22° C. However, because people have different levels of tolerance, it is a good idea to suggest that participants dress in layers or bring a coat or sweater with them to your programs. This allows them to address personal comfort needs.

If possible, use a training site in which you have control of temperature settings. This is important because being in a room that is either too hot or cold can dramatically affect learner concentration and ultimately negatively impact learning. If you must decide between having the room warmer or cooler, choose cooler. This is especially important following a meal, when people normally become sluggish. If the room is somewhat too warm and you cannot control the temperature, make sure that there are plenty of breaks and activities as well as liquid refreshments for participants.

Electrical Sources and Controls

Many training rooms are designed by non-trainers and without consultation with the people who will actually use them. As a result, it is not unusual for you to have limited access to controls and electrical plugs. Often the controls for lighting, sound, and temperature will be located in the back of the room away from where you are standing.

An ideal training environment will have ample electrical outlets spaced approximately every 6–8 feet to allow access to various training and computer equipment. There should definitely be one multiple plug outlet at the front of the room approximately 6–8 feet from the wall. Having maximum outlets provides flexibility in designing training activities and in using a variety of training aids and equipment. One backup plan for any training program is to have a multiple plug extension cord that is at least 25 feet in length, just in case outlets are not readily available or working. Light controls should be found at both the front and back of the room for ease of access no matter where you are located as a facilitator.

BRIGHT IDEA

Increasing Your Training Options

Depending on your session topic, consider setting up either VCR/monitor or personal computer (PC) stations along the walls of your training room. You can then have small groups work through either video or CD-ROM scenarios related to the program topic or through self-paced instruction lessons to address issues or problem solve. They can then report back to the rest of the class. In addition, you can have them electronically review key session concepts.

Acoustics and Sound

Too often a trainer or presenter will opt not to use a microphone because he or she feels he or she has a sufficiently loud voice, yet people in the rear of the room cannot hear what is said. When this occurs, frustration results because learning is not transferred. In effect, those who cannot hear are wasting valuable time sitting in the room and often either tune out or leave. It is critical that everyone in the room is able to hear what you and others say. Otherwise objectives will not be met and your effectiveness and professional image will be reduced significantly.

To ensure that a problem does not occur and that learners can hear you, do a sound check from various points in the room before participants arrive. If there is an area in which sound is muffled, try to avoid putting participants in that section or make sure you can be heard by using a microphone, repositioning yourself, and directing comments toward those learners. In doing your sound check, test all of your training aids (e.g., video or music) to ensure that the volume is loud enough to carry to every point of the room. Also, if you are presenting to a large audience or in a large room, consider putting a stand-up microphone in the middle of the room so that anyone asking a question can use it and be heard by others. An option to this is for you to repeat questions asked by participants before answering them. In addition, try a short practice where you use your normal presentation voice and have someone stand in various parts of the room to see if you can be heard easily.

Another element that impacts your ability to be heard is the noise level in the room. If you can do so, eliminate any excessive or unnecessary noise from air conditioners, heating, ventilation, or other sources. Many older models of projectors have noisy cooling fans that can generate a distracting humming sound. Try to either upgrade to a quieter model or turn the projector off when not using it to make a point. One strategy that is employed by many organizations for noise reduction is to pump in **white noise** or other low-frequency sound to mute room noise.

Participants also contribute to noise levels by using cell phones and beepers and by having side conversations or speaking in loud voices during small group activities. This type of noise can actually cue you that learners have completed a small group task because when participants finish discussing an assigned topic, they will typically begin networking, laughing, and in other ways causing the noise level to escalate. At any rate, all distracting noise should be controlled or eliminated to the best of your ability to enhance the learning experience.

External Noise

Other sources of noise include people and things outside the room, such as passers by; maintenance, custodial, or catering workers performing tasks; or passing vehicles. Distractions in the form of noise can detract from learning by causing participants to refocus their attention or take their minds off the task. Typically, external noise is generated from people or equipment in and around the classroom. You should try to minimize or eliminate such distractions. The following suggestions can help accomplish this:

Where possible, do not position training rooms near roadways, construction areas, lunch tables, building entrances, or other locations where people gather.

Select rooms that have acoustic tiles on the ceilings, carpet on the floor, and cloth coverings on the walls in order to absorb excess noise.

Use audiovisual equipment that is well maintained and that does not create excess noise (e.g., fans).

Use a speaker system in any room that is 40 feet or longer in any direction to overcome room noises and aid hearing.

Put in work requests on any equipment that creates noise (e.g., air conditioning and heating vents, humming light fixtures, or squeaky doors).

Close doors after participants arrive to reduce noise from people outside the room.

Music

It has been said that "Music soothes the savage beast." Whether that is true or not is irrelevant. What is important is that brain researchers have found a direct correlation between certain types of music and brain functioning.

In 1993, an important study was conducted on the impact of music on the brain.[18] This experiment resulted in what has been termed the "Mozart IQ Effect" because it was the music of the famed composer Amadeus Mozart that was selected for use in the study. During the research, students at the University of California, Irvine listened to relaxation music, Mozart, or white noise for 10 minutes as they performed spatial tasks. Afterwards, it was determined that those listening to Mozart outperformed others.

Eric Jensen points out that although this study alone cannot adequately confirm the conclusion that listening to music was the reason for improved performance, the effect also occurs in rats exposed to music. In addition, people with epilepsy show increased spatial reasoning. Twenty-seven studies replicating the original resulted in at least some positive "Mozart Effect." Subjects of **electroencephalogram (EEG)** studies who listened to Mozart and then performed spatial-temporal tasks showed enhanced brain activity compared to a control group who listened to a reading of a short story.[19]

Although there is controversy regarding the significance of the Mozart Effect, there seems to be little doubt that music can positively impact brain functioning. In reality, many researchers now believe that it is not the type of music played, but the melody, harmony, and rhythm of the music that mostly influences the brain.

Interestingly, as more researchers are finding how important music really is to brain development, many school systems are cutting extracurricular activities such as choir or band programs, or what they call "fluff," from school budgets. Recent discoveries have shown, however, that the right type of music incorporated into a learning environment can reduce anxiety and stress, impact physiology, influence mood, and aid learning.

If you play musical selections during individual and group activities, make sure that the volume level is loud enough to be heard, but low enough that it does not distract or interrupt concentration or conversation. For background music, you are probably better off using nature sounds or instrumental selections instead of vocals. Also, select instrumental music that does not have words (e.g., jazz, new age or classical) so that participants do not subconsciously focus on the songs and sing along mentally or out loud. To benefit most from the research when using music in your sessions, choose selections that have approximately 40–60 beats per minute if you want to slow the pace of activity, for individual work, visualization activities, or relaxation. If you want to stimulate creative thinking and assist in problem-solving, increase the tempo to 60–70 beats per minute. Finally, if you want to really energize participants and get them moving, use music that has 70–140 beats per minute.

As a trainer, you can add music to the background to break the awkward silence that sometimes exists as participants enter the room or return from breaks. You can also use such music to signal the end of one event and the beginning of another. This works because the abrupt silence that occurs when the music is turned off attracts attention. Nonverbally, you are signaling that something is about to happen or that it is time to begin.

Music can definitely assist in setting the tone for a session, and if used correctly, can actually contribute to the theme. For example, in a class on time management, I recorded an hour of songs with time in the title (e.g., "Time won't let me" by the Outsiders, "Time has come today" by the Chambers Brothers, and "Time in a bottle" by Jim Croce). I played the songs as learners arrived and during breaks; in my opening remarks I commented about how time influences every aspect of our lives, including our music. In another session on motivation, I ran in from the back of the room with the theme of the movie "Rocky" blaring away. Once in front of the class, I turn off the music and in animated fashion welcomed everyone with a loud "GOOD MORNING! ARE YOU READY TO LEARN SOME TECHNIQUES TO IMPROVE YOUR WORKLIFE?" I then get everyone to stand up, and lead them through a fast-paced stretching or other fun activity. That leads to small group brainstorming activity into what gets people pumped up in today's workplace. We review their ideas and get into the program content.

When selecting music for your programs, do not forget that each participant has preferences related to music type (e.g., rock, rap, new age, and country), format (e.g., instrumental versus vocal), and volume level. Also, recognize that some people will enjoy the music and others will complain about it. Experiment to find a happy medium and ask for participant input. You may even want to discuss the issues mentioned in this section related to music and learning at the beginning of the session. Depending on how much music you plan to use, build in small competitions in which the winner gets to assume the role of the disc jockey who selects the next phase of music you will play during breaks or whenever. This is a fun way to involve participants and give them some control while relieving you of the task of making selections.

Lenn Millbower points out the need for cultural awareness by explaining the role of music in different parts of the world. "Music fulfills different needs in diverse locations around the world, and we are all prisoners of our cultural assumptions. Individuals, even professional musicians, have a difficult time appreciating the nuances of music outside their heritage. Erroneous music placement based on mistaken cultural assumptions is a potential source of embarrassment when training with music. You must know the cultural assumptions and expectations of your audience before selecting material."[20] The key to selecting the right type of music is to consider the organizational culture, topic, geographic location, and cultural background of learners. For example, although upbeat country and western music might play well as break music for a session being taught in Texas or other parts of the western United States, it might not be well received in major cities of the northeastern part of the country or in other countries. Similarly, heavy metal or modern rock might generate frowns from an audience of age 50 plus corporate executives. Eric Jensen's book *Music with the Brain in Mind* gives hundreds of ideas related to which types of songs can aid various training activities (see Creative Presentation Resources in the Resources for Trainers section of the appendices).

As previously mentioned, there are many ways to include music in your sessions. You can use prerecorded classical music or songs that you record yourself from CDs or the Internet. A variety of Baroque, nature sounds, and classical music selections have been recorded on CDs to use specifically with activities in which the goal is productivity, creativity, relaxation, or fun. You can also purchase songs, television theme songs, and specially created game show type music for use in games or other group activities (see Creative Presentation Resources in the Resources for Trainers section of the appendices). The choice is really yours.

Another point to remember about music is that you should not make it a major part of your program. Like any other training aid, music should be used to support your material and delivery, not substitute for it. Keep its use to no more than 10–20 percent of total learning time.

BRIGHT IDEA
Using Music Creatively

In addition to using prerecorded music to accomplish a variety of goals and affect learner moods, you can get participants actively involved. One suggestion is to form small groups that are then asked to come up with a creative team name for each group. Next, have them create a rap song or modify the words to a well known song (e.g., "Mary Had a Little Lamb," "Happy Birthday," or "Somewhere Over the Rainbow"). When creating their song, have participants use key characteristics possessed by team members (e.g., skills, abilities, attributes, and so forth), or key concepts from the session.

Be conscious of the diversity of your group when selecting songs. Select songs not likely to offend, such as tunes with political or religious themes (e.g., Christmas songs or historical songs connected to events such as the U.S. Civil War).

A final consideration when using music is to respect and comply with copyright laws. The law is very specific about when and how copyright protected material, such as music, can be used. In 1998, the United States Congress passed the Sonny Bono Copyright Term Extension to the Federal Copyright Law. It changed the length that a piece is copyrighted from the end of the life of the originator plus 50 years to life plus 70 years for 1978 works and beyond, and from 75 to 95 years for pre-1978 works.

Any failure to comply with federal and international copyright laws can result in liability and embarrassment for you and your organization. Before using written material or songs, obtain written permission from the copyright holder or become licensed to use material. The name of the copyright owner is usually found on the first few pages of a book; in the front of a periodical; and on the cover/case of a CD, cassette, or videotape.

There are two organizations that represent the artists and producers of most modern music that is published—**BMI** and **ASCAP** (see the Music Licensing in Resources for Trainers section in the appendices for contact information). For a yearly licensing fee paid to these organizations, you can obtain copyright permission to play songs by the musicians they represent.

Music reduces stress, relieves anxiety, increases energy and improves recall. Music makes people smarter.
—Jeannette Voss
The Music Revolution

PUTTING YOUR BRAIN TO WORK: ACTIVITY

What other noise sources that you have experienced in training? _____

_____

What obstacles do such noises present to you as a facilitator or trainer? To learners? _____

_____

How were, or could have been, these noises better eliminated or controlled? _____

_____

Vegetation

The importance of fresh air on brain functioning has been known for years. The brain needs air rich in oxygen and free of contaminants to operate at peak performance levels. Unfortunately, many organizations now occupy closed environment type buildings where air is recycled and windows cannot be opened. The result is often reduced air quality that in some cases even results in what has been termed "sick building syndrome." According to the Environmental Protection Agency (EPA), indoor air pollution is one of the top environmental hazards of our time. It is a leading cause in the rise of asthma

Table 5-2. Common Plants for Use in the Classroom

Areca palm	Norfolk Island palm
Bamboo palm	King of hearts
Boston fern	Golden pathos
Corn plant	Peace lily
Christmas cactus	Lady palm
Dracaena	Poinsettia
Dumb cane	Rubber plant
Dwarf date palm	Snake plant
English ivy	Spider plant
Ficus	Wax begonia
Chrysanthemum	

cases. To counter this negative effect, strive to have open windows and/or good air exchange throughout your sessions.

Plants have been found to be another simple, yet effective, way to offset some of the pollution that exists in offices and training rooms. In research for the National Aeronautics and Space Administration (NASA), Dr. B. C. Wolverton[21] conducted studies using plants to remove pollutants in controlled, closed environments. He and others have found that a number of common house plants successfully remove contaminants. The study concluded that placing plants within an individual's breathing zone (approximately 6–8 cubic feet surrounding the person) improves air quality. It is recommended that two to eight small or two large plants be placed every nine square meters (900 square feet).[22]

BRIGHT IDEA

Increasing Air Flow

Because the air breathed in most training environments is likely marginal, and the average person uses less than 25 percent of his or her lung capacity, your participants need air! To help them accomplish better air exchange, include stretching and deep breathing activities periodically throughout your sessions. Also, depending on outside air quality, consider opening windows whenever possible rather than recycling air through air conditioners or other equipment.

Smells and Odors

For years, researchers have been exploring the impact of smells on learning and memory. In one study,[23] the odors of pine, peppermint, and **osmanthus** were used to determine if odor had an impact on the brain. In the testing, subjects were taken into a room where an odor was present and attention called to the smell. Each person was then left in the room for 10 minutes while he or she filled out a questionnaire. Following the questionnaire, the experimenter read a series of 20 common nouns. After each word, subjects were asked to describe some event that the word reminded him or her of. Forty-eight hours later, each subject was tested to see how many of the words could be recalled. When the unusual odor of osmanthus was present during the learning (when words were read and mentally imprinted) and testing, recall was best. Of the other two odors, recall was better when peppermint was introduced in a contextually inappropriate manner. Based on this study, the researchers determined that smell is a good contextual cue for learning.

In another experiment by Dr. Herz,[24] 40 students were given a word test for which they were not told they would need to recall the words later. Half of the subjects were in a room with no smell and the other half were in a room that smelled of violet leaf (an unusual and unpleasant odor). Seven days later, all students were tested in the same environments in which they had learned the words. Those who had been in the violet scented room did significantly better on recall than those in the room without an odor.

Dr. Alan Hirsch has also found a direct link between odors and mental processing. In a variety of studies, he found that environments with floral odors increased creativity, learning, and thinking ability.[25] A similar finding occurred when a floral odor was introduced as subjects took the Halsted–Reitan Test Battery. In that study, 17 percent of the subjects completed the test faster when the fragrance was present.[26]

Shimizu Technology Center in Japan has also conducted studies to determine how smells influenced workers. That experiment involved the introduction of different fragrances into a work area where keypunch operators were positioned and monitored for entry errors. The results showed that:

Keyboard errors dropped 21 percent when a lavender fragrance (a relaxant) was introduced.

Errors dropped 33 percent when a jasmine (an uplifting scent) fragrance was introduced.

Errors dropped by 54 percent when a lemon fragrance (sharp, refreshing, stimulating odor) was introduced.[27]

Other researchers have found that women are more sensitive to odors than men and that smells definitely impact levels of relaxation and agitation. In addition, when bursts of peppermint or lily of the valley odors were introduced every 5 minutes as subjects complete certain tests, performance jumped as much as 15–25 percent. Also, when spiced apple scents are encountered, brainwaves and blood pressure drop within 1 minute.

Overall, it appears that pleasant, natural aromas increase efficiency and encourage more risk taking. They also cause people to negotiate more amiably, form more challenging goals, and behave less combatively.[28]

BRIGHT IDEA

Adding Aromas to Training

To help stimulate the learning environment, experiment with different aromas. Try using plug-in air freshener fragrances (these plug directly into an electrical socket and gradually dispense aromas into the air). Choose some of the aromas mentioned in this section (e.g., sandalwood, floral, or lavender scents). Ask for feedback on the smells and flavors and explain the research behind their use. Also ask for additional aroma suggestions that participants believe stimulate and enhance brain functioning.

For additional information on the impact of various aromas, search the Internet under the term Aromatherapy.

Hydration

Medical authorities encourage the average adult to drink 8–15 glasses of water per day. This helps keep the body temperature regulated, aids bodily functions, and keeps the brain, which is estimated to be 90 percent water, well saturated.

When planning your sessions, always put a pitcher of water and glasses on participant tables and in the rear of the room along with other refreshments. Encourage your learners to drink water throughout the day. In addition, you may want to provide a variety of beverages such as coffee, tea, soft drinks, and juices so that learners have a choice based on preference and personal need. Remember that some people have special dietary needs with which you must comply for legal reasons in certain situations.

Dehydration can lead to your own reduced physical and mental performance as well. Keep plenty of water on hand as your facilitate and pause to drink regularly. Water is better than drinks containing caffeine (e.g., coffee, tea, or soft drinks), as such drinks can cause irritation and hyperactivity. Also, carbonated beverages can cause embarrassing stomach gas that might escape unexpectedly as you speak.

Food and Refreshments

There is scientific proof to substantiate the saying "Breakfast is the most important meal of the day." Starting in childhood, many people are taught the importance of eating a balanced diet made up of the major food groups. They are also often warned of the results of using or abusing drugs, alcohol, and caffeine. Even so, these early lessons are often overlooked or ignored when trainers plan their sessions.

To make sure that you and your learners operate at peak potential and that effective learning occurs, you should consider various elements related to nutrition as you prepare your sessions. Many trainers provide food and refreshments for learners in the morning, at lunchtime, and for breaks. This is a great idea as long as you provide the right foods, include an assorted variety, and provide ample beaks so that learners can take advantage of whatever you provide.

Because many people fail to eat breakfast, providing food when participants arrive can be beneficial for them and you. Studies show that the brain needs complex carbohydrates found in fruits, grains, cereals, and breads to function effectively. To assist in fulfilling this need, you might want to ensure that a variety of nonsweet as well as sweet items are offered (e.g., muffins, croissants, and bagels) along with fresh fruit. Simply offering donuts and other sweet pastries often overloads learners with simple carbohydrates (e.g., sugar) that provide a spike, then a letdown as energy levels subside. On the other hand, if you want to provide a quick stimulant and pump up sugar and performance levels for a specific activity or task, consider providing candy, cookies, brownies, or other sweet treats.

If you are providing lunch, consider carefully what you will serve. Keep the meal light and healthy and ensure that you provide proteins in the form of fish, shrimp, or chicken instead of heavier red meats. Avoid turkey because it contains a natural chemical amino acid called l-tryptophan that acts as a sedative and relaxes participants after lunch. Also, provide a variety of fresh vegetables and fruits.

In mid-afternoon, you may want to replenish nutrition levels by providing complex carbohydrates, such as fruit, juices, or grains. If you supply sweets, make sure that you also provide nonsweet alternatives. Also, if you provide popcorn or other snack foods, take it easy on salts and oils.

BRIGHT IDEA
Stimulate Learning

Remember what you read about the effects of apple and peppermint scents? Maximize the benefits of that research by offering small pieces of candy with those flavors as rewards for task or activity completion.

PUTTING YOUR BRAIN TO WORK: ACTIVITY

What types of foods and refreshments do you normally provide or receive in training sessions?

_____

_____

Based on what you have read, what other options might you want to consider? Why? _____

_____

INTERIM REVIEW

Take out a sheet of paper and draw a straight line down the middle from top to bottom. On the left side of the line write the word DOING and on the right side write NEEDED. Next, think of the program that you most often facilitate. Look back on the environmental factors you just read about and list the ones you actually address before your participants arrive on a regular basis in your programs. On the right side, list the ones that you need to remember to work on in future sessions. Use your responses as a checklist when preparing for future sessions.

Furniture

An important determinant of successful outcome of activities and training is the quality and configuration of seating. There is an old training adage that says, "The brain can only absorb as much as the rear can endure." In layperson terms, that means have comfortable chairs that are properly placed and do not keep learners in them for too long. Depending on the room, size and makeup of your group, and planned activities, you need to select an appropriate room configuration.

Where possible, choose furniture that fits training activities and participant needs. Select rectangular tables that are wide enough for materials and task completion. Rectangular tables are typically available in 6- to 8-foot lengths and in widths of 24, 30, and 36 inches. I personally like folding tables that are 30 × 72 inches. These allow for a variety of configurations and flexibility along with ease of movement and storage. If learners are using computers, or if both sides of the table are occupied, 36-inch widths seem to work better. Great alternatives to rectangular tables are round ones. These typically are designed to seat six to ten participants. I like to use the larger tables, but seat only five to six people per table. This allows me to position learners in a crescent or semicircular configuration facing the front of the room so that no participants are seated with their backs to me. Otherwise, some learners are inconvenienced by having to turn around to face the front of the room and end up with no firm writing surface.

A third option is to eliminate tables altogether and simply use chairs. Although this saves space and increases the number of participants you can get into a room, writing surfaces and personal space are sacrificed. This latter element varies according to individual preference; however, research has found that most participants feel more at ease when they have approximately 10 square feet of personal space in any setting with theater style seating. Therefore, space should not be casually dismissed just to increase numbers. If effectiveness and learning are negatively impacted, it may be a bad return on investment. When using only chairs, make sure that they are ergonomically structured to provide back support, without causing undo physical stress on any area. Adjustable, cushioned chairs, and those with arms, are often preferable to hard, solid straight-backed chairs.

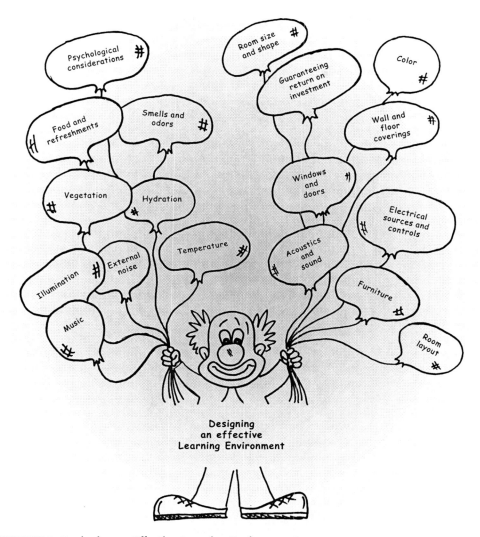

MINDMAP 1. Designing an Effective Learning Environment

As you decide on the configuration of furniture you will use in a given program, answer the following questions:

Does the arrangement provide adequate personal space?

Does it facilitate learning?

Will ease of movement be possible (e.g., during activities)?

Will it contribute to an energized, interactive environment?

Does it mirror planned content, delivery, and trainer style?

Does it allow ease of visibility and hearing for everyone in the room?

● MAXIMIZING INVOLVEMENT AND LEARNING

A key element in getting learners involved and in encouraging information and knowledge exchange revolves around how you set up the learning environment. Depending on what your learning goals are and how involved you want participants to be, there are many options for furniture configuration. **Figures** 5-1 through 5-19 show the most common types of possible seating style options available to you.

BRIGHT IDEA
Facilitator Table and Equipment Location

For your work area, eliminate overhead projector stands that are typically too small. Add a 6-foot instructor's table in front of the room instead. Rather than arranging the table in the traditional horizontal position, place it vertically (lengthwise) toward the audience. This eliminates the physical barrier between you and your group. It also provides a platform on which to put your overhead projector at the end closest to your participants. This gives you the remainder of the tabletop, partially obstructed from participant view, to place a watch out of sight. In addition to allowing private time monitoring, you can also lay out transparencies, lesson plans, props, and other resources you need for the session. You can further clean up your tabletop area by using an Overhead Projector Organizer Pockets (see Creative Presentation Resources in Resources for Trainers section of the appendices) that consists of three small plastic pouches with Velcro attachments to the edge of your projector frame. You can keep noisemakers, markers, pointers, and other small items in the pockets, ready to use, but out of the way.

When using flip charts in conjunction with an instructor's table, position them for maximum effectiveness and access. For example, if you have a remote control, you can place the VCR/monitor on a stand opposite of where you are located while placing a flip chart closer to you. The position of the flip chart will be dependent on whether you are left or right handed as you'll want to use your nondominant hand to turn pages as you write with your dominant hand (see Seating Style configurations to see how this would look in conjunction with furniture).

Reduced Learner Involvement Configurations (with Tables)

Classroom Style Seating (with Tables)

Setup
Start with the first row of tables approximately 6–8 feet from the trainer or facilitator. Place chairs facing the front of the room with approximately 2 feet between each participant. If the room permits, offset each table so each participant has a line of sight between the two participants in front of him or her. Round or rectangular tables can be used (Figure 5.1).

Maximum no. of participants
Twenty-four. This number can increase or decrease, depending on room size, shape, and the setup of tables (see Variations).

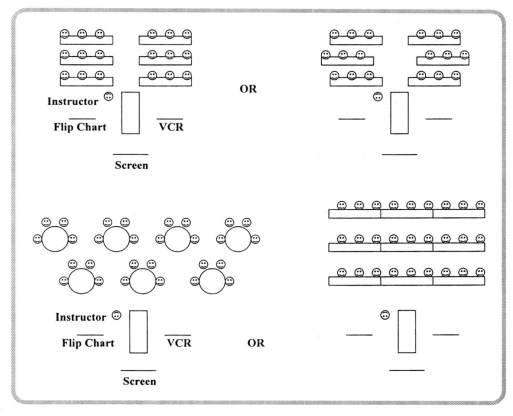

FIGURE 5-1. Classroom style seating (with tables, using overhead projector) *Variations:* "V," fishbone, or chevron style seating (with tables).

Advantages

Provides writing surfaces for all participants.

Participants can view the trainer and audiovisual aids.

Adds structure and control for the trainer.

Facilitates eye-to-eye contact between the trainer and learners.

Disadvantages

Very formal

Can conjure up images of early school years for some participants.

Reduces interaction between the trainer and participants and also among participants.

Physical barriers exist between trainer and participants and between participants. This can subconsciously impact trust and possibly communication.

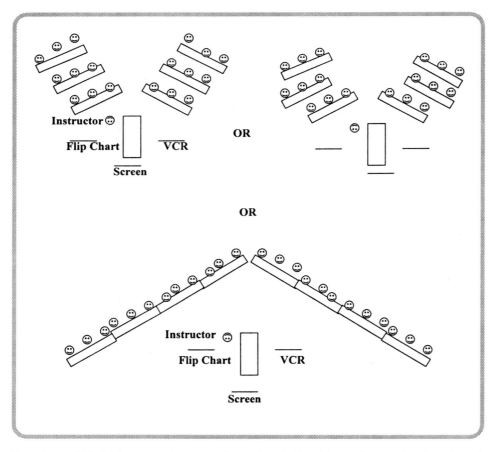

FIGURE 5-2. "V", Fishbone, or chevron style seating (with tables, using overhead projector)

Can promote a more passive "I talk; you listen" mentality among participants.

Can create a challenge for people with physical disabilities unless accommodations are planned.

Variations

"V", Fishbone, or Chevron Style Seating (with Tables) (Figure 5-2)

Variations of classroom style seating are named based on the resemblance to the letter V, the bones of a fish, and the shape of military chevrons. Advantages and disadvantages are basically the same as for the classroom style seating. Offsetting even numbered rows of tables can aid the view that participants have of the front of the room by allowing learners to look between the two people in front of them. By using only one row of tables, the effectiveness can be upgraded to a moderate participant involvement level; however, the maximum number of participants is decreased to 16–18. Although adding chairs in front of tables in the "V" can increase those numbers, some participants lose their writing surface when they have to turn in their seats to view the trainer. Round or rectangular tables can be used.

Perpendicular Style Seating (with Tables) (Figure 5-3)

This variation to the classroom style seating provides face-to-face contact between participants and access into the group by the trainer. Additional chairs can be inserted on the insides of tables to increase the number of participants and to facilitate networking and small group interaction.

Round or rectangular tables can be used.

Reduced Learner Involvement Configurations (without Tables)

Theater Style Seating (without Tables) (Figure 5-4)

Setup

Align rows of chairs, spaced 2 inches apart, approximately 6–8 feet away from the trainer or speaker. Also, stagger rows so that every other row is offset to allow a line of sight between the two chairs directly in front of each person.

Maximum no. of participants

Unlimited, depending on program content, audience makeup, program objectives, room size, shape, availability of sound system, and audiovisual support.

Advantages

Increases audience size potential.

Relatively easy to set up.

Good for information sharing in lecture format (sometimes called information dump).

Allows easy viewing of visual aids (e.g., projected visuals or videos).

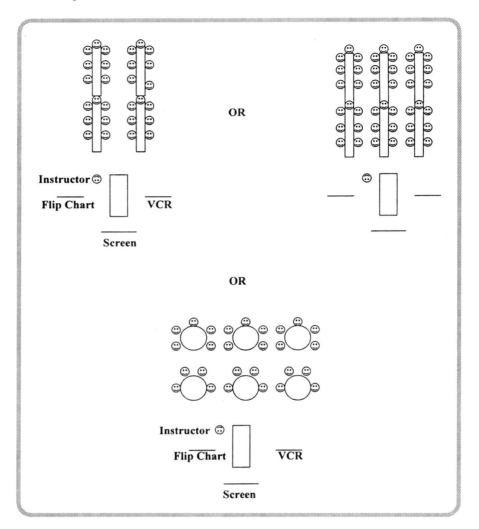

FIGURE 5-3. Perpendicular style seating (with tables, using overhead projector)

Disadvantages

Can be a challenge for someone with a physical disability unless space is planned. Psychologically presents an unfriendly configuration with the trainer/speaker facing the audience. This is especially true if a table or lectern is between the trainer and participants.

Communication is lecture-based with little opportunity for discussion or small group activities.

Potentially lowers learner retention because interaction and sharing is restricted.

Resembles early education settings where students are seated in rows and "talked at."

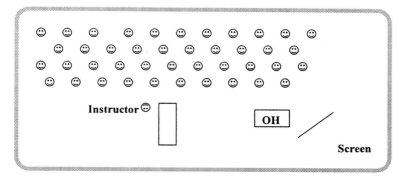

FIGURE 5-4. Theater style seating (without tables, using overhead projector)

Limits close trainer access to participants.

Eliminates eye-to-eye contact by participants.

Reduces networking and communication between learners.

No writing surfaces for participants.

Some visual aids (e.g., posters, flip charts, VCR/monitor) are ineffective.

Variations

Semicircular Style Seating (without Tables) (Figure 5-5)

This arrangement takes more space than theater style seating; however, it can give a slight feeling of interaction because some participants see the faces of others. Rectangular or round tables can be used.

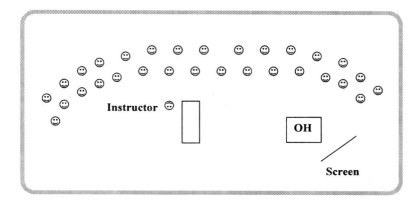

FIGURE 5-5. Semicircular style seating (without tables, using overhead projector).

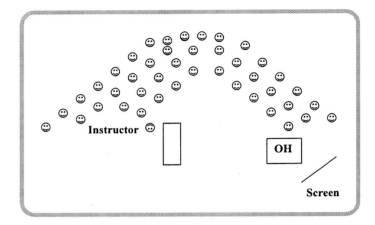

FIGURE 5-6. "V", fishbone, or chevron style seating (without tables, using overhead projector)

"V", Fishbone, or Chevron Style Seating (without Tables) (Figure 5-6)

It offers all the advantages and disadvantages of the theater style seating. Some limited trainer access to the group can be provided by placing an aisle down the center of the room and putting chairs on either side; however, more room is required when this is done. Participants can be provided better viewing of the front of the room by offsetting even numbered rows, which will allow viewing between the two people sitting in front of each participant in those rows.

Moderate Learner Involvement Configurations (with Tables)

U-Shaped Seating (with Tables) (Figure 5-7)

Setup
The end of the first participant table on each side of the facilitator should be positioned approximately even with the front edge of the instructor's table. Chairs are placed around the outer edges of the participant tables so that all learners are facing the center of the "U." Additional participants can be added by also placing chairs inside the "U" so that learners are on both sides of tables. This can help increase networking and communication while better facilitating small group activities. To prevent the feeling of being in a bowling alley (e.g., long distance from the front of the room to the farthest table in the "U"), the width and length of the table setup should be approximately the same. Additional tables or chairs can be placed in corners of the room for use with breakout activities.

Maximum no. of participants
Twenty-four. This number can be increased by placing chairs on the inside of tables within the "U."

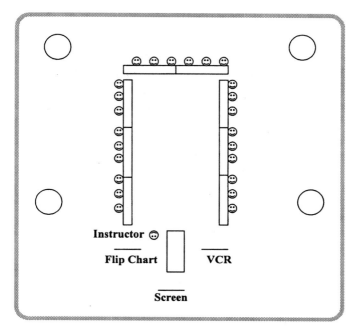

FIGURE 5-7. U-shaped seating (with tables, breakout tables, and using overhead projector)

Advantages

Facilitates close contact between facilitator and participants.

Allows easy distribution of materials to participants.

Most participants have eye-to-eye contact with one another and with the trainer.

Participants can easily view audiovisual aids at the front of the room.

All participants have writing surfaces.

There is room for small group interaction (chairs can also be placed inside the "U" or in corners of the room for this purpose).

Disadvantages

Physical barriers (tables) separate participants from one another.

Regular eye contact with some people in the room is awkward owing to the linear configuration of the tables on either side of the "U." For example, participants at each end of the table cannot easily see those to their far right or left.

Instructor-dominant configuration where the trainer is placed as the center of attention and perceived as being in charge.

If an instructor resource table is used, especially if it is turned horizontally between the trainer and participants, there is a physical barrier separating the two.

Requires more space than some other configurations. Limits the number of participants to approximately 24.

Variations

Double U-Shaped Seating (with Tables) (Figure 5-8)

Although providing the same advantages and disadvantages as the single U-shaped seating, this configuration provides a forum to have one group (inner U) conduct an activity or discuss a topic while the outer group observes, critiques, and/or provides feedback.

Crescent Style Seating (with Tables) (Figure 5-9)

This alternative to the U-shape seating configuration offers the same advantages and disadvantages except that the number of seats is reduced. Also, putting participants in the center becomes more awkward because most of the learners on the insides of the crescent would have to turn to face the front of the room and would lose their writing surfaces.

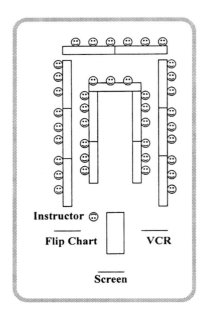

FIGURE 5-8. Double U-shaped seating (with tables, using overhead projector)

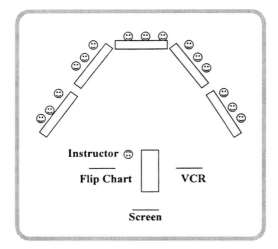

FIGURE 5-9. Crescent style seating (with tables, using overhead projector)

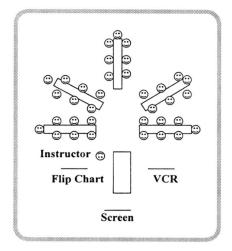

FIGURE **5-10.** Horseshoe style seating (with tables, using overhead projector)

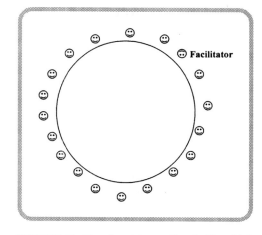

FIGURE 5-11. Circular style seating (with table)

Horseshoe Style Seating (with Tables) (Figure 5-10)

This configuration to U-shape seating can increase the number of participants. It can also allow easier grouping of learners into teams for activities. However, the disadvantage is that large group cohesiveness and networking can suffer if you do not move people among groups throughout the session. Rectangular or round tables can be used.

High Learner Involvement Configurations (with Tables) (Figure 5-11)

Circular Style Seating (with Tables)

Setup
Place tables in a circular formation with chairs on the outside of tables facing in.

Maximum no. of participants
Limited by activity and table and room size, however, the participant number should be kept to a size that allows each person to interact and offer input in a nonthreatening environment. Typically a group of 18 or fewer participants works well.

Advantages
Fosters a relaxed, informal atmosphere.

Eliminates a "front of the room" and puts the facilitator in a less authoritarian role.

Everyone is on an equal status level.

Encourages problem-solving, decision-making, creativity, exchange and exploration of ideas, and interpersonal communication.

Learners are subconsciously encouraged to participate.

Allows eye contact among group members.

Disadvantages
Potentially limits the number of participants.

Visual aid usage is eliminated. This could be a challenge and loss for visual learners and people with hearing impairments.

Variations

Rounds Style Seating (with Tables) (Figure 5-12)

This alternative to circular style seating provides an opportunity to add learners and to have them participate in small groups. If you will be doing a large amount of facilitation from the front of the room, reduce the number of chairs and place them in a crescent configuration on the sides of tables that face the front of the room. This precludes anyone from having to turn around to view you or audiovisual aids, and thus losing their writing surface.

Hollow Square and Solid Square Style Seating (with Tables) (Figure 5-13)

This configuration uses rectangular tables in two different variations and offers the same advantages and disadvantages as the circular style seating configuration.

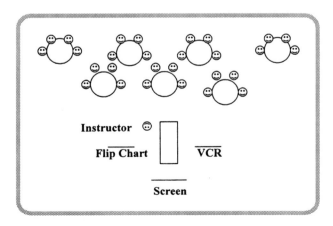

FIGURE 5-12. Rounds style seating (with tables)

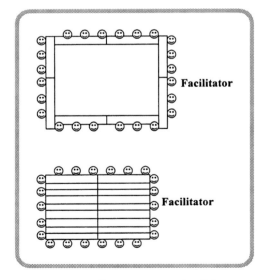

FIGURE 5-13. Hollow square and solid square style seating (with tables)

Open Square Style Seating (with Tables) (Figure 5-14)

Similar to the hollow and solid square style seating, this option to the circular style seating allows good group interaction. By removing one of the tables, you can enter the square to better interact and make eye contact with learners. You can also use a flip chart for capturing ideas and comments. All advantages and disadvantages of the hollow square and solid square style seating are the same, except that the facilitator is no longer on an equal status with participants. As a result, communication can be affected. In addition, because of the arrangement of tables, some participants may have difficulty viewing a flip chart.

Rectangular or Conference Style Seating (Figure 5-15)

This variation of the hollow square and solid square arrangement is created by arranging tables in a longer (rectangular) formation. Eye contact among the group members thus is reduced at far ends of the tables. A psychological "head of the table" is established, which can create the impression that people at either end of the table are of higher status or in charge. As a result, communication and idea exchange could be negatively impacted. The configuration also sets a more formal atmosphere.

High Learner Involvement Configurations (without Tables)

Circular Style Seating (without Tables) (Figure 5-16)

Setup
Arrange chairs in a large circular pattern.

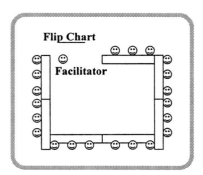

FIGURE 5-14. Open square style seating (with tables, flip chart)

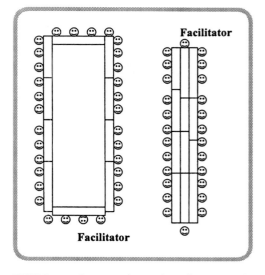

FIGURE 5-15. Rectangular and conference style seating (with tables)

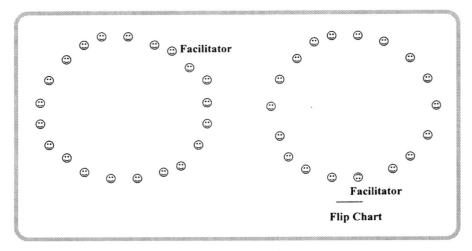

FIGURE 5-16. Circular style seating (without tables)—with and without flip chart)

Maximum no. of participants
Limited by room size and planned discussion, however, when more than 18–20 learners are present, communication could be affected.

Advantages
The trainer has close contact with all participants (from a seat within the group) and learners can see and interact with others. To achieve this relationship, the trainer should assume any seat within the group to be on equal status with participants and encourage discussion.

This configuration also provides an informal forum for discussion and idea exchange.

Access for participants with disabilities is easily possible.

As an alternative, a few chairs can be eliminated so that the facilitator can assume a different position in which a flip chart can be used to capture comments or ideas.

Disadvantages
Attendance is limited to approximately 18–20 learners, as larger groups can limit open exchange of ideas and discussion.

Participants have no writing surfaces.

Variations

Crescent Style Seating (without Tables) (Figure 5-17)

This arrangement offers many of the advantages of circular style seating while creating a central trainer position. The crescent configuration is also a little more formal than the circular style, yet less so than with the use of tables. Audiovisual aids can also be used. There is no writing surface for participants.

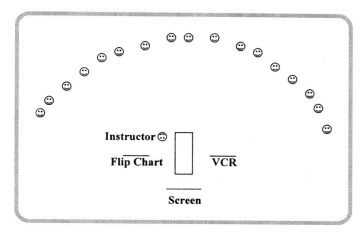

FIGURE 5-17. Crescent style seating (without tables—with VCR, overhead projector, and flip chart)

Cluster Style Seating (without Tables) (Figure 5-18)

Setup

Arrange chairs in groups of two to eight throughout the training room so that small groups can assemble to brainstorm, discuss issues, or role-play.

Maximum no. of participants

Limited by room size, planned activities, and number of facilitators. There should be a minimum of one facilitator per 20 participants to monitor activities and provide feedback and control. Each facilitator should monitor no more than three groups in order to ensure that teams remain on task, that all questions are answered, and that timely feedback is provided.

Advantages

Provides an opportunity for small group interaction.

Practical application and skill practice can occur with immediate feedback from peers and a facilitator.

Idea exchange and peer coaching are encouraged.

Potentially reduces anxiety for learners who have difficulty asking questions or expressing thoughts in front of larger groups.

Fosters strong networking and teambuilding.

Can lead to a high-energy environment.

Facilitates experiential, active learning.

Disadvantages

Can be a noisy environment.

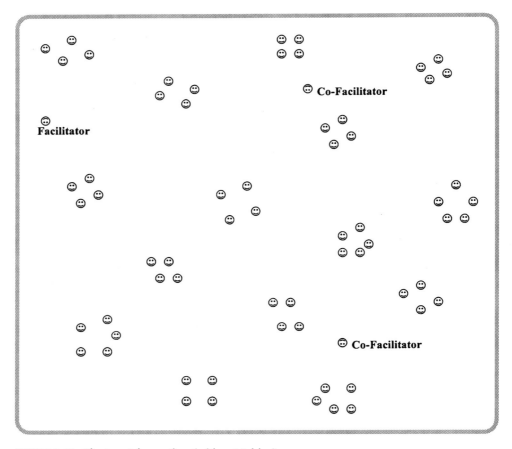

FIGURE 5-18. Cluster style seating (without tables)

Requires an assistant facilitator to help monitor activities.

Notetaking is difficult because there are no writing surfaces.

Attention is dispersed between different groups and facilitators may miss opportunities to observe and give feedback to all learners.

Time is lost in forming small groups for activities, then reassembling the larger group for discussion.

Fishbowl Style Seating (without Tables)

This arrangement is excellent for role-plays and demonstrations. A small group of active participants are located in a small circle inside a larger circle of observers who later provide feedback and comments. Again, there are no writing surfaces.

All Life is an experiment.
—Oliver Wendell Holmes

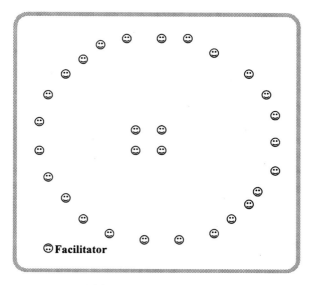

FIGURE 5-19. Fishbowl style seating (without tables)

Think about the types of programs you normally conduct and the audience sizes.

Which of the seating configurations that you have read about would best facilitate learning with small groups (24 or fewer participants) that you train? Why? _____

_____

Which of the seating configurations that you have read about would best facilitate learning with large groups (24 or more participants) that you train? Why? _____

_____

What other seating arrangements have you used or seen used? _____

_____

● ADDING CREATIVE PERIPHERALS

After you have ensured that all the necessary facility and equipment components are present in your classroom, give some thought to adding a bit of pizzazz. Go beyond the typical classroom components and put on your creativity hat as you read in Chapter 2. Develop and purchase items that help set the tone for your program theme and to inject a bit of humor, excitement, competition, and diversion into your program. You can even create a theme for your program (e.g., "South of the border") for a hot new project or product rollout, "safari" for problem-solving or decision-making when you are brainstorming ideas, or "Las Vegas" for programs related to new programs or projects that your company is launching that might involve a gamble or risk. Be creative and have fun as discussed in Chapter 2.

Depending on the program topic, you can purchase items that will complement and reinforce your message. The following are some ideas for peripheral materials that can be used to enhance the learning environment for a variety of topics. Go to a teacher supply or party/novelty store and look for these items or others that can be modified or used as tie-ins to your program topics. If you have trouble locating local sources, contact Creative Presentation Resources in the Resources for Trainers section of the appendices.

Cardboard Wall Borders

These borders come in various shapes and designs and can be used to add color and context to your theme. They are available as pieces of various lengths and can be taped or thumb tacked along the top edge of the wall around the room. You can either get solid-colored poster type borders just to add a splash of color, or ones that have a theme (e.g., diversity figures, money, or numbers). The latter could be used in classes on diversity topics, finance, accounting, cashier training, or other programs dealing with money or figures.

Modeling Clay (Play Dough®)

It is easy to bring out the child in your learners by placing modeling clay on participant tables to allow them to manipulate it and quietly create little figures during the program. You can also use this for teambuilding or individual competitions by having learners create specified figures within a set timeframe.

Party Hats

Party hats, available at party and novelty stores, allow you to fashion your session theme around any holiday or festive event. Various hats can be tied to a program, event, or holiday theme. Participants might be given hats that identify them as part of a small group for activities or you may just give them random hats as part of a celebration or activity. For example, crowns (as used by royalty) can be used to signify group leaders during activities. As the role of leader is passed to

someone new for subsequent activities, the hat is passed to the next leader. At the end of the day, the person ending up with the hat receives a prize. This encourages people to volunteer early since they do not know how many activities you have planned.

Noisemakers

Not only are noisemakers great for grabbing the attention of your learners, but they can also be used by participants to applaud others, signal they have finished an activity, or just to add a festive mood. By using various types of noisemakers, you can allow participants to signal an answer, to show appreciation for something said or done by others, or simply when you want them to get excited and become a bit rowdy to celebrate a successful completion of an activity. Noisemakers can be in the form of clickers, sports whistles, train whistles, musical instruments, cow bells, squeeze balls that make noise, hand clappers, or party favors. For example, plastic hand clappers can be placed on each participant's table and used to applaud someone else's correct answer to a question or to sound when they have the answer to a question (e.g., the first person signaling wins a prize and gets the chance to answer the question for additional prizes). Such usage adds a bit of noise to the room and helps keep participants alert as they listen for an opportunity to sound off.

Party Glitter or Confetti

Just as at parties, confetti can provide a festive mood to your training room while adding color. You can purchase table and doorway curtains made of metallic tinsel. The color, sparkle, and flowing nature when the wind blows attracts attention and sets a mood of fun because such items are typically seen at parties. You can also sprinkle paper or metallic glitter in various shapes on participant tabletops. Again, it sends a message that the session is going to be different and fun.

Crepe Paper

If your goal is to add color to the room, crepe paper is a great vehicle. It comes in long rolls of various colors and can be wound along walls or across rooms from the ceiling to add color or pizzazz to the room.

Foil or Tissue Balls

Think of all the parties, weddings, and other festive events in which there were metallic and paper balls, shapes, and figures hanging from the walls and ceiling or on tables. Their presence added color and said "Fun!" Why not take advantage of similar memories that your learners also likely have? Place these festive shapes around the room to attract attention and spark the environment. They come in various shapes and can be purchased at many party and novelty stores (see M&N International in the Resources for Trainers section of the appendices).

Mylar Balloons

Balloons inflated with helium can be purchased in a variety of shapes such as stars, moon, sun, smile face, and so forth. These easily tie to a variety of program themes and add color and fun. You can even buy your own portable helium tanks for use at your organization. The biggest challenge with using these is that some hotels and organizations with closed systems (windows will not open) forbid using the balloons because any escaping helium goes into the air circulation systems. Check before planning to use them in your programs.

Party Balloons

The use of balloons is limited only by your imagination. You have already read a number of ways to incorporate them into your sessions. Later chapters contain even more suggestions. By using various colors, sizes, and shapes you can brighten your environment and add a plethora of activity possibilities to your sessions. You can even have balloons imprinted with messages or words related to your program topic.

BRIGHT IDEA

Festive Review

Hide bits of paper with key program terms or content issues inside balloons that you hang on classroom walls. During the session the balloons add a festive tone; later, when you are ready for an interim or final review of program content, have participants select a balloon. Randomly, have learners pop their balloons and read what is on the piece of paper inside. Have them tell as much as they can about what is on their paper, based on what they learned in the program. Then have anyone else add to what was said before going on to the next person, who repeats the process.

Props

You can use props to grab attention and while facilitating, and to set the tone for activities or make a point. In addition to the hats mentioned earlier you can use some of the following items:

Toy police badges

Light-up wands or swords

Hard rubber chickens that can be used as flip chart pointers

Foam rubber animal masks

Rubber animal noses

Clown noses, hair, and shoes

Costume masks

Holiday Supplies

If your training happens to take place on or near a special day (e.g., Easter, Valentine's Day, Secretaries' Day, Halloween, Hanukkah, Kwanza, Mardi Gras, super bowl, and so forth) you can buy supplies to decorate for the theme. If the holiday has already passed, you can stock up on discounted materials for use later. You can generally find everything from hats, masks, balloons, napkins, plates, and other items supporting the holiday theme.

Streamer String

This foamy material comes in an aerosol can and can be sprayed around the room or at some specific time in your program to signal an event. As you spray, a long stream of the "string" shoots out of the nozzle. You have to clean up after the fun is over, however. Still, it adds another dimension to your sessions.

International Theme Items

With participants coming from all over the world, you may want to give thought to incorporating items from different countries into your sessions (e.g., Mexico, Italy, Germany, France, and Ireland). These can be found in many party and specialty stores. Use these to decorate your room for diversity training.

Smile Face Items

Most people have been exposed to the proverbial "smile face" (bright yellow with two eyes and a silly grin). This recognizable character comes in all types of shapes and products. You can buy balloons, cups, shirts, pencils, balls, buttons, and virtually anything else with smile faces on them. Use these for programs such as customer service, communication, or to give as incentive prizes.

As you read in Chapter 2, you are limited only by your imagination when it comes to decorating your classroom or creating a theme. Ask peers for ideas and observe other trainers to see what they are doing and copy them. Keep in mind that your purpose in using peripherals is to garner interest and to add a bit of excitement and fun to your environment.

● GATHERING YOUR TOOLS AND TOYS TOGETHER

A final aspect of creating a stimulating environment is to ensure you have given thought to the tools that you could use to reinforce and encourage learning. You'll read more about other tools in later chapters; however, let's explore some options for preparing to have some fun in training. Remember the fun you had in a toy, craft, hobby, or variety store when you were a child? You could probably have spent hours just walking around and trying out all the interesting things they had. And every time you went back, there were likely new things to attract your attention. It's possible that, like me, you likely haven't changed much. If that is true and you have not been to a store that supplies toys, incentives, and other fun things in a while, take some time to do so. Many of your old favorites are probably still there, as well as hundreds of new things! Here's a partial listing of the types of stores you may want to visit:

Toy

Craft/art supply

Bookstores

Discount department (e.g., K-Mart, Target, Wal-Mart)

Closeout stores (e.g., Big/Odd Lots, or others that specialize in purchasing end of year or stock from stores going out of business).

Greeting card

Warehouse clubs (e.g., Sam's Club, BJ's, or COSTCO)

Drugstore chains

Science/discovery

Teacher supply

As an alternative to visiting a store physically, you can scan through catalogs or visit Internet websites of companies specializing in children's toys or training aids for trainers and teachers (see Creative Training Resources and the Trainers Warehouse in the Resources for Trainers in the appendices).

As you wander up and down the aisles, put some of those creative ideas discussed in Chapter 2 to use. Examine things closely to determine how they could possibly tie into a program or workplace theme.

BRIGHT IDEA

Brainstorming Uses for Fun Things

As you explore all the items you find, ask yourself these questions:

How could this item be used as an incentive to reward employees in the workplace?

How could it be used as a reward in a training program(s)?

Could this item tie into a training theme and thus be used as a training aid to reinforce a learning point?

In what variations could the item be used? (e.g., Does it relate to several issues or themes?)

What similar items have you found elsewhere that could be used, possibly at a lower price? (We often get additional ideas by "thinking outside the box.")

Could the item be used as a team activity?

What specific skill(s) or learning objective(s) could be addressed with the item?

What audience level would it best suit?

How difficult would it be to incorporate the item into training or the workplace?

Does the item require additional pieces of items to be effective?

APPLYING WHAT YOU LEARNED
Strategies for Stimulating the Brain

1. In what ways can you use research findings related to the environment to improve the places where you deliver training? _____

_____

2. How have you seen the psychological needs of learners described in this chapter exhibited in your training programs? _____

_____

3. How can you better ensure your learner's return on investment by modifying your learning environment? _____

_____

4. What environmental issues in your organization's training area need immediate attention?

_____

_____

5. What room layouts do you feel are best suited for the type of training that you regularly conduct?

_____

_____

_____

ENDNOTES

[12] Heath, R.P., The wonderful world of color, *Marketing Tools and American Demographics,* Oct 1997.

[13] Howard, P.J., *The Owner's Manual for the Brain,* 2nd ed., Bard Press, Atlanta, GA, 2000, pp. 704–705.

[14] Walker, M., *The Power of Color: The Art and Science of Making Colors Work for You,* Avery Publishing Group, Garden City Park, NY, 1991, p. 21.

[15] London, W., (1998) *Brain/mind bulletin collections, New Sense Bulletin,* Vol. 13, Los Angeles, CA, April, 7c.

[16] National Research Council of Canada, Institute for Research in Construction, Ottawa, ON, K1A 0R6.

[17] Veitch, J.A. and McColl, S.C., *Full-Spectrum Lighting Effects on People: A Critical Review,* National Research Council of Canada, Institute of Research in Construction, Ottawa, ON.

[18] Rauscher, F. and Ky, K., (1993) Music and Spatial Task Performance, *Nature* 365:611.

[19] Jensen, E., *Music with the Brain in Mind,* The Brainstore, San Diego, CA. 2000, p. 37.

[20] Millbower, L., *Training with a Beat,* Stylus Publishing, Sterling, VA, 2000. pp. 134–135.

[21] Wolverton, B.C., *How to Grow Fresh Air: 50 Houseplants That Purify Your Home and Office,* Penguin Books, New York, 1997.

[22] Vermeulen, A. and Maritz, N., *Brain Ergonomics: Humanising the Lecture Room to Increase Learning and Performance,* Presentation at the 40th World Education Federation Conference, Laineston, Australia, January 1999.

[23] Herz, R.S. (1997) The effects of cue distinctiveness on odor-based context dependent memory. *Memory and Cognition,* 25, 375–380.

[24] Herz, R.S. *The American Journal of Psychology,* 110, 489–505.

[25] Hirsch, H.R. and Johnson, L.H. (1993). Floral odors increase learning ability. Presentation at the annual conference of the American Academy of Neurology and Orthopedic Surgery.

[26] Hirsch, H.R. and Johnson, L.H. (1993) Odors and Learning. *Journal of Neurology and Orthopedic Medicine and Surgery,* 17:119–126.

[27] Howard, P.J., *The Owner's Manual for the Brain: Everyday Applications from Mind-Brain Research,* 2nd Ed., Bard Press, Atlanta, GA, 2000, p. 713.

[28] Vermeulen, A. (ibid).

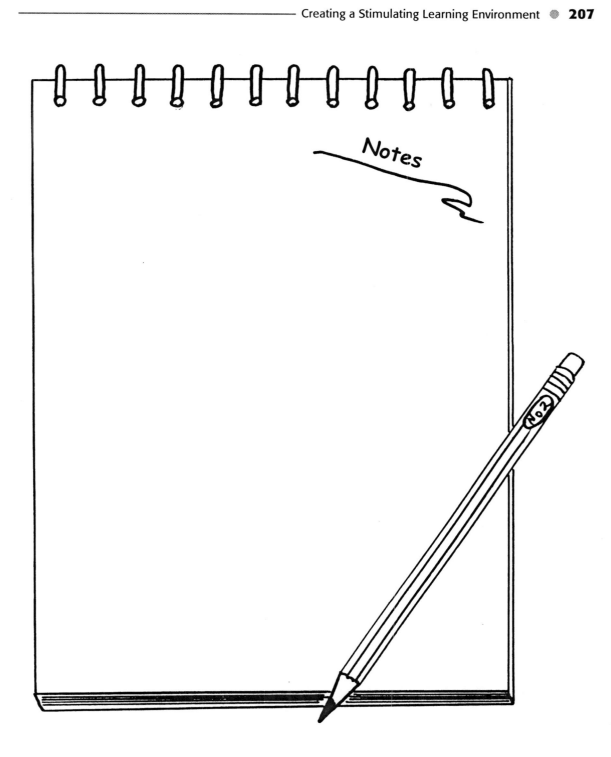

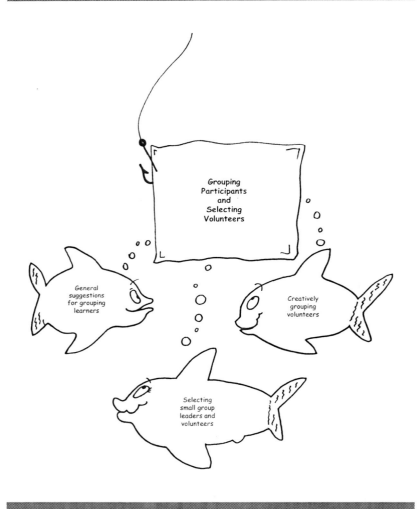

Grouping Participants and Selecting Volunteers

People influence people.

—Robert F. Mager
Developing Attitude Toward Learning

Learning Objectives

At the end of this chapter, and when applying concepts covered, you will be able to:

- Group participants in a manner that facilitates learning, idea exchange, and networking.

- Randomly select group members in a variety of creative ways.

- Select group leaders and scribes in a fun and innovative manner.

- Use various props, toys, and incentive items to group participants and identify roles within the team.

- Utilize clever techniques to identify group topics for discussion and review.

- Reward participants and encourage further involvement through distribution of incentives and other motivational strategies.

Toys, props, and fun. What do those words mean to you? To many adults, they bring to mind memorable times as a child, or as an adult, in which life was less stressful and more energized. They communicate a less hectic pace of life where enjoyment of the moment was all that mattered and fond memories were formed. Whether it was on the playground as a child, around a table playing card or board games with friends, wearing silly costumes at a party, or just relaxing and celebrating free time with others, such terms conjure up stored thoughts. Learning took place when these items and concepts were present.

How can you capitalize on what you just read? Think about it for a second. Can you recall how it felt when you were playing games in the past or how much fun you had walking into a party room full of friends with some props or costume on? Transfer the same devices and techniques that gave you joy and fond memories to your learners. It is easy to do, if you just mentally escape back to your youthful freedom.

In this chapter, you will read about strategies and techniques for energizing learners and helping them enjoy their learning experience. As you explore using a variety of toys and props to group participants and select volunteers, you will also identify concepts that can transfer to other areas of your training.

● CREATIVELY GROUPING PARTICIPANTS

Separating participants into smaller groups is a standard practice for trainers and facilitators. It is one technique for securing participation by people who might otherwise hide in the background without sharing their knowledge and ideas. It also divides those who reduce networking and information sharing opportunities by gathering with people they already know or with whom they work.

Why Group?

You may say, "Why bother separating people into smaller groups?" There are a number of reasons. Some of the more important ones include the following.

Behavioral Style Preference

Because of their behavioral style preference, some people are reluctant or too embarrassed to stand in front of a large group to speak. Placing them in smaller work groups, where they can comfortably share ideas in a conversational setting, may help to get them to open up and participate more freely. Thus, more ideas are generated and ownership of the final result belongs to everyone rather than just the vocal minority.

Networking Is a Crucial Success Factor

Getting to know others is always one of the valuable added benefits for people attending a meeting or training session. When people are divided into smaller groups, they have a better opportunity to get to know more intimate details about someone's background and to share important details about themselves. This doesn't always happen when you have a large number of people in a group setting.

Information Exchange Is Important

The amount of lively discussion and exchange of ideas often increases when there is an equal number of people in each group for discussions. This is particularly valuable if you want a consensus or discussion on a topic. If brainstorming of ideas, solutions, or issues is expected, this also helps in generating a potentially higher number of comments.

Planning Time Is Gained

By dividing participants into smaller discussion groups, then assigning tasks, you can allow time for yourself to plan another activity, get ready for the next phase of a program, and to better manage interaction during discussion. As participants work on assigned tasks, you can check your lesson plan to mentally prepare for what is to follow the small group activity.

In addition, as participants are interacting, you can walk around to eavesdrop and offer appropriate comments. Participants often view this as personal attention by the facilitator. They may even ask questions that they felt were inappropriate in front of the larger group. For example, maybe they would like your feedback on how to handle a specific workplace situation.

The major challenge this latter instance creates is that, if lengthy conversations evolve, you might take participants off task and they might not finish along with the rest of the groups.

People Tend to Cluster

By randomly grouping learners, you break up cliques of friends and co-workers. This helps encourage the sharing of ideas among different groups and individuals because people often congregate with those with whom they feel most comfortable. When they do this, they often tend to talk and joke more, while paying less attention to you and program content. This leads to disruption and distraction for others. It may also make it necessary for you to deal with the disruptive behavior and possibly discipline someone. In any event, it's a lose–lose situation.

In breaking up these insular groups, it is important to make group member selection seem "random," so that it does not appear you are singling anyone out. To convey this perception you may want to prepare before anyone arrives, by placing props or other items that you will use to group participants at their tables.

The key to getting small groups off to a good start is to plan your technique for smooth division of participants. I typically outline my strategy in my lesson plan. By doing so, I don't have to remember which approach I had planned to use when the time comes for grouping learners for an activity.

Recall the last time you attended a program and the facilitator decided to divide participants into small groups for an activity or discussion and how they did it. To group participants, many trainers revert to the old standby of "Let's count from 1 to whatever . . ." Although this certainly is effective in determining who goes to which group, my personal feeling (and that of many others I know) is that this technique is boring.

To accomplish the same results and provide a little variety and fun in your sessions, try developing a varied repertoire of techniques for grouping people. You can do this by thinking outside the box and using everyday items, toys, props, or whatever you have available to identify individuals as members of a group.

To add a bit of anticipation and creativity to the course delivery, I try not to use the same strategy twice in any one session. It also keeps me alert because I have to think of what technique I'll be using next.

● GENERAL SUGGESTIONS FOR GROUPING LEARNERS

Over the years, I have used dozens of approaches for grouping participants. I also use a wide variety of items or props to help energize and add fun to the environment. With most strategies I try to tie into the program theme when possible. For example, in a customer service class, I might choose a toy or something else that comes in a variety of colors and has a smile face on it.

Whatever item I use to separate participants must be available in multiple colors and/or shapes and sizes. The total number of groups will determine how many different colors or shapes, and how many of each, will be required. For example, if I wanted to divide 24 participants into four equal groups, I'd need at least four shapes or colors. I'd also need at least six of each shape/color (one for each participant). On the other hand, if I wanted six groups of four people, I'd reverse my required numbers and colors/shapes (six shapes/colors and four of each type).

PUTTING YOUR BRAIN TO WORK: ACTIVITY

Before we examine techniques for grouping participants, take a few minutes to think of techniques you have used or seen others use in programs. Without looking at examples I've provided, list as many as you can think of here or on a sheet of paper:

_____

_____

_____

_____

_____

Techniques for Dividing Participants

Now that you have brainstormed some possibilities, let's take a look at some of the techniques that I have developed or used regularly in training adults.

Toys/Props

Prior to participants arriving in the room, I decide how many activities I will use, how many groups I'll need for each activity, and based on total participant number, how many people will be in each group. Once I have accomplished this, I'm ready to think of ways to select participants for each group.

To introduce participants to the concept that I'll be using props and techniques for grouping, I usually emphasize at the beginning of a session that, "We'll be using a variety of toys, games, and incentives today to add a little FUN to the session." I tell them that they'll find toys and other items on their tables that will be explained when the time comes to use them. I also tell them that the items are theirs to keep at the end of the session. In doing this, I have rolled functionality and reward into one idea.

The following are some of the items that I use in a variety of shapes and colors, often based on the course content. (Also see Creative Presentation Resources in the Resources for Trainers section of the appendices.)

Eraser Shapes

Telephones are great for telephone and customer service training.

Light bulbs enhance creativity and brainstorming sessions.

Computers are perfect for software/PC training.

Sailboats, cars, planes, or trains expand the theme in travel/transportation classes.

Numbers and letters of the alphabet work for any topic area.

Seasonal erasers can be used during a specific holiday or special day just to add a festive note (e.g., Halloween—ghosts, Thanksgiving—turkeys, Easter—bunnies).

Dinosaurs work well when teaching change programs (reluctance to change).

Jungle animals are great for stress and time management (especially if you can find ones in the shape of monkeys—to illustrate "keeping the monkey off your back").

Ice cream cones relate to "licking the competition" or motivation.

Crayon erasers can help focus attention on self-improvement or goal setting. (Color your world.)

Star shapes tie nicely into motivation. (You're a star.)

Small Toys

Smile faced items can be used for customer service programs or virtually any other topic, for example, stuffed animals, hacky sacks, or foam balls.

Currency or coins are effective for bank teller or cashier training.

Fish exemplify successful programs/projects when things are "swimming along."

Zoo animals can add fun to virtually any subject or when discussing stress or a high-energy topic when things are hectic, (e.g., It's a zoo around here.)

Insects or bugs help in activities when discussing pet peeves or things that "bug" participants, either in customer interactions or the workplace.

Spinning tops made of plastic can emphasize high sales or improvement levels (on top of the world).

Back scratchers made of wood or plastic can be related to ways of "reaching or attaining a goal."

Sheriff's badges can be tied into concepts of taking charge, leadership, authority, or ownership of an issue.

Ducks made of rubber or plastic might be used to remind people that sometimes things are not always what they are "quacked up" to be (when discussing problems or how things can go wrong in a specific situation).

Hand-held pencil sharpeners can point out the need to ask direct questions or "get to the point" when doing a customer service or interpersonal communication program.

Footballs, baseballs, sponge balls, or similar small items may help emphasize teamwork or "getting on the ball."

BRIGHT IDEA

Idea Excursion

Take an *idea excursion* to find as many different toys and incentives as you can for all the programs you conduct. This is best done on a weekday if possible as some stores may not be open on Saturdays.

First, make a list of all the programs, then take a full day to just window shop. Visit all types of stores—teacher supply, art/craft, toy, discount/closeout, department, discount book, drug (chain stores), card shops, malls with science and discovery type stores, and any other potentially fertile place for ideas in your area. As you visit, *really* look at small items, toys, stickers, books, and incentives. Also, because it is more cost effective if you can get a variety of benefits from an item, ask yourself three questions: (1) How could I tie that into my program content? (2) Can it be used in multiple ways (e.g., incentives, rewards, grouping)? and (3) What audience(s) would the item appeal to? Make a list or purchase those items that you feel best serve your purpose. You're now on your way to presentation pizzazz!

Rubber Stamps

Stamps are very popular and come in hundreds of shapes. They are fairly inexpensive and readily available. There are entire specialty stores currently selling them; you can also buy them at art/craft stores, teacher supply stores, toy stores, and many department stores that sell toys. In addition, you can custom design your own and have them made by many print shops.

Just as with erasers and toys, you can use them to indicate group assignments. Simply stamp an image onto the participant name tents before they arrive and you are ready to go when the time for an activity comes around.

PUTTING YOUR BRAIN TO WORK: ACTIVITY

Take a few moments to list other shapes or items you could use for the specific training programs you conduct. These might be from the list I've provided or others you can think of. _____

_____

_____

Colored Markers

Colored flip chart markers also can be used for grouping participants. They provide a group identifier and, when ready to brainstorm, each person has a marker to write with on a flip chart. There are several ways to use markers to group participants. The first technique is to indicate groupings by placing a series of colored markers at participant locations. For example, start with red for the first person; then go around the room with blue, green, and black; and then start over with the same color pattern until each person has a marker. You could then either group all like colors together for an activity or state that they have "X" number of minutes to form groups, ensuring that all groups have a person with each color represented (e.g., one red, one blue, and so forth). Either way, you separate people who were sitting together and change the groupings.

A second use for markers is to simply put a letter or number on name tents or nametags (e.g., A–F or number 1–6) depending on the size of groups desired.

A third approach is to use various colored markers and put a colored dot in the upper corner of each person's name tent or nametag. For example, the first person gets a red dot, the second, a green, and so on until you have enough colors to meet your group size needs. You then repeat the pattern clockwise around the room until everyone has a colored dot. Colored adhesive dots available at office supply stores serve the same purpose.

PUTTING YOUR BRAIN TO WORK: ACTIVITY

What other creative ways can you think of to use markers to group participants? (Include techniques you have used or seen used.) _____

_____

Pencils

Colored pencils or ones with designs or slogans printed on them are another easy and fun way to tie into program content and divide participants. As with the toys and erasers, you can reward participants by allowing them to keep the pencils at the end of the session.

I use a variety of colored pencils, both plain and the type with phrases on them. Either way, people now have something to write with and you have a way to divide into groups when the time comes. If you're using themed pencils with phrases or symbols that tie to program content, they now have a reminder to take back to the workplace. Whenever they see or use the pencil at their desks, they may recall the program and topic. This is a simple way to reinforce the learning after the training has ended.

Themed pencils can often be found in novelty stores, at shopping malls, and in teacher supply stores (see Creative Presentation Resources in the Resources for Trainers section in the appendices for training specific phrases).

BRIGHT IDEA

Create Your Own Specialty Items

If you have an idea for a particular phrase that would tie into a program theme, contact some of the local promotional incentive item companies in your area. They can create specialty pencils customized for your program. You can even put your company logo on them so that subconsciously participants get the message that they are attending a special program just for them.

Some examples of themed pencils that I use in my sessions are:

For train the trainer or other similar sessions
Training Can Be Fun!!
Learning Is Exciting
Learning Is FUN!!
Training Opens Doors
Training for Excellence
Learning Expands Horizons

For change management programs
Facilitators Promote Change
I'm Working for Change

For customer service sessions
Smile faces
Customer Service Excellence Award

Supervisory/management training
Super Supervisor Award
Caught Doing Good

During teambuilding
#1 Team Player
Team Player Award
Teaming for Excellence

In interpersonal communication classes
Good Listener Award

Stickers

Stickers are easy to obtain, relatively inexpensive, and can add sizzle to your sessions. You can select from hundreds of shapes and themes. They are available in virtually any store that sells greeting cards, school supplies, toys, books, and novelties. There are also specialty companies that cater to trainers and presenters (see Creative Training Products in the Resources for Trainers section in the appendices).

As with the toys and erasers discussed earlier, stickers can tie into a variety of themes or topics. For that reason, trainers in just about any industry can find something to enhance their sessions.

Just as with the erasers and toys earlier, you'll need enough of various colors and shapes to select participants into equal groups. To do this, simply put a sticker in the corner of each person's name tent or nametag, as you did with the markers, before they arrive. The following are a few ideas for specific types of stickers that can relate to an industry/topic:

Animals: any topic or industry

Cars and trucks classes for the automotive industry

Computers: PC/technical skills training

Clock faces: time management

Clown faces: humor training

Eyes: optical industry classes

Food shapes: restaurant/food services training

Mouths and lips: nonverbal/verbal communication skills

Seasonal: can be used for any type of training based on a special day (e.g., St. Patrick's Day, Halloween, New Year's)

Safety signs: OSHA or workplace safety training

Smile faces: any industry or class

Stars: any type program

Teeth and mouths: dental classes

Traffic signs: transportation/safety training

PUTTING YOUR BRAIN TO WORK: ACTIVITY

Think of the types of programs that you do. List them here, then imagine and list a type of sticker that could tie into the topic. Next, go on a shopping trip to locate them for future use. _____

Paper Products

There are many ways to divide people randomly using various products made of paper. Keep in mind that your goal is to have an equal number of people in each group. Whatever method you use should include a variety of colors or shapes. Here are a few ideas that might help.

Playing cards can be used to divide people into four equal groups. To do this, find out how many attendees you will have, then select that number of cards sequentially from each suit in a deck of regular playing cards (e.g., assuming a group of 24, you'll need to pick out all the 1–6 cards of spades, hearts, clubs, and diamonds). Next, mix the cards up so that the suits are not together. As people enter give them a card randomly. When the time comes for an activity, you now have two ways to divide participants. You can either have all people with a like suit join together, or you can have all 1s, 2s, and so on group. Either way, you end up with four equal groups.

Using construction or colored paper in various colors is a second technique. Select the number of colors based on groups desired. Cut the sheets into equal pieces or use entire sheets. Either pass them out as participants enter or put the paper at their tables/chairs. And, just as with the cards, when you're ready for an activity, have people group by the color of their paper.

The paper can also be used in an activity in which participants list items or share ideas by passing written comments from one person to the next. Each person adds an additional piece of information to the sheet, then passes it on. This is a variation on a brainstorming process called **brain writing** often experienced using a flip chart page. In that activity participants go from one flip chart sheet to the next adding comments or ideas to a prestated question or issue at the top of each page. Basically, they use previous ideas stated by their peers to stimulate new ideas of their own.

Colored 3 × 5 (7.5 × 12.5 cm) or 5 × 7 (12.5 × 17.5 cm) cards also can be used to group people. Another alternative to colored paper is to put various colored dots in the corner of white 3 × 5 or 5 × 7 cards.

Cutout shapes can be created and used for many activities to gather information and to group your participants. For example, you can create a variety of shapes (e.g., stars, hearts, light bulbs, circles, squares) using the templates found in the Tools for Trainers section of the appendices. Reproduce these on bright colored paper, cut them out, and put them in a pile in the center of participant tables before a session. When ready to group, ask each participant to select from the pile so that there are an even number of each shape from each table (e.g., two stars, two hearts, and so on). Next, based on the subject matter for your activity, have them write comments, statements or ideas on their shapes. They then gather with other participants based on the shape they all selected. Once grouped, they discuss the issue or topic. When they finish, the shapes are taped to a wall or flip chart page. During the break others can view all the ideas, suggestions, or comments.

BRIGHT IDEA

Feedback

To gather feedback on how things are going during your session, pass out a single-shaped cutout (e.g., a light bulb). Use a variety of colored paper—bright neon colors add a splash of color and pizzazz to the room. As with other grouping methods, ensure you have an equal number of colors.

Next, draw a large image of a hand on a flip chart page and at the top write "Give Me A Hand. . . ." Spray this page with artist's adhesive (available at craft/art supply stores or see the Resources for Trainers section in the appendices) and post it on the wall or on a flip chart easel by the exit door. Before a break, or lunch, conduct an activity in which participants write on one side of their cutout "plus" (+) and list one idea, concept, or suggestion that they have experienced thus far in the program that will be useful. Then, have them turn the cutout over and put "minus" (−) and list one thing they would change about the program if they were facilitating it. Tell them that they can pass if they can't think of anything to write.

Divide participants into groups based on the color of their cutout and have them share the positive ideas they've gathered. By doing this, they are rethinking what has been covered as they list something, then again as they discuss it and hear what others have written. All three opportunities to revisit information covered helps to reinforce the learning that has already taken place when the original idea was presented earlier.

Party Props and Supplies

Another fun and entertaining approach to grouping participants begins when you make a trip to your local party supply store in search of a different kinds of props (see also Party Supplies and Decorations in the Resources for Trainers section in the appendices). Numerous items can be used for dividing people into smaller groups for various activities.

The following are a few ideas I've used over the years.

Rubber animal noses or foam animal face masks are great for grouping people based on the type of nose they receive. You can use these in a couple of ways.

For an opening icebreaker, get small paper bags, have a rubber stamp created that says "Please do not open until told" (you can also write this on each bag), count out an equal number of various shapes, then put an animal nose or mask in each bag and staple shut.

When ready to use, tell participants to open their bags, put whatever they find in the bags on their faces, then locate all the other people in the room who "look" like them. Once grouped, you can give instructions for an activity. Some people may feel silly wearing these, so you may want to walk into the room initially with a nose on to show that you are not above having people laugh with you. This can help reduce their apprehension. If they don't want to wear the nose, they can stretch the strap around the back of their head and let it rest on their forehead so others can see and locate their teammates (see Creative Presentation Resources in the Resources for Trainers section in the appendices).

A second method for using animal noses is to wait until you're ready to start, then randomly pass one to each person. Ask them to put it on and find their team.

What other ways can you think of to use animal noses? _____

_____

Hawaiian leis in different colors can be distributed as participants enter to add a festive mood to the session. You can then have learners assemble by color to introduce themselves or discuss something.

Hats come in virtually any color and dozens of shapes. There are neon colored baseball caps; crowns; colored sun visors; straw, animal, western, alpine, clown, and derby hats; and many more. Select one that adds to your theme or just fits your interest and go for it. Either pass them out at the entrance, or have them ready on tables before participants arrive.

Plastic kazoos can be used to have people locate teammates. Participants get a different colored kazoo based on their group assignment. On slips of paper, assign a song title to each group that everyone is likely to know (e.g., "America," "Old McDonald," "Happy Birthday," and "Jingle Bells"). Have them use their kazoos to hum their songs as they walk around the room in search of teammates. Once found, they group for an activity.

Small party favors those given at birthday parties for children can also be used effectively (e.g., rings, whistles, barrettes, animal stencils, spinning tops, and prisms). They are great because along with helping group people, they also provide immediate incentive rewards for them. In addition, throughout the session, as attention naturally wanders, participants now have something to "play" with.

Buttons

Buttons with phrases related to your program topic (e.g., "Satisfaction Guaranteed" or "Smiles Will Be Returned" for customer service programs) or colorful graphic images (e.g., a smile face, clown face, or shape such as a square, circle, rectangle) are inexpensive and easy to obtain. You can even create your own customized versions (see Creative Presentation Resources in the Resources for Trainers section in the appendices). Also, as with some of the items discussed earlier, these can be given to participants as prizes at the end of the day, if desired.

Miscellaneous Items

In addition to the items mentioned thus far, you can also use everyday materials to identify participant groups. Some of the more easily accessible are:

Colored paperclips attached to participants' name tents. You can use either the jumbo plastic type or the rubber-coated metal ones. Either works fine and can often be found in a typical office supply cabinet.

Colored Post It® Notes stuck to name tents or simply placed at each participant's table area along with handout materials.

Poker chips of different colors placed at each participant location prior to their arrival.

Coins of different denominations (pennies, nickels, dimes, and quarters). Plastic play coins or play currency can also be used effectively to identify group members.

Color-coded handouts for easy participant grouping. When you produce handout materials for your session, simply print the cover sheets in a variety of colors. You then have automatically assigned groups based on where each person has chosen to sit.

Other Grouping Techniques

In addition to simply placing items or identifying people, you can also use some random techniques that can tie directly into an activity. For example, you can put questions or issues related to your topic inside small plastic colored eggs, the kind used at Easter. Have an even number of each color and enough for all participants. Put the eggs in a bag or bowl and pass it around. Each person takes one egg, thus identifying his or her group assignment. He or she then opens the egg to determine what question or issue he or she must present or offer within the group during the activity. This is also a great interim review technique when the items inside the eggs are key issues presented up to that point in the session.

A second technique for grouping people without the use of props is to write the names of either flowers, sports, colors, cars, and so forth (ideally something related to your session topic) on individual sheets of flip chart paper posted around the room. There should be a sheet for each group needed for the activity. Next, starting with the first person to your left, participants move in sequence to the various sheets of paper. Once there, leaders and scribes are selected as indicated later in this chapter; then they are given their assignments.

Another, more time consuming technique is to place numbered strips of paper in a box, bag, or bowl prior to participant arrival. You will need a strip for each person. When ready for an activity, have participants start counting at "1" and continue until each person has a sequential number. You then randomly draw numbers one at a time to group participants.

Another option is to place similarly colored toothpicks, marbles, pieces of wrapped candy, pieces of ribbon, or other items (equal to the number of participants and groups you need for an activity) into a container. Pass the container around the room and have each person select one item. He or she is now assigned based on the color drawn.

● SELECTING SMALL GROUP LEADERS AND VOLUNTEERS

By randomly selecting people to take on various roles throughout your session, you reduce the likelihood that one or two individuals will dominate or control the session, discussions, and activities. You also encourage interaction and input by all participants.

To set the stage for participants playing an active role in the program, discuss the leader/scribe process at the beginning of your programs. It also helps when you plan to give small incentives (e.g.. buttons, toys, candy, or other fun items) to your "volunteers" and let them know this at the beginning. Doing so can actually generate some friendly competition as people rush to volunteer throughout the day.

BRIGHT IDEA
Rewarding Initiative

At the beginning of your session announce that, throughout the day, you will be using a variety of techniques to randomly select small group spokespersons (leaders) and notetakers (scribes). Also let participants know that you will be rewarding these "volunteers" and others who actively participate. Tell them that, for their efforts, they will get smile face stickers on their name tents each time they answer questions first, volunteer, or play a leadership role. Emphasize that with initiative goes reward. Inform them that the person with the most stickers at the end of the session will get a prize. You may even want to say jokingly something to the effect that although you won't tell them what their prize will be, it will not be a new car!

At the end of the session, count the stickers and reward the winner(s) with an inexpensive prize. Be sure to have a tie-breaking process in mind or multiple prizes in case more than one person has the same number of stickers.

Some prizes might include:

Bag of candy (which often can be shared with peers)

Small stuffed smile face characters at the end of customer service programs

Copies of books, such as Deborah Tannen's "*Talking 9 to 5: Women & Men in the Workplace* at the end of an interpersonal communication course, or one of my books at the end of a supervisory program.

The ideal reward will tie into your program content.

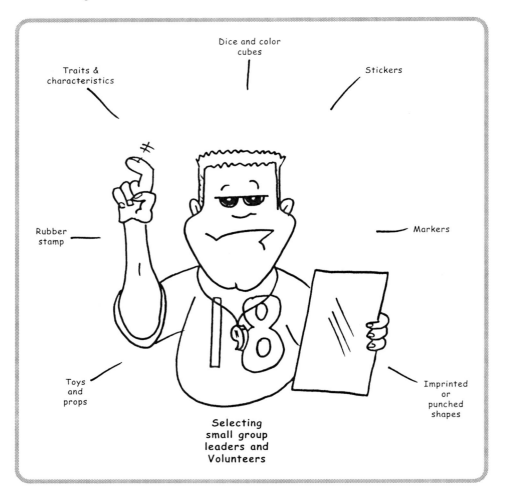

MINDMAP 1. Selecting Small Group Leaders and Volunteers

In considering ways to involve people in activities, it is important to remember that some people are "private" and might become embarrassed if forced to take a lead role, or if they are put on the spot.

It is also usually a good idea at the beginning of a session to identify trainer and participant expectations in some way. One of these means might be to state that, if a participant does not want to take a leadership role or volunteer, he or she can "pass" without being embrarassed. When you are ready to select small group spokespersons (leaders) and notetakers (scribes), use your imagination to make the event fun and add a little interaction and activity to the session. Just as with grouping participants, this task is limited only by your imagination and desire to think outside the box.

The following are some possible ways to select randomly "volunteers."

Die or Color Cube

Die

One truly random technique involves placing a regular or large foam rubber die on each group's table. Instruct the participants in each group to roll the die in turn, with the first person getting a "6" first becoming the leader. Have them continue until someone gets a "1." This person has then "volunteered" to be the scribe.

Color Cube

A variation of the die is to use a *color cube* (see Creative Training Resources in Resources for Trainers section in the appendices), which has different colors (instead of numbers). Designate the color that will determine both the leader and scribe and have participants start rolling until someone gets them.

Stickers

As with the technique for using various types of stickers to identify group members, you can designate leaders and scribes in a similar fashion. The easiest way to accomplish this is to use colored or themed stickers on name tents as described earlier in this chapter. To appoint leaders and scribes, either use a larger version of the stickers or a second sticker added to name tent for each group. You may even want to put the extra sticker underneath the folded name tent out of sight. Some "seasoned" session attendees may see the dual stickers and shy away figuring that they must be there for a reason.

Markers

By placing identifying marks (e.g., letters, numbers, dots, and symbols) on participant name tents or nametags, you can easily designate certain individuals from each group to play specific roles.

Toys and Props

As with the use of various items to identify team members, you can also designate leaders by placing special items at their seat locations. These items might be the same thing everyone has, only differently colored, or they may be completely unique. By using a "symbol of office" you can even have a bit of fun by having the item passed from one volunteer to the next for various activities. The person with the "symbol" is visibly either the leader or scribe. These items might be a special marker (e.g., jumbo size) for the scribe, or a special toy for the leader (e.g., magic wand, paper crown, or some other item associated with authority or power).

> **BRIGHT IDEA**
> ## Symbols of Office
> Use Mondo Koosh® or foam rubber/sponge balls as symbols of office for your leaders. Place one ball at random locations so that each group will have a leader for your first activity. For you second activity, have the former leaders gently toss their balls to anyone else in their group. That person just "volunteered" to be the new leader. Have the scribes similarly pass their symbol of office.
>
> A variation on this is to allow the leaders to "delegate" their leadership responsibilities to another member of their group. Before starting an activity, identify who the group leaders are for each group. Next, announce that one of the competencies of a good leader is to be able to delegate tasks effectively. Tell them that the leaders may now delegate their leadership during the activity to anyone else in their group, if they so desire. This technique usually generates a few chuckles and a flurry of activity as people quickly transfer their symbol of office to someone else.

Identifying Traits or Characteristics

Dozens of participants' traits or characteristics can be used to designate them for specific tasks. However, be cautious not to choose something that will embarrass an individual, such as a physical characteristic that he or she cannot change, for example, weight, height, nose/shoe size, or eye/hair color. Nor should you focus on items related to a group that they represent, for example, religion, sexual preference, or race. Doing so might even lead to charges of discrimination or favoritism.

Some more acceptable possibilities include:

Birth date closest/farthest to the date of your program

Most/least pets

Longest/shortest time with organization

Person who most recently purchased a particular item (e.g., car, electrical appliance, piece of clothing)

Person wearing the most of an item or color

Person carrying the most coins

Person with the most/least siblings

Person who traveled farthest/least to get to the program location

Person with decorative metal on his or her shoes

Person who has most recently participated in an athletic event

Person who has had the most cups of coffee/tea/juice since arriving at the session

Person with most/least letters in his or her first name

Person with the longest middle name

Person born in the city in which the program is being conducted

Person who has most recently attended another professional development program

PUTTING YOUR BRAIN TO WORK: ACTIVITY

What other techniques for designating small group leaders have you experienced or can you think of?

_____

_____

BRIGHT IDEA

Idea Exchange

Conduct a *creative idea exchange* with peers in your area. If you have a local chapter of The American Society for Training & Development this is a great resource for networking and exchanging ideas (see Resources for Trainers in the appendices for ASTD information). Either meet with, mail, or e-mail a questionnaire, or make telephone calls to trainers you know. Elicit ideas that they have used for creatively selecting leaders and scribes in their training sessions.

As with any other aspect of training, you probably also have many ideas or techniques that you have developed, seen, or heard about to make small groups more effective. Take the time to catalog all of these, then compile them into a list with the ideas you gather from others. Share the list with everyone who participated in your idea exchange.

APPLYING WHAT YOU LEARNED
Strategies for Grouping Participants and Selecting Leaders

1. What techniques will you use in your next session to form small groups in a creative way?

_____

_____

_____

2. What are some techniques that you can use to select randomly group leaders and scribes?

_____

_____

_____

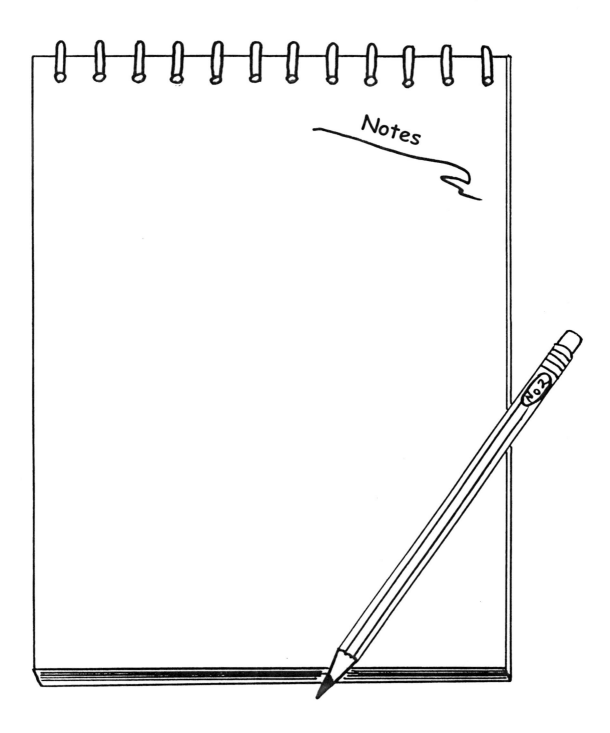

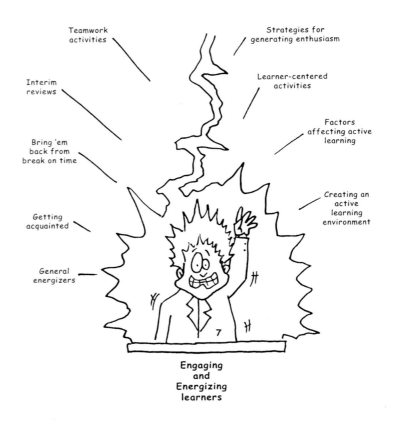

Teamwork
activities

Strategies for
generating enthusiasm

Interim
reviews

Learner-centered
activities

Bring 'em
back from
break on time

Factors
affecting active
learning

Getting
acquainted

Creating an
active
learning
environment

General
energizers

Engaging
and
Energizing
learners

Engaging and Energizing Learners

Alas! How enthusiasm decreases as our experience decreases!
    —Louise Colet

Learning Objectives

At the end of this chapter, and when applying concepts covered, you will be able to:

- Use innovative training strategies and techniques that generate learner enthusiasm.

- Build learner-centered activities into your sessions.

- Plan for active learning by anticipating and handling factors that can impact your training.

- Create an active learning environment.

- Review program materials at various points during a session to ensure that learning is occurring effectively.

- Encourage networking among participants as they get to know one another.

- Get participants back from breaks using a variety of innovative techniques.

- Use various energizers to invigorate participants.

Adult learners typically expect to be challenged and to be involved in their own learning. To address both of these expectations in training requires some pro-activity on your part. By taking an approach that cultivates learner enthusiasm through use of the proven strategies described in this chapter, you will be able to elicit greater participant involvement and help ensure transfer of knowledge.

◉ STRATEGIES FOR GENERATING ENTHUSIASM

Think about what you read in the earlier chapter on creativity. There are many ways to spark excitement and enthusiasm in your sessions. Take the time to search out and develop strategies and techniques that are innovative and require learners to think while having fun and enjoying their experience. Here are a few ways that you can help stimulate enthusiasm in your classroom.

- *Be enthusiastic in your facilitation.*
  Through your own interest and excitement, you can engage and stimulate learners.
- *Plan and deliver activities that add value.*
  Your goal is the overall accomplishment of learning objectives. Do not add activities just because they are fun. Make sure that anything you do in your programs is relevant to session content and aids learning.
- *Ensure that initiatives are well organized.*
  Take time to prepare and practice before learners arrive.
- *Clearly and concisely deliver directions.*
  To ensure that participants get maximum benefit from all activities in a session, take the time to explain what learners are to do.
- *Communicate the purpose and AVARFM of the activity.*
  It is crucial to explain to learners the value of what they are doing so that they will understand potential benefits. Making an assumption that the objective of an activity should be obvious could be a serious mistake. Remember that people learn and process information differently.
- *Elicit questions, comments, or suggestions.*
  Before participants begin an activity, take the time to ask if everything is clear and to determine if all their questions related to the activity have been answered before they begin.
- *Give adequate time for successful completion of activities*
  Little is more frustrating to adults than to be assigned a task only to have someone stop them before they have time to complete it. When this occurs, most participants will feel they have just wasted time and that sticking to a schedule of events is more important to you than their learning. Cutting time short or rushing learners though an activity can cause them to participate reluctantly in future activities. It is better to reduce the amount of material delivered and to allow quality

time for each segment than to cram a great deal of information into a time frame that is too short to allow processing.

- *Provide the tools and support learners' need to be successful.*
  Keep in mind that one of your primary roles in a session is to facilitate the exchange of information and knowledge and to help participants learn.
- *Encourage success.*
  Take time throughout the session to provide positive feedback on learner performance. Using small rewards can also help in this area.
- *Hold an end of activity review.*
  In addition to using periodic interim reviews during a session, build in a thorough review of session objectives at the end of a program. Also, point out how they were addressed.
- *Conduct a follow-up discussion.*
  Take time after every activity to answer questions and to facilitate mental bridging from the classroom to the workplace. This helps ensure all learners "get it" and know how potentially to apply what was learned.

PUTTING YOUR BRAIN TO WORK: ACTIVITY

When you attend training sessions, what strategies have you seen used to excite participants and get them involved? _____

_____

In what ways do you think that you can generate learner enthusiasm in future sessions that you facilitate?

_____

_____

● LEARNER-CENTERED ACTIVITIES

To engage and energize your participants effectively, you must build a variety of learner-centered activities into each of your sessions. As you read in other chapters, participants learn and retain more when they are an active part of the learning process. Such involvement can be the result of individual and/or group activity. In whatever format, involvement can lead to more confident, independent, and self-managed learners. Later in this chapter I will outline a variety of group activities and energizers that I use to accomplish this in my sessions and that you can also use to stimulate, motivate, and foster an enjoyable learning environment.

As Carla Hanaford[29] stresses, "To 'pin down' a thought, there must be movement. A person may sit quietly to think, but to remember a thought, an action must be used to anchor it." Just as children learn through experimenting, so do adults, through experiential and accelerated learning strategies. To maximize the potential of such activities, provide a variety of opportunities for learners to process and practice information and skills mentally and physically.

One way to get learners involved is through the use of visual imagery exercises. In such an activity, participants are asked to close their eyes and imagine or visualize themselves in an environment that you suggest and using the information or processes they have learned to complete a task successfully. For example, you might ask them to relax and imagine an environment in which they are using the steps to a decision-making process that you have taught them to solve workplace problems. Encourage participants to use as many senses as possible and guide them through the imagery by asking questions such as:

What does the environment look like currently?

How does it feel to do (whatever the process entails)?

How does it look as you are performing (the activity)?

What positive feedback do others give you as a result of your actions?

What is the final outcome after you successfully perform the task?

BRIGHT IDEA

Visioning

An alternative way of conducting a visioning activity is to have participants open their eyes and write down or draw pictures of their images. As participants are introduced to the activity, you can provide some light classical, Baroque, or instrumental music in the background. Some current musicians whose music is suitable for this purpose include Enya, Dave Koz, Kenny G, Giovanni Marradi, Jai Peng Fang, George Winston, and Daniel Kane.

Other individual activities for learning include the use of:

Puzzles

Mental challenges (e.g., brainteasers)

Stretching or deep breathing exercises

Journal or diary writing of key ideas learned

Mindmapping of concepts

Participant presentations

Artistic expression (e.g., drawing)

● FACTORS AFFECTING ACTIVE LEARNING

Consider the following factors when you sit down to create activities and initiatives that will involve and stimulate your learners.

Audience Makeup

Ensure that you choose activities and content that are appropriate for the group you will be facilitating. Some activities (e.g., role-play) work best when participants know one another well or are comfortable with one another. Talk to program sponsors and/or participants to discern who will comprise your audience.

Participant Knowledge and Experience Levels

To build successfully on what learners know, you must first determine current capabilities. You can do this through the needs assessment processes that you read about in Chapter 3. Also, ensure that the planned activity suits the audience level (e.g., frontline employee, supervisor, manager, or executive); otherwise, you can easily either intimidate or bore your learners.

Desired Involvement

Decide how, and to what extent, you want to involve participants. Although much self-discovery is possible, you will need to intermingle your own involvement with that of your learners.

Available Time

One mark of a professional trainer is to be able to accomplish established learning objectives and planned activities within the allotted time frame in a seemingly effortless manner. When selecting activities, ensure that the time limit set is realistic and allows for successful completion and debriefing without intruding on other planned program segments.

Training Venue

Take care to select a facility that has the space and equipment needed to conduct planned activities. When possible, actually visit the site so that you can visualize layout and activities.

Also, talk to the people who will set up that room to ensure that they understand your needs. Do not count on a third party relaying your needs to the setup crew.

Group Size

Choose activities that are appropriate for the size of your audience and ensure that co-facilitators are planned if necessary.

Plan for Contingencies

Too often, training will not go as planned. There are often many factors out of your control, especially if you are visiting or training in a facility that you are not in charge of. Accept this fact and prepare for it by having a backup plan in place. For example, if you plan to use a computer projection system, have transparencies or flip charts available in case equipment fails and you need an alternate training aid. Know your material well enough so that you can modify or cut things as necessary because of time overruns or other unforeseen occurrences. This sometimes happens if your presentation is just one of a series being offered in which other presenters or trainers go over their allotted time, thus creating a ripple effect where subsequent trainers have to either speed through material or go past the scheduled ending time. The latter is sure to irritate participants and get you negative remarks on evaluations. It is always better to end early than run over.

BRIGHT IDEA
Finding Activities

Many resources exist for creative and fun activities that can be used for various topic areas. Try going to major Internet search engines (e.g., Yahoo, Excite, WebCrawler, Ask Jeeves, or Google) and typing in key words such as icebreakers, training activities, energizers, or creative training techniques. You can also go to www.ASTD.org for a bulletin board on training issues. While there, you can look up the contact person for the local chapter of The American Society for Training and Development where you can network with other trainers and share ideas.

Several publishers focus on books and magazines in the active or creative category. Try searching the Internet for books by the following publishers:

American Management Association

American Society for Training and Development (ASTD)

Gulf Publishing

HRDPress

Jossey-Bass

Lakewood Publications

McGraw-Hill

Pfeiffer & Company

The Brain Store

Movement is the door to learning.
—*Paul E. Dennison*

PUTTING YOUR BRAIN TO WORK: ACTIVITY

Do you feel that changing activities on a regular basis is a good idea? Why or why not? _____

_____

What other factors can you think of that should be considered when designing or selecting activities to involve participants? _____

_____

What are some additional sources of creative and fun activities do you know of? _____

_____

● CREATING AN ACTIVE LEARNING ENVIRONMENT

To really take advantage of the concepts of brain-based learning and get participants actively involved takes more than lecturing. Be careful not to assume automatically the role of "expert" as you step into a training room. Use activities that will draw participants out so that their knowledge, skills, and abilities are also tapped for learning.

With all the creative resources in print, on the Internet, and available through other sources, there is little reason for you do all the work in stimulating learning or to become stagnant yourself. Literally thousands of ideas and experiential learning activities have already been developed. They are proven to teach knowledge and skills on virtually any topic. These activities can be adopted or adapted, or you can create your own to provide an effective high-energy training environment for learners.

When you are using active training strategies, make sure one of your primary goals is to engage participants. You want them to think, feel, act, and react through many senses with each concept presented. Rather than giving learners answers, provide the theory, tools, support, and an opportunity to resolve issues themselves. Tap into the broad base of experience, knowledge, and ability that is present in any adult group. Do not make the mistake of selling learners short or thinking that because they have not dealt with material or subject matter before they cannot handle current material. Remember that one of the driving principles of adult learning is that participants bring with them

Table 7-1. Comparing Traditional and Active Training

Traditional	Active
Bland, traditional environment	Colorful, upbeat environment
Formal; somewhat stressful	Informal; relaxing
Theory stressed	Application stressed
Focused on memory	Focused on creative thinking
Instructor-centered	Participant-centered
Lecture-based (one-way communication)	Activity-based (group dialogue)
Taps instructor knowledge and skills	Taps learner knowledge and skills
Cognitive-based (intellectual)	Cognitive and affective-based (self-knowledge and feelings)
Limited preparation time needed after initial session	Planning and preparation needed for each session
Learning measured through tests	Learning measured through on-the-job application
Participants work alone	Participants work as teams

knowledge and prior experience that can be harnessed and modified to address other issues. **Table 7-1** shows how active training compares to traditional methods.

Take the time to choose appropriate learning techniques as you design your training programs. Mix up the format to provide variety, contrast, and stimulation for yourself and your learners. The following are some options for engaging and energizing your learners.

Open-Ended Questioning

By asking questions in a format that encourages participant input and feedback you can encourage involvement while eliciting ideas, comments, and suggestions. At the same time you can gauge understanding of material covered.

Small Group Learning

Using activities in which participants form small groups and then work together to address issues or solve problems is an effective technique. You can also add an element of fun by building in strategies for selecting and rewarding volunteers in creative ways.

Trainer-Led Discussion

Using dialogue that you initiate and control can stimulate learning while drawing from the collective knowledge of participants.

Group Learning

Activities in which the entire participant audience works together on an activity that you lead can help build group consensus and camaraderie. For example, you could conduct a review activity in which key terms or concepts from the program are flashed onto a projection screen and participants shout out responses.

Team Activities

By having learners form small teams and participate in exercises, games, role-plays, or similar activities, discovery and reinforcement of ideas can occur.

Peer Coaching

Following the introduction of a concept or process, participants can work in dyads (two learners) or triads (three learners) to practice or rehearse and provide feedback to one another.

Individual Learning

In some instances, participants can take an active role in their own self-discovery. For example, learners could be tasked with conducting interviews with experts. In doing so, they gain new knowledge and insights from the interviewees while actively participating in their own knowledge and skill acquisition.

Participant Teaching

One of the best ways to learn a new skill or topic is to prepare and deliver a presentation on it. Participants can gain a lot by delivering a presentation on some element of your session content to other learners and then receiving feedback on their presentations.

PUTTING YOUR BRAIN TO WORK: ACTIVITY

List five people or sources that you can contact for additional ideas on creating an active learning environment. Try searching the Internet for sources too. _____

_____

_____

● GENERAL ENERGIZERS

Building quick energizing activities of 5 minutes or less into your programs can help increase participant alertness and enhance learning because the blood will start pumping and ultimately stimulate the brain. Many brain researchers have discovered that giving learners a break every 60–90 minutes can help invigorate and rejuvenate energy levels.

When you see energy levels and enthusiasm dropping in your session, or directly following a break, take a few minutes to move people around in the room. Even if it is just to have everyone stand and do some deep breathing or stretching, get learners active. Doing so is important because even though the brain is about 3 percent of total body weight, it consumes about 20 percent of the oxygen taken in by the body. Deep breathing and exercises can help produce a more efficient exchange of oxygen through the blood, thus reinvigorating the brain.

The following activities can be used to energize participants and add a short diversion to the training routine.

Moving On

After you have been in a session for 90 minutes or so, you should give learners a quick break for refreshments, restroom use, and so forth. On their return to the room, try this activity to stimulate them. It is also good for regrouping people and breaking up small gatherings of friends and co-workers who inevitably sit together in a session. By regrouping people you can encourage networking and communication while also reducing the amount of side conversations that occur when participants who know one another well sit together. For this and other activities, keep in mind what you read in an earlier chapter regarding allowing people with disabilities to remain in chosen seats that best accommodate their disabilities.

To conduct this activity as participants return from a break, simply have them gather all their belongings and move to a new location that is at least 10–15 feet from where they are currently seated and not next to someone who is beside them at present. As this is taking place, put on some lively music (e.g., an Irish jig or other upbeat melody). With participants in a new location, you can then continue, or possibly have them participate in an activity that involves their new group in order to facilitate getting acquainted.

Cross-Laterals

You read about the importance of movement in stimulating learning in an earlier chapter. By getting learners up and active, you help the brain refresh itself and become more efficient. You can accomplish this result by using Brain Gym[30] activities such as cross-laterals that cause learners to use both hemispheres of the brain in coordination. In doing such activities, the parts of one side of the body cross over the midpoint of the participant's body to the other side. To have learners participate in and benefit from such activities, have them stand behind their chairs and follow your instructions as you lead them through a series of slow movements. In doing these activities, muscles and bones are being activated along with both brain hemispheres through nerve endings that control various senses (e.g., sight, hearing, and touch).

Here are some possibilities.

Have participants walk in place by raising the left knee, touching it with either the right elbow or hand, then alternating with the left hand or elbow to the right knee. Have them do five to ten of these together.

Reach across the front of the body with the left hand and gently pat the right shoulder, then alternate a number of times.

Raise the left foot behind the right knee and pat the sole of that foot with the right hand, then alternate. If necessary, have participants hold onto the back of their chairs for balance while performing the task.

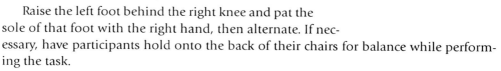

While standing up on tiptoes, reach as high up in the air as possible with the right hand while at the same time reaching as low as possible down to the side toward the ground with the left hand. Relax back to feet flat on the floor and hands hanging to the side, then alternate and stretch again.

Have participants pat their heads with their left hands and at the same time rub their stomachs with their right hands. Alternate.

Reach behind the head with the left hand, grasp the top of the right ear, and gently pull up. Alternate.

Have participants do some air swimming movements. Just as if swimming in water, have them extend the right arm and hand up and out, then down in a swimming motion while the left arm goes down, back, then up in a circular motion.

Rest the side of the face on either the left or right shoulder, extend the arm of that shoulder straight out, and point the index finger straight ahead. Then starting in the center of the body, draw imaginary lazy 8s. Do this by slowly making the form of the number 8 by rotating the arm up and circling to the right and down, crossing the midpoint of the body and then up and circling down to the left, then back to midpoint. Repeat the figure 8 several times, then alternate by putting the face on the opposite shoulder and using that arm and hand to draw the imaginary figure 8s in the opposite direction.

A note of caution should be given to learner prior to starting the activity. Give each person a choice of opting out of the exercise or participating to their own level of comfort and capability.

Stretch and Breathe

To help increase blood flow and participant alertness, have them stand and do periodic stretching and breathing activities. Build these in as transitions between key concepts, before beginning an activity to clear thinking, or to introduce an interim review.

Simply have everyone stand and on your commands (e.g., inhale and exhale) take slow deep breaths. Also, have them reach as high as they can above their heads, fingers extended, up on tiptoes, and stretch. Repeat 10 times, then have them relax, and drop their hands to their sides and shake them vigorously. Another alternative is to have participants bend at the waist and slowly reach as far toward their feet as possible. This can also be done while seated. The key is to get people moving and to do it slowly and in a relaxed fashion. Playing light, easy listening instrumental or nature sound music can assist in setting the mood.

● GETTING ACQUAINTED ACTIVITIES

The amount and quality of in-class communication between you and participants, and among participants, can often directly impact the success of a session. One of the key differences between **pedagogy** and andragogy is the experience level of adult learners. Providing opportunities for participants to share their knowledge and expertise is important.

Often, communication can be facilitated through activities in which learners have a chance to get to know one another, build rapport, and share what they know. Such activities are often called icebreakers when used at the beginning of a program because they provide a vehicle for learners to get acquainted and start to meld as a group. Later in a session, such activities might be called energizers, or simply activities focused on accomplishing a variety of course-related objectives, including enhancement of communication. As with other elements of the human resource development (HRD) process, there are many books and published activities on this subject that you can adapt or adopt. In deciding which is the most appropriate activity for your needs, consider the objectives of the activity, session goals, audience demographics, resources, facility, available equipment, and time that you read about earlier.

Rather than using the same activity each time you facilitate, build a repertoire of at least a dozen and alternate them when you train. This prevents you from becoming bored and appearing practiced and gives participants who attend many of your sessions some variety. This latter point is crucial in keeping learners stimulated and alert so that they want to learn and participate. The last thing that you need at the beginning of a program is for a participant to decide early that he or she has "been there" before and to turn off to what is being offered. If they are required to take part in activities that they have experienced previously, they could very easily shut down and even undermine the activity for others out of boredom.

MINDMAP 1. Getting Acquainted Activities

I'd Like to Introduce . . .

To provide a different approach for participant introductions, do a little advance preparation. Create a colorful flip chart page with borders or small art characters (e.g., flowers, a smiling sun, or cartoon) somewhere on the page. Across the top, write in bold capital letters, "INTRODUCING . . .". Spray the page with artist's adhesive or photo mount so that items will stick without tape. Display the page by the room entrance.

As participants arrive, give them a 3 × 5 colored index card (use a variety of colors to add pizzazz to the room) or a small piece of blank colored paper about the size of the cards. These paper strips can be cut in shapes (e.g., stars or geometric shapes, such as those found in the Tools for Trainers section in the appendices). Have each person print his or her name, title, and organization on the card along with one strength (e.g., knowledge, skill, or attitude) that he or she possesses related to the session topic. Once finished, participants should put their cards on the flip chart page. After everyone has arrived and is seated, move the flip chart page to the front of the room. Ask for a volunteer to come up and take any card other than his or her own. That participant should then read the name that is on the card by stating, "Good morning. I'd like to Introduce . . . ." The person whose name was read should then stand and the entire class should enthusiastically shout in unison, "GOOD MORNING _____." This participant should remain standing until the person holding his or her card reads the remaining information about him or her. Both people can then be seated. This process should continue, with people randomly coming up to select a card and reading the name and information until all participants have been introduced. After everyone has finished, you can say something such as, "What a great group with wonderful strengths to add to today's program. Let's get started by giving a round of applause." Remember that you are trying to create an environment of enthusiasm and excitement. Little things such as applause for acknowledgment can help by recognizing and rewarding while raising the noise and energy levels in the room. A nice side effect is that by clapping, participants increase their heart rate and blood flow to the brain.

It's My Birthday

This activity gives participants an opportunity to get acquainted and learn a bit of information about one another. Have everyone stand. Tell them they have 3 minutes to form a single line based on their birthdays. Once correctly in line, you can have them form into groups of three or four participants to get acquainted or for any other activity you designate.

Help Yourself

This is a standard get acquainted activity used by many trainers to help participants learn more about one another in a fun manner. As such, you may want to caution anyone who has participated in the activity in another session to not disclose how it is done and to play along. To start, give each person a 3 × 5 index card in bold numbers (use markers) and pass around a bag of shelled roasted peanuts, hard candy, plastic coins, or any other easily handled item. You can also use a box of facial tissue, or a roll of toilet paper or paper towels. As you pass the items around, encourage people to "help themselves" and take as much as they like.

Once everyone has taken a share of the item, have them count the number that they took and write the number on the 3 × 5 card. After they have done so, ask for a volunteer to show the number on his or her card. Once they do so, tell them that the purpose of the activity is to get to know one another and that they should tell who they are, their organization or job title, and bits of information about themselves equal to the number on their 3 × 5 cards. For example, if soemone took 15 squares of toilet paper or peanuts, he or she must share 15 professional or personal pieces of information abot him- or herself. For example, someone might disclose that he or she is one of nine siblings.

Truth or Fiction

Here's another classic training activity that you can use to help learners get to know details about one another that might not typically be disclosed during a training program. Have participants form groups of two to four people. Give participants 3 × 5 index cards and ask them to write down three things about themselves that others in the group do not likely know. Two of the items should be truth and one should be something they make up. The fiction items should be plausible. To get them started, you may want to share three items about yourself and have them guess which is untrue.

Next, have participants find a partner and get to know one another by trying to guess which of their partner's items is false.

You can also do this as a group activity in which participants form groups of four or five members, then each person does a self-introduction and shares what is written on his or her card. After they have done so, the members of the group should come to a consensus on which item was not true.

After all participants finish their introductions, you may want to ask randomly which were some of the truths and the untruths. This activity will work for any size group.

My Potato

This is a fun activity that can be used to help learners get acquainted or as an activity in classes on communication, presentation, or selling skills.

To get started, pass around a bag with potatoes in it and have each participant take one. After everyone has a potato, tell learners to take 3 minutes to get to know their potato well. Tell them to note unique characteristics about their potato. Once participants have had time to learn about their potatoes, have each person in turn stand, introduce herself, and tell what is unique about her potato and why she feels that makes it unique. You might also want to have her tell how her potato's unique qualities are like her. For example, "My potato has many eyes and I am constantly observing others."

If using this for an activity in a class on selling, you could have participants tell the features (characteristics) and benefits of each of those features to get them used to the traditional selling model.

Me Too!

Tell participants that they have 10 minutes to move around the room to find one or more people who have the same birth month that they do. If someone has no matches, have them find someone with a birth month that is closest to their own. Once they find a match, they should spend the remainder of the time getting to know one another. At the end of the designated time, have participants introduce themselves to the group, tell where they work, and anything else about them that they think others should know. It is best to limit this introduction to 30 seconds in case you have a participant who enjoys talking and being the center of attention.

Toy Story

Collect a variety of small toys (kitchen items, tools, or similar groupings also work well) and put them in a large box or bag that you pass around the room. Have participants reach in and select something. Give them a few minutes to examine their toys and then have them introduce themselves telling why they selected the toy they have and how its characteristics are similar to their own. For example, someone might get a small GI Joe or other military figure. They might disclose that they or someone in their family is or was in military service.

Let's Get Together

This is a great activity for providing some interaction when pairing participants or forming small groups.

Start by randomly selecting half as many playing cards from a deck as you have participants. For example if you have 24 participants, choose 12 cards. Cut the selected cards in half and mix them up. Randomly distribute one half of a card to each participant. Tell everyone to get up and move around the room looking for their other half. Once all participants are paired, have them participate in an activity.

An alternative to pairing participants is to have each person find the person holding the other half to his or her card, then those two participants would continue jointly to locate four other cards (eight other people who are holding cards) that will help their team end up with the highest poker hand in the room. Set a time limit of 5 minutes to do this and at the end of time, people who still do not have a group of 10 participants will randomly be grouped with others. The team having the best poker hand should be rewarded with small prizes.

Variations of this activity can be done by writing famous quotes (e.g., "Time is money," or "Waste not; want not"), capital cities and states (e.g., Tallahassee, Florida), or any other recognized statement, thing, or title that can be divided in two. Cut these in half and distribute instead of cards.

What a Zoo

As participants arrive for a session, attach a stick-on nametag, or safety pin a piece of paper, with the name of a wild zoo animal on it to their backs. Tell them that they have the names of zoo animals on their backs; however, they cannot look at what is written on the tag or paper, or have anyone read it to them. Once everyone has arrived, have all participants walk around the room meeting others and ask one closed-end question (e.g., yes/no or short answer) of each person they meet. The goal is to try to determine what kind of animal one is. They cannot ask open-ended questions. Instruct participants to shout out the name of their animal once it is known. If correct, reward them; if not, have the introductions continue. This activity integrates well into interpersonal communication, interviewing skills, customer service, or team-building sessions where better communication or effective questioning is an objective. Instead of zoo animals, you can substitute countries, flowers, states, or other categories. Just keep in mind the demographic makeup of your audience and choose things that everyone is likely to know.

Remember Me?

Here is a fun activity that can help participants learn each other's names as well as a detail about one another. I often use this activity when I teach sessions involving memory. To conduct the activity, have participants form circles of no more than nine people. Remember what you read about memory in an earlier chapter related to the brain's ability to retain approximately seven bits of information, plus or minus two?

Once in a circle, explain that each person will do a self-introduction by giving his or her first name and the name of one flower (or car, vegetable, tree, country, state, or whatever you designate) that she likes. The item she chooses must start with the same letter as her first name. For example, someone with the name of Lisa might choose a lily as her flower. After the first person has self-introduced, subsequent participants must repeat the names and flowers of each person before them, starting with the first person and going in order of previous introductions. For example, if I were the third person in a circle following Tom and Michelle, my introduction would be. (Gesturing toward Tom) Hello, this is Tom and he likes tulips; (gesturing to Michelle), this is Michelle and she likes mums; I'm Bob and I like babies' breath. When it gets back to Tom, he must name everyone starting with the person to his right or left (depending on the direction in which introductions went).

This activity builds on the concept of repetition and is helpful in getting people to know one another in a fun manner.

PUTTING YOUR BRAIN TO WORK: ACTIVITY

What are some additional techniques you know of to help participants get to know one another?

● BRING 'EM BACK FROM BREAK ON TIME

A major frustration for many facilitators and trainers is having participants come back late from breaks and lunch. Rather than spending precious classroom time delaying getting restarted or chastising tardy learners, build in some creative activities that can help motivate participants to return on time. Being late is often a sign that a participant does not appreciate the full value of what is being offered or that he or she is there unwillingly. Try to overcome such obstacles by making the session more interesting and breaking the flow with pre- and post-break strategies.

Start with the basics of either having a clock in the room or having all participants synchronize their watches together. If you have a separate break area outside the classroom put a clock, synchronized with the one in the classroom, in there too. Next, make sure you convey expectations of promptness and describe any reward systems you use at the beginning of the session. With these details taken care of, plan some creative reminders and/or rewards to get people back on time.

Make Time Visible

An alternative to using a timing device is to point out the return time on the classroom clock, then write the time when the break ends on a flip chart page or other writing surface that is left visible in front of the room. When that time arrives, get started.

> **BRIGHT IDEA**
>
> **Keeping Time**
>
> You can purchase plastic spin dial type transparent clock faces for use on your overhead projector. You can also purchase battery-operated chronological times (called Meeting Minders) that count time from "0" up or from a set time down. These can be used on an overhead projector to keep the designated return time visible to participants. There is even an audible alarm to let people know when time has elapsed. Both of these devices are available through Creative Presentation Resources in the Resources for Trainers section of the appendices.

Build in Productivity Time

In an era in which most companies are doing more with fewer resources, it is a real challenge getting people into a training session and holding their interest. There are just too many deadlines and other requirements distracting and competing for their attention. This is real life; face it and build in time for learners to handle administrative details during the day. You can do this by offering a longer break at some point during the session or by adding an extra 15 minutes to lunch. During your opening remarks, tell participants that this is being done so that they can plan to check voicemail, make calls, and check e-mail during those designated times rather than being distracted or building in their own extended break. The latter disrupts the flow of the session, especially when you have planned an activity that involves everyone immediately following breaks or lunch and some learners do not show up on time.

Schedule Returns at Awkward Times

Try selecting an unusual time for returning from breaks. For example, have people return at 10:07 rather than 10:00 or 10:15. Write this time on a flip chart in front of the room. The unusual time tends to stick in participants' minds better.

You may also want to schedule lunch at different times. For example, allowing learners to go to lunch at 11:45 instead of at noon can get them to eating facilities before the normal lunch crowd and will result in their not wasting time standing in line. When the latter occurs, many people often extend their lunchtime to make sure they get the full lunch period of 30 or 60 minutes. You might also want to give an extra 15 minutes for lunch to allow for productivity time and to allow participants to return to work areas for quick administrative functions. Of course, the risk of doing this is that their boss, co-workers, or customers will detain them once they get back to the office. That might also happen if they go back anyhow, so the extra time may offset such an occurrence.

Give Them Nourishment

By providing a variety of snacks and drinks in the classroom or nearby, you not only refresh participants, but also eliminate one more reason for them to leave the area. If learners have to go off in search of coffee or food, they will waste their break time and likely extend the break to compensate. A side benefit of having food in the classroom is that while participants remain in the area, they get to network with each other and you.

Do a Commercial

If you have noticed how television and radio stations pique viewer and listener interest, you already have one strategy for getting people back. Those sources announce throughout the day or during a show what is coming up, for example, "Stay tuned for three tips that will make you wealthy" or "Tune in at five for ways to improve your lifestyle." They give people something to look forward to and stimulate interest by providing a preview of coming attractions. You can do the same in your sessions by telling participants what is coming up right after the break. Make it something they will value rather than a passé statement said in a monotone such as, "When you get back from break, we'll continue to brainstorm." Instead, try something like an enthusiastic, "When you return from break we'll look at some ways that are guaranteed to reduce your workplace stress levels," or whatever your topic relates to. Also, remind participants of their return time and that you will begin at that point.

Have an Audible Signal

By turning music on as soon as a break begins, you fill the room with something to listen to. The music serves as a great timer as well, because when the break time has elapsed and you turn the music off, silence attracts attention and quietly signals that something is about to happen. Most people will automatically look to see why you turned the music off and will likely return to their seats. You can also set egg timers, projected timers, alarm clocks, or similar devices to signal the end of the break. In addition, you can use noisemakers, such as cowbells, whistles, noise spinner party favors, musical instruments, bicycle horns or bells, sirens, or any similar device for producing a sound that will attract learner attention. You can then calmly ask participants to have a seat so you can begin. This is much better than trying to get attention by yelling above a room full of people who are laughing and talking loudly while focusing elsewhere. Another strategy is to introduce an attention getting technique at the beginning of your session such as telling participants, "When they hear me clap three times, you should repeat the clap." When you use the technique, more and more people eventually hear the clap and join in. Soon everyone is focused back on you.

Start on Time

The only thing worse than some participants having to wait for others who are late is for you to delay restarting and waiting too. If you fail to start on time you are in effect saying, "We will start whenever you get back." That might encourage others to take their time in returning from future breaks because they will figure, "We won't start on time anyhow."

Even if you are missing a large percentage of your group, close the door and get started in some fashion. Doing so penalizes those who are tardy and rewards those who returned promptly. There are a number of techniques for doing this.

Hold a Mini Contest

Before participants leave for a break or lunch, explain that they will be given a puzzle, riddle, or other brainteaser when they return. The first person to get the correct answer will win a prize. You can even turn this event into a team competition if teams are formed early in the session. This can help encourage communication, camaraderie, networking, and teamwork while adding a bit of fun. There is also subtle peer pressure because for a team to win, all members must be present and participating.

Give Quick Tips

Similar to having a mini contest and commercials, you can encourage prompt returns by providing something available only if participants are present. For example, without telling participants prior to break, give those who return on time a few quick helpful hints related to the topic. These might be shortcuts (as with computer applications), suggestions for implementation or saving time (for work-related processes), or tips on handling irate people (for customer service, train the trainer, or communication programs). These tidbits should be above and beyond planned course content and should not be repeated for those who arrive late. If you are giving valuable ideas, the word will get to those who are tardy. They will likely begin to show up on time so they do not miss out on things that can ultimately make their lives easier.

Reward Promptness

Use a variety of creative techniques to reward participants who return on time from breaks and lunch. You can either give an immediate reward, such as candy or a small prize (e.g., inexpensive toy or organizational incentive items such as key chains or cups) or give participants an opportunity to earn chances toward a reward later. For example, you might give each person who returns on time a poker chip, a plastic coin, a playing card, or a carnival ticket (the kind for which you keep one part and give the other one with the same number to the participant). At the end of the session, you can have a drawing, or give a prize to the person who has accumulated the most items given, or who has the highest or lowest poker hand based on the number of cards he or she received.

An alternate to giving awards is to list team names on a flip chart that remains posted throughout the session. During the session, points can be awarded for activity completion, successes, or returning on time. The team with the most points at the end of the session can then be rewarded or you might have different levels of reward for the first, second, and third place "winners" so that all participants walk away with something and no one feels like a loser. You can even purchase first, second, and third place ribbons for something like this (see Creative Presentation Resources in the Resources for Trainers section in the appendices). Many people will hang this type of thing in their office and when they view it, or someone asks about it, they are reminded again of the program and topic. This subtly reinforces learning.

Use Peer Pressure

Social stigmatism is a powerful deterrent for many people. Most people want to be accepted and liked by their peers and others. You can use this phenomenon to your advantage by setting up systems that reward team participation and success. To do this, let everyone know that individuals who return on time will be rewarded; however, if an entire team is back on time, there will be an extra incentive. You will likely see those in the teams who value rewards shepherding others who would normally be delinquent back to their seats on time.

Imagination is more important than knowledge, for while knowledge points to all there is, imagination points to all there will be.
    —Albert Einstein

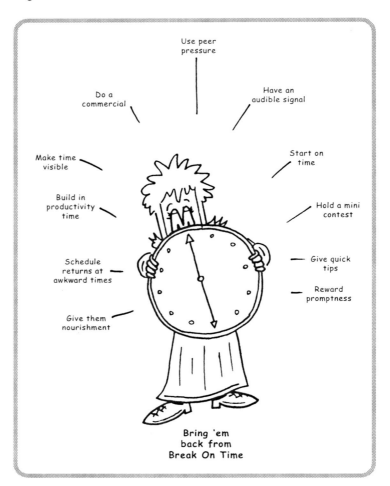

MINDMAP 2. Bring 'Em Back From Break on Time

PUTTING YOUR BRAIN TO WORK: ACTIVITY

What other practices might you use to encourage prompt return from breaks and lunch? _____

_____

_____

What rewards can you use in your organization that might help generate a fun environment while encouraging participants to return on time? _____

_____

_____

To recapture childhood wonder is to secure a driving force for grownup thoughts.
—Charles Sherrington

BRIGHT IDEA
Interim Review Status Check

To determine how participants perceive session content, stop after an hour or more has passed and form small groups of four to eight learners. Explain that you will give an introductory statement that each one in their group will complete based on course content. The statement can be anything you wish or you can use, "Up to this point this session is . . ." or "The most useful thing I have learned thus far is . . ." Tell participants that they cannot repeat something another person in their group has already said. As they proceed through the activity, walk around the room and eavesdrop to see what they are saying.

Through this type of an activity, you can help determine if there is an unresolved issue you need to address, what participants feel is important, or to what extent the session is meeting their needs. Make any adjustments in the session as necessary or reemphasize key points they seem to have missed once you have heard their comments.

● INTERIM REVIEWS

Earlier in the book, you read about interim reviews and how they can be used at various points to verify that participants are getting key information from the session. Placed at various points throughout your sessions, the reviews provide an opportunity to reinforce learning, cause a break in the flow of information, identify issues or points that need additional review or reinforcement, and provide fun while rewarding participants. While doing the reviews, learners consciously review material presented. This effort helps solidify the material in their memories so that they can later recall and act on it.

The following are some possible review techniques that I have used in a variety of training programs. After completing some of these reviews, you may also want to spend time discussing session content and discussing real-world applications as a class.

Play "What if"

Ask a series of open-ended questions that start with, "What if . . ." related to session concepts. Have individuals randomly answer the questions. For example, in a session on conflict resolution, you might ask, "What if someone disagreed with you and instead of saying 'Yes, but . . .' you simply listened before responding. How do you think he or she would feel?"

Peer Coaching

Have participants form pairs, then tell them that one partner is to pick any concept, process, or other component covered in the program thus far. The selected point is to be explained to the partner and applications for on-the-job use discussed. As participants discuss, casually walk around to listen in on what is happening. Offer appropriate comments, as necessary.

After one partner has finished, have participants switch roles and have the second partner repeat the coaching process used by the first. Once everyone has completed this exercise, randomly ask what concepts were covered and address any additional key ideas that were not reviewed. A group of any size can use this activity; however, if there are more than 25 participants, you may want to get help from co-facilitators.

Put It to Use

Depending on the session topic, you might be able to have participants actually practice skills learned. For example, if you are teaching computer, verbal or nonverbal communication, customer service, or similar skills, participants can form dyads, triads, or small groups and practice skills, then give one another feedback.

Ball Toss

Use a permanent marker to write key words or questions related to the session content on a large inflatable beach ball. Have participants form a circle and toss the ball as described previously, except that when they catch the ball, they read a question or term aloud and briefly answer or explain it to the group before tossing the ball to someone else. Each person must choose something not already covered by a previous learner.

At the end of the review, have everyone give a round of applause and then you can cover any key points that were missed.

Bean Bag Toss

Use games to review program content. For example, you could set up an area in the corner of your room in which participants could compete individually or as teams. One option is to use a bean bag toss in which each participate tries to get the bag to a designated target point after calling out a key term or concept learned in the session. Reward for the term and again if the target is hit.

You can either put a tape line on the floor and have participants attempt to get closest without going over or you can make more sophisticated ball toss grids with spinning scoring blocks available in many children's educational and toy stores. Give rewards based on the criteria you set before the toss begins.

Puzzlers

Pass out crossword, word match, or word search type puzzles based on program terms and content. Have either individuals or teams try to finish the puzzle within an allotted time frame. Have an answer key on a transparency, or another handout page that you can share with learners. You can reward winners, then review program concepts as a group.

Balloon Review

As you read in a previous chapter, you can use balloons to add color and a festive mood to a room. As you blow them up, you can place small strips of paper with key program concepts written on them inside. When you want to conduct an interim review, have each participant, in turn, select and pop a balloon. Have him or her retrieve the paper strip and randomly read aloud what is written on the paper. As a group, discuss each of the concepts read and discuss what it means and how it might apply in the workplace.

Easter Egg Basket

Similar to the balloon review, place strips of paper with key concepts on them inside colorful plastic Easter eggs. Put the eggs in a basket or bag that you pass around. Each participant in turn selects an egg, opens it, and then reads what is on the paper inside. Group discussion follows each concept read.

Spin the Football

Remember the game of spin the bottle from childhood? This is a similar version without the kissing! (You know that you have to be politically correct!)

To conduct this type of review, purchase a couple of small, inexpensive toy footballs or Nerf® footballs. Draw an arrow from the center of the ball toward either end on several sides. Have eight to ten participants sit in a circle. Form several circles if you have more than ten people. Starting with a designated learner and moving either left or right, have someone spin the ball in the center of the group. The person the arrow points to must give a key idea or concept that was covered in the program, and that no one before him or her has named. Others in the group must then provide additional information about the identified idea or concept so that a joint review takes place. Have participants continue spinning until everyone in the group has had a turn. During the review, if the ball points to someone who has already given a term or concept, the person to his or her immediate right must provide a term or concept instead. If that person has also had a turn, spin again.

Bring the participants back together and ask which concepts or terms were identified; add any additional ones missed.

Musical Chairs

Take learners back to early childhood learning days by having them play musical chairs as a review activity. Set up chairs in an oval shape with one fewer chair than you have participants. If you have more than 15 participants, you may want to form several ovals. Have participants line up one after the other facing the center of the oval, then have them all face either left or right. Explain that when the music starts, they should start to walk slowly around the oval until the music stops. At that point everyone should quickly try to sit in a chair. The person left without a chair must give a key idea, term, or concept from the program and everyone else then adds information about it. The standing person is then eliminated from the activity and can observe while one more chair is removed from the oval. Start the music again and continue this activity until only one person is left in a seat. At the end of the activity, discuss any key concepts not named by participants.

When choosing music, pick an upbeat song such as "Celebration" by Kool and the Gang, "I Just Want to Celebrate" by Three Dog Night, or something similar. Another option is to go to a teacher supply store and buy a CD with children's songs such as "All Around the Mulberry Bush." End with a round of applause from everyone.

Popups

This activity can be used as a vehicle for energizing participants or as a review. To do the former, start at some point in the room and proceed either right or left by having each participant in turn stand (pop up) and shout out any designated information, such as the name of a flower, song, state capital, tree, and so forth, then sit down.

As an interim or final review, start with any designated learner and have the motion go to either his or her left or right. When you tell them to begin, the designated learner stands, shouts out a key concept or terms from the session, then sits down. Subsequent learners repeat the process until everyone has popped up and been seated. Participants should be told that they cannot repeat any concept or term already given by someone else.

After everyone has finished, have participants give themselves a round of applause and then review any key concepts or terms that they missed.

Tic, Tac, Toe

To review key concepts using teams, you can use a variation of the game tic, tac, toe. Start by creating a transparency or flip chart of a tic, tac, toe board (get the tic, tac, toe template in the Tools for Trainers in the appendices). Write a clue for key concepts, terms, or issues, addressed thus far in the session, on one of nine numbered strips of paper. Answers are written on the reverse side of the strips. For example, assume that you discussed the contents of this chapter in a session. A clue for paper strip 1 might be " A technique used to have learners go back over key program ideas, terms, or concepts." On the back of the strip is the answer "interim review." After you create nine clues, fold the strips and place them in a bowl, bag, box, or other receptacle from which you can randomly draw them later. You will need separate sets of clues for each round of the game that you will be playing because of the number of teams you have.

Have participants form two small groups of six to eight learners. If you have more than 16, but fewer than 24 participants, you may want to form four small equal sized groups. Designate one team as "X" and one as "O." If you have four teams, you will need to play two rounds of the game using two teams each time. Project the tic, tac, toe transparency onto the screen. Give all players a hand clapper, bell, whistle, or other noise-making device and tell them that if they know the answer to a clue they must sound off first in order to have a chance to attempt to provide the answer for their team. Randomly select a helper (see Chapter 6) who will write in the Xs and Os on the transparency or flip chart that you created.

When ready to begin, toss a coin or otherwise randomly decide which team has a chance to answer first. Randomly select a numbered clue from the pile and read it aloud. Any player on the selected team can sound off with his or her noisemaker and then attempt to answer the clue. If he or she is incorrect, any member of the opposite team gets to sound off and attempt to answer. Keep going back and forth until someone provides the correct answer. You may want to reward those who answered correctly with candy or an inexpensive prize.

As you proceed, have your helper place either and X or O, depending on which team the participant represented, onto the tic, tac, toe transparency in the appropriate numbered box that corresponds to the number on the strip of paper with the clue. Continue this process until one team has three team symbols (Xs or Os) in a row on the tic, tac, toe board. Reward the winning team, then continue reading each of the remaining clues, for which any participant on either team can sound off, attempt to answer, and be rewarded for correct answers.

Once all clues have been read, start round two, if there are other teams.

Reward your helper and winners and have everyone give a round of applause. You may want to give everyone a small piece of candy as a reward.

Color of Knowledge

To prevent the embarrassment caused by your calling on a participant who does not know the answer during a review you can use colored paper strips. Create a set of colored strips from construction or other heavy paper for each participant. You will need one red, green, and yellow strip in each set. On a flip chart page or other writing surface in front of the group, list what each color represents: green = I know the answer; yellow = I think I know the answer; and red = I do not know the answer.

As you ask questions pertinent to session content during a review, each participant should quickly pick up and display the appropriate colored paper strip. You can then call on someone from either the green or yellow group.

Using a color coding system allows you to gauge general knowledge about topics, determine which participants are "getting it" and which are not, and will prevent you from embarrassing someone who does not have an answer. You can build in rewards for participants providing correct answers, and at the end of the review give everyone something, such as a piece of candy, for their efforts and so that there are no feelings of losing, feeling undervalued, or being left out. You should review any concepts not known by the group.

Let's Talk Trash

Have each participant write down on a piece of paper one key concept, issue, or term learned in the session. Once all participants are finished, have them crumple their pieces of paper into a ball and toss them into an empty trash can that you pass around. After collecting all papers, start the can back around the room and have each person select one piece of paper, then form a group with three or four other learners. Give each group a sheet of flip chart paper and tell them they have 15 minutes to uncrumple their papers, write down each issue on the flip chart page, and discuss how the issue applies to their workplace. At the end of 15 minutes, have a spokesperson for each group briefly share their issues and how they apply to the rest of the class. Reward the group spokespeople with candy, points, prizes, or whatever you are using as incentives.

Let's Toss About Some Ideas

An alternative to the Let's Talk Trash activity is to write key ideas, issues, concepts, or terms on pieces of paper crumpled into balls. On your command, everyone gently tosses his or her paper to someone else in the room. After all participants have retrieved a piece of paper, have them uncrumple the pages and randomly call on people to read what is on their paper. As a class, discuss the value of the idea or issue. If someone has an idea or issue that has already been discussed, ask if anyone has more to add to the earlier discussion, then move on. At the end of the review, add any additional key points not brought out and discuss them.

BRIGHT IDEA

Capturing Feedback

Many participants do not take time to provide valuable feedback on evaluation forms at the end of a training session. They are typically in too much of a hurry to leave and often circle rating numbers on the form, then rush out.

You can help increase the likelihood of receiving comments that can assist in upgrading program content and delivery. To do this, provide session evaluation forms at the beginning of the day rather than handing them out at the end. Following a quick interim review, have participants take out their evaluation form and jot down at least one thing that they have liked or disliked about the session to that point. Tell them not to worry about the rating numbers until the end of the

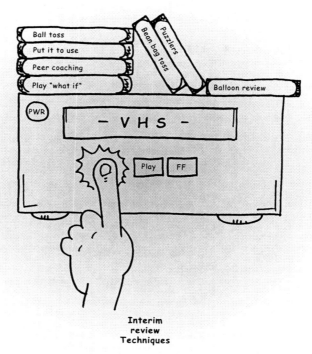

MINDMAP 3. Interim Review Techniques

program. Using evaluations in this manner potentially increases the amount and quality of learner feedback. You may want to have them use a pencil for comments because they may want to change something at the end of the session.

PUTTING YOUR BRAIN TO WORK: ACTIVITY

In what other ways can you get participants actively involved in a review of program material?

_____

_____

What benefits can you think of to inform participants why you are conducting reviews throughout a session? _____

_____

Nothing is interesting if you are not interested.
—Helen MacInness

● TEAMWORK ACTIVITIES

Keeping the action moving in your sessions not only makes training time pass quickly, but it also helps stimulate the brains of your learners. The end result is increased learning and retention. There are many books and articles on the market explaining energizers; the following are some of my favorites.

Team Lift

This activity can be used to grab attention, as you read about in Chapter 4, or as a group activity.

You will need five people for a demonstration. Four should be relatively small (approximately 150 pounds and no taller than 5'8") and one person larger (200 pounds or more and 5'10" or taller).

Start by placing a chair in front of the room facing sideways from the audience. Have the larger participant sit down. Position the other four participants so that two are in front of the person facing him or her and one is on either side facing the participant. Explain to the five volunteers, so that the audience can also hear, that this is a demonstration of how teamwork can allow people to do things that might not seem possible, or that they might otherwise not accomplish. For the demonstration, show the standing participants that they are to form a fist with both hands and then extend their index fingers as if they were going to point at someone. They are then going to connect the two index fingers by bringing the tips of both index fingers together. The people to either side will connect their fingertips under the seated volunteer's armpits while the other two volunteers will connect their fingertips under the knee of the seated volunteer. Tell them that on your count of 3 each person will simply keep his or her index fingers connected and, using nothing else, lift the seated volunteer straight up. Emphasize that with any successful team activity, all must act in unison and in a fluid motion without stopping.

Once they have lifted the participant, have them gently place him or her back into the chair. Have participants give a round of applause. You can then form teams of five participants and let them practice the maneuver if they'd like to.

To help protect from injury and liability, offer participants the opportunity to opt out of the activity. Also, monitor their actions carefully and stand ready to intercede, if necessary.

Knot Me

Form teams of 8–10 participants and have them stand in small circles facing one another. Have each person in the team reach out with his or her right hand and grasp the hand of someone across the circle from him or her. Next, have each participant reach out with his or he left hand and grasp someone else's left hand (not the person whose right hand he or she holds). Tell them that when you say "Go" they should try to untangle the knot of people without anyone releasing hands. Before they begin, designate two people who will release either a right or left hand and have them do so. Everyone else in the group should maintain a grip with both hands. Give participants 10 minutes to end up with everyone in a straight line.

If you plan to use this activity, you may want to inform women to wear comfortable flat shoes and slacks or shorts. Also, tell participants that if anyone has a physical condition that might be irritated by the activity of bending and twisting they can coach and cheer their group on. End with a round of applause.

Have a Seat on Me

Here's another simple team activity that demonstrates how important working together and supporting one another can be. Start by having everyone form circles with 8–12 participants per group. Have everyone face to either the right or left, feet together, and ensure that they are all about 6 inches apart. Tell everyone to place his or her hands on the hips of the person in front of him or her. Without releasing their grasp on the person in front of them, tell participants that on the count of 3 they should carefully sit down on the knees of the person behind them. Once everyone has done so, they can release their grasp and sit comfortably. To have everyone stand, tell them to again grasp hips and on the count of 3 stand up. In debriefing the activity discuss how similar support is necessary in the workplace to achieve success. Have learners applaud themselves.

Simon Sez

Remember the fun game, Simon Sez, that you played as a child? Adults often enjoy an opportunity to revisit childhood memories. In the game, you will give instructions, such as "Simon Sez put your left hand on your head." Explain that unless you say Simon Sez, no one should execute the action. Anyone who does is eliminated from the game. After explaining the rules, ask if there are any questions before you start, then go though a series of commands until only one person remains standing. Have everyone give this person a round of applause and then reward him or her with a small prize. You may want to give everyone a piece of candy or other treat for their participation and so they do not feel like they failed or are being punished.

Team Juggle

This activity is a good way to wake people up and get the heart pumping. It also helps participants to get to know each other's names and emphasizes the need for team communication. Start by getting everyone into a large circle. You will then need three balls made of soft material (e.g., Koosh®, Nerf®, or tennis ball). Explain that you will get the process started by calling someone's name, then gently tossing him or her a ball. That person then calls someone else's name and tosses the ball to the next person, who repeats the rotation to someone else. Tell participants that they should remember from whom they got the ball and to whom they tossed it. Explain that they cannot toss to someone who has already had it. Once the last person receives the ball, stop the action. Talk a bit about how participants felt the activity went and how it could have been done better. Ask how they might speed up the process. This is a good technique to tie into discussions of quality improvement, communication, creativity, or teamwork in the workplace.

After the debriefing, tell participants that they will go through the process again in the same order as before but this time you will introduce two balls into the circle. Toss in one ball to the same person who started the first round, then toss in the second to that person as soon as he or she gets rid of the first ball. Again debrief after the last person catches the second ball. Have participants give a round of applause for their success and debrief again. Finally, tell them that they have done so well that you think they are ready for three balls. Give them time to brainstorm on how they might improve their time further, then repeat the process using three balls. Debrief the activity by asking how what they just did resembles their workplace (e.g., doing more in a shorter time and sometimes without adequate preparation time; breakdowns in process or communication; or the need for teams to plan, coordinate, communicate, and work together).

Have everyone give a round of applause.

Team Grid

If you are not fortunate enough to have a carpet with a grid of squares woven into it, you can make your own with a roll of 1-inch masking tape. To do so, clear an area in the back of the room, or close by, that will allow for a grid that is approximately 8 × 8 feet with room to walk around it. Lay down your outer edges of a square first to ensure that you have a large enough area. To do this, measure eight distances of 12 inches apart along the top of the square strip and mark the edge of the tape at those points. Next, measure eight distances of 12 inches apart along the left or right strip and mark those points. Add the bottom and remaining side strips, mark them, then put additional strips of tape from one mark on the top strip to a corresponding mark on the bottom strip and then do likewise on both side strips. When you finish, you should have a grid that has 64 twelve by twelve inch squares (see **Figure 7-1**).

When you are ready for the activity, have all participants gather at the bottom edge of the square for instructions. If you have more than 10 learners, create two teams. Teams

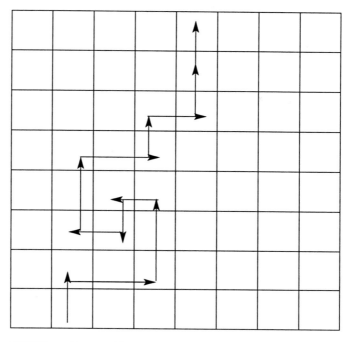

FIGURE 7-1. Team grid

should have no more than 8–10 participants. If there are multiple teams, you may want to create a second grid and find a co-facilitator so that large numbers of participants are not standing around waiting as one team goes through the square.

You can conduct this activity in a number of ways. The plan that I use is to create a small grid on a sheet of paper that corresponds with the tape layout on the floor. Next, I map out any random pattern from one grid square to the next that I choose. This is the directional pattern that participants must follow to cross the grid successfully and should not be shown to participants. The directional pattern can consist of having participants go forward, sideways, or back (see **Figure 7-1** for sample grid and directional pattern). The primary objective is for the entire team to move across the grid one at a time until every member has gotten all the way across in the allotted time.

To tie into real-world situations, I stress that time and effort should be used wisely and that we should learn from our mistakes so that we do not waste time and effort in the future. To emphasize this, I give each person 10 one dollar bills in play money. They can gain additional money through success; however, they can also lose money for mistakes. To emphasize this, they earn $1 for each new box to which they advance the team through the square and lose $1 for every incorrect step that they make backing out of the grid. For example, if the participant successfully got two squares into the grid before stepping on a third incorrect square and then correctly exited the square the same way she went in, she would earn $2 for the two correct squares. If, on the other hand, the participant advances two squares before stepping onto the third incorrect square, but then inadvertently steps on one incorrect square in attempting to exit the grid, she would lose $1 because of an error. Subsequent learners moving through the grid do not earn money for stepping on the correct squares identified by previous participants. Only those new squares that they discover as they move forward are rewarded.

Should one person run out of money, others on the team can choose to give some of theirs. I relate this to the workplace where time and effort are money and where working together to pitch in and help each other often leads to successes for the entire team. I relate all this to the workplace by telling them that we have to be creative and sometimes borrow resources from one project (person) in order to be successful in other areas.

Even though they work as a team, the person with the most cash left at the end gets a prize. By stressing personal gain, seemingly at the expense of the team, I stress that organizations often set up individual rewards for a team environment, thus frustrating and confounding employees.

To control movement, I typically sound a whistle or other fun noisemaker to signal incorrect square choices. I also take one dollar for each incorrect square that a participant steps into with both feet in attempting to move into or back out of the grid. If a mistake is made and the noisemaker sounds, the participant in the grid must reverse direction and move back out of the grid in the same way that was used to come in (stepping in the same boxes) before the next team member starts.

The rules for playing follow.

1. Participants have 45 minutes to get their team successfully across the grid.
2. Participants can have up to 10 minutes to plan their strategy before beginning, if they desire. This is in addition to the 45 minutes to cross. If they choose to plan for only 2 minutes, they can add the remainder of the planning time to crossing time.
3. The primary objective of the activity is to get all members of the team through the grid (simulating a workplace project).
4. A secondary objective is for team members to have as much cash as possible at the end of the session.
   Note: To preclude a number of members from having the same amount of money, I typically will use play money as a reward throughout the entire session so that they can earn for such things as being back from breaks and lunch on time, offering bright ideas, and answering questions. Otherwise, you may end up rewarding a large number of trainees at the end of the day. Depending on your budget and the type of prize you plan to award, this might not be a bad thing.
5. As learners progress, they are rewarded or penalized individually or as a team, as they would be in the workplace for successfully completing or failing to complete a project on time.
6. Each person gets 10 one-dollar bills in play money to start.
7. One additional dollar can be gained or lost for each correct or incorrect square stepped into.

8. Progression through the grid squares must be in the exact order as planned by the facilitator.

9. If a participant steps on an incorrect square that a previous team member also stepped on, $2 will be forfeited. This happens because they just repeated a mistake and did not learn from others. In the workplace, this can cost their organization money and other resources as well as lost customers and embarrassment.

10. Putting two feet in a square indicates that the square has been selected.

11. Once the activity starts, only one team member can be on the grid at a time.

12. Other than the person on the grid, no other team member can move beyond the bottom taped line.

13. If two members end up in the game grid at once they each forfeit $5. I relate this to not effectively communicating and to violating company policies, regulations, or laws that could subject them and the organization to severe penalties.

14. There can be no talking, although nonverbal signals can be used between the participant on the grid and other team members. This ties to the concept that communication often breaks down in organizations because e-mail and other communication vehicles are used instead of face-to-face or telephone communication. Also, many people work at remote locations and getting clarification of messages is sometimes delayed or difficult.

15. Participants in the grid should progress as far across it as possible without stepping on incorrect squares. In doing so, it is important to remember the wrong squares encountered by previous team members and to remember the route taken into the grid so that they can retrace their steps back out of the grid if they make an error. Otherwise they can lose money.

16. As each person successfully gets across the grid, he or she will receive a bonus of ten dollars. When all members of a team successfully reach the other side and exit the grid, they are rewarded with $20 each.

17. Once all participants of a team cross the grid, have them give a round of applause, reward appropriately, then discuss what happened and lessons learned. Relate all of this to workplace issues and answer any questions that participants might have.

As part of the debrief, I often talk about the importance of such issues as communication, quality improvement, time and resource management, teamwork, effective planning, follow-through, and creativity. An example of the latter is that even though I tell groups that they can plan and must not talk to one another after the activity starts, I do not tell them that they cannot write down patterns taken by each participant to ensure that they do not inadvertently step on an incorrect step a second time. Even so, few groups ever think to create a map. Related to this, I make this point about the workplace and how each person should be questioning why things are done and making recommendations for improvement.

A final note about the direction of travel that you set. Making it more complicated with many twists and turns will add time to completion and frustrate participants. Remember that the purpose is to learn and not just win.

APPLYING WHAT YOU LEARNED
Strategies for Engaging and Energizing Learners

1. What are some innovative ways in which you might stimulate your learners' interest?

_____

_____

2. How can you change current activities to encompass better participant-centered concepts?

_____

_____

3. What can you do to create a more physically active learning environment?

_____

_____

4. What techniques can be used to build in material reviews throughout your sessions?

_____

_____

5. Based on what you read in this chapter, what can you do differently to encourage networking?

_____

_____

6. How will get participants back from breaks on time in the future? _____

_____

7. In what ways can you better energize your learners or provide activities to invigorate them?

_____

_____

ENDNOTES

[29]Hanaford, C., _Smart Moves: Why Learning is Not All in Your Head,_ Great Ocean Publications, Atlanta, GA, 1995, pp. 98–99.
[30]Dennison, P.E. and Dennison, G.E., _Brain Gym, Teacher's Edition,_ Edu-Kinesthetics, Venture, CA, 1994.

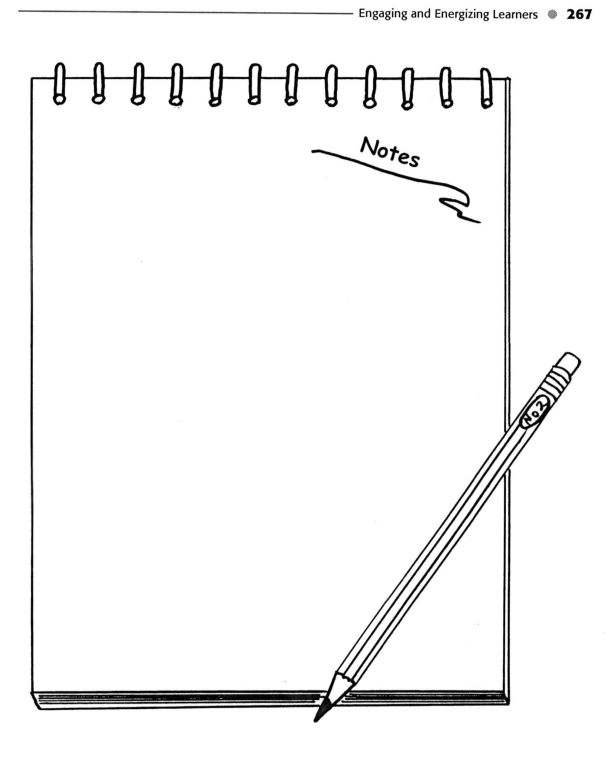

Making Your Visual Message Sizzle

There's no excuse for not being great.

Tom Peters
The Circle of Innovation

Learning Objectives

At the end of this chapter, and when applying concepts covered, you will be able to:

● Create a more professional image through design and use of written materials that communicate effectively and add pizzazz to your programs.

● Provide training reinforcement on the job.

● Use creative strategies for generating flip charts, that attract interest and send a message.

● Identify ways to use posters, charts and diagrams to enhance the environment and get your message across.

● Help participants brainstorm effectively using Post-it Notes®.

● Develop and use cloth boards as an alternative to static messaging in your classroom.

● Use electronic visual aids in an effective and creative manner that aids comprehension and adds pizzazz to your material.

Many trainers and educators make the mistake of thinking that their knowledge alone makes them good at helping others learn. Although what you know certainly can be a cornerstone for effective training, it will make little difference if you do not know how to engage the minds of your learners effectively. Words alone will not ensure transfer of knowledge to others. To facilitate better getting what you know in front of participants takes preparation and skill in a variety of delivery strategies. You must be able to use all of the information you have learned about brain-based learning and how to apply it in the classroom.

A common fallacy is that by your speaking or having learners read words, they will be able to absorb and apply what they encounter. In truth, only by engaging participants on different sensory levels will they be able to gain and retain information, concepts, or ideas. A simple technique for presenting information is to develop a theme for your session and the key concepts contained in it. Once you do so, think of words, acronyms, and visual images that conjure up mental visions and aid memory and recall. For example, if you were delivering training on interpersonal communication, think of words that relate to positive communication. Possibly come up with an acrostic device (e.g., an acronym) created from the first letters of key words, factors, concepts, or other program components. Use the device to present the model visually and to accompany the words. Add visual aspects (e.g., pictures, clip art, or other elements) to supplement and reinforce your message. You can use any graphic display as long as it is in congruence with the written message and adds to understanding rather than confusing learners. Repeat the theme you develop throughout your presentation. Hang posters, have participants write it, project various images of it, and create job aids to take back to the workplace. You can also place the theme on pencils, mugs, hats, ribbons, buttons, or anything else you can think of as incentive takeaways. Doing this reinforces the model or message each time your learners look at the items in the future. An example of this involves the *Basic Concepts* that are the core of a program that I developed for a program titled *Working Effectively with Others: The Legal and Ethical Aspects of the Workplace*. In addition to stressing these concepts throughout the 1-day program, I have learners participate in activities designed to have them apply the Concepts in class. They then have to explain how and why they used each of the Concepts during the activity. I also have posters with the Concepts displayed on several walls, give pocket-sized cards (job aids) to take back to the workplace for future reference, and I provide coffee mugs imprinted with the Basic Concepts. By bombarding participants with the Concepts throughout the day and afterwards, there is a better chance for absorption and application of the material.

You can take the theme idea to another level by presenting information during your sessions, then having participants brainstorm how what you taught applies to them and their workplace. Taking such an approach helps make the learning more personal for them and they will likely take more ownership of implementation. You might even either create a logo from the theme for the session or have learners do so. Use this logo as a watermark (faintly screened background image) that appears in the center of each page of printed handouts or on projected images (e.g., transparencies or slides).

By seeing and encountering program relevant information more often learners are more likely to retain and act on it.

BRIGHT IDEA

Control Your Classroom Traffic

I recently found a wonderful means of communicating classroom rules and other messages to participants by placing messages on the walls around the room. These messages come in the form of signs you hang that look similar in design to various road signs. Messages include the following:

QUIET: LEARNING IN PROGRESS

DANGER: TALKING OVER CLASSMATES CAUSES IRRITATION

SERIOUS LEARNERS ONLY BEYOND THIS POINT

NO SNORING 8:30 AM TO 5:30 PM

CAUTION: CELLPHONES IN USE MAY DISRUPT LEARNING

NO HOGGING THE SHOW

They are interesting, colorful, tasteful, and can be purchased from The Trainer's Warehouse (see Resources for Trainers section in the appendices).

● CLARIFYING WRITTEN MESSAGES

Printed messages can provide a comprehensive explanation of a topic supplement what you say verbally, and work in concert with visual images. Whether you put text in handouts or onto visual aids, such as transparencies, slides, or flip charts, the written message should be clear and concise. It should also be checked for correct spelling, grammar, and syntax. This is crucial because what you write sends a message about your abilities and professionalism. Improperly composed messages can actually distract certain personality types. Instead of focusing on you and your intended message, they will spend time editing and criticizing your written messages. They will also likely point out your errors on the end of session evaluation.

In addition to ensuring accuracy in your written messages, remember to format them in a manner that addresses brain-based principles that you read about in earlier chapters. Also, keep in mind that there are likely some people in your audience with vision or learning disabilities, and who may have difficulty reading certain textual messages. Make sure you address their needs, as discussed in Chapter 3.

Putting a Face on Writing

There are literally thousands of font typeface styles (types of lettering characters) from which you can choose. To get an idea of some of the variety available, go to your computer and open your word processing program. Look on your toolbar for the button titled *Font* (in Word, this is under the toolbar heading *Format*) and open it to display the names of various lettering style types. Review some of these to compare their appearances. You will find dozens of fonts and an array of style options (e.g., bold, italics, and bold italics), as well as different font sizes.

There is no definitive source that outlines what type of font to use in the creation of training materials; however, a good rule of thumb is to consider the following factors in selecting a typeface and style you will use for printed materials.

1. *Who will be in the audience?* Think about the age, gender, education, ability levels, and national origin of participants. Each of these factors can impact how well someone reads, and his or her ability to see and decipher what he or she sees.
2. *What is the purpose of the text?* For example, is it a handout for reference during the session and afterwards? Will the text be enlarged for a poster or other large image? Depending on how the material is to be used, the type of the font and the size of each letter can impact visibility.
3. *Does the content lend itself to use of a combination of fonts and sizes?* Typically, better visibility is gained through use of complementary fonts used for headers and accompanying text. In addition, headers that are a bit larger than text tend to stand out and are quickly identified.
4. *Will special characters appear in the document?* This is important because some font families do not contain certain characters (e.g., #, *, or numbers). If such characters are to be used, you will need to make sure they exist in the desired style.

Font Size

The type size used for text in most books and reading materials in the United States ranges from 10–12 points (one point measures 0.0138 inches). Most materials average about 12 points for text, with larger fonts (e.g., 14–24 points) being used for headers and subheaders. Larger sizes are used for projected visuals with large groups.

BRIGHT IDEA

Get Graphic with Fonts

For participant guides or workbooks, you can effectively use larger, fancier font types, as well as artistic lettering and graphics to add pizzazz. Take a look at **Figure 8-1a** and **Figure 8-1b** to see the difference made by adding graphic borders, clip art, and artistic fonts. You can also add color to the border and fonts and print on brightly colored paper to enhance the image further.

Typeface Styles

Generally, fonts used for training materials fall into two classifications—serif and sans serif. Serif fonts look like the text (Times New Roman) in this section up to this paragraph and have little finishing strokes at the end of each letter. Sans serif fonts look like the font in these sentences (Arial) and do not have the finishing strokes. These are sometimes referred to as "block" letters. They provide a clean, crisp look and as you will read later, work well on flip charts and projected visual aids because they are easy to read from a distance.

Typeface Appearance

Because most books, newspapers, and other printed material have a similar printed appearance, your learners will come to class with expectations of seeing a similar look. If you deviate too much with typeface appearance, you may actually distract participants and reduce their comprehension of what they read while increasing the time it takes them to read it.

Case Usage

ONE ASPECT OF READABILITY IS THE ALTERNATE USE OF UPPER- (CAPITAL) AND LOWERCASE (SMALL) LETTERS. WHEN YOU VIOLATE THIS PRINCIPLE AND USE ONLY UPPERCASE, IT CAUSES READERS TO PAUSE AND MAKES READING MORE DIFFICULT. To reduce participant anxiety and aid comprehension, stick with the standard practice of using a combination of uppercase letters at the beginning of a sentence or proper noun. Use lowercase for the remaining letters and words in a sentence. An exception to this guideline is when writing headers. Using all capital letters for headers can actually help draw attention and make the word(s) stand out from other text.

Bold and Italics

Other aspects of typeface style include making words **bold** and using *italics,* as I have just done, or combining bold and italics to emphasize key words or text. Throughout this book, I have used bold primarily to indicate words defined in the Glossary and italics to indicate the title of books, articles, chapters, and other referenced or important material. I have used a combination of bold and italics for certain text (e.g., quotes) and primary subheaders.

Color

As you read in earlier chapters, brain-based research has shown the importance of color in attracting attention. You can use this fact to draw attention to headers, special words, text, and graphics that accompany text, or to make certain letters stand out in your materials. If you do use color, remembering the following points can increase the ability of learners to follow your message easier.

PRESENTATION PIZZAZZ:
Adding Impact to Learning

by

BOB LUCAS
President, **Creative Presentation Resources, Inc.**

FIGURE 8-1a. Sample workbook cover sheets

Use consistency in selecting colors. For example, if you start using navy blue for headers at the beginning or a participant workbook or in printed material, use the same color for headers throughout the entire piece.

Participants have varying preferences for colors based on cultural and personal experiences. If you know of such sensitivities through your needs assessment or knowledge of the learners and their organization, select colors accordingly. If you are not aware of their preferences, do some research.

PRESENTATION PIZZAZZ:
Adding Impact to Learning

A Special Presentation

by

BOB LUCAS
President, **Creative Presentation Resources, Inc.**

© Copyright 1993, 2001
Creative Presentation Resources, Inc.
P.O. Box 180487
Casselberry, Florida 32718-0487.
(800)308-0399/(407)695-5535.
E-Mail: blucas@presentationresources.net
All Rights Reserved.

FIGURE 8-1b. *(Continued)*

Use of a few colors can aid appearance whereas too much color can distract and make material look thrown together and unprofessional. If you are unsure how to match colors, seek the advice of someone who has that knowledge (e.g., artist, marketing professional, or books on arts and graphic design).

Color can aid learning and appeal to emotions, as you read in Chapter 5.

Black ink works well on lighter colored (e.g., pastel) and white paper; however, it does not show up well on dark papers (e.g., purple and red).

Use red sparingly, as people who are color blind have difficulty reading large sections of text in that color. It is also puts a strain on the eyes.

Spacing and Margins

A general tip when creating written materials is to leave plenty of white space. This aids ease of reading and provides areas for writing notes. Most people use 1-inch margins at the top, bottom, and on each side of text pages. They also leave blank line space between key points and paragraphs. Headers typically have at least two blank line spaces above and one below so that they stand out. Subheadings usually have one blank line space above and below them. If you are going to bind (e.g., put in a notebook, glue, or staple) a participant workbook, leave at least 1½–2 inches on the left margin so that participants can easily read the beginning of sentences once the material is bound.

BRIGHT IDEA

Provide Note Space

When creating multiple-page participant workbooks or guides, leave plenty of white space on pages. Also, consider including blank pages that have a graphic border with a header *NOTES*. If you are using a chapter or section format for your guide, leave at least one of these per chapter. If there are no distinct section breaks, insert a few note pages throughout the guide. There is a sample *NOTES* page in the Tools for Trainers section of the appendices at the end of each chapter.

Text Length

Although there is no hard and fast rule on the length of sentences and paragraphs, your goal should be ease of reading, holding participant interest, and comprehension. To achieve this when writing, keep your average sentence length to between 20 and 30 words. Anything longer may require rewriting. Making sentences too complex limits their effectiveness and can confuse readers.

Related to sentence length, pay attention to the length and complexity of paragraphs. Remember that paragraphs should contain only one key idea or focus. You can reduce paragraph length by limiting the number of key points or **subordinate clauses**, which are separated by commas.

New paragraphs are set off by either indenting the first line, or by separating it from the previous paragraph by a single blank line.

Adding Artwork

There are many software packages and books that provide cartoons, pictures, borders, creative fonts, and other graphics that you can use to make your visual message sizzle (see Resources for Trainers in the appendices). Visual images can reinforce the meaning of your written message or enhance what you are saying. Use care to select images that complement or are in congruence with the words.

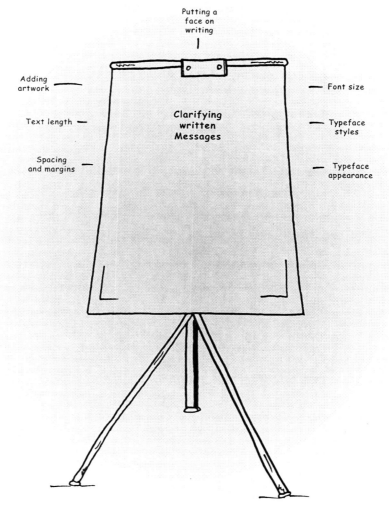

MINDMAP 1. Clarifying Written Messages

As you saw in **Figure 8-1a,** adding art to your cover sheets can make a difference in appearance. You may also want to consider including pictures, graphs, diagrams, clip art, caricatures, graphic bullets, or other visual images in your text. As I have done throughout this book, you can entice learners to your written message by placing graphics to attract attention or to reinforce a point. This often works because many people grow up reading newspaper comics or comic books. For that reason, they are already conditioned to seeing a combination of written and graphic messages. This can work to your advantage because they subconsciously see a cartoon or graphic image, which often attracts them because of fond childhood memories. Once they get to the image, they will likely read the text to see what it is about. It is then that you hook them and hold their interest through the text.

Obtain a copy of a participant workbook from any program that you or your organization has produced or purchased. Using the information you just read, do an analysis of the material to see what improvements or changes you night make.

What is your immediate reaction to the appearance of the material when you look at the cover or thumb through contents? _____

_____

What do you like about the material? _____

_____

What changes might you make? _____

_____

● JOB AIDS

There are many ways to aid learners during and following a training session. One economical means is to develop a job aid that can be used during training and as a reference by participants later. These reinforcements to learning come in many forms and can range from a single-sided page or poster to a guide kept on a bookshelf or in a desk. They offer step-by-step checklists for the procedures of a given process or task. Common examples of job aids include the following.

Posters

Posters show information, models, or diagrams of processes. They can be displayed in training rooms and the workplace for easy access.

Pocket Guides

Small pocket-sized reminders of key steps, models, procedures, or important information are often given so that learners will have an easily accessible resource in their cars, on their desks, in a purse, or in a pocket.

On-line Computer Help Screens

As a supplement to classroom or technology-based instruction, you may want to develop an on-line site that allows learners to access information by topic to assist in using software features or to refresh memory of information received in training sessions.

Reference Guides

Guides for workplace referral that contain key terminology can be designed to complement classroom concepts taught. These are handy quick-reference guides providing important information that someone needs to perform a task or assignment. They can range from a couple of pages to hundreds.

Flow Charts

Charts consisting of a series of intervals plotted on lines or to show a series of parallel lines can be used to illustrate progress, a schedule of events, time lines, a chronological sequence of events, or other paths from start to finish. These are especially helpful to remind learners about key elements or events and to assist visual learners recall information.

Computation Guide

Statistical, numerical information and computation charts, such as a multiplication table, can be developed for use by those who have to deal with such information or with formulas so that they have a readily available source of the information and do not waste time recomputing or figuring out needed data.

Sales Tax Guide

Handy guides to assist merchants in determining how much sales tax to charge for a sale can save many hours over a period of time, as such numbers do not need to be calculated.

People's minds are changed through observation and not through argument.
  —Will Rogers

● FLIP CHART MAGIC

Flip charts, sometimes referred to as newsprint because of the type of paper used, have been around training rooms for decades. They are a handy, versatile tool available to trainers, facilitators, and anyone else who needs a visual writing surface for ideas or information. They are great for quickly capturing participant comments, for creating prepared information and graphics, and for displaying material for reference later in a session. One of their greatest assets is the simplicity of use. Virtually anyone can use them to write or draw in a session. Even so, you should take the time to plan their usage and practice your technique so that what ends up being displayed is perceived as valuable by participants. Learning basic presentation techniques and using flip charts effectively adds another dimension to your professional abilities. They can be used in ways that are limited only by your creativity and ability (see *The Big Book of Flip Charts* in the Resources for Trainers section in the appendices).

When designing flip chart pages for use in your sessions, ask yourself the following questions:

Are they clear (meaning)?

Are they concise (well written)?

Are they simple (creative without detracting)?

Are they graphic (right colors, clip art, and images used)?

Do they add value (will they aid learning)?

Are they necessary (can points be made in other ways)?

General Tips for Use

Flip charts are inexpensive yet effective training aids for small groups of up to about 25–30 participants (depending on room configuration). They provide an easy way to capture key thoughts or to highlight information in small group settings. Many tips for using flip charts are found in *The Big Book of Flip Charts*[31] and are shown on the following pages. In general:

Make sure the easel is locked into position and balanced.

Place the easel so that ceiling lighting shines onto the front of the page and does not come from behind where it can cast a shadow and make viewing difficult.

Do not write on the flip chart and talk at the same time. Write first; then face your participants and talk.

Stand to the right side of the easel, as you face your audience, if you're right-handed; stand to the left side if left-handed. This allows you to face your participants and easily turn to capture key discussion points on paper with your dominant writing hand while turning pages with your free hand.

Do not block your participants' view when pointing to preprinted information on the flip chart.

When not writing, PUT THE MARKER DOWN! Playing with it or using as a pointer can be distracting and communicate nervousness.

Leave a sheet of blank paper between each sheet of text to prevent participants from "previewing" the next page as you discuss the current one. It also prevents damage to the next printed page should your marker "bleed" through.

Use large pointers made of wooden dowel rods with a black tip (available at craft, teacher, and home supply stores). You can also use arrows cut out of poster or other heavy colored paper or other props (e.g., plucked chicken pointer available from Creative Presentation Resources in the Resources for Trainers section of the appendices).

If appropriate, tear off sheets and tape them to walls for future referral.

Put two-inch strips of masking tape on the side or rear of the easel for use in posting torn pages.

Consider putting tabs (e.g., a strip of tape attached to the back of the sheet, then folded forward attached to the front edge of the page) on prewritten pages to ease in topic identification. You can then number or label topics on the tabs for easy location when needed. The tabs allow you to refer quickly back to pages later in your presentation and to turn them. Instead of tape you can also use the clear colored stick-on strips produced by 3M. Reference the colors in your lesson plan or notes so that you can easily find a desired page.

Always have extra markers and pads of paper available.

You may want to write comments or key ideas lightly in pencil in the upper corner of the pages. This allows you to refer to them unobtrusively, as you appear to be looking at the flip chart topics. Your participants will never know you "cheated" because they can't see the remarks from a distance!

A creative technique used by some experienced trainers and presenters is to use two flip charts in tandem (together) during a session. They either alternate prepared images between the two charts, or they have prepared pages on one easel and use the second to capture participant comments or to add more information to a topic during the session. If you plan to use two easels, I suggest numbering the easels (1 and 2) and indicating in your lesson plan or session notes which easel you will use to make a point. This can prevent embarrassing confusion during your presentation. The other key is to PRACTICE with your easels before participants arrive. I find it helpful to have a set of similar colored markers on both easels. This prevents me from carrying a marker used to the other easel and leaving it, only to be without it when I return to the second easel later.

Design Considerations

Lettering about 1–2 inches is usually large enough to view from a distance of approximately 30–60 feet (see **Figure 8-2**).

Use block lettering—uppercase for title or header lines and combined upper- and lowercase for text.

Limit the number of words to six to eight per line and the number of lines of text to six to eight (six by eight rule).

Use horizontal (across the page) versus vertical (down the page) lettering for ease of reading.

Use numbers, symbols, and abbreviations. Avoid unnecessary words.

If using vertical columns of information, use no more than three columns per page.

Keep your page simple and uncluttered.

Limit yourself to one topic per page. Don't dump everything together—it will only confuse participants.

Underline title lines and key words or concepts with bright colored markers to draw attention to them.

Use no-bleed type, water-based markers to prevent ink from going through the page onto the next one.

Use dark colors to write. Black, dark green, and dark blue work well. Red is good for highlighting key words or phrases and drawing icons but should not be used for text. That is because from a distance red is difficult to see and words appear to run together, particularly for people with deficient color vision. Pastels and lighter colors can be used for borders and art to add color and pizzazz; however, they should be avoided for text.

Avoid using the bottom one third of the page because some participants will have difficulty seeing it over the heads of others.

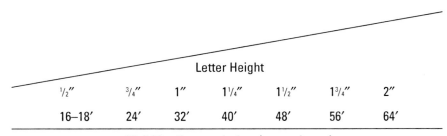

Letter Height

½″	¾″	1″	1¼″	1½″	1¾″	2″
16–18′	24′	32′	40′	48′	56′	64′

Visibility distance in feet (approximate)

FIGURE 8-2. Visibility distance in feet (approximate)

Flip Chart Page Layout

Flip charts that you create before a session can save time and help project the image that they are professionally prepared if they are planned well and neatly designed. No matter what you plan to put on your pages, always leave plenty of white (blank) space to aid ease of visibility. In general, it helps to leave a margin similar to that of your printed materials. Two inches of blank space on the top, bottom, and sides of a page gives your flip charts a clean, finished appearance. This image can be conveyed further by the use of bullet points or icons before each concept, sentence, or idea (see Tools for Trainers in the appendices for sample icons) Also, leaving about 1 inch between lines of text helps participants better read what you have written. If you are writing information or capturing ideas from participants during the session take your time and do not clutter a page with too much content. You may even want to leave the bottom one third of a page blank so that the participants in the rear of the room can see over the heads of others.

If you use captions on your flip charts to label items, follow the same guidelines that you see graphic artists use in printed materials. Put them in the upper left hand corner of the page. If they describe an image shown, place the caption directly under the image. This is helpful because people see such an over/under format used in various media and come to expect such a standardized use. Doing anything else might distract them from your message.

Adding Artwork

You can greatly enhance the appearance of your flip charts by adding relevant artwork or images to your pages. You do not have to be a great artist to include basic characters or images. Pick a couple of simple images and practice them on paper, then transfer them to your flip chart. There are many books available to help you learn how to draw images and cartoons (also see Tools for Trainers in the appendices section for simple drawings that you can copy).

When using art or images of people, always have them facing in toward text, rather than on the edge of the page facing outward. The reason for this is that your participants' eyes are naturally drawn to wherever the image is focusing. Plus, it makes more sense to have a purpose for the image (e.g., looking at the text). See the use of my caricature at the end of the Introduction to this book to get an idea of graphic usage.

Graphic artists have researched and fine tuned techniques for putting material on a page for best visibility and maximum impact. I suggest that rather than ignore what they know, take advantage of it and use the strategies to strengthen your own visual messages in whatever format or media you use. Some of the basic concepts to consider are balance, pattern, and unity.

Balance

When designing your transparencies and other written materials, consider how you weight the items on the page. From a graphics standpoint, information is viewed as either having *formal balance* (equal on both sides of a page, as in **Figure 8-3**) or *informal*

FIGURE 8-3. Formal Balance   **FIGURE 8-4.** Informal Balance

balance (pictures or more information on one side than the other, as in **Figure 8-4**). When you use only a balanced format, your images can become boring or monotonous because everything appears the same. This is because items are equally matched or displayed on the page so that the attention of your learners is not drawn one way or the other. To achieve such a balance, you would use an equivalent sized image on the left and right side or at the top and bottom of the page.

Unlike the balanced image, an informal perspective is achieved by having only one image placed on the page without a corresponding one opposite it. The effect is that the eyes of your participants are drawn to the image. This is one of the reasons stated earlier for ensuring that any image used in your material should have a purpose and compliment written messages. You want your learners to be aware of the image subconsciously and not to consciously have to focus on it to try to figure out how it applies to the message being presented.

BRIGHT IDEA

Maintaining Balance

To get the feel of formal and informal balance and what the concepts look like on your flipchart, draw and cut out a variety of images and shapes that you may want to continually use in the future (e.g., smile faces, boxes, rectangles, simple people figures, or whatever, such as those in the Tools for Trainers section in the appendices).

Spray them with artist's adhesive, and then practice placing them at various locations on your page. Next, try adding some lettering and move your images around.

Text should be evenly spaced and start at the same position on each page to present a uniform appearance. To maintain visual balance, consider leaving the same margin on all sides of text, for example, 2 inches from the top and bottom edges of paper and 2 inches from the left and right edges. When adding graphics, keep their size in proportion to the rest of the information shown.

Pattern

When designing your flip charts, the pattern of the word flow and image positioning can affect the way information is received and understood. The visual pattern you create is called an *arrangement*. The key in layout is to use the K.I.S.S. process (Keep It Short and Sweet). Too much information or artwork clutters the page and loses the interest of your participants. When laying out text and graphics, choose a pattern that resembles one of the following letters: C, O, S, L, T, or Z. (see Figure 8-5)

FIGURE 8-5. Flip Chart Patterns

Typically a C, S, Z, or T pattern shown in Figure 8-5 appears more dynamic and will likely capture and hold learner attention better. Whichever pattern you choose, remember that the words or message should be the focal point, not the artistic intent. You do not want to overshadow or diminish your written message.

Unity

The final aspect to consider when designing your flip charts or other visual material is unity (see Figure 8-6). By grouping figures or like items you can connect them visually. For example, if you wanted to use three large circles to enclose three key steps of a process, you can achieve unity by allowing the edge of each circle to overlap that of another slightly. Now, instead of appearing as three separate and distinct individual steps, the three appear connected or as one (Rule of Thirds). In effect you have subconsciously sent a message that this is a single process with three parts or steps. A good rule of thumb to accomplish this effect is that there should be more room between the edge of your transparency frame and a figure you are using than there is between the figures.

BRIGHT IDEA

Creative Shortcut to Drawing

If you are like me, you are artistically challenged. To overcome that deficit, I suggest that you find an image you would like to include on your flip chart, enlarge it to the size desired, and then copy it onto a piece of clear transparency film. Place a flip chart easel with pad directly in front of an overhead projector (a couple of feet, as necessary), then project the image onto the paper and trace the image (see Figure 8-7). If you want to wow your participants, lightly draw the lines of the projected image on paper; then when ready to use that page, trace the lines with the broad

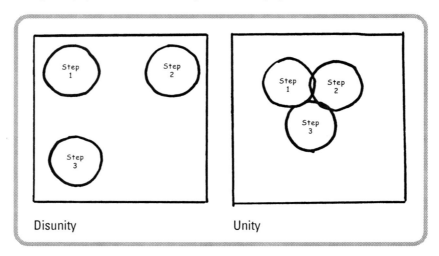

Disunity   Unity

FIGURE 8-6. Flip Chart Unity

FIGURE 8-7. Creative Shortcut to Drawing

edge of colored markers and make it look as if you are drawing freehand. Voila! Instant artist and your learners will likely be impressed with your talent.

Keep in mind that if you are using copyrighted images, you should obtain written permission to use them. Also, give the originator credit for the images. This is especially important if you are conducting seminars open to the public or for which you are charging a fee.

An alternative to using copyrighted material is to find a friend, co-worker, or participant with artistic ability and ask him or her to draw a few images for you. If you pay for the images as a "work for hire" you can use them in any way you please in the future. This strategy has worked well for me over the years. I have gathered a collection of caricatures of myself by stopping by caricature artist stands I have found in malls and festivals. I pay them to draw images of me in different poses, for example, pointing to a flip chart, or standing next to an overhead projector or behind a lectern. I now have art that I can use on transparencies, in handouts, or on flip charts.

Text Appearance

It is important that learners be able to read what you write. To facilitate reading, take your time so that your handwriting is straight and legible. You can purchase flip chart pads with line grids on them to help facilitate this or you can use a yardstick or other straight edge to guide your writing.

Also, as you read in the section on printed materials, use block lettering, upper- and lowercase for text and all capital letters for titles or headers (see **Figure 8-8**). These practices can enhance legibility.

Creative Accessories

There are many accessories on the market today that can enhance the appearance and add pizzazz to your flip charts. Here are some of my favorites available from various sources.

A	B	C	D	E	F	G	H	I	J	K	L
M	N	O	P	Q	R	S	T	U	V	W	X
Y	Z										
a	b	c	d	e	f	g	h	i	j	k	l
m	n	o	p	q	r	s	t	u	v	w	x
y	z										
1	2	3	4	5	6	7	8	9	0		

FIGURE 8-8. Sample "Block" Lettering

Pantograph

Many people remember the wooden or plastic expandable gatelike devices they used as children to trace an image or picture from one page to another. These pantographs can be purchased at art supply stores (or from The Trainer's Warehouse in Resources for Trainers) and used to enlarge or reduce an image from a page onto your flip chart when preparing for a program. At one end of the pantograph, there is a point for tracing along the lines of an image. The other end holds a pencil that moves along your flip chart page in concert with the tracing end. You can then use colored markers to trace the drawn image and add some impact to the flip chart page.

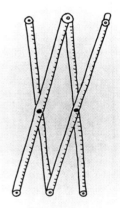

Pantograph

Projection Device

If you wish to trace an image from the page of a book, photograph, or other solid source, you can use a small projection unit (opaque projector) found at many art supply stores. You simply place the item to be enlarged or reduced and traced under the projector and turn it on. A disadvantage is that on some models the source item might be damaged from heat if you leave it on for too long.

Circle Devices

If you need to draw perfect circles of various sizes onto your flip chart pages, you have a number of options. Many are available in art and teacher supply stores. Others are as close as your kitchen (e.g., bowl lids). Another technique involves taking a standard

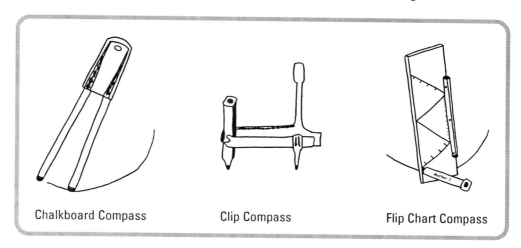

Chalkboard Compass   Clip Compass   Flip Chart Compass

FIGURE 8-9. Commercial Alternatives for Drawing Circles

wooden ruler or yardstick, drilling holes at every inch point, and using it to draw circles of the circumference you need. You do so by inserting a pencil tip through a hole, holding the end of the ruler/yardstick in place with one hand, then drawn in the shape of a circle. There are also at least four commercial alternatives for drawing circles:

Chalkboard compasses (see Figure 8-9) can be used to hold chalk or small markers when drawing on chalk or dry erase boards or flip chart paper. These can be found at most teacher supply stores.

Clip compasses (see Figure 8-9) are sold in art supply stores and have a spring loaded clip for holding a marker, pencil or crayon and can draw circles up to nine inches round.

Flip chart compasses (see Figure 8-9) are actually multipurpose drawing tools that have been modified for use as a protractor, compass, straight edge, angle template, and horizontal ruler. You simply insert a marker at one end, position it on your paper and start drawing perfect circles (see Trainer's Warehouse in the Resources for Trainers section).

Shape templates are available with various sized circles and can be obtained at craft, art or other stores selling school or office supplies.

Flip Chart Stickers

These colorful stickers come in a variety of shapes and colors and can be added to your flip charts to highlight or bullet a line of text or key points (see Trainer's Warehouse in Resources for Trainers section).

Fluorescent Tape

You can add impact and color to single words or entire lines of text by covering them with this transparent tape that allows the words underneath to be read. You can reposition the tape, which comes in green, orange, yellow, purple, and blue (see Trainer's Warehouse).

Flip Chart Border Tape

These colorful tape borders can add impact and color to your written message. Simply cut strips from a roll and attach them along your flip chart pages for instant pizzazz (see Trainer's Warehouse).

Error Correction Paper

If you have ever created flip charts before a session and realized that you misspelled or used the wrong word, you know the feeling of frustration. You can correct the problem by cutting two blank sections the size of the error from a blank flip chart page, then taping the sections over the mistake with transparent tape (from the reverse side of the page) and rewriting your message. You can also purchase rolls of white correction tape onto which you can write a new message after covering a mistake.

Double-Sided Adhesive Tape

Many organizations and conference facilities will not allow you to tape or pin things to their cloth wall coverings. To get around such restrictions, there is now a new double-sided tape that is made of felt and does not damage wall surfaces. Simply cut off a long strip, run it along the wall, and then stick clip chart pages along the strip. When the session ends, peel it off the wall, put it back on the roll, and you're done (see Trainer's Warehouse).

Magnetic Shapes

If you have a metal writing board (some flip chart easels and dry erase boards are) or metal strips around the wall of your room, you can hang individual flip chart pages and posters. To do so, either buy refrigerator magnets in shapes related to your session topic (e.g., cars, trucks, planes, or boats for travel-related classes, telephones or computers for customer service) or create your own. To do the latter, cut out various shapes (e.g., stars for service stars) from brightly colored poster board or construction paper and buy a roll of magnetic strip at an office supply store and cut small pieces of the magnet to glue to the back of the shapes. An added bonus is that you can award the magnets as prizes at the end of the session as a reminder of the training experience.

BIG Pencils

You can buy actual pencils that are several feet in length, along with other huge props such as Band-Aids, aspirin, notepads, and many other everyday items. Use the pencils as flip chart or screen pointers and the other items as props to tie to program themes (e.g., a Band-Aid for a big problem). I used to get these from a company called Think BIG!, which is now out of business. If you know of an alternate source, please let me know.

Cloth Panel Wall Clips

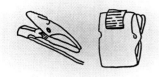

Cloth Panel Wall Clips

If you are training in a room with cloth wall coverings, you can purchase special clips designed for use in modular office cubicles. They have two long pins on the back that insert into the cloth and a plastic clip on the front that hangs onto your flip chart paper or posters. They are available at office supply stores.

Hang Tabs

As an alternative to tape, you can purchase plastic adhesive tabs to affix to the front or back corners of your pages. Simply peel off the covering and adhere the sticky part to the paper. These tabs come with a small hole punched in the top center so that you can either hang the poster by string or with push pins. The tabs are useful if you have laminated items and want to hang them for display in programs, as they will hold the additional weight that masking tape sometimes will not.

Corkboard Display Strip

In rooms that you use for training regularly at your organization, there is a more permanent means of hanging flip chart pages and other items. You can mount wooden or metal strips that have corkboard (the same as found on bulletin boards) around the perimeter of the room at a height of approximately 7 feet. When ready to display items, use push pins (the kind with the large plastic colored heads) or thumb tacks that you can get at office, school, and art supply stores.

Multiple Purpose Labels

These handy clear, multicolored, and white labels come in packets of 500 or more, and in shapes such as large circles, squares, and rectangles. They can be used to substitute for masking tape when you need to hang a sheet of flip chart paper. Two labels (at least 1¼ inch) at the top of the sheet should be all you need.

Flexible Curve

There is a tool called a "flexible curve" that is used by graphic artists and technicians who need to be able to draw special shapes (e.g., circles, curves, squares, and so forth). It is a 24-inch plastic covered, flexible, square metal core that can be bent in virtually any shape and traced. It is made by Staedtler and can be purchased in office supply and graphic art supply stores (see Graphic Arts Material in Resources for Trainers in the appendices). The tool comes in handy when creating a shape on your flip charts and other written materials. Simply form your shape, lay it against the paper, and trace around it.

In what ways can you add art images to your training materials? (Be Specific.) _____

_____

_____

Who do you know who can help you learn to draw basic characters or create them for you? _____

_____

_____

Cling-On Surfaces

A clever alternative to flip chart paper is a vinyl substance that comes in individual sheets mounted to pads like flip chart paper and in rolls. These sheets are reusable because you use dry erase markers to write or draw on them. They cling to virtually any wall surface through static electricity and therefore there is no need to use masking tape. Also, their flexibility and light weight make them handy when you have to travel to a site to conduct a session. Of course, with many creative products there is a downside. Because the surface is erasable, you cannot prepare and reuse the sheets unless you place them between cardboard or other storing material to prevent smearing (see Presentation Equipment and Accessories in the Resources for Trainers in the appendices).

● POSTER PRESENCE

Printed posters are an excellent medium for making or reinforcing a point, or for enhancing your training environment. Depending on your topic, there are a variety of ways to use posters in your sessions. For example, if you are facilitating a program on how to do cardiovascular resuscitation (CPR) you can hang posters around the room that show each step in the resuscitation process. Following a demonstration of the procedure, participants can refer to the posters as they practice the skill.

In classes, such as supervisory skills, customer service, or employee motivation, you can hang posters with models of behavior or inspirational quotes related to the topic around the room (see Motivational Posters/Products in the Resources for Trainers in the appendices).

Because posters are portable and can be colorful and graphic, they are effective tools for reinforcing or expanding learning. Through the use of pictures, vibrant colors, and appropriate word context, posters add another dimension to the room and tie into the brain-based learning concepts that you read about in earlier chapters.

A shortcoming is that posters cannot be seen from a distance. For that reason, if you plan to refer to them or they are an intricate part of the program, purchase multiple copies of the same poster and put them at various points on walls throughout the room. Another downside of posters is their cost and short lifespan, because they are not durable unless protected. If they become tattered or dirty, they can actually distract learners who focus on the defects of the posters. To extend their usefulness and protect your investment, you can have your poster framed with glass or purchase the large plastic sleeve protectors designed for flip chart pages. These come in 10 different sizes and have a clear, write-on matte plastic surface, with Velcro on the back edges. The Velcro holds the covering to the frame once you peel it back and insert a poster or flip chart page (see The Training Warehouse in the Resources for Trainers in the appendices). You can also purchase tripod easels developed for the display of your mounted posters.

PUTTING YOUR BRAIN TO WORK: ACTIVITY

How can you incorporate posters into your upcoming training sessions? _____

_____

_____

What are some key themes from sessions that you regularly facilitate that might be put into a poster?

_____

_____

_____

BRIGHT IDEA

Customizing Posters

If your organization has a graphics department and print shop with four-color separation capability, create your own posters to fit exactly into your sessions. You can also use outside graphics companies. Find generic pictures (most graphics departments subscribe to services that provide such photos) that blend with your program themes, then add either motivational quotes (see Resources for Trainers in the appendices for graphics software) or program models and concepts. You can even add your corporate logo at the bottom. Doing so sends a subtle message to participants that this program was actually designed for them and the organization, rather than being an off the shelf product. The latter can cause resistance in some learners.

INTERIM REVIEW

Getting Visual

Review all of the techniques explored to this point for making a message visual. Take out a pencil and paper and write down the one idea that you think has the most value and that you can use in your training programs. Also, list the reasons for its value.

● VISUALIZING THROUGH CHARTS AND DIAGRAMS

Charts and diagrams come in many forms and allow you to communicate statistical and other detailed information visually. Such an approach can supplement your textual descriptions and really appeal to analytical and visual learners. Many managers who are pressed for time typically like and use charts and diagrams to portray things such as numbers, trends, dollars, percentages, and patterns.

The key to using charts and diagrams effectively revolves around your ability to design and explain what you create, as well as the ability of your audience to understand it. There are several excellent books explaining the different kinds of charts and diagrams, their use, and how to create them on the market (see Resources for Trainers in the appendices). According to Zelancy,[32] "Choosing the correct chart form depends completely on your being clear about what *your* message is. It is not the data—be they dollars, percentages, liters, yen, etc.—that determines the chart. It is not the measure—be it profits, return on investment, compensation, etc.—that determines the chart. Rather, it is *your* message, what *you* want to show, the specific point *you* want to make."

The nice thing about charts and diagrams is that many word processing and other computer programs will create the image for you after you input the data. All you have to do is hit the "Create" button and the computer will do the rest.

You can display your charts and graphs on flip charts, posters, in handout materials, on job aids, and in slide shows. These help reinforce your message.

● PICTURING WITH STICKY NOTES

Sticky notes are a terrific invention, which trainers and facilitators adapt for many uses. In addition to using them to capture small bits of information from participants during activities, they can be used to brainstorm, storyboard ideas, and do many wonderful team activities. They are easy and fast to use and can be repositioned as necessary, without the use of any other materials. They also tie directly into research that has found a value in using graphic organizers to communicate knowledge visually. Bromley, Irwin-De Vitis, and Modlo reference numerous studies that support the concept that when such tools have been used in schools, comprehension and recall of information increased.[33]

Here are a few of the ways that I use sticky notes in my training programs. *Brainstorming* can be greatly enhanced in small groups through the use of the small sticky pads that allow participants to jot down a quick point and add it to others that are posted on a wall, flip chart, dry erase board, or blackboard. To conduct such an activity, write the theme, issue, or objective for the brainstorming at the top of the solid writing surface or on a piece of paper taped to a wall. Tell learners how much time they have to brainstorm, remind them of the rules of brainstorming by posting a flip chart page or poster containing the rules on the wall (see Sample Brainstorming Guidelines in Tools for Trainers in the appendices), pass out pads of the notes and a pencil, and have them begin. Suggest to participants that they lump or group like or related items after they capture all the ideas from group members. They can then generate solid ideas or suggestions by combining similar concepts into one solid idea or recommendation. Following the brainstorming, have each leader share his or her group's ideas with the rest of the class. A nice thing about using sticky notes is that you do not have to worry about markers bleeding through and staining the surface or paper underneath.

Prioritizing Ideas

Groups sometimes have difficulty with problem-solving because a consensus must be attained. To make it easier, I have everyone write down their ideas, then through a voting process, prioritize what everyone wrote. They do this by using multicolored stick-on labels (the small ones purchased through office supply stores in packets). Give participants three labels and tell them they can vote for any of the posted items on the board that they like by placing one or all of their stickers by their favorite idea. The top two vote winning ideas get priority and are used for whatever the purpose was (e.g., goals for the coming year, ideas to assign to a committee, or issues for further discussion). As facilitator, I get one sticker and can vote for one of the top two options to break a tie, if necessary.

Identifying Relationships and Problem-Solving

Sticky notes can aid in showing relationships between common issues, situations, components, and so forth. To do this, have participants write down all the parts or aspects of an issue. For example, assume sales are down in your organization. Have learners write down any possible contributing cause (e.g., deliveries are slow, there are delays getting component parts to build a product that you sell, there have been problems with the computer database used for fulfillment and tracking orders, the economy is sluggish, several new salespeople were hired this year, or a new competitor just surfaced and is marketing heavily). Once the possible causes are identified and written onto sticky notes, start grouping similar items. For example, in the list you just read, deliveries, the computer database, and the new salespeople are internal issues controlled by the organization; the remainder are outside of organizational control. Once you have lumped common elements, set objectives for each group and have them set about identifying how to address the issues. Perhaps one group of participants would work on internal and one group on external issues.

● CLOTH BOARD COMMUNICATION

These are items that have been around in schools and military programs for years. They are sometimes called "flannel boards" because of the material that covers them. You can display poster board strips with images, words, or sentences on them just as you would on a flip chart easel.

I occasionally use cloth boards as a break from traditional training aids to add variety. You can make one by buying a piece of thin plywood; a very thick piece of cardboard from a box will also work. Cut it about the size of a flip chart easel backing (approximately 30 × 36 inches). Next, go to a store that sells sewing cloth and buy a piece of black or navy blue felt, flannel, or other rough weave material that is large enough to cover the entire board with about 4–6 inches extra on each side and end. This will serve as your display surface. Wrap the material so that it is smooth on the front and so that the edges overlap to the back. Affix the edges with staples or strong tape (e.g., duct, wide electrical, strapping, or packing tape works well). Once you have finished place the board either on a flip chart easel, chalk/marker tray of a writing board, or on a chair placed on a table to allow easy viewing (see Figure 8-10).

To add text and images to your board, cut strips of poster board or flash card sized pieces for printing your message in large letters (minimum of 2 inches high) using the guidelines for flip charts that you read. Use a separate strip for each thought, topic, sentence, key word, or idea.

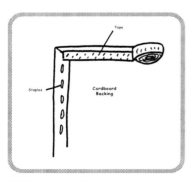

FIGURE 8-10. Clothboard Construction

Use glue to attach a 1-inch piece of barbed (adhesive portion) Velcro strip to each corner of the cards on the back. You can get Velcro at office and sewing supply stores.

You are now ready to present. As you make a point or discuss a topic, attach the appropriate card to the cloth board just as if you were using the **revelation technique** of uncovering one item at a time on the flip chart or an overhead transparency. You can also cut out brightly colored shapes that tie to the program theme or to represent key concepts or words and place them on the edges, much like you would use clip art on flip charts or transparencies.

An alternative to a permanent cloth board is to use stick pins to hang a piece of cloth on the wall, thus saving your flip chart easel or other solid display surface for other purposes.

BRIGHT IDEA

Participant Presentations with a Cloth Board

To add variety to learner presentation of ideas following a brainstorming or team activity, give them colorful poster board strips and markers to write down their ideas. Have them use a cloth board rather than a flip chart page to present their ideas to the class. Rather than use Velcro, they can use a couple of pieces of masking tape rolled into a circle and attached to the back of their cards (the wider 2-inch tape has more sticking surface and holds better to the cloth).

● ELECTRONIC MESSAGING

Technology has created many new and exciting ways to deliver messages in your sessions. In addition to the old standby equipment described earlier in this chapter, there are now pieces of equipment that allow you to expand your delivery repertoire and get information to your participants creatively.

Electronic White Boards

Similar to traditional dry erase boards, electronic white board devices allow you to write with dry erase markers so that your learners can see and follow along with your message. They are lightweight and mobile like a flip chart easel. The twist is that some of the electronic boards allow you to save what you have written to a computer as either a BMP, JPEG, or TIFF image file. You can also print copies of what you have written or drawn onto standard 8.5 × 11 inch paper. You can then make copies and give participants a copy for future reference. The benefit of this technique is that your listeners who prefer not to take notes can focus on your message and not on writing. Of course, as you read in earlier chapters, taking notes visually reinforces a message and is helpful for visual learners. At any rate, the new electronic boards are an additional tool in your presentation toolbox that might be considered in certain situations (see Resources for Trainers in the appendices for information sources or log onto the Internet and enter Electronic White Boards).

Poster Printers

Developed a number of years ago, these convenient devices can create posters and banners (up to 100 feet) from a computer connected directly to the unit or from a piece of paper. Posters can be created in varying sizes (from 17 to 36 inches).

Many improvements have been made since the first models surfaced in the early 1990s. A nice advantage of the newer models is that they can print directly from your computer. If you have poor handwriting or cannot draw, this allows you to use a variety of creative software to generate flip chart pages with fancy borders, fonts, or clip art and then print poster sized sheets that you can mount and hang (see The Big Book of Flip Charts in the Resources for Trainers in the appendices for ideas on hanging and storing your flip charts). Newer models also allow the use of paper that is heat resistant and can be laminated, if desired. Plus, various colors of ink are available, including metallic and fluorescent. You can also get paper that is bright yellow and has print images, as well as letters in black ink and vinyl-backed adhesive paper. These can be used for more permanent displays. For example, you may want to make quotes or important information stand out while adding color to your room. Check the Resources for Trainers in the appendices and the Internet for more information.

● PROJECTING A POSITIVE IMAGE

Delivering information to larger groups or to those in rooms that are longer than 30 feet from where you are presenting requires visual aids other than flip charts. Projected visuals can satisfy this requirement. Overhead projectors, computer-generated slide shows, or videos on large screens can make your message visible from further away. The key in using these tools is to plan well and to position your screen correctly so that it can be seen. Also, practice using the actual equipment you will have during your session before participants arrive so that you are thoroughly familiar with it.

Opaque Projectors

Many technological improvements have been made in this old classroom standby since the 1950s; however, the same value comes through. You can project images from actual items, pictures, books, art, or any printed source. Your participants will see the same thing on a screen that you are seeing on the image under the projector base.

Some of these projectors are now designed to substitute as an overhead projector by making a minor adjustment; thus you get two pieces of equipment for the price of one.

Overhead Projectors

Overhead projectors are a versatile staple tool for many trainers all over the world. They are simple to use, relatively inexpensive, and durable. They are also easily adapted to project a variety of images. According to HOPE Reports, published by an organization that covers all aspects of the media-AV communications industry, "The first overhead projector used a 3¼" × 4" slide on a flat stage . . . Victorlight designed the VisualCast, a large classroom overhead projector (known as the 'monster') first used by the U.S. Army. In 1945–46 a New York dealer asked the Charles Beseler Co., which made 3¼" × 4" overhead projectors, to design one with a round 8" diameter stage. That became known as the Vu-Graph."[34]

3M Corporation claims the bragging rights to the development of the Fresnel Lens early in the 1960s. This lens is a key component in the overhead projector as we know it today and helped launch an entire line of products. Since the 1960s, trainers and educators have found dozens of ways to incorporate the overhead projector into program delivery.

Overhead Projector Usage Tips

The overhead projector is a very user friendly and effective training aid when incorporated correctly into your sessions. Just like any piece of equipment, however, you should familiarize yourself with the actual projector you'll be using because different models vary slightly in design and operation. You should also rehearse using actual transparencies that you'll be using in the workshop. Some basics of usage include:

Select the appropriate type of projector. I find that models that project the light from underneath the transparency work best. The alternative is a unit that bounces light onto the transparency, then back up to a mirror (portable types). The latter can create light glare in your eyes and prevents viewing of uncovered lines of text when using the revelation technique. The portable type projector also prohibits the use of the older LCD projection panels (no longer manufactured) if you plan to show a computer-generated slideshow.

ALWAYS ensure that you have a spare bulb or backup projector before starting your session.

Have at least a 25-foot extension cord with multiple outlets handy in case there is no electrical outlet near the projector setup area.

Before participants arrive, check the focus of the projector by projecting a transparency image and viewing it from different locations in the room.

Position the projector to allow a clear line of vision to the screen by participants.

Ensure that the screen is set up at a 90-degree angle to avoid the keystone effect.

Dim lights nearest the screen to ensure a sharper image and reduce glare on the projected image.

Do not stand between participants and the projection screen, or between the projector and the screen.

When using a transparency, paraphrase the information by reading from the transparency, not the screen. This keeps you facing your audience.

If you want to emphasize a key item, point to the transparency with a pen, pointer, or other similar item rather than trying to stretch to reach it on the screen. Once you've finished with the pointer, PUT IT DOWN! If you are nervous, I suggest you not use a laser pointer because the dancing red dot on the screen will certainly let the audience know of your anxiety while distracting participants.

Time the usage of transparencies so that you display only those items you are actually addressing. A maximum suggested length of viewing time is about 3–4 minutes. The minimum time for projection is 1 minute to allow notetaking.

If you find that the projected topic generates considerable conversation, turn the projector off (remember—light attracts attention and so does the buzz of the motor), discuss the issue, then turn the projector on again. This also helps extend bulb life.

Have backup training aids (e.g., flip charts, handouts, pictures, job aids, or posters) available in the event your projector stops functioning. This allows you to project an air of professionalism as you continue with you presentation using the alternate aids without excuses, and as if nothing happened.

Transparency Design Considerations

Like any other part of your presentation, you want to ensure that your transparencies are designed to send a powerful message that reinforces what you say. Many of the rules for flip chart design and art usage also apply when creating material for projection. The following are some specific considerations when preparing materials for use with a projector.

Prepare an introductory transparency for you presentation. You might have a graphic, program title, your name, corporate logo, date, or other information on it.

Transparencies should follow a standard format, all printed either vertically or horizontally. Switching between horizontal and vertical formats can be frustrating for you and your participants. Because most overhead projector models have a glass surface that is approximately 10 inches wide and high, horizontal formats work best. In addition, the vertical format does not work well because the size of a normal transparency is 8.5 × 11 inches. Using this entire area for text causes portions of the message to be off the viewing surface and the transparency has to be moved up or down to get the image onto the screen.

Sans serif ¼-inch lettering (approximately 30-point font) is usually large enough for text. Title lines should be slightly larger to make them stand out. A quick rule of thumb— place the page of text that you will use to make the transparency on the floor and stand above it on a chair. If you can read it easily, it's probably large enough for about 40–50 feet.

When preparing projection transparencies, use uppercase for title lines and for the first letter of a word on a new topic line or for proper nouns, followed by lowercase for text. This makes reading easier.

Use bold lettering to make the words stand out on the screen.

Limit transparencies to eight to ten lines of text and to six to eight words per line to avoid a cluttered look.

Add color to your transparencies by having the title line a different color from that of the text. You can use any dark color or even red to make the title stand out.

Try choosing two dark colors (e.g., dark green and dark blue) for use on text lines. For each new point made (line of text), use an alternate color. For example, point one would be in blue, point two in green, point three in blue, and so forth. Stay away from red for text lines because it is difficult to read, especially from a distance or for people who have red color blindness.

Consider using color transparency film (acetate). You can purchase in blue, green, yellow, and red; however, as you have seen in other chapters, red is difficult to see and should be kept to a minimum when possible.

To add some additional color to clear transparency film over the top of your transparency, some companies sell special acetate. You can also cut out shapes and fit the color around your text to give some interesting variety. For example, you can cut a large star shape from the center of a piece of yellow acetate and then fit the remaining acetate (with the open star shape in the middle) on top of a transparency so that the words appear to be inside the star. To do this, mount your clear transparency to a cardboard transparency frame, then tape the color cutout over it.

Adding Art

Include graphics in the form of clip art, pictures, graphs, charts, or other images.

Use colorful borders or simple background templates to help make transparencies look more finished and professional. If you use them, choose one format for use on all transparencies to show consistency.

When placing a figure of a person onto a transparency, make sure that the person is facing toward the text rather than off the side of the film. This will help direct learner attention toward the text rather than away from it.

Use the Rule of Thirds that you read about earlier to determine where to place an image on your transparencies.

Creative Usage Alternatives

As noted previously, there are a number of ways to use the overhead projector. The following are additional things you can do to increase the usefulness and effectiveness of the overhead projector.

Show one piece of information at a time. Use the revelation technique to accomplish this. To do this, place a piece of blank white copier paper beneath the transparency on the viewing surface. By placing the paper under the transparency instead of on top, the weight of the film holds the paper in place as you near the bottom. This prevents the paper from falling off and revealing the last couple of lines prematurely. As you are ready to discuss an item, move the paper down slightly to reveal that point only. When ready to show additional elements of your message, move the paper down further until you have covered all parts of the transparency.

Instead of turning the projector off after each transparency is shown and a new one is put into place, you can cover the entire glass surface with a piece of dark paper, for

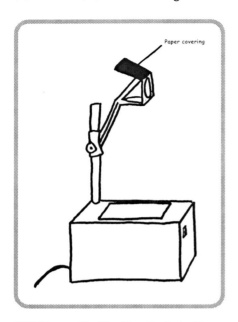

FIGURE 8-11. Blocking Your Projected Image

example, construction or cardboard backing from a writing pad. This prevents projected white light which can distract from your comments; however, you still contend with the noise of the motor. On older projector models you also have to deal with air from the cooling fan, which can blow paper items off your instructor's table and can overheat, causing the paper to become hot and potentially ignite. Some people prefer this method; however, remember what you read in earlier chapters regarding how light and noise can distract learners.

Another alternative to turning the projector off is to tape a small piece of paper to the top of the lens cover where the mirror is located (Figure 8-11). When you are projecting an image, flip this paper up and out of the way. When you do not want participants to look at the screen, flip the paper down. If you decide to use this technique, be aware that several problems exist with it. The first is that paper (especially dark) left over the magnifying lens for a long time will ignite. (Remember what happened to leaves when, as a child, you held a magnifying glass over them and allowed the sun to shine through? The same is true of concentrated light from the projector through the lens onto the paper cover.) A second problem is that while the screen light and image are blocked, the blinding light from the bulb is reflecting up into your eyes and is also visible to learners. Finally, the noise of the motor can be distracting.

Some presenters like to add another dimension to their presentation by setting up two overhead projectors or using a combination of overhead projector and slide projector or video projector. This is sometimes done when there are co-presenters during a session. When using two pieces of equipment, screens are typically placed to the right and left of the presenter in opposite corners of the room. The key to success when using multiple training aids is PRACTICE. Make notes in your lesson plan or session guide related to which piece of equipment you should be using and refer to the notes as you proceed so that you do not get confused.

Toys and Accessories for Your Overhead Projector

There are a variety of materials and training aids that you can adapt to use with your overhead projector. Each can add a different element of creativity and pizzazz. Here are some that I have found over the years.

Pointers

If you need a pointer for use on your projector's glass surface to draw attention to a specific line of text or word as you talk about it, ensure that it will not roll off. Rather than using round pencils, try a more creative approach. Purchase a small pointer in the shape of an arrow or finger, or create your own out of construction or other heavy paper (see Tools for Trainers in the appendices for a template that can be copied and cut out). Another creative alternative is to collect the little plastic indicators that you see in some steak houses (the ones that say rare, medium, or well done) or the swizzle sticks from drinks in bars, restaurants, and on airplanes. You can also go to an arts and crafts store to buy plastic cake decorations in various shapes, or you might even use the plastic card holder that comes in flower bouquets and normally have a point at the bottom end. Think outside the box and you will find pointers everywhere! If you want to buy a plastic finger pointer, you can also do that (see Resources for Trainers in the appendices).

Transparency overlays

Add another dimension to your transparencies by creating an overlay to show complex models or processes. An overlay is developed by producing a basic transparency, then adding additional transparency sheets to the first by taping them to a cardboard frame. Overlays are great for helping learners visualize a complex process or model step by step. You can add additional pizzazz by making each transparency image of the overlay a different color.

To create an overlay, start with the first step or point to be addressed on a transparency. Tape this transparency on four sides to a cardboard frame (available at office supply and many art stores). Attach subsequent transparencies, each of which contains one additional step or point, by taping it along one edge to the frame from the top. This allows the transparency to flip open like a box top (see **Figure 8-12**). Continue this

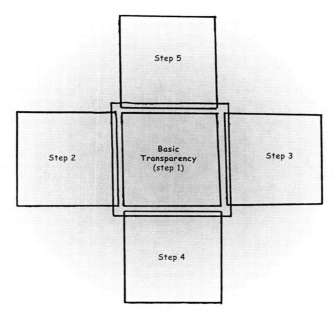

FIGURE 8-12. Transparency overlay

process by attaching each additional transparency on a different edge of the original transparency. Before taping, make sure that the images line up correctly over the top of the original image.

You can use the overlay in two ways. The first is that when you are ready to discuss the process or model, you can show only the first step of the process and explain that others will follow. As you are ready to discuss the next step, flip the appropriate transparency into position. The second approach is to show all steps overlaid briefly, and explain that the process has X number of steps or points that are to be examined. You can then flip all but the original image up and start discussing step or point number one, followed by subsequent steps in turn.

Meeting Minders™

These handy pieces of equipment are actually chronological clock timers that you can use on top of your overhead projector to project time onto a screen. They perform a variety of functions, some of which include counting down the time from a preset point to indicate when the time for an activity or test has expired (a buzzer sounds to alert the end of time), performing as a standard digital clock to show time, and acting as a stop watch to time events (see Creative Presentation Resources in the Resources for Trainers in the appendices).

Transparent plastic clock faces

These static clock faces have a spinner that holds the hands in its center. Before sending learners on a break, have them synchronize their watches with the classroom clock and then set the clock face at the return time. When that time occurs, you can reward those back in their seats, start an activity, or restart your session (see Creative Presentation Resources in the Resources for Trainers in the appendices).

Plastic spinner

You can use a generic plastic spinner that consists of one small acrylic dial on top of a larger one. You can write your own numbers, letters, and so forth onto the dial and use it for games, activities, random leader and volunteer selection, or for any other purpose you desire. The device comes with a variety of number templates and suggested usages (see The Trainer's Warehouse in the Resources for Trainers in the appendices).

Overhead scoreboard and game pieces

If you use team games in your training programs, these helpful devices make scoring for activities easy and visual. You can either use an overhead projector marker to track progress for up to seven teams or use the small game chips.

Shapes and images

Take another idea excursion to a local craft store and spend some time wandering the aisles to examine what you find there. Open you mind to possible uses with the overhead projector. Here are some that I found on a recent trip.

PLASTIC SUNCATCHERS. These come individually, or in packages with paints. They come in all types of animal, celestial, geometric, and other shapes. Their real purpose is to paint and hang on windowpanes so that light shines through them. From a creative training perspective, you can place these shapes on your overhead glass to project onto a flip chart page placed close to the projector. You can then trace the image onto the paper and color it in. You can also project images onto a dry erase or chalkboard to add graphics to your text, or to jazz up the appearance of your written messages.

WOODEN SHAPES. There are a variety of shapes (e.g., animals, houses, and flowers) that are designed to be painted and used in various woodworking projects. These can also be used like the suncatchers to project a shape onto a surface for tracing.

SHAPE TEMPLATES. By purchasing a variety of plastic shape templates, you can trace images onto your handouts and transparencies, or project them as I explained earlier. Templates can be found in craft, teacher and office supply, department, and many other types of stores that sell school, art, or office supplies.

STICK-ON SHAPES. Many infant, bath, and home improvement supply stores sell stick-on adhesive shapes that can be used on walls on in bathtubs. Like the wooden shapes, these can be traced onto handouts, or can be projected and traced.

STENCILS. While searching a local craft store, I found some wonderful little books that sold for a dollar and contain stencils that, like the shape templates, can be used to trace various images.

STAINED GLASS COLORING BOOK. These inexpensive little craft store books have very intricately drawn images of butterflies, animals, flowers, and shapes. They are on translucent paper that can be placed on paper or onto a projector and traced. Don't forget about copyrights.

BRIGHT IDEA

Package Your Presentation

Use plastic transparency protectors or cardboard frames, onto which your transparencies are taped. Either one allows ease of handling and the storage of your transparencies in a three-ring binder. Put copies of you handout originals and lesson plan in document protectors, along with a diskette containing all presentation-related materials in the binder also. Finally, label the spine of the binder with the session name and file it neatly on your bookshelf. When you are ready to present or pack for travel to a training location, you simply grab the binder and head out with the confidence that you have everything you will need to prepare for the program. If you decide to use cardboard frames, you get the advantage of having an area right beside your transparency to write key points, words, or transition phrases to your next transparency. You can reference these notes as you project and view the transparency during your presentation.

The creative mind plays with the objects it loves.
—Carl Jung

Projection Units and Slideshows

Manufacturers are continually updating and inventing new types of image projection equipment. These units are used to project computer-generated slide presentations that can be seen by large audiences. Many of the principles discussed for designing transparencies also pertain to creating computer-generated slides.

Although slide shows have some drawbacks, they also offer room for creativity because you can add such things as sounds, animation to words and images, movie clips, music, and there are many predesigned backgrounds that you can choose from that save design time. You can also move to other areas of the room and operate equipment if you have a remote control and laser pointer.

On the other hand, they limit your ability to project actual small items for discussion or to trace onto a flip chart. They also do not allow you to use various fun props such as shaped pointers.

Projection Software

Technology continues to provide a variety of stimulating and easily developed visual aids. With the software currently on the market, you can create eye-catching visuals and handouts that were available previously only through professional graphic artists and printers. In a short period of time, most trainers who know their way around the basics of a computer can learn to use presentation and layout graphic software. Such software offers maximum flexibility by allowing the creation and modification of materials in a matter of minutes versus days that previous production processes required. With programs such as PowerPoint, Harvard Graphics, Freelance Graphics, Quark, PageMaker, and later versions of Word and WordPerfect, an average trainer can do much of the layout work that used to be done by graphics professionals. With programs like Corel Draw, Adobe Illustrator, PrintMaster, and other many other graphics and clip art programs, you can create wonderful handouts and projected visuals by moving (importing) art, font, and a variety of images around in different programs (see Resources for Trainers in the appendices for more information on these sources).

Usage Tips

The following are suggestions for using slide shows.

Before participants arrive, check the operation and focus of your computer and projection units.

If you are using an LCD projection system that sits on top of the overhead projector glass and uses the projector's light to display an image on the screen, look in the owner's manual to ensure that the overhead projector has a bulb that is bright enough.

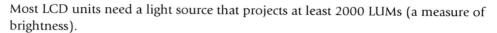

Most LCD units need a light source that projects at least 2000 LUMs (a measure of brightness).

ALWAYS plan backup training aids in case of equipment failure. This is crucial if you are taking your own laptop computer to another location where someone else will provide a projection unit. Too often, the equipment does not connect well, a connector cord is missing, or your computer may be damaged in transit. I generally make transparencies of my computer slides and have them with me in case I need to switch to an overhead projector presentation. If you plan to use a mounted projection unit, it is also a good idea to request an overhead projector as a standby resource. I also request a flip chart for smaller groups and rooms.

Place your projection screen where the audience can easily view it. Check the visibility before participants arrive by projecting an image, then going to various points in the room to verify a clear line of sight.

Have a 25-foot extension cord with multiple adapters on it available in case there is no electrical outlet conveniently located at the front of the room.

Dim the lights directly over the projection screen to prevent glare.

Follow a standard format—all printed either vertically (portrait) or horizontally (landscape).

Limit to 8–10 lines of text and to six to eight words per line to avoid having materials look too cluttered.

Sans serif ¼-inch lettering (approximately 30-point font) is usually large enough for text when presenting to groups of 100–200. Title lines should be slightly larger to make them stand out. These sizes assume that your room configuration is simple (e.g., theater style) and audience view is unobstructed.

When preparing slides, use uppercase for title lines and uppercase for the first letter of a word on a new topic line and for proper nouns, followed by lowercase for text. This makes reading easier.

Use bold lettering to make the words stand out on the screen.

Add color to your slides by having the title line a different color from that of the text. You can use any dark color or even red to make the title stand out.

Try choosing two different colors (e.g., yellow and white) for use on text lines when using a dark background. For each new point made, alternate the colors. For example, point one would be in yellow, point two in white, then point three in yellow, and so forth. Stay away from red for text lines because it is difficult to read, especially from a distance or for people who have red color blindness.

Ensure that your slide fonts and background colors are complementary. If you are unsure about a combination, either refer to a graphics source (e.g., book, artist, or other person with good color perception) or do not use the combination.

Do not use excessive special features when designing your slides. Select one or two options and carry that theme through the entire presentation so that the medium does not become the focal point and distract from your message. For example, choose only one or two types of slide opening (e.g., drip, dissolve, or fade).

Add clip art that complements the written words to your slides to help attract and hold attention. Keep your images small so they do not distract from the words.

If you use a commercial video segment, preview it and become thoroughly familiar with the content before learners arrive. Have prepared comments to introduce the segment, give participants specifics to watch for in the clip, and review what they saw afterwards, if appropriate.

When possible, use a remote control to allow you to move around the room and still operate the slide show. This frees you from having to stand next to the computer to punch a button when you want to advance a slide. An alternative is to have an assistant positioned to change slides when you are ready. This often takes considerable practice and coordination, so think about using a helper before participants arrive.

As mentioned with the use of transparencies, if you are nervous, DO NOT use a laser pointer to direct learner attention to something on the projection screen. Your hands will be shaking and the nervousness will be obvious and magnified as the red dot dances around the screen. Also, if you are going to use a laser pointer, be very careful not to shine it into your eyes or someone else's because eye damage can occur.

Creative Slide Design

Depending on the computer program used to create your presentation, you can do a multitude of things to enhance the images and impact of what you show your learners, some of the more common of which follow.

Insert sound or movie clips that can demonstrate or explain short segments of information into your presentation at appropriate points.

Include animation in which you have characters, such as dinosaurs, with your actual face or that of various learners as the head, walking across your screen to drag in text (see Resources for Trainers in the appendices). Use such features conservatively so that the images add value and are not there just for amusement.

Add graphics or text that seems to float around the screen by changing locations. This effect might be used with a graphic that you project for the duration of a break, for example, a smiling sun face that moves around.

Try using creative graphic fonts for title slides or title lines to add a bit of variety.

Flip objects or images so that the same image is used in a different position. For example, you might have two versions of your own caricature facing one another on either side of the slide at the bottom.

Add a three-dimensional effect in which letters or words appear stretched or to come in from the distance.

Make words or images appear to have a shadow behind them.

Insert charts, tables, or text boxes into slides to help explain key points of the presentation.

BRIGHT IDEA

Welcoming Slide Show

Set the mood for your session by running a slide show in which the images continually rotate on the screen as participants arrive. Depending on the session topic and format, you could project pictures of previous participants going through various portions of the training and session activities, pictures of current participants with their name and titles, motivational quotes that relate to the topic, information about the organization or key employees (shown in a new hire orientation program), or whatever you deem appropriate. You can even add upbeat background music to accompany the images.

Videotapes

Videotapes are an excellent vehicle for supplementing your program material. They provide a break for you and learners by having an automated presenter give information. This is often a welcome change of pace, assuming that the video is of good quality, current, and contains accurate and pertinent information. Content should be focused at your audience level and session objectives and not used just to fill time or as another prop.

Videotape Usage Tips

The following are tips that can help make the use of videotapes more valuable and successful in your sessions.

ALWAYS preview
When planning to use any video in your training, it is important that you know what is in it before participants arrive. You should be thoroughly familiar with its content and how you plan to use it with the group. In previewing, look for outdated or controversial content and information that might be contrary to what you plan to say, organizational policy or procedures, or regulations and laws. Such material can undermine your efforts and cause learners to lose interest or view the program as less valuable. If a video has any of the aforementioned features, consider finding another resource or not using the video.

Practice

Like all other elements of your session, make sure that you practice with the equipment that you will actually use and know how it functions before the start of your session.

Cue up the video to the opening scenario

Unless there is a textual message at the beginning of the tape that adds value or credibility, do not show it. An example of introductory information that might be shown would be a series of vignettes that are preceded by a statement that they are based on real events, current laws, or that the presenter in the video has special qualifications (e.g., a lawyer).

Keep it short

When possible, show shorter sequences rather than an entire video, especially if the video is more than 20 minutes long. This complies with the concepts of attention and brain-based learning you read about in Chapter 1.

Jot down key points

Prepare a short guide or talking points of things that you want to reinforce from the video. You can cover such items before and after participants view it. Points might include character descriptions, their roles, or some specific content element (e.g., things that are controversial or for which law or policy may have changed).

Prepare learners

Let participants know what they are about to see by briefly explaining content. Assign participants to look for specific information (see Video Evaluation Sheet in Tools for Trainers in the appendices). You may even want to turn it into a competition where one side of the room looks for certain information while the opposite side looks for other things. Award the team that finds the most issues a prize.

By assigning tasks, you raise expectations that participants are supposed to watch and will be held accountable. Following the video, have a quick review of key points, relate the information to program content, and stress how the material ties to the real world or their workplace.

Stay in the room

Do not start a videotape and leave the room for extended periods. If you are not present, you cannot monitor learner reactions to what they see. Also, if the equipment malfunctions, you have wasted valuable training time and will likely appear unprofessional for not being there to handle the situation.

Respect copyrights

If you are conducting a public seminar (paid) and use clips or an entire video in your program, obtain written copyright permission. Also, remember that you cannot legally borrow or lend a training video for use in a program. Only the original purchaser or

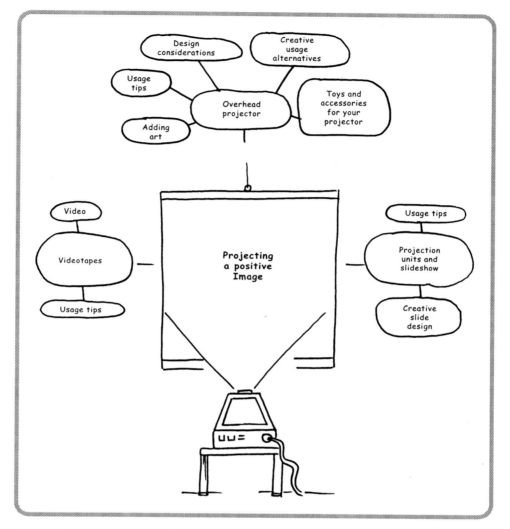

MINDMAP 2. Projecting a Positive Image

owner of a commercial training video has the right to use it in training unless the man-ufacturer tells you otherwise in writing. Read the literature that comes with the video and the opening FBI warning that appear on most professional training videos produced in the United States. Comply with the guidelines presented to avoid possible liability for yourself and your organization.

In addition to using video that you locally create yourself with a video camera, you can purchase or rent commercially produced videos that are excellent for helping make a point. Many companies that produce and market training videos have purchased the rights to commercial films or have licensed the use of famous individuals for use in training videos. Your organization can buy these and use them as you like in organizational training programs. For other videos from which you wish to extract scenes to use in your programs, find out who distributed them and obtain written permission first.

To help identify potential videos/films for use in training, go to the website www.teachwithmovies.org. This site provides the names of various movies, their potential use, a synopsis of the film, possible problem areas, and other useful information. Many of the video reviews on that site also contain additional links to films on related topic material.

Video Gems

To get you started, here are some examples of some video gems that I like to use in training. Some of these are available through training video distributors. Others can be found at your local video store.

Who's on First with Abbott and Costello

This is a great video to show how communication can break down even though people speak the same language.

12 O'Clock High

The entire video can be used as a study in situational leadership and planning under stressful conditions.

Rush Hour

This video provides some wonderful humor with a scene at the airport when a black police officer from Los Angeles goes to pick up a Chinese counterpart from Hong Kong. The black officer applies an inappropriate communication technique used by many Americans, who assume a person from another **culture** does not understand what is being said—they talk in a loud voice. The scene provides a perfect example of communication and cultural breakdowns.

Airplane

This is another humorous movie that shows an example of cultural and **subcultural** communication. In one scene, two black people are sitting on the plane talking in street language common to their subculture. Accompanying their spoken messages, the director inserted subtitles explaining what they are talking about in what some consider standard English. This is great for emphasizing how many groups within the United States and other areas of the world sometimes develop a language or communication style that others outside their group do not understand. Even children come up with such techniques to mask their messages from outsiders (remember pig Latin and the song "The Name Game?").

Karate Kid

There are numerous scenes in which the main characters Mr. Miyagi and Daniel are interacting and communicating. Two scenes that I like to use in coaching programs show Mr. Miyagi teaching Daniel how to wax a car (wax on/wax off). He does not explain at the time why this is so important and ultimately Daniel gets upset because he feels that he is not learning karate, which was his purpose for working with Mr. Miyagi in the first place. In a later scene, Mr. Miyagi shows Daniel that by using the same hand and arm movements taught for waxing the vehicle, he had in fact learned and perfected several protective karate moves.

Dead Poet's Society

Throughout the movie, there are examples of creative teaching techniques involving brain-based learning concepts. At one point, the professor jumps up onto a table and gives a motivating speech to students. Such segments are good for reinforcing the power of thinking outside the box and using unorthodox strategies for communicating your message. Good for trainer development and presentation skills sessions.

Patch Adams

This video provides numerous examples of how being compassionate toward others, taking a creative approach to work, and accepting personal responsibility gives great returns in the workplace. In one scene, Patch (a doctor) goes into the wards of terminally ill children and through a series of comedy and other humorous techniques raises the spirits of children who have otherwise somber lives.

Roots (Episode 1)

In a series of five episodes, the life of captured slave Kunte Kinte and his successors is detailed. In Episode 1, Kunte and another slave concoct a plan to communicate with the 100 plus slaves chained in the galley with them even though many spoke other languages. This is an excellent discussion generator for ways to use creativity, ingenuity, and teamwork and for taking individual responsibility and leadership to plan and execute a goal. Also, good for showing a creative alternative to intercultural communication.

Roots (Episodes 1 and 2)

There are numerous scenes in these episodes that show how Kunte Kinte established and worked toward achieving a goal and vision (breaking free from slavery and returning to his native Gambia, Africa). I use such examples to show the power of commitment to a purpose and how self-determination can help people weather difficult situations. Also good for emphasizing goal setting and moral courage.

GI Jane

The first female candidate in the tough Navy SEAL Team training program has to deal with harassment, stereotypes, preconceived ideas about her abilities, and a demanding physical and psychological work environment. Various segments in this video are good for demonstrating personal leadership, commitment, goal setting, and motivation.

An Officer and a Gentleman

Similar to GI Jane, the lead character in this video has to face stressful events and pressures to overcome personal challenges to reach his goal of becoming a U.S. Naval officer. Good for goal setting, leadership, motivation, determination, and overcoming stereotypes.

Black Hawk Down

This highly emotional movie shows the rigors of dealing with extreme physical and psychological obstacles to achieve workplace objectives and survive. Provides good scenarios for discussion related to the importance of planning, communication, teamwork, preparation, motivation, and individual responsibility when under stress.

Patton

The opening speech is a wonderful catalyst for discussion on the need for and impact of strong leadership in organizations. Can also be used in programs on motivation.

Flubber

Through a series of errors and efforts, Flubber (a highly reactive substance) is applied in a variety of unusual ways (e.g., on the bottoms of the shoes of basketball players and on a car). Demonstrates the power of creative thinking.

PUTTING YOUR BRAIN TO WORK: ACTIVITY

As you view videos and movies in the future, remember what you read about idea excursions in which you look at everyday items and try to envision how they might be used in training. As you think of using videos in your sessions, answer these questions.

In what sessions can you begin to use videos to supplement your program content? _____

_____

_____

How can you use such videos effectively to reinforce learning? _____

_____

_____

What are some videos that you can think of that might be useful to support training topics? _____

_____

_____

APPLYING WHAT YOU LEARNED
Strategies for Making Your Visual Message Sizzle

1. How can you use what you read in this chapter to improve the design of your written materials?

_____

_____

2. What materials can you think of to use as job aids for reinforcing what participants get in the classroom? _____

_____

3. In what ways can you add pizzazz to your flip charts using information found in this chapter?

_____

_____

4. How can posters, charts, and diagrams be incorporated into future training programs?

_____

_____

5. What are some creative training uses that you can think of for Post-It Notes®?

_____

_____

6. What role do you see cloth boards and other static displays playing in future training sessions?

_____

_____

7. How can electronic visual aids effectively be used in your training programs?

_____

_____

ENDNOTES

[31] Lucas, R. W., *The Big Book of Flip Charts,* McGraw-Hill, New York, 1999.

[32] Zelancy, G., *Say It with Charts: The Executive's Guide to Visual Communication,* 3rd ed., McGraw-Hill, New York, 1996.

[33] Bromley, K., Irwin De Vitis, L., and Modlo, M., *Graphic Organizers: Visual Strategies for Active Learning,* Scholastic Professional Books, New York, 1995.

[34] *HOPE REPORTS Perspective,* Vol. 2, No. 1, September 1976, Rochester, NY.

Notes

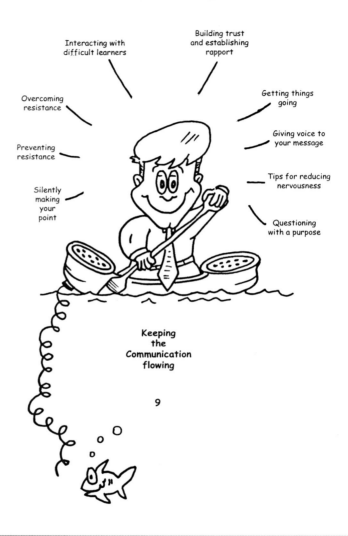

Interacting with
difficult learners

Building trust
and establishing
rapport

Overcoming
resistance

Getting things
going

Giving voice to
your message

Preventing
resistance

Tips for reducing
nervousness

Silently
making
your
point

Questioning
with a purpose

**Keeping
the
Communication
flowing**

9

Keeping the Communication Flowing

Communication is the process (either verbal or nonverbal) of sharing information with another person in such a way that he (she) understands what you are saying. 'Talking' and 'listening' and 'understanding' are all involved in the process of communication.

Dr. H. Norman Wright

Learning Objectives

At the end of this chapter, and when applying concepts covered, you will be able to:

● Build trust and establish credibility with learners.

● Use behaviors for introducing your session in ways that stimulate interest and foster a positive atmosphere.

● Apply key elements known about voice usage to enhance the effectiveness of your presentations.

● Send and receive nonverbal messages that can result in a more professional and well communicated session.

● Use questioning techniques that get better responses and facilitate information exchange.

● Implement strategies for preventing or reduce learner resistance in your training sessions.

● Address the behavior of resistant participants in a productive and efficient manner.

In any facilitated training session for which you are responsible, YOU are the messenger. What you do, or fail to do, will often determine the success or failure of the program in meeting stated learning objectives. All the expensive and glitzy props, equipment, techniques, and training aids in the world will not compensate for the inability to communicate and manage information flow with your learners.

If you watch experienced trainers and presenters in action, you will likely note several things about their behavior:

They care about their learners.

They are passionate about their topic and their role in facilitating learning.

They understand the importance of their role.

They are consummate professionals in their appearance, language, and actions.

They are prepared for the session and as many contingencies as possible.

They focus on using whatever strategy or technique is available to aid learner comprehension.

They have practiced and honed their presentation skills before coming before the group.

They immediately engage learners.

They strive to build trust and credibility as soon as they come into a training environment.

They use humor and a variety of creative approaches to facilitate communication.

● GETTING THINGS GOING

As you read in Chapter 4, your first few minutes with a group can impact ultimate success later. In addition to the strategies discussed in that chapter, here are some additional thoughts for getting your session off to a positive start.

Review Notes

Before your participants arrive, review your session notes one more time. Even if you have done the program many times before, it is a good idea to refresh your mind and fix opening remarks into short-term memory.

Create an Open Learning Environment

You read about the importance of the learning environment earlier in this book. Ensure that you have planned and organized effectively. Once learners arrive, set the expectation of exchange, openness, fairness, and an opportunity to share and learn.

Dress Professionally

As described earlier in the book, appearances do count and impact participant impressions of you.

Greet Each Participant

Shake hands, smile, and welcome everyone entering the room. This means that you must have adequately prepared and gotten to the training room at least an hour before the arrival of your learners. This will allow you to set up materials and equipment, make last minute adjustments, and be ready when participants begin to arrive. Greeting people is important because the physical act of coming in contact with someone as you shake his or her hand, smile, make eye contact, and use his or her name forms a psychological bond. You become "friends" and friends do not normally attack or criticize one another. Thus, you can potentially reduce the chance of challenge or disagreement later in the program.

Listen Actively

Pay attention to names, comments, and questions at the beginning of the program and throughout the session.

Do Not Apologize

If something goes wrong, does not work, or is not present, deal with it without telling participants. For example, if you were going to show a videotape, but the sponsor forgot to bring a VCR and monitor—improvise. It will do no good, and can actually do harm, if you try to blame others or elicit sympathy from participants. Your learners do not know what you had planned. If you do not tell them they are not going to see a planned video, they will never know. The result will be a seemingly well planned and executed session by a professional. This is opposed to a nonprofessional crybaby who points fingers at others and did not have a backup plan!

Gain Attention

A variety of attention-getting ideas have been offered throughout this book. You can use whatever you feel appropriate for getting the attention of your group. For example, flicker the lights, use a loud sound (e.g., whistle, music, or bell), or have someone else dramatically introduce you (e.g., Herrrrrre's Johnny!).

Be Personable

A technique used by experienced trainers and presenters for reducing their own nervousness is to look into the eyes of participants in the front of the room and smile. If someone smiles at you, you feel good and smile back. Then, you smile at someone else and they smile. The pattern continues until you feel relaxed among friends and they see you as warm and approachable. The reason for choosing people from the front of the room is that those are usually the people who are most interested in being there and to learn. Thus, they are likely to be more receptive and friendly.

Provide an Overview or Update

In your opening remarks, you will generally cover session learning objectives, explain the AVARFM to learners, discuss what will be covered, and handle administrative details. If you are doing a multisession program, starting with the objectives, a quick review and tie-in of material covered previously is always helpful, as it allows participants to mentally tune in to you and the session.

Verify Understanding

Before moving into session content, I find it helpful to verify that learners understand what I have explained in the overview. I also give them a chance to add their own objectives or information that they need from the session. These are written on a flip chart page and posted to ensure they are not overlooked and to demonstrate their importance. Posting them also allows me to review them at the end of the session to make certain that learners feel they were adequately addressed. During verification, I give participants a chance to ask any questions they might have about the schedule, session topics, or processes that will be used.

Be Politically Correct

Avoid and prevent stereotyping, off-color humor, and behavior considered offensive or unprofessional (e.g., an arm around the shoulder of a participant as you stand talking to him or her, or others). Even if you are good friends or related to a participant, maintain professional decorum. Remember that first impressions count and someone seeing you from across the room may not know of your relationship.

● BUILDING TRUST AND ESTABLISHING RAPPORT

As in any interpersonal interaction trust is a crucial element for successful training. Without trust, there is no relationship or chance for effective communication exchange. Many factors can impact the trust level between you and your learners. Here are some strategies that can foster a more trusting relationship with trainees.

Start Your Session on Time

As you read in an earlier chapter, time is important. Even though it may seem like a trivial matter, most people are trying to squeeze out every minute possible in today's fast-paced world. If you fail to start or resume your sessions on time, you are in effect disrespecting your learners' time and needs. This can lead to resentment and reluctance to attend future programs. It can also send a message that it is all right to be late and participants are not likely to return from breaks and lunch on time, thus reducing your ability to cover all planned material.

Be Consistent

Participants start forming an opinion of you early in your session. To ensure that their image is positive, explain roles (yours and theirs), processes, and expectations at the beginning of your programs. This lets learners know what to expect and mentally to plan their time. Throughout the session do what you said you would do or what was agreed on at the start of the session. For example, if you announce that a reward system will be used during the program, strive to honor that commitment and look for opportunities to recognize positive behavior with a reward for participant achievements and participation.

Respect Your Learners

To get respect, you have to give it. Many trainers, especially those with less experience, believe that they are the "expert" and know best how to conduct a session or activity. Also, technically proficient people with little training experience sometimes default to their knowledge to carry a session. In either instance, participants can be offended or may develop an indifference to the training because of a feeling that they are being disrespected. As adult learners, most participants bring prior topic knowledge and experience from earlier training programs. They want to be recognized for what they know, their expertise, intelligence, and ability. When those elements are ignored, they might become antagonistic.

To prevent such a scenario from occurring in your sessions, take the time to listen and actively involve your learners. Give them a forum for sharing what they know. Let them exercise creativity and brainstorm solutions rather than giving them all the answers. By allowing them to participate in role-plays, demonstrations, presentations, and discussions, you can show them that they are an important part of the learning process. Allowing such involvement can lead to learners feeling empowered and shows that you do not see yourself as the omnipotent leader with all the answers.

Make Eye Contact

By looking into the eyes of your participants as you meet them and throughout your training session, you send a message of concern, warmth, and friendship that can lead to open dialogue. You can also reduce potential resistance from people who might otherwise view you as an authority figure who represents only the interest of management or human resources.

Pay Attention to Learner Needs

By being vigilant and watching for verbal and nonverbal cues from your participants, you can better identify what they need. Because people typically like it when others focus on them or are attuned to their needs, doing so can go a long way in establishing rapport. You can indicate that you are on the same wavelength as participants by listening as they speak, giving appropriate verbal and nonverbal feedback, asking questions to draw out dialogue, and using training strategies that actively involve them. For example, you can start your session with an in-class needs assessment as described in Chapter 3.

Mirror Participant Behavior

Researchers in the area of **neurolinguistic programming (NLP)** have examined human behavior for years in an effort to determine why some people seem to attract others (charisma) and build almost instant rapport, whereas others do not. They found that matching the pacing of someone's speech pattern and movements can build trust and acceptance. Some salespeople and therapists have used this technique successfully for years, becoming rich and famous as a result.

You can incorporate the NLP technique into your training. For example, through conscious effort to observe and listen to a participant's speech and gestures you might hear her say, "I cannot quite see your point." You clarify and mirror, you might respond, "So the example that I gave is hazy to you?" In effect, you are speaking similar language and giving back what she gave you. Once she responds, "Yes," you then try a different approach to explain your point. Similarly, if a learner is excited about something and is animated in voice and actions, you can respond in kind to indicate that you are on an equal emotional level. This might involve increased vocal inflection or movements on your part. Or, your expression of emotion might include high-energy words, such as exciting, stimulating, or wonderful.

Remember what you read about visual, auditory, and kinesthetic learners in Chapter 1? By matching the language of participants exhibiting one of the three preferences, you are incorporating NLP concepts (as in the preceding example of the visual learner). The key to mirroring successfully is to do it intermittently based on what learners say. If you react to each behavior or speech pattern presented by a participant you may be perceived as mocking, insincere, phony, or making fun of the person. For more on NLP (see Books under Resources for Trainers in the appendices). Howard[35] gives some good examples of ways to establish rapport though NLP.

Be Credible

If you quote research or other sources, give specific citations to back your claims. Simply saying, "Research has found . . ." is not enough. Such a statement actually opens you up to challenge by some of the participant types described later in this chapter.

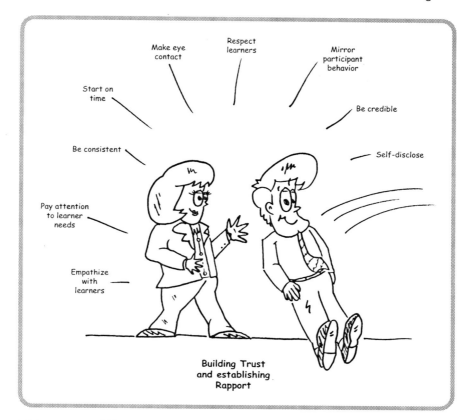

MINDMAP 1. Building Trust and Establishing Rapport

Empathize with Learners

Let your participants know that you have done your homework, been in their position, and researched your topic thoroughly. Also, let them know that because of your preparation you can relate to or understand their situation. Possibly share one or two personal experiences to demonstrate that fact. Also, talk about things you and they have in common.

Self-Disclosure

One of the quickest ways I have found to gain acceptance with a group is to disclose information about myself. This does not mean bragging about accomplishments; you can list those on a biographical description included in handout materials. What I am referring to is personal information (e.g., about background or family) that makes you appear human and lets learners see you as a typical person like them. I also share a story about myself, such as personal experiences of situations in which I was successful or unsuccessful using techniques similar to those in the session I am facilitating. Often, self-disclosure encourages reciprocation from learners. I often provide a vehicle for such reciprocation by having learners participate in a trust-building icebreaker activity.

BRIGHT IDEA

Self-Disclosure Icebreaker

To help participants get to know more about you and each other, create a prepared flip chart page listing information such as that shown below. Fill in the blanks with your own personal information as an example when you introduce the activity. With small groups (20 or fewer participants) you can have everyone in turn stand and introduce themselves giving appropriate information about themselves for each category. For more participants, form small groups and have them share among themselves.

Name:

Place of birth:

Birth month:

Number/type of pets:

Favorite car:

One thing desired from the session:

PUTTING YOUR BRAIN TO WORK: ACTIVITY

Think about training programs you have been part of in the past.

What instructional techniques worked well for building trust and rapport? Why?_____

_____

_____

What techniques led to a breakdown in resistance between the trainer and learners? Why?_____

_____

_____

You may be deceived if you trust too much, but you will live in torment if you do not trust enough.
—Frank Crane

● GIVING VOICE TO YOUR MESSAGE

Have you ever been in a training session or presentation in which the trainer or presenter spoke too softly? Too rapidly or too slowly? With little or no emotion? If you answered "yes" then you probably understand the importance of effective verbal communication. If you cannot communicate your knowledge well your learners will not benefit regardless of how much you know about a topic.

Dynamic trainers use a variety of techniques and tools similar to the ones described in this book. They are also polished speakers who know how to use their own voice and body effectively to deliver their messages. Here are some key elements to consider related to verbal communication in your classroom.

Think Before Speaking

There is an old adage that I recall when I think of this element of communication: "Be sure your brain is in gear before putting your mouth in motion." Take the time to plan and write down key points you want to make so that you have a guide during your session. Practice your presentation so that you know exactly what you are going to say and how it will be said.

Speak to Be Heard

You voice should be loud enough for everyone in the room to hear without straining. To check this, do a quick rehearsal with a friend or someone else standing at far points of the room to see if he or she can hear. If not, use a microphone. The latter allows greater latitude in raising and lowering your volume for dramatic effect or to emphasize key points.

Speak Clearly and Concisely

Strive to enunciate each word clearly. This is especially important and effective if you have learners with hearing impairments or who normally speak another language. Acronyms (NAFTA, for North American Free Trade Agreement), contractions (e.g., I'd or you'll), technical jargon, slang, or slurred words (e.g., wouldja, didja, or hafta) can all cause difficulty in comprehension. If you are going to introduce acronyms, technical terms, or slang words, write them down on a flip chart or other writing surface so that everyone can see the spelling. Then, define the term before going on.

Avoid Verbal Fillers

Many people pick up annoying favorite words or phrases and use them throughout a conversation or training session. They also use nervous nonwords. Be on the alert for verbal fillers such as, "You know," "Right," "Like," "Etcetera," "Whatever," and "Uh" or "And uh." Have a friend listen to your session to note such habits.

BRIGHT IDEA

Check Your Performance

Periodically videotape your sessions. Watch the video and rate yourself objectively on the following areas:

	Low				High
Overall presentation	1	2	3	4	5
Volume level	1	2	3	4	5
Rate of speech	1	2	3	4	5
Diction (word clarity)	1	2	3	4	5
Fillers used	1	2	3	4	5

Modulate Your Voice

By using inflection or a change in the pitch of your voice, you can add vocal punctuation to your message. Pitch is formed by the vibration of sound waves and is influenced by your emotional state. Think of times when you were excited or joyous about something and spoke. Your voice pitch likely was likely higher than normal. Likewise, when you ask a question, your inflection usually goes up and you end the sentence with a vocal question mark. Many women tend to use increased inflection at the end of many statements, whether they are asking questions or not. This can lead to confusion in listeners who are not totally focused because they hear the vocal question mark and mentally think, "She just asked me a question." Once they consciously realize that was not the case and you have continued to speak, they may have missed an important point. For this reason, female trainers may want to have a friend or others listen to their speech pattern or to audiotape and listen to their presentation of information to see if they have such a tendency when speaking.

Another pitch problem occurs when you speak in a matter-of-fact or monotone. In such instances, your pitch is lower and sounds flat and unenthusiastic, which can affect the enthusiasm level of learners.

Practice changing your pitch by saying the following statements, emphasizing only the italicized word in each one. Audiotape yourself and listen to the difference in inflection and how it can change the meaning of your message.

I cannot believe you said that.

I *cannot* believe you said that.

I cannot *believe* you said that.

I cannot believe *you* said that.

I cannot believe you *said* that.

I cannot believe you said *that.*

Monitor Your Rate of Speech

The average adult in the United States speaks at a rate of about 125–150 words per minute (wpm). This may vary with emotion and the region of the country from which the person comes. It may also vary based on his or her normal living environment. For example, many people from the southern and rural areas of the country live in an environment where the pace of life is slower, and this often is mirrored in the speech patterns. Other people who come from urban and northern areas live in an environment where the pace is more rapid and frantic; thus, they speak quickly to save time.

Often, some trainers will speak rapidly at the beginning of a session and slow down later. This is sometimes the result of anxiety or nervousness. You can guard against this tendency by using some of the stress reducing techniques listed in this chapter. To give you an idea of how different rates of speech sound, listen to speeches by John F. Kennedy and Martin Luther King. Kennedy spoke at an average of 180 wpm while King's "I Have a Dream" speech started at around 90 wpm and ended at around 150 wpm. To help you regulate your rate, think about how fast you are speaking and consciously speed up or slow down for dramatic effect. Also, use pauses occasionally after statements and questions. This allows you and your learners to think and gives you time for a deep breath.

PUTTING YOUR BRAIN TO WORK: ACTIVITY

To develop an action plan for vocal improvement, answer the following questions. If others know your presentation style well, ask them for their honest feedback as well. Use the responses to work on improvement of your delivery.

What vocal delivery skills do you consider strengths? _____

_____

What areas of your vocal delivery style need improvement? (Be specific.) _____

_____

What techniques can you think of to help improve areas identified in the preceding? _____

_____

> *The right word may be effective, but no word was ever as effective as a rightly timed pause.*
> —Mark Twain

● TIPS FOR REDUCING NERVOUSNESS

Stage fright or the jitters is normal when training. According to some researchers, people fear public speaking more than death. Even experienced trainers feel some degree of apprehension when stepping in front of a group for the first time. Such feelings often stem from a desire of wanting to be accepted or liked. You are probably going to have butterflies in your stomach. The key is to get them to fly in formation rather than swarm. Any stress or anxiety symptoms normally go away within the first few minutes when you begin to see people smile and you begin to relax.

Anxiety manifests itself differently for each person. I have heard of people complaining of rapid heart beat, trembling hands, clammy palms, sweaty armpits, dry throat, shaky knees, shortness of breath, rashes, flushed face, quivering voice, and diarrhea. Remember that your symptoms are normal and do not focus on them. Also, do not act in ways that project the fact that you are nervous. Certainly do not apologize or draw attention to it. For example, if you are shaking, do not position yourself so that it becomes obvious (e.g., pointing to items illuminated on the overhead projector with your finger or using a laser pointer with slides so that your participants see magnified shaking on the screen). Just remember that your learners cannot see and are unaware of most of the symptoms and that it is only in your head that they are a problem. There are ways to reduce your anxiety level before and during a session. Try the following strategies.

Get Plenty of Rest

Do not stay out late partying the night before a training program. Try to get your normal amount of sleep rather than throw your system off balance by being tired. You want to be in prime condition for your learners.

Gain Experience

The more you speak in front of groups, the easier it gets. Take opportunities to speak to school, civic, church, and volunteer groups. Get involved with Toastmasters (see Resources for Trainers in the appendices), where you will have the opportunity to practice various types of speeches in a safe environment and receive nonthreatening peer feedback.

Prepare Adequately

Taking more preparation time will likely add to your confidence level because you will feel ready for most contingencies. As a rule of thumb, I recommend that new trainers who attend my train-the-trainer programs take at least 8 hours to prepare material for every hour they will present. This helps ensure that they will have answers to unplanned questions and will spend little time saying, "I do not know the answer to that, but will get back to you with it later." If this is done too often, a trainer can lose credibility and trust.

Plan Your Opening Well

The only portion of your presentation that you may want to memorize is your opening remarks. Once you get off to a good start and your participants start reacting positively to what you are saying your nervousness will likely go away quickly.

Concentrate on Your Audience

Rather than focus on the nervousness, concentrate on your learners and how you will address their needs. Think about the activities and potential outcomes. Get caught up in your material to take your mind off yourself.

Practice, Practice, Practice!

This does not mean to try to memorize all of your session content. That will likely end in failure because short-term memory can hold only a limited amount of information. Also, if someone asks a question or gets you off a topic, you may have trouble refocusing and remembering what you were going to say. This is one important reason for ALWAYS using notes or a lesson plan. Rehearsing what you will say in the actual room and with the actual equipment you plan to use can mentally help fix the process in your mind. That way, when you are actually speaking to learners, it will be like a déjà vu experience in which it feels as if you have been there in the setting before (because you have). One technique that I find highly useful is what is called a **wall talk**. When I was training to become a Marine Corps Drill Instructor in the early 1970s we stood before full-length mirrors practicing for hours. This allowed us to hear ourselves and see our gestures simultaneously. Although this was effective for what we were trying to accomplish, I encourage use of the wall talk before a blank wall instead. The reason is that you eliminate the distraction of watching yourself or seeing other things in the mirror. Instead you can concentrate on your voice articulation and quality. The wall reflects your voice, making it a useful tool for hearing what you have said. Adding a tape recorder and listening to the presentation later is also helpful.

Do Not Place Undue Stress on Yourself

You are your own worst critic. Lighten up. Some people strive for perfection, which is a lofty goal. Certainly do what you can to be successful, but acknowledge that some things are out of your control. Do the best you can to plan, organize, and prepare, but if something goes wrong, shake it off and go to your backup plan.

Think About What You Drink

Drink water instead of milk or caffeine products, especially carbonated drinks that produce gas. They can upset your stomach or increase your stress levels.

Breathe Deeply

As you are being introduced or before you step in front of a group, take a few slow deep breaths to replenish the oxygen supply to the brain.

Use Visioning

As discussed earlier in the book, visualizing an event is a powerful tool for learning. As you are preparing for your training program, go to the actual delivery site and envision what the setup will be. Practice facing different parts of the room at certain points in the program to remind yourself to make eye contact during the training. Also, envision what a successful program will look like, then do whatever is necessary to make that happen. After all, much of being successful is your mental attitude.

Take a Short Walk

I often use the time between checking last-minute room details and the arrival of my learners to take care of myself. I get a drink of water, use the restroom, and walk around the perimeter of the training room or facility. I also use the time to do a mental check-list of things and to rehearse my opening remarks one more time for peace of mind.

Do Something Physical

You read about how activity stimulates the brain and learning. It is also good to help take your mind off any nervousness and to stimulate your muscles, increase your breathing, and enrich the brain with oxygen. Try some stretches, cross-lateral activities, or some isometric exercises. For example, stand an arm's length from a wall, position your feet at shoulder width, and place your palms on the wall. Tense your upper body as you push against the wall trying to push it over. Hold this for 15–30 seconds, relax, and then repeat a couple more times. Sit in a chair with hands on your knees and feet flat on the floor. Press down with your hands, relax, and repeat. Now try it with your feet.

Pause Before Speaking

If you have seen professional speakers after they are introduced, you have possibly noted that once they step onto the stage, they pause for dramatic effect. They might glance around the room, smile, gesture openly to the crowd, and say something such as, "Look at this audience! You are wonderful! Give yourself a hand." All the time, while the audience is applauding, the speaker is mentally preparing opening remarks. You do not need to rush in talking as you enter the room. Take your time, breathe, and pause before beginning.

Use Gestures

As you will read later, nonverbal gestures can aid and impact your delivery. Gestures allow you to channel your nervous energy rather than standing frozen not knowing what to do next. Start out with a few simple movements, then get more creative as you loosen up.

Use Creative Visual Aids

You have read about dozens of ideas for creating visual aids that sparkle. Use them to assist in capturing attention rather than standing alone in front a group of strangers feeling naked. The visual aids you choose can help divert some attention away from you while they reinforce what you say. As people are reading information shown, they are not concentrating all their attention on you.

Be Enthusiastic

My final tip is to be enthusiastic in every presentation. It is contagious. If you look like you are having fun and enjoying the material, chances are that your learners will too.

INTERIM REVIEW

To practice your articulation and inflection skills and to review key points you have read up to now, find a tape recorder and stopwatch. Start the timer and recall as many of the concepts learned as possible while you record your responses. After 1 minute, stop, verify, and review your answers. To simulate a presentation start off with, "I'm here today to talk with you about. . . ."

In a classroom, you could do a similar review by forming triads of learners. Have two people write each point recalled as one participant reviews and names key concepts. Using triads versus dyads helps ensure that more points will be captured. Perhaps even have the two recorders alternating and writing every other concept stated so that none are missed. At the end of specified time frames have learners switch roles and repeat until all three people in a group have done a review. Doing this type of review reinforces the key concepts covered a number of different times and helps solidify the learning as participants mentally review and repeat the concepts and as others listen and absorb them.

BRIGHT IDEA

Learn from the Experts

Giving information to large groups can be a stressful event. Some researchers have found that public speaking is the number one fear of most people (glossophobia), even before fear of death. Presenting information or giving a speech can be especially unnerving if you are unsure of what you will say or do. That is why practice is your best tool for success.

Fortunately, many people have presented before you and have left behind valuable advice in the form of audio- and videotapes. Take advantage of their expertise by going to a library, searching the Internet, or visiting a video or audio store to get tapes or CDs of dynamic speakers of our time. Listen to books on tape and follow their model for inflection and emphasis when you facilitate. Some of the more powerful speakers of the twentieth century were Dr. Martin Luther King, John F. Kennedy, Winston Churchill, Ronald Reagan, Adolph Hitler, and Jesse Jackson. Whether you agree with their messages or politics does not reduce their success. You can also study the voice and mannerisms of nationally known radio and television personalities.

● QUESTIONING WITH A PURPOSE

One key tool you have for gaining involvement and gathering information from learners in your sessions is the art of questioning. I believe that asking questions appropriately is truly an art because not everyone can do it well. The result of inappropriately worded questions is that you get what you ask for. If you ask the wrong question, you get unintentional, useless information that can lead to frustration and the need for additional questions. A humorous example of this occurred in an exchange I had with my 85-year-old mother, who lives with my wife and me. Mom is a delightful person, is very active, and likes to help around the house. One night, when I was working on a book manuscript and my wife had not come home from work yet, mom wanted to be helpful and get dinner started. As I worked on the computer, she came in and asked if I would like her to cook baked potatoes for dinner (a closed-ended question). I stated that would be fine and went back to work as mom left. A few minutes later I noticed her standing in the doorway and asked what she needed. She asked, another closed-ended question, "How many potatoes do you want? I was half listening and a bit irritated at the second interruption because I was behind deadline for the manuscript. I replied, "One is fine, thanks," and went back to typing. I quickly realized that mom was still standing in the doorway and as I looked up, she responded with a third closed-ended question,

"Well, what are MJ (my wife) and I going to eat?" I sort of laughed and said, "I don't know mom, I only want one potato. If you two want a potato, then feel free to fix them." It occurred to me at that moment that we had just experienced the type of communication breakdown that often occurs in classrooms when trainers ask the wrong type of question. They do not get the information needed or expected, more questions are required, time is wasted, and frustration can result. My mom wanted to know how many potatoes to fix for dinner, but she did not ask that. I responded only to the closed-ended questions she asked and, as a result, we were both frustrated.

In your training sessions, questions are an excellent tool to give yourself a break from speaking while involving learners. Through effective questioning, you can gauge participant understanding of a point made, determine interest and willingness to participate, and elicit ideas, issues, or solutions.

I have found that the most effective way to keep communication relaxed and more informal is to ask more open-ended questions (e.g., when, where, how, why, what, or to what degree). Such questions often stimulate and nonverbally let participants know that I want more than a short answer. To verify, validate, confirm, reinforce, or gain commitment, I also use closed-ended questions (e.g., generate short answer, one-syllable responses such as yes/no, a number, or name). The challenge created by closed-ended questions is that I do most of the talking and get little information. This is the reason I use them carefully.

One question that I have found to create some degree of irritation starts with the question "Why?" There is no way to inflect that word and make it sound friendly. Try it. No matter how you try, the word sounds harsh and abrasive. I often relate the reason for potential irritated reactions to the "Why" question as being learned behavior from childhood. To understand what I mean, think about the times when, as a child, your caregivers restricted you from an activity when you asked permission. Following their response, you likely responded like most other children (including your caregivers when they were young) and asked "Why?" Your caregivers probably heard this as a challenge in a whiney, high-pitched voice. And, they (like thousands of other caregivers before them) likely responded, "Because I said so and I'm the mommy/daddy (or whatever)." For this reason, when your adult learners hear your question "Why?" in response to something they said, they hear their own whiny challenge and resent it just as their caregivers probably did. The potential logic is that they are now adults and should have authority (of a caregiver) and should not be challenged in their thinking. This psychological memory might actually create a barrier to effective communication in your classroom. For that reason, I encourage you to rephrase a question such as "Why do you say that?" to "What causes you to believe that is true?" The same question is posed using different words and inflection, and I believe a potential psychological minefield can be avoided.

Here is a good questioning technique that I learned from a wise former boss and friend, Leon Met. He suggested that there are two ways to ask a question. Each can get a different response or cause different emotional reactions.

Technique 1: APC

Ask a general question of your group, such as, "What do you think would happen if we applied this technique in the workplace?"

Pause to let the question sink in and for all learners to consider a response.

Call on one person by name to answer the question.

This technique is more informal and indirect. As you pause, you can scan the room for a volunteer or someone who appears to have an answer or idea. This is usually better than calling on a person who has his or her eyes down toward the desk to avoid being seen. The technique also potentially puts everyone on alert that they may be called upon so they start thinking of an answer.

Technique 2: CPA

Call on a specific participant by name.

Pause to let the person realize that his or her name was called.

Ask the question.

This second technique is a more direct, in-your-face approach. As a result, I use it selectively so that I avoid unduly offending or embarrassing learners. It is not a technique that I often use with introverted participants or those whose nonverbal cues indicate that they might not have an answer. It does come in handy for the difficult participants who are distractive or or inattentive during the session. Calling their name snaps them back to refocus, the pause allows them time to prepare to listen, and the question is offered for their response.

As a final thought related to questioning, you might want to post some questioning guidelines on your training room wall (see **Table 9-1**). Explain and reference these in your opening remarks. Point them out when someone violates the guidelines to help them learn effective questioning techniques and to prevent their offending anyone.

BRIGHT IDEA

Questioning Practice

As a way of helping your learners recognize the value of asking the right questions, have them participate in an activity such as this.

Explain the purpose of open- and closed-ended questions. Then, to help learners understand the difference between the two types, have them participate in a fun activity for which you reward them. Have participants separate into pairs with partners sitting back to back. Pass out blank paper and pencils to all. Tell learners that they are going to practice closed-ended questioning and that they cannot ask

> ### Table 9-1. Questioning Guidelines Sample
>
> Ask friendly questions—what, how, where, when, or to what degree.
>
> Avoid "why" phrased questions.
>
> Do not cross examine—questions are to stimulate thought; not harass or probe.
>
> Remain objective—focus on issues or behaviors, not on people.
>
> Elicit details—if an answer is incomplete, follow up with other open-ended questions.
>
> Use closed-ended questions sparingly—verify, validate, gain commitment, or reinforce information.
>
> Ask "what if" questions to stimulate thinking and problem-solving.

open-ended questions. Give one person in each pair a copy of **Figure 9-1— House 1** and tell them they are not to let their partners see the image. Tell the participants without the image that they will have 15 minutes to ask closed-ended questions only in an attempt to determine what the other person is looking at. As they question, they are to attempt to draw what they think the image that their partner has looks like. At the end of the alloted time, sound a whistle or other noisemaker and have partners compare images. Once the laughter dies down, have partners switch roles, give the partner who did not have an image the first time, **Figure 9-2—House 2,** and repeat the process. At the end of the second time frame, debrief the activity by asking what worked and what didn't as they proceeded. Ask what would have helped them do a better job. If someone does not offer, asking an open-ended question such as, "What does the house look like?" suggests how helpful such a simple open-ended question might have been. Relate this to their workplace and own interpersonal situations.

● SILENTLY MAKING YOUR POINT

Much of the emphasis you add to your message, and the attention you gain in front of a group, comes from movement and other nonverbal cues. The key is that such movement must be planned and purposeful. Inappropriate gesturing that contributes no particular meaning or seemingly nervous pacing actually distract.

Dr. Albert Mehrabian[36] and other researchers have found that as much as 55 percent of emotion extracted from messages between two people comes from nonverbal

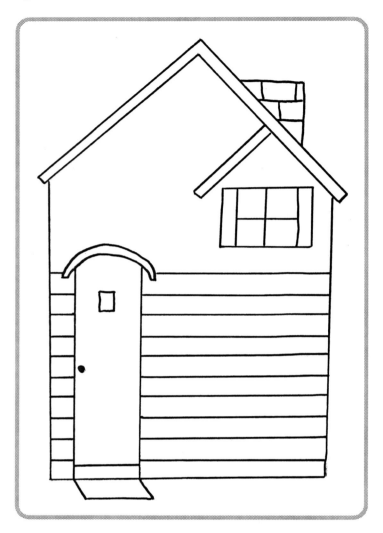

FIGURE 9-1. House 1

sources (e.g., facial expressions, or use of hands, shoulders, arms, and legs). Further, an additional 38 percent of meaning comes from verbal cues (e.g., rate of speech, volume, inflection, and tone). That is a total of 93 percent of message meaning from sources other than words. That does not mean that words are not important, it simply means that when a person receives a verbal message accompanied by a nonverbal cue, he or she is more likely to believe or act on the nonverbal message first. Although Mehrabian's research was not focused on large group communication, his findings do emphasize the

FIGURE 9-2. House 2

importance of being aware of how you stand, sit, gesture, and move when in front of a group or interacting with learners. Everything from the way you dress to where you put your hands or position yourself in front of a room is watched by someone in your participant group. If you are conscious of this fact, you will likely be more conscientious about what you do as a trainer or facilitator.

The following are some general guidelines that can help improve your effectiveness and enhance your message delivery.

Gather Participants

It is helpful from a psychological perspective to group people together in a training room, especially in a large conference room. You read about the importance of room size and configuration in **Chapter 5.** By having participants move to the front of a room, you bring them into closer proximity and can better see and interact with them. People who are shy or resistant typically often sit in the rear of a room. By forcing them forward, you help them better bond with the group and mentally form a more cohesive entity not present when people are scattered. Doing this also saves time when forming small groups because they can more quickly assemble. Dale Carnegie[37] once noted, "A man in a large audience tends to lose his individuality. He becomes a member of the crowd and is swayed far more easily than he would be as a single individual. He will laugh at and applaud things that would leave him unmoved if he were only one of half a dozen people listening to you."

Move with a Purpose

Each time you change locations in the room, you should do so for a reason. Continuous walking from one point to another can appear as nervousness, whereas planned movement can actually aid facilitation. Experienced trainers have known for years that you can control your audience and the quality and amount of discussion by moving closer or farther from participants throughout a session. For example, if you want to emphasize a point or engage a specific individual in your group, you might casually move forward toward the person as you continue to talk. Or, if you have two participants who have lost focus and are having a side conversation, you can often stop the discussion without having to say a word. Simply by closing the distance, making eye contact with the learners involved, and continuing to speak, you nonverbally say, "I'm talking to you," or "This is important, pay attention."

From a learning standpoint, consider that for the brain to maximize potential, it needs a continual stream of new information or input. If you stand in one place, the brain becomes bored. This accounts for refocused attention on the part of many participants. They then look elsewhere—doodle, work on or read other material, or start mentally processing material outside of the program content (daydream)—when you are stagnant or do not visually and mentally stimulate them.

As you read in earlier chapters, the brain processes information actively as it memorizes it. As part of that effort, a participant's eyes will typically move to a known area. Many researchers believe that there are at least six basic eye "thinking" positions (see **Figure 9-3**). Law enforcement professionals and others who interrogate and interview for a living have attempted to use this knowledge to gauge whether a person is being truthful. Unfortunately, an experienced liar or someone with certain psychiatric conditions can easily deceive and modify his or her behavior.

You can also use this research as an additional tool for helping determine participant understanding and brain activity. However, like any other element of human nature, this is only a general guide because each person differs in ability and brain functioning.

Creating new auditory messages/
information

Accessing stored auditory messages/
information

Creating new visual messages/
information

Accessing stored visual messages/
information

Self-talk

Experiencing emotions/feelings

FIGURE 9-3. Eye Positions (for most right-handed learners; reverse for most left-handed learners)

> **BRIGHT IDEA**
>
> ## Capitalizing on Brain Functioning
>
> To maximize the benefit of research related to eye movement, stand to the right side of the room (from your learners' perspectives) whenever you are presenting concepts, ideas, or information. That is where the brain looks for new information or auditory messages. When conducting questioning or a review activity, move to the left side (where the brain looks for stored information). This can aid retention and help learners access material later.

Face Your Learners

Because your participants are the reason for you being in the training room, give them your full attention—not just because it is the polite thing to do and because caregivers likely taught you to look at someone when you're talking to them, but because you want them to get your message. If you turn away they might miss or misinterpret what you said. Also, if someone has a hearing deficit, he or she cannot see your mouth movements to get the message.

When in front of a group, face them, and stand with your weight evenly distributed over both feet and shoulders to the front. Keep your head up and shoulders relaxed as you smile (depending on your topic) and use other open nonverbal gestures. Also, when writing on a surface, write, then turn and talk to your participants. Do not attempt both actions simultaneously.

Gesture Appropriately

Some trainers gesture a great deal, others hardly at all. One large challenge, for new and experienced trainers as well, is what to do with their hands as they speak. Some people clasp them behind their back, others in front. Some cross their arms; others rest them on a lectern or the arm of an overhead projector. (This should never be done, as it can bend the arm and make future adjustments of images onto a screen difficult). Still other trainers put their hands in their pockets, on their hips, or simply let them hang limply by their sides. A good stance is facing your learners with elbows bent and hands at about waist level in front of you. From this position you can easily gesture left, right, or in unison to emphasize a point or attract attention. For example, if asking a question from the group, you might simultaneously spread your arms and hands out, palms up, toward learners in a gesture indicating that you are giving them the floor or putting them in control. You are verbally and nonverbally eliciting a response. When asking for feedback or encouraging input of ideas, you might say something such as, "I would like to hear what you think about this" while gesturing with open arms toward your learners, then sweeping them inward toward you in a gathering motion.

As a general rule, gestures are used to highlight (similar to training aids) your vocal presentation of information. With the right motions, the hands can add punch or impact to a speech or message. Movements should appear natural and spontaneous, rather than forced or artificial. Do not wring your hands, keep fingers interlaced or clasped, crack your knuckles, pick your fingernails, play with rings, or repeat other nervous hand gestures. Use gesturing correctly to clarify or emphasize. One point to remember about using nonverbal gestures is that some cues have different meanings in various cultures. Some of the common gestures in Western cultures (e.g., thumbs up, forming a circle with the thumb and index finger, or motioning for someone to come to you palm up while bending joined fingers back and forth toward you can actually offend in other cultures; see Books in Resources for Trainers in the appendices). Be familiar with possible nonverbal meanings and use gestures appropriately.

Use Congruent Messages

Your verbal and nonverbal messages should match. For example, if you said, "I'd like you to remember four things. . ." while holding up three fingers, confusion is likely to result and learners might be distracted. The reason is that when verbal and nonverbal cues are used together, the nonverbal use normally overshadows the verbal message; in addition, more people are visual than auditory or kinesthetic learners.

Keep an Eye on Your Learners

Eye contact is a crucial element in building and maintaining trust. There are a variety of suggestions on how to use it during a training program. I have found that by making eye contact with a few select individuals who appear receptive or friendly, and smiling at them, I can relieve the initial anxiety felt during a presentation. Later, I casually make eye contact with other participants while sharing information throughout a program. To make everyone feel connected to me, the program, and the content, I periodically maintain eye contact with one or two learners as I speak before moving on to other learners and another point. Having practiced my material, I need to glance only occasionally at my lesson plan or notes. This allows me maximum time for participant eye contact.

The amount of time spent looking at your learners will vary. It is not necessarily the quantity but rather the quality of your eye contact that will make a difference. Concentrate on smiling and sending confident, friendly looks rather than challenging stares or blank gazes (e.g., over their heads or at the ceiling or floor).The latter can cause participants to believe you are nervous or unprepared as you blankly search for an answer or thought.

Eye contact is not only a way for you to send emotional messages to your learners. You can gain audience feedback by making eye contact with them throughout a session. For example, by noting blank stares you can often determine when someone has lost focus (MEGO effect—My Eyes Glaze Over) or it is time for a break (if large numbers of people exhibit MEGO). You can also determine confusion (constricted facial expressions), disagreement (frowning or shaking their head), or distraction (looking elsewhere) through eye contact.

PUTTING YOUR BRAIN TO WORK: ACTIVITY

What role have you seen nonverbal gestures play in managing learners in the past? _____

_____

_____

What types of nonverbal cues do you believe are least effective in a classroom? Why? _____

_____

_____

What types of nonverbal cues do you believe are most effective in a classroom? Why? _____

_____

_____

BRIGHT IDEA
Highlighted Notes

To help me quickly find key points in my notes or lesson plan, thus helping me spend more time making eye contact with learners, I use a color-coded highlighting system. First I capitalize and bold all headers, subheaders, and indications for training aids and activities in my lesson plan. I then use yellow highlighters to indicate visual aids such as slides, transparencies, posters, or flip charts. I use green for any handout materials that I will give to learners, such as workbooks, flyers, or job aids. I use orange for videotapes or audiotapes. Using the bold and highlighted indicators, I can quickly glance at notes and know what to do next because I have adequately prepared and know my material well. The result is that my focus stays on my learners and not my written materials.

Movement is the door to learning.
—Paul E. Dennison

● **PREVENTING RESISTANCE**

In any session you are likely to encounter people who for one reason or another do not want to be there or who feel they must compete for attention. Either type can create a challenge by interfering with planned activities, annoying people, and disrupting the learning process. Here are some things you can do that I find help reduce the amount of disruption encountered in training programs.

- **Be Approachable—smile!**
  You have already read about the power of smiles. Use them freely.
- **Use solid "people" skills.**
  Continually strive to improve your interpersonal communication skills such as the ones you read about earlier in this chapter.
- **Encourage questions and honest challenges.**
  People learn by questioning and processing ideas. Provide as many opportunities as possible in your session for doing this.
- **Set an environment of trust.**
  Take positive actions to ensure that participants feel safe and psychologically comfortable in your sessions.
- **Stress a safe environment.**
  Eliminate threats, intimidation, and put downs, and ensure that learners feel protected from unwarranted judgmental criticisms when voicing ideas, questions, or thoughts.
- **Facilitate, rather than direct learning.**
  Apply techniques such as the ones found in this book and others to engage and stimulate learners through active involvement.
- **Plan and practice.**
  Being ready for any situation helps ensure that instructions and activities will flow well and that your material delivery will appear seamless to learners.
- **Seize opportunities to recognize.**
  Develop a reward system and look for opportunities to compliment and honor achievement. Outline the system to learners at the beginning of the session and use it during the session.
- **Use attentive silence.**
  You do not have to talk all the time. Pause regularly to allow thinking and questioning. As participants talk, listen actively and react appropriately to their comments.
- **Provide appropriate feedback.**
  As Ken Blanchard, author of The One Minute Manager series, says in his book, "Feedback is the breakfast of champions." Take the time to recognize positive behavior (e.g., correct responses, contributions, or volunteerism) and give feedback. This encourages all participants to duplicate the action or behavior so as to receive their own positive stroking.

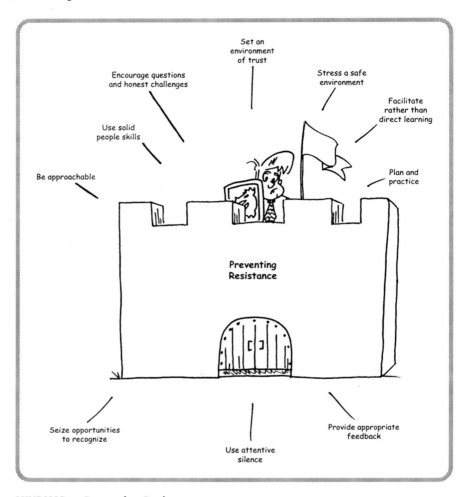

MINDMAP 2. Preventing Resistance

- **Accept, rather than deflect input.**
  When learners provide comments, ideas, responses, suggestions, or other input, even when you know it is incorrect, accept it. Thank the person for offering the information and either respond to it or open the floor to others with, "What do the rest of you think about what _____ just said?" This acknowledges the input as important and encourages future participation. Eliciting comments from others takes you out of the position of being the expert or disciplinarian, or possibly having to dispute a point. It also prevents the learner who offered the comment from looking "dumb" in front of peers, which might cause him or her to withdraw and shut down.

- **Offer credible evidence.**
  When you state facts or make references to material, provide professional citations or source information to add credibility. This can reduce opportunities for someone to challenge or dispute your information.
- **Mediate effectively.**
  When the inevitable disagreement occurs between individuals or groups, professionally and calmly intervene to redirect comments or head off inappropriate criticism or feedback.

● OVERCOMING RESISTANCE

Learners are typically in your sessions because they want to gain new knowledge, insights, and tools for enhancement of performance; however, there are instances when some participants do not have those goals or are reluctant to participate for a variety of reasons. The result can be resistance or challenges to learning for them and others during the program.

Indicators of Resistance

Here are some of the more common types of resistance that trainers encounter in sessions. See if you recognize any of them.

- **Coming to the Session Ill Prepared**
  People show up with no pencil or paper, have not done preclass assignments, and have no idea what the session is to be about.
- **Reluctance to respond**
  When questions are asked, participants refuse to answer or give only minimal responses, prompting follow-up questions. When this happens, make sure it is not because of the type of question you asked.
- **Side conversations with peers**
  Throughout the session, some learners hold side conversations about what is being discussed in class or about totally unrelated topics.
- **Making humorous remarks**
  To attract attention or as part of a personality that causes a learner to be fun loving, comments and jokes are made that elicit laughter from others. This is not necessarily bad unless it becomes continual, disruptive behavior.
- **Excessive breaks**
  Some people continue to return late from breaks or regularly excuse themselves throughout a session.
- **Questioning designed to derail**
  Some learners challenge ideas or comments that you or others make during the session, seemingly just to see if they can throw you off balance or to stimulate controversial discussion.

- **Doodling or working on outside items**
  Throughout a session, you may note some learners doodling (scribbling or drawing on a piece of paper), working on nonsession materials, or looking through their calendars.
- **Failure to complete assignments**
  When given an individual or group task (e.g., read information or write down ideas) some participants will ignore the assignment or will take a half-hearted approach and perform only minimally.
- **Disruptive behavior**
  Learners who exhibit juvenile behavior (e.g., shooting rubber bands or tossing paper balls) can distract others.

Because training time is too valuable to waste, controlling resistance is crucial. Unfortunately, many trainers revert to methods learners to control disruptive behavior that they learned as children from their caregivers (e.g., parents or teachers). They attempt to use intimidation (e.g., "Because I'm the trainer, that's why . . . ") or threats (e.g., "If you don't stop/settle down, I'm going to have to skip the break so we can cover all the material we have left), or accommodation (e.g., "We'll just wait until you finish your conversation so we can continue"). All of these strategies can lead to further resistance in the form of frustration and anger because you likely are going to embarrass the participant(s) involved and you are ultimately penalizing other learners. These approaches can also damage your credibility because you appear weak and powerless.

Strategies for Handling Resistance

To handle resistance effectively, you must first determine the reason for it. The behavior being exhibited by difficult learners is often not directly related to you or your program. Outside influences sometimes impact a trainee's desire or ability to focus and actively participate in a session. However, there might be some things that you are doing, or not doing, that may be causing adverse reaction or behavior. Some common causes of resistance follow.

Session-Related Causes

- **Program format or content**
  In some instances, you may have inappropriately planned content or targeted the wrong level of participants. For example, because of a limited or omitted needs assessment, you failed to determine that your audience is made up primarily of mid-level managers and supervisors. Yet, your program content is focused more on entry-level skills. The result is a bored and frustrated audience who feel they are wasting valuable time.
- **Delivery style or format**
  Perhaps you are tired or complacent about the topic and as a result are coming across in a low-key manner. Such a performance will likely drain enthusiasm or energy level and demotivate your learners.

- Trainer attitude

  Projecting an arrogant (e.g., I'm the expert), nonsupportive, or indifferent attitude, in which you are seen to be there because you have to be rather than want to in order to help can have a negative influence. If it appears that you have a canned presentation and are just going through a routine performance, participants might be offended and stop listening to your message.

- Training environment

  As you read in Chapter 5, the training atmosphere influences learning, retention, and application. If you are in a dull, colorless environment with ineffective lighting and temperature, or fail to provide refreshments and other elements to stimulate, participants will likely react accordingly.

- Your knowledge or expertise

  It is important to demonstrate that you are worth listening to. Because time is in such short supply these days participants need to believe that they will get value for their investment of time and money. This is especially true if you are an unknown coming from outside the organization. Providing advance marketing and background information can help encourage learner confidence in your abilities.

External Related Causes

- Preexisting expectations

  Learners may come with expectations based on the training environment or organization in which the training is being conducted. For example, they might show up without a pencil or notepad because they are in the habit of having such items provided by trainers. This is one reason why prior planning on your part is so crucial to your success. In addition, participants might not be enthusiastic because they know that their supervisor is not an advocate of training and sends learners only because management requires it. Once back in the workplace, participants are not encouraged to apply what was learned and instead hear things such as, "I hope you had a nice day off. Welcome back to the real world."

- Directed training

  A common reason for resistance that I have encountered is having participants who are required to attend a program, often as either part of an employee's professional growth performance goals or because of perceived deficits in knowledge, skills, or attitude.

- Misperceptions

  Participants sometimes register for a program without adequately reading program objectives. They register based on a session title (e.g., Communication Skills for Professional Advancement) thinking it will fit their needs. When the content turns out to be focused differently, the learner can become frustrated. For example, the preceding sample title might be a session about how to write business correspondence effectively, but the participant needed a course on interpersonal communication skills, including effective listening.

- Emotional baggage

  Many participants have experienced negative educational or training sessions in the past and bring their perceptions about such training with them to your sessions. Other emotional issues come in the form of learner immaturity, insecurity, and feelings of inadequacy or superiority. All of these can impact learner behavior and your session.

- Professional issues

  Distractions can occur when a participant is dealing with workplace issues, for example, project deadlines, workload, performance appraisal issues, supervisory or peer conflicts or changes, job changes, or other similar issues.

- Personal issues

  Like professional issues, events in a learner's personal life can also distract from his or her ability to focus on session topics, for example, financial, family health, marital, dependent problems, or other home life issues.

- Previous experiences

  If a learner has attended programs similar to the one that you are offering, you may have to prove why yours is better or will help him or her further. Some organizations continually offer professional development opportunities for employees and require that they attend. The result is that you must show AVARFM to participants so they recognize a personal value to learning. Otherwise, they may come in with the attitude that your program is just a rehash or what they know, or is the flavor of the month, which will pass if they just attend and sit quietly, then return to work. Chances are that in such situations, there is no accountability to apply what was covered once employees return to the workplace. So, it does not really matter whether they learn anything or not.

Taking Action to Reduce Resistance

Resistance can be annoying and detrimental to the success of your session. It must be dealt with professionally and swiftly. In dealing with resistant learners, make it appear as smooth and effortless as possible. This is a sign of your professionalism and is accomplished through planning and research on dealing with such behavior in advance. Attend courses and read books on training techniques and on interpersonal communication skills. Learn a variety of strategies for dealing with difficult personality types and behaviors, then use them. Become a student of human behavior.

BRIGHT IDEA

Taking Action to Reduce Resistance

To help you decide on a course of action, review the causes for resistance you read earlier. Also, get answers to the appropriate questions below. Some of these can be answered through a needs assessment conducted prior to or at the beginning of your session.

How are typical sessions organized and prepared?

What expectations might learners bring with them to the session?

Why are learners attending the session?

Were objectives and a program description accurately and adequately distributed prior to registration?

Has appropriate contents and activities been planned based on scheduled audience makeup?

How has program format and delivery been organized?

What might learner reaction be to the planned program?

Am I adequately prepared and enthusiastic about the session?

In what ways will the planned environment contribute to a successful program?

Are all materials, equipment, and supplies available and working?

What negative external workplace factors may hinder learner participation, interest, and success?

What professional issues are participants dealing with that might interfere with their learning?

● INTERACTING WITH DIFFICULT LEARNERS

We train in a diverse world in which learners bring a variety of ethnic, cultural, and other personal factors with them. The result is that you are likely to come into contact with someone you might consider a "difficult" learner each time you go into a training environment. As you read in Chapter 3, you are constantly coming into contact with people who are demographically, culturally, mentally, and physically different from you. The strategies outlined in that chapter can assist you to interact effectively with diverse groups of people. In this section you will read about techniques I have learned and used to handle people who, because of personality or attitude issues, can create confrontational or awkward situations for you and their peers. To maintain credibility and some degree of control, you must take a head-on approach in handling participants who distract or disrupt training. Your learners look to you to do so. The important thing to remember in dealing with any of these learners is to be firm, but fair and consistent. Also, do not publicly ridicule or embarrass learners. Failure to follow this advice can lead to confrontation and animosity from the participant involved. It can also cause you to lose respect in the eyes of others, especially friends of the participant involved or whom you embarrassed. Participants tend to stick together when someone outside their group "attacks" one of them. The following are descriptions of a variety of participant behaviors that can create learning challenges and some ideas for addressing them.

Talkers

A learner who is a talker can be one of two types.

Conversationalist

The first is one who continually holds side conversations in a low voice with those sitting nearby. When asked if he or she would share his or her comment with the rest of the group, the response is usually, "No" or "That's okay." To handle such participants I use one or more of the following tactics.

Tactic 1

Without drawing attention to the person verbally, I casually move in his or her direction as I continue to talk to all participants. I position myself near the person, possibly increasing my volume to draw attention to myself. I also make direct eye contact with the person as I speak. The power of nonverbal communication (e.g., closing proximity, raising my voice, and making eye contact) is powerful and will normally say to the person, "Pay attention." Once I have refocused the learner's attention I can move back to the front of the room. This technique works well in rooms configured for interaction, as outlined in Chapter 5.

Tactic 2

A simple strategy that also ties to brain-based learning concepts is to move a person who is talking to another location or group. This is helpful for dividing small cliques of friends or co-workers who often sit together out of choice or a feeling of obligation to do so. People who know one another are often more likely to have side conversations, often about non–session-related topics. To accomplish such movement, use one of the random techniques discussed in other parts of this book so that it is not obvious that you are doing so primarily to relocate a talker. This can prevent the perception that you are singling one person out or picking on him or her. I often put extra grouping systems in place when planning a session even though I may not use them (e.g., colored dots on name tents, color-coded pencils, and so forth). Doing this allows me to group participants spontaneously as needed.

Tactic 3

A more direct approach to handling a conversationalist is to ask a blanket question of the entire group and then directly call on the person talking to answer it (CPA questioning technique described earlier). For example, "Earlier, we discussed ___. Can someone give an example of how that would work in the workplace? (Talker's Name)?"

I generally reserve the use of this tactic for learners who have been an ongoing nuisance, and after I have tried other strategies with little success. In this manner, I do not unduly embarrass anyone. By the time I use this third approach, other participants have started to show nonverbal displeasure with this person for his or her behavior.

Tactic 4

When all else fails, you may need either to call a break or take the talker aside during a scheduled break. When you do so, be polite and tactful, but firm. Inform the learner that he is creating a diversion and try to determine if anything is wrong. Often a talker is just friendly and not aware of creating a distraction. Other possibilities are that he did not want to attend the session voluntarily or is not feeling challenged by the strategies and techniques you are using. He may also feel that he already knows what is being covered and is bored. The first possibility might need to be handled by asking the person to leave and the second by soliciting suggestions for making the material more meaningful to them.

Non-Stop Talkers

The second type of Talker includes participants who start talking in front of the group and do not want to quit. These learners are sometimes difficult to control because they either enjoy being the center of attention or simply have poor communication skills and tend to ramble. Whatever the cause, such a participant can distract and ultimately annoy others. If you do not control these talkers, you very likely will get off schedule and have trouble covering planned content. There are a variety of ways to address this second type of Talker.

Tactic 1

Once it becomes obvious that a participant likes to talk, use tactful interruptions to regain control. For example, while the participant is talking, politely interrupt and say something such as, "That's an interesting point you just made. Let me stop you and get input from some others." Then, quickly call on another learner. If the talker seems to need other ideas or perspectives related to an issue being faced, you can offer to discuss during breaks.

Tactic 2

If the Talker tends to get off on tangents, especially by going off the original topic, interrupt with, "That sounds like it is important, however, we need to stay on topic. Can you and I discuss your point further at break?" Then quickly start talking or call on someone else.

Tactic 3

Use closed-ended questions to gain control of the conversation, then quickly ask someone else for input. For example, ask the Talker, "Does that happen often?" If he or she says yes, then quickly ask others for suggestions to offer the Talker. If he or she says, "Not really," then state something such as, "Well then, maybe we should spend our time more wisely on issues that do occur regularly." Then quickly proceed or ask others for input.

Shy Participants

In contrast to the Talkers, you will often encounter the learners who do not want to respond in front of a large group. Because of personality, or perhaps from a feeling that they do not know enough or have nothing valuable to contribute, these participants quietly melt into the group. They are attentive and proactive in capturing information, just quiet. By being alert for such behavior, you can possibly draw them into the program. This offers them a chance to learn and grow and provides additional perspectives and ideas to other learners. Many technically skilled people have introverted personalities, yet they obviously have much knowledge to share. To get shy learners involved, I often try one or more of the following strategies.

Tactic 1

Smile, greet them by name, and use open body language to put them, and others, at ease. You also send a message of being approachable.

Tactic 2

Take time to get to know shy learners at the beginning of the session or during breaks and introduce them to other participants. If they feel comfortable around others or know them, chances are they will be less reluctant to interact or talk during the session.

Tactic 3

I start involving shy participants by asking them several easy closed-ended questions to which I am sure they have an answer. This is an old sales technique. The idea is that you ask a series of short-answer questions that elicit positive responses or affirmative answers, then you ask for the sale. Psychologically, because the person has been talking for a while and agreeing, he or she often agrees to the sale. After answering several easy questions, the confidence of shy learners grows, and you then can ask them an open-ended opinion question (e.g., "How do you think that would work?" or "In what ways do you see that as being useful?").

Tactic 4

I often use dyads (two people) and triads (three people) and small groups. Many shy people feel comfortable speaking in smaller group settings and interactions.

Experts

A third category of difficult learners are the ones who have (or think they have) a great deal of subject knowledge and skill. This group can cause potential problems or confrontation if handled incorrectly. They are often people who are technically skilled, knowledgeable, and well trained or educated. My experience is that many of these people are confident and have a need to be heard. They will often challenge what I say or give additional information following each point presented because they want to show their knowledge.

The reason that you should not put yourself into a position in which you arbitrarily say, "Research shows. . . ." is that an Expert will likely ask for a source, thus putting you on the defensive or damaging your credibility if you cannot provide one.

Here are some ideas for handling this type of learner.

Tactic 1

Be polite and do not show signs of irritation when an Expert speaks up. Listen to what he or she has to say, then defer to other learners (e.g., "How does that sound to the rest of you?"), rather than confronting or saying that you disagree. Other participants will often disagree. This peer pressure can potentially soften the Expert's approach. You can always add more information following what is offered by other learners or you can cite expert sources. If the expert challenges dates, credibility of sources, and so forth, I simply state, "I wasn't aware of that. I'll research it and get back to you." I then state, "Let's get back to our topic and move on." Obviously you should not use this latter approach often because others may begin to see the Expert as more knowledgeable and start deferring to what he or she says rather than to what you are providing.

Tactic 2

Identify any experts in your group through a pre-session needs assessment or a quick in-class assessment once everyone arrives. Introduce yourself to them before the session begins, if possible, and ask if they would mind you calling on them for additional input from time to time. Once the session starts, acknowledge their presence or expertise. This stroking of ego can help defuse their need to try to take control. You might also make such a person a small group leader during an activity. Be careful to monitor them in group sessions, however, or you may find all other participants deferring to this person's knowledge or experience when they are supposed to brainstorm or come to a group consensus. If this seems to be happening, take the Expert aside and again appeal to their knowledge by encouraging them to guide the thinking of others rather than providing all the answers because they are in a learning environment. I have found that by being professional and partnering with experts, there is normally little problem having them in a session.

Pessimists

There are some participants who for a variety of reasons will try to squelch the ideas of others. These learners automatically respond, "Yes, but. . . . ," no matter what is offered. My personal belief is that what they do is learned behavior they got from caregivers as children. Their role models likely were poor communicators who failed to give positive feedback or reinforcement to these people often. Pessimists will typically use such phrases as:

We tried that before and it did not work.

Sounds good in theory, but it won't work here.

That will never work in the real world.

Upper management (supervisors) will not support that.

Policy (law/regulations) prevent us from . . .

We don't have time/money/resources to . . .

I have found that a number of strategies can help in dealing with Pessimistic learners.

Tactic 1

Ask for the pessimist's reasoning of why an idea will not work, then offer his or her response to the group for their input or feedback. Ask, "What do the rest of you think about what ___ just said?" Be careful and prepared for what you will do if they agree with the pessimist. Sometimes, there are real unspoken issues that you are not made aware of that prevent application of training concepts. If important issues have surfaced you may want to either flip chart them for later discussion, give to management (assuming learners agree to that), or take a diversion and discuss the issue, then brainstorm possible courses of action for a short period of time. Otherwise, learners may be distracted by the issue and you will end up with a roomful of Talkers.

Assuming that others do not agree with the Pessimist, they will likely wear the person down. Peer pressure is a powerful tool for quieting dissention.

Tactic 2

Assume that the pessimistic learner may have a point and ask, "What alternate ideas do you have?" or "What do you suggest instead?" Often he or she will not have given any real thought to the issue and cannot think of another option. If that is the case, suggest that the group discuss the original idea presented further and that if the Pessimist thinks of something later you are willing to consider it. On the other hand, if the Pessimist does have an alternate suggestion, listen to it, then discuss the merits as a class or take other action deemed appropriate.

Agitator

Some learners have a personality, and display behavior, that is a constant irritant to others. If you are unfortunate enough to have such a person in your session, your patience will be tested, as will that of other participants. The reasons for such behavior vary, however, my experience seems to indicate that these people are inwardly insecure and feel they need to demand attention in whatever way and form possible. Likely, such people have done so or been rebels all their lives. They have probably resisted authority in many forms, so you are not likely to succeed in appealing to their better side or win them over.

You probably represent the organization or management to them, especially if you work for or were brought in by Human Resources or upper management. As such, you are fair game to them because they probably would not take pot shots at HR or upper management representatives directly. The following strategies might help in dealing with Agitators.

Tactic 1

Be firm, polite, and take charge of the situation immediately. Other participants look to you to intercede, especially if the Agitator is attacking one of them or their ideas. In a cordial manner react to a negative or sarcastic comment with, "That may be how you feel ___; however, we should hear from others about their views." Then call on someone else immediately. Do not let the Agitator corner you into a one-on-one confrontation. Others who are friends of the person may side with him or her.

Tactic 2

Partner with the Agitator to diffuse his or her argument and thereby regain control of the session. Look for something in what the person says that you can agree with. For example, if an Agitator says something such as, "You stand up there and give us all these great ideas without ever having worked in this organization." To counter, I would agree, "You are correct. I have not worked in this organization; however, I have held similar positions in other organizations, have done research on the issues you brought up, or spoke with a number of employees from this organization before the session to gather background information. These strategies have worked in similar situations and this program's content is based on my experience and findings." This is all assuming I have done these things. Do not lead the Agitator or any other participant into believing you have done something that you have not. If they catch you in a lie you can lose and never regain credibility.

Tactic 3

Simply agree with the Agitator and ask if anyone else has a comment, then move on.

Tactic 4

State, "We seem to have differing opinions on the issue. Can we simply agree to disagree and move on? You and I can discuss it further during a break if you would like."

Revolutionary

Some trainees come to a session with their own agenda. Even though you may have clearly stated the program objectives and given an accurate description of content in promotional material, they want something else. As a result, they try to take control of the session by stating, "What we really need is. . . ."

Tactic 1

Do a quick in-class needs assessment via either a show of hands or anonymously have participants respond on a strip of blank paper. Ask, "Who agrees with ____?" If the majority feels the issue is important, you may want to do a quick content adjustment and build it into your program. You can do so by either modifying and shortening other less important topics or replacing something altogether. To do this you obviously need a strong subject knowledge base and have confidence in your ability to think on your feet. One way to accomplish the inclusion of unplanned agenda items is to have small group brainstorming on the issue and the possible solutions. Thus, you give them time to air the issue and walk away with real-world suggestions they can use, so they are likely to be more satisfied with the training experience.

I have found in such situations that a contributing cause for participants' need to address extra issues is that they never have time or opportunity to do so during their normal days. The only time they all come together is in training or other organizational sponsored event. They likely know the problem and probably have good ideas for solving it; they just need a forum to put it all together. When this type of issue surfaces and I deal with it in the preceding manner, I traditionally get my highest session evaluation markings for providing valuable tools they can use. In reality, all I did was get out of the way and facilitate their problem solving.

Tactic 2

Let the Revolutionary know that although the issue being surfaced by him or her is important, the group needs to get through the session content first. Tell them that if time permits at the end of the program, the issue can be addressed then. Capture the idea, and any others that surface, on a posted flip chart page to make it visual, to show its importance, and to be reminded of it later. Some trainers call such a page a "Parking Lot" of ideas or issues and even use colorful graphics to make the sheet look like a parking lot. If time does not permit at the end of the session, offer to discuss it with the Revolutionary after the program. If others agree that it is an important issue affecting them all, try to get an additional session scheduled to address it or pass it along to management with the recommendation that action needs to be taken on it.

Clown

In many groups, you will encounter one or more people who are fun loving and seek attention through practical jokes or humorous words or actions. While such behavior can help liven a session, it can also distract if carried to an extreme. It can be compounded when friends of the Clown continue to encourage the behavior or contribute their own.

To address Clowns, try the following strategies.

Tactic 1

Ignore the behavior or comments if possible. This eliminates the psychological reward of the person being recognized before the group.

Tactic 2

Appeal to the learner's serious side by asking session-related questions or opinions of him or her.

Tactic 3

If friends in a small group are contributing to and encouraging the behavior, separate them in a random manner. Use some of the techniques described in this book.

Tactic 4

If the Clown's behavior is really a problem, call a short break, meet with the Clown, and discuss the need to remain on task.

PUTTING YOUR BRAIN TO WORK: ACTIVITY

1. What are some additional types of disruptive participants whom you have seen in the past?

_____

_____

2. What strategies have you seen used to deal with the types of learners you listed in question 1?

_____

_____

Although these are not the only challenging types of behaviors you will come across in your sessions, they are some of the more common. See Books in the Resources for Trainers in the appendices for additional resources on the topic.

APPLYING WHAT YOU LEARNED
Strategies for Keeping the Communication Flowing

1. How can you use what you read in this chapter to improve the design of your written materials?

_____

_____

2. What materials can you think of to use as job aids for reinforcing what participants get in the classroom on the job? _____

_____

3. In what ways can you add pizzazz to your flip charts using information found in this chapter?

_____

_____

4. How can posters, charts, and diagrams be incorporated into future training programs?

_____

_____

5. What are some creative training uses that you can think of for Post-It® Notes?

_____

_____

6. What role do you see cloth boards and other static displays playing in future training sessions?

_____

_____

7. How can electronic visual aids effectively be used in your training programs?

_____

_____

ENDNOTES

[35] Howard, P.J., *The Owner's Manual for the Brain,* 2nd ed., Bard Press, Atlanta, GA, 2000, pp. 663–668.

[36] Mehrabian, A. (1968), Communication without words, *Psychology Today*, September, pp. 52–55.

[37] Carnegie, D., *How to Develop Self-Confidence and Influence People by Public Speaking,* Pocket Books, New York, 1956, p. 115.

Celebrating Successes

It is what we do easily and what we like to do that we do well.
—Orison Swett Marden

Learning Objectives

At the end of this chapter, and when applying concepts covered, you will be able to:

- Use the criteria for an effective reward to select appropriate incentives for your learners.

- Apply some basic concepts related to motivation in setting up the proper learning environment.

- Identify intrinsic and extrinsic motivators.

- Avoid doing things that stifle or destroy learner motivation.

- Reinforce learning through various types of review activities.

- Bring your sessions to a formal close so that learners feel the experience is complete.

- Recognize the elements of an effective formal session closing.

- End your sessions in a memorable fashion.

To add a bit of festivity and fun while reinforcing learning that occurs during your training sessions, try using rewards, recognition, and celebrations. Many adult learners enjoy having an opportunity to have their knowledge and efforts recognized or to culminate an activity with some form of celebration or ritual. Such acknowledgment and reward can be something as simple as a verbal compliment or feedback on performance. It can also be a more tangible form, such as a small prize or group celebration with gifts. In effect, when recognition occurs in a safe environment where threats and negative stress are minimal or eliminated, creativity, problem-solving, interaction, and transfer of knowledge often result.

According to some researchers and educators, rewards, also known as bribes, do not work well in reinforcing learning for younger people. Their position is that rewards merely reinforce rote behavior or mindless compliance to the teacher or instructor, and may actually inhibit learning. These researchers contend that although small or short-term rewards can encourage and stimulate action, longer term behavior (e.g., learning and memory) can actually be impeded. However, adults have already formed basic behavior and values. As a result, rewards and incentives can be used to provide in a light-hearted manner, reminiscent of younger days. Still, usage of rewards should be well planned and should never distract from learning activities. Like training aids, they should reinforce learning and tie into the session theme rather than appearing arbitrary. Further, Pierce[38] indicates that research reports, ". . . Rewards for effort are more encouraging in the long run than rewards for success. Research suggests that no one general rule defines the best way to encourage creative excellence. People are different. Do what works. To encourage creativity in a person, match his or her personality and its attendant values. Reward extroverts with a part, introverts with a good book!" Pierce goes on to say you should emphasize verbal encouragement and time your encouragement for occasions of special effort and achievement from learners.

● CRITERIA FOR REWARDS

The key to the effective use of rewards is to do so in a manner that promotes a bit of diversion and not have rewards become a goal of the program. Some trainers use so many games, gimmicks, and rewards that learners lose sight of why they are there—for learning. Instead, they get caught up in the competitions and the rewards that result. Although use of rewards can be helpful in encouraging participation and desired behavior to some extent, they should be used for fun, variety, and novelty, and not as a primary learning vehicle in your programs.

Rewards come in many tangible forms. Anything that you use to inspire, encourage, motivate, or compensate a learner can be a reward or incentive. For something to be categorized as a reward, it should generally meet the following criteria.

- **Valuable**

   Learners need to recognize the item you are giving as a reward as having positive value. Examples of such rewards include candy, stickers, toys, food, prizes, or gifts. The dollar value is irrelevant because each learner places importance and desirability on his or her own experience and need. Some people treasure small toys or mementos whereas others other crave larger, more expensive gifts.

- **Predictable**

   Predictability is a second criterion for determining if something is a reward. For example, you announce that you will use small prizes, such as candy, cookies, or other incentives as a reward for group accomplishment following activities.

   Behavioral researchers have developed the following schedules for reinforcing behavior.

- **Continuous reinforcement**

   This schedule for giving rewards provides a learner an incentive or prize each time an action is taken, behavior improves, or the person meets established criteria (e.g., following each correct response volunteered).

- **Intermittent reinforcement**

   When a predetermined ratio or time schedule is met and a reward is provided, learners are being intermittently compensated (e.g., at the end of each activity or on the hour).

- **Fixed ratio reinforcement**

   You might provide a reward at specified intervals or at a fixed time (e.g., after someone answers five questions correctly, he or she receives a reward).

- **Variable ratio reinforcement**

   When learners are rewarded based on group average, or an average number of responses, they are receiving variable reinforcement (e.g., if the average test score is 80, then everyone scoring 80 or higher on a test would be rewarded).

- **Fixed interval reinforcement**

   When you spread rewards out over a uniform time period, you are using a fixed pattern of reinforcement (e.g., rewards are given at the beginning of each break and lunch period).

- **Variable interval reinforcement**

   There may be times when you want to give rewards at unannounced or unpredictable times (e.g., you arbitrarily decide to give everyone on a learner's team a reward because each group member offered ideas during a discussion or returned from break on time).

- **Purposeful**

   Your purpose for giving or taking away something is the third criterion used to determine if something you give qualifies as a reward. If your goal in providing or withdrawing something is to change participants' behavior or to influence them to be more motivated, then it is a reward.

BACK TO THE BASICS

You are probably aware of the major schools of thought and theories related to human motivation and behavior. Classic studies by noted researchers such as B.F. Skinner (Behavior Modification), Ivan Pavlov (Operant Conditioning), Frederick Herzberg (Motivation/Hygiene Factors), Abraham Maslow (Hierarchy of Needs), and Douglas McGregor (X/Y Theory), continue to provide trainers with insights into how to encourage and influence learner motivation and behavior. According to such researchers, motivation that drives behavior is something that each person has within or something provided by his or her environment. As a trainer, you cannot make learners become motivated or learn. Nor can you make them change their behavior. However, you can influence them through a variety of creative strategies by setting up an environment in which learning is not only expected, but also encouraged and supported. You can do this by identifying what is important to learners (e.g., through a needs assessment), then either providing it or giving them the tools they need to attain it on their own.

Many times, learners believe that they do not want or need what your training offers. When this occurs, you have to become a salesperson or therapist of sorts. You must first determine why they are resistant (as you read in Chapter 9), or what they need. You then have to address barriers to learning and seek ways to remove them to fulfill learner needs. Keep in mind that what motivates one does not motivate all. Although some of the small toys and incentives discussed in this book might work well to encourage some, they may appear childish and insignificant to others. This is why your ability to assess your participants' needs in advance is crucial. For example, I once had a group of upper management members, including several vice presidents, in a teambuilding program. Analysis showed that they needed to communicate better and to learn to work as a team. One way to accomplish this was to allow them an environment in which they could relax and have fun while getting to know one another better. We used an off-site location and wore very casual clothing. I also decided to use some of the incentive processes described in this chapter and others. When I first introduced the idea that I would be using stickers on name tents to reward participation I could see some of the more autocratic people bristle. However, after we got into the program and I started rewarding some people during the first hour, the competitive nature of these managers emerged. At one point I even had a Senior VP call out, "Hey, Bob, you forgot to give me a sticker for that last answer." What I likely was witnessing was a "need" to be recognized and to excel. They saw peers (some junior) with more stickers than they had. The prize that I was going to give at the end of the session for the person with the most stickers was not important. They

did not even know what that prize was. What was important was their internal need to reach a goal of being the best (self-actualization, according to Maslow) while satisfying their own intrinsic need.

For any reward program to be effective in your training, it is important to outline the guidelines for usage. I generally discuss my reward philosophy and system at the beginning of a session and stress the fun aspect. This sets the tone for later implementation.

As it is for me, your challenge in using reward and incentive programs is to do so in a manner that does not distract from the learning. In my preceding example with the upper managers, I explained to them that they did not get a sticker every time they said something (random reinforcement). Otherwise, I would have spent all my time running from one name tent to the next placing stickers rather than facilitating. This would have been ineffective and distracting.

> **BRIGHT IDEA**
> ### Mastering the Basics
> To understand more effectively the importance of human motivational theory, do an Internet search for information on the researchers listed in this section. Also, type in key words, such as "Motivation," "Learner Motivation," and "Intrinsic and Extrinsic Motivation." By learning as much as possible about human nature and behavior, you can become a more effective trainer of adults.

● TYPES OF MOTIVATORS

Performance satisfaction comes from two sources—internal (intrinsic) or external (extrinsic)—depending on what a person values and needs. Because each of your learners will have differing perspectives on what is important to him or her, you should build in a combination of activities, recognition, and rewards to help fulfill both intrinsic and extrinsic needs of all your learners.

Intrinsic Motivators

Throughout life, learners are exposed to many experiences that shape their values and beliefs. Their exposure leads them to appreciate, desire, and covet certain things over others. Some people become more materialistic, seeking to collect "things" or build their resources. Others strive for a more cerebral balance in which emotional experiences and intangible opportunities create more enjoyment for them. For this latter group, self-satisfaction or a feeling of accomplishment is more important than receiving material rewards. For example, such learners are often just as pleased when receiving sincere, descriptive feedback about their performance as they would be getting a gift certificate.

This is because a gift certificate may be a physical sign of appreciation, however, once it is used, nothing remains. On the other hand, when you provide such learners with meaningful commentary on a task well done, they can later recall the emotionally happy experience of getting the recognition. This feedback might be one-on-one or in front of a group of their peers, depending on their personalities and beliefs (some ethnic and religious groups do not seek individual gain or personal recognition; they strive for group achievement and harmony instead).

People who are intrinsically motivated often tend to be self-starters. They do things for the satisfaction of completing them. These are the learners who continually volunteer to take leadership roles or answer questions, offer ideas, and provide input during problem-solving. Factors such as personal interest, self-fulfillment, positive **self-talk,** desire, and initiative drive their behavior.

Intrinsic Rewards from Training

Many internal factors or needs drive a learner's behavior. Although receiving tangible items and recognition is important, many participants gain a greater sense of satisfaction from within. The following is a list of some of the internal factors that cause a person to speak up, volunteer, and become active in your sessions.

Personal Enjoyment

Many participants gain enjoyment from the learning process itself. Some people simply like the challenge of having their brains engaged or trying to learn new information or skills. The simple process of gaining new perspectives (the "ah ha" factor) can lead to personal satisfaction.

Self-Satisfaction

By being part of a team or group as it searches for new ideas, knowledge, or discovery, some learners feel that they are achieving personal satisfaction—one that comes from reaching a goal or being part of something beneficial.

Elevated Self-Esteem

Participants who enjoy growing personally and professionally and those who believe that knowledge is power often get a sense of confidence through training. This leads to learners feeling better about themselves and often comes from having their ideas or efforts accepted during a training session.

A Feeling of Control

Some participants enjoy the academic challenge of being in a training session with peers. They thrive on the feeling that comes from directing activities as volunteer group leaders and the learning of others or from being in charge of their own learning.

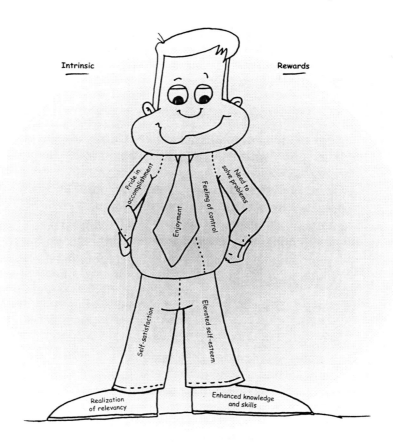

MINDMAP 1. Intrinsic Rewards

Need to Solve Problems

With so little time to address problems or issues in the workplace, many participants welcome the opportunity to have dedicated periods in training during which they, and others, can brainstorm potential solutions that will make their jobs easier. They enjoy a chance to come up with alternate answers to issues. This is especially gratifying if the solution adds significant value to the workplace, team, others, or the learner's personal life.

Realization of Relevancy

When training is clearly related to the workplace, participants often feel a sense of accomplishment that comes from recognizing that what they are learning or experiencing has a direct link to their lives and jobs. Material that is pragmatic and not just theoretical is seen to provide a purpose for the learning.

Pride in Accomplishment

There is a certain pleasure or sense of self-fulfillment that can be derived from learning or mastering difficult subjects or skills. This is especially true when only a few before the learner have met such milestones.

Enhanced Knowledge and Skills

Through an investment of time and effort, many learners recognize that their efforts to learn and apply what is gained can ultimately lead to an improved status in the workplace or life as a whole.

By creating an environment in which learners can attain intrinsic goals or rewards, such as those listed in the preceding, you can encourage involvement and ultimately success. Giving participants choice in what and how they learn, and some degree of control over the learning process, increases the chances of your success in facilitating learning.

Recognition of Achievement

Like rewards, recognition can help motivate learners to participate, share ideas, and give input during a session. When you recognize someone, you have potentially demonstrated some degree of appreciation or approval for his or her behavior. The major difference between rewards and recognition is that the latter comes in a variety of intangible forms. For example, someone raises a hand to ask a question or offer a response to something you said and you call on the person. In taking this simple action, you have potentially satisfied a need the participant has for attention or to be acknowledged as significant.

Recognition can also sometimes be accompanied by giving tangible rewards. For example, in addition to asking the group to give someone a round of applause for a creative idea, you can also reward the learner with a piece of candy or a small prize.

There are many ways in which you can recognize learner performance and thus respond to intrinsic needs. Here are a few ideas to consider.

Use the Names of Learners

An old adage says that "There is nothing sweeter than the sound of one's own name." Maybe this is why successful business people use their customers' names often during interactions. If nothing else, using a person's name cuts down on confusion when you refer to them in a group.

Have a Dress Down Day

If your organization does not already have them, get permission for trainees to attend your session in business casual clothing. This will send a message that they are getting special treatment and help relax the environment. This latter benefit can enhance learning opportunities because psychologically a level of stress is eliminated or reduced.

Get Senior Management Involvement

Request that a member of senior management come in at the beginning or end of the session. Ask the manager to stress the importance of the program and thank attendees for their involvement and investment of time.

Incorporate Ceremony and Ritual into Your Programs

You can add ceremony and ritual by doing simple things. For example, whenever someone offers a solution or a perspective related to an issue or problem, have all participants join in a round of applause for the person. You can also recognize some important learner event such as an anniversary with the organization or a birthday. You might bring in a small cupcake with a candle or sparkler on it and have everyone sing. Be cautious about celebrating birthdays unless you are sure that it is acceptable. Some individuals do not celebrate such events because of religious or cultural beliefs. When in doubt do not celebrate; find an alternative way to recognize the person.

Decorate the Room

Use colorful signs or posters to make learners feel that they are appreciated and anticipated. For example, put up a brightly decorated "Welcome" banner in New Hire Orientation programs. You can buy vinyl-bordered blank banners at party stores and use dry erase markers to write in whatever information you please or you can create paper banners with computers. Personalize the banner or sign by listing the names of new employees on it. Perhaps even take a group photo and give each new hire a copy later as a memento. They can later review the pictures on an anniversary date with others who started working at the organization when they did.

Schedule Training Offsite

Whenever possible, conduct your sessions away from the workplace. This prevents learners from going back to their office during breaks and returning late, but it also keeps supervisors from sending someone to get learners or ask questions. In addition, it often makes participants feel special or important to go off to a program.

Arrange Site Visits

There is something about an effectively planned site visit that makes a program seem more valuable. Most learners love the opportunity to see how others are using the techniques or tools that they are being taught. They also like to see how problems similar to their own are being handled. Such trips can also enhance the perception of a program's importance and usefulness.

Provide Ongoing Kudos

Throughout your session, give **kudos** for achievements by learners. These might be coupled with tangible rewards.

Give Feedback

Whenever a learner does something well, or perhaps when expectations or goals are not met, let them know what you observed. If necessary, let learners know how they might improve their performance. When giving feedback, focus on the behavior and not the individual. Give the feedback that is sincere, specific, and timely (as soon after the event as possible).

Note Exceptional Behavior

Take time to point out examples of exceptional behavior in your sessions. Compliment the participant demonstrating the behavior. Doing this can encourage that participant, and others, to repeat similar behavior. For example, during a break, you can use a colorful cutout shape, such as a star (see Tools for Trainers in the appendices) to write a personal compliment. Put the note on the seat of the learner who exhibited the behavior while she is on break. She will find it on her return and know that what she did was noticed and appreciated. This type of recognition would be in addition to any public acknowledgment she received from you with the group present (e.g., a sticker on her name tent).

Photo Wall of Fame

As learners enter the room, take a Polaroid or digital photograph of them. Once they develop or are printed from a computer, have each person write his name and a strength he has, related to the session topic, on the bottom of his picture. Post these on the wall for all to view during the breaks. This is a good way to help people put a name with a face and to learn what resources they have in the room, should they need assistance later or in the future.

Help Learners Succeed

Throughout your program, share experiences (positive and negative) along with tidbits of wisdom. Offer any information (e.g., the type of material I have offered in the Resources for Trainers in the appendices) that will assist participants in growing professionally. This could be done by sharing research findings, giving contact information for future networking, or offering your ideas on a particular issue.

Create a Credit Chart

Prepare a flip chart with the name of each attendee on the left side of the page. Before beginning your session, have each person write down one creative idea related to accomplishment of stated learning objectives. Next, have each person in turn offer his or her idea to the group while you write it next to his or her name. Post this list for reference during the session and institute any ideas that are feasible.

Have Participants Co-Facilitate

If you have someone with a special talent or knowledge related to your session topic, ask them to share what they know with others. You might learn some new things also. They can share a best practice, explain a process they use, or otherwise share expertise. Recognize their efforts with group applause or a ceremony and/or a reward.

Use a Traveling Trophy or Award

Create an award or buy a plastic trophy that you can use in class. Present it to the first person who comes up with a solution, volunteers to assist, or whatever else you decide. Tell learners that the recipient gets to hold the award until someone else offers a creative solution or takes some other designated action. If you use these to designate group leaders, you may want to have a trophy for each group. The award provides visual confirmation of positive performance.

Arrange for Peers to Say "Thank You"

Build in activities during and at the end of your session in which learners can give one another thanks or positive feedback. For example, you can have participants turn to one another to say "thank you" for offering information or helping make the learning experience better. You can also have everyone form groups at the end of a session, then pass out small strips of paper so that each person has one strip for every member of his or her group. Have all learners write the names of peers on the strips of paper so that they have one for each teammate. Finally, have members of each team write one positive thing on the strips that they liked about their teammates. Encourage them to sign the strips so that people know who the comments were from. Collect all the strips and separately group the comments for each participant. You may want to do this as participants fill out their session evaluations. Without reading the strips yourself, distribute them to the appropriate learners. Each learner now has nice comments from his or her peers with which they can end their day.

Give "Thank You" Letters

If you cannot get a member of senior management to attend your session closing, ask that one of them (ideally the president or CEO) at least provide a letter addressed personally to each learner. Ask him or her to stress the importance of using what was learned to improve themselves and the organization and thank them for their participation. You can draft this letter for signature, thus increasing the likelihood of getting one done and that it will say what you need. At the end of the session, present the letter in an official organizational envelope, possibly along with a Certificate of Achievement, diploma, and/or a small present.

Establish a Special Award

An award for some special performance can be used to enhance participant pride and spirit. The award does not even have to be serious in nature. For example, you might create a *No. 1 Team Player* certificate. Have learners vote for the winner at the end of the session. The certificate can be colorful with balloons or a group of cartoon characters on it along with the wording. I recently used something similar to this at a leadership retreat and the learners loved it.

Say "Thank You"

In addition to having learners say "Thank you," take the time at the end of your session to thank participants for helping make the session a valuable learning experience and for what you learned from them. Follow this expression of gratitude with a reminder that you are available as a resource in the future, then provide your contact information if you have not done so.

Point Out Successes

Too many facilitators look for things that learners do wrong. For example, mistakes on tests are typically highlighted with red ink. Try highlighting "correct" and creative answers with a neon highlighter marker or giving positive strokes in class regularly.

PUTTING YOUR BRAIN TO WORK: ACTIVITY

What value do you see for addressing the intrinsic motivators of your learners? _____

_____

_____

What other intangible strategies can you think of to recognize your learners? _____

_____

_____

BRIGHT IDEA

Mystery Learner

This is a variation of a technique used by the Central Florida Chapter of the American Society for Training & Development in Orlando, Florida, to make new members and guests feel welcome at monthly meetings.

As learners arrive for a session, select one at random to be your "mystery learner" whose role is to network and enjoy refreshments without drawing attention or identifying himself or herself as a special person. Ask the learner to remember the name of the second member of the group who comes up and voluntarily introduces himself or herself. During your opening remarks and participant introductions, explain the "mystery learner" process and ask the selected person to do a self-introduction and to identify the second person whom they met. Give both learners a round of applause and a small prize. The purpose of the process is to encourage people to communicate and network, and to get them thinking that through involvement comes tangible and intangible reward.

Good words are worth much, and cost little.
—George Herbert
English clergyman and poet

Extrinsic Rewards from Training

Participants who prefer tangible rewards or incentives for their efforts are said to be extrinsically motivated. These learners often thrive in environments in which competition and effort lead to receipt of rewards. They enjoy receiving money, prizes, gift certificates, ribbons, buttons, and other physical forms of recognition that have value for their performance. Such people often have shelves or walls in their offices or workspaces where they proudly display certificates, diplomas, trophies, or other performance recognition memorabilia. They also have small toys, buttons, and other mementos received in training programs, on their desks, computer monitors, bookcases, or hanging from the walls. You may know the type. They are the ones who have their nametags from all the conferences they have attended each year displayed on their cubicle walls. These nametags are a great conversation starter when others visit their office and serve to remind the person what he or she has accomplished in attending the conferences.

Tapping the motivation of these extrinsically driven learners can often be accomplished by setting up games, competitions, or activities. You can reward the learners for their successful performance and participation in any number of ways. In addition, whenever participants answer a question, offer a creative idea, volunteer to lead or scribe in a group, arrive on time, or assist in any way, you can reward their behavior. Even if they are randomly selected using the techniques outlined in this book, you may want to reward them to encourage further involvement by them and others.

Types of Extrinsic Rewards

Here are some examples of rewards sometimes used in training programs.

Stickers

Use stickers in various shapes (e.g., stars, animals, or smile faces) placed on name tents to reward behavior or activity.

Erasers

The same erasers discussed in Chapter 6 can be used as incentives. These inexpensive, creative prizes come in many shapes that often relate directly to various training topics (see Creative Presentation Resources in the Resources for Trainers in the appendices). Like stickers, erasers can be given to reward a variety of learner behaviors.

Coupons

At the beginning of a session, I often describe how coupons or tickets that I will distribute throughout the session can result in a prize at the end of the program. I explain that participants receive a coupon or ticket for arriving on time, volunteering, responding first to a question (or raising their hand), or otherwise participating. The coupons can be the carnival type that come on rolls and are numbered (see Creative Presentation Resources in the Resources for Trainers in the appendices). They have duplicate tickets—one for the participant and one for you to retain for a drawing later. You can also create your own with graphic images and the program title on them printed on bright colored paper. You can make eight to ten of these on a sheet of paper, then cut them apart for distribution. At the end of you session, have participants write their names on the back of the coupons they have received, and then toss them all into a box for a prize drawing. You may want to have candy bars or small incentives for all the participants who do not win the major reward so that you do not have any losers in the group.

Toys

Many toys and props can be adapted to relate to program themes. For example, I use Magic 8-Ball key chains as incentives for workshops on creativity, train-the-trainer, problem-solving, and decision-making. These creative little balls also come in larger hand-size versions. The way I adapt them to training is to have a learner ask a closed-ended question to which he or she wants to know an answer (e.g., "Will I get that raise next week?"). On the back side of the ball is a little viewing area. Inside is a floating cube with 12 possible responses (e.g., "Yes," "Can't tell," and "Try later"). By turning the ball upside down, an answer appears to the question. This is a lighthearted way to add some fun to your programs and learners can have a key chain for their own use later. Each time they see the reward in the future, they are likely to think of the program and thus learning potentially will be reinforced.

Like so many other things addressed in this book, your ability to apply creative learning strategies rests with your desire and effort to think outside the box. As I have mentioned in other parts of the book, visit local toy or educational stores and purchase various items. Really look at the items and ask yourself, "To what topic does this relate?" or "How could I use this as a training aid or incentive?"

Imprinted Items

Most phone directories contain the names of various companies that create custom imprinted or promotional items. You can develop a slogan or theme for your programs, and then have it imprinted on a variety of products. Better yet, have learners come up with several suggested themes during programs and select the best. Reward the person whose idea was adopted later. Once you have a slogan, have one or more of the following items produced for use in future training programs:

Mugs

T-shirts

Mouse pads

Key chains

Pencils or pens

Buttons or badges

Note pad cubes

Drink coasters

Glass/Bottle cozies (insulated covers)

Paper weights

Toys

Magnets

Screen Savers

There are a variety of inexpensive software programs that allow you to create your own screensavers. Find copyright-free color landscape or animal photos, or use other creative graphics along with your program theme, topic, tips for success, quote, or organizational logo. Save copies of the custom screen saver(s) you produce onto CD-ROM disks and give them as prizes or for attendance at a session. You can also use them as giveaways to promote the program and encourage registration at trade shows, organizational expositions, or gatherings. Make sure that the disks are virus-free.

Candy or Food

Do not overlook giving inexpensive prizes such as candy bars or packages of snack foods (e.g., chips or cookies). Many people enjoy these and often share them with peers when they receive them. You are also addressing the motivational needs of learners discussed earlier in the book.

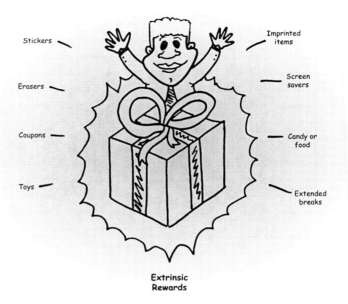

Stickers
Erasers
Coupons
Toys
Imprinted items
Screen savers
Candy or food
Extended breaks

Extrinsic Rewards

MINDMAP 2. Extrinsic Rewards

Extended Breaks

All rewards need not cost money. Consider giving extended breaks or lunch periods as a reward for individual or group accomplishment. You can even turn the determination of time length into a game of chance using spinners, dice, cards, or other creative means (see Resources for Trainers in the appendices).

BRIGHT IDEA

Books for Behavior

Books are excellent incentives because they can be chosen for their content to reinforce and supplement classroom information later. If you have major bookstore chains in your area (e.g., Borders, Barnes & Noble, or Books-a-Million), check their discounted bookshelves located in the front of their stores. If these chains do not have a store nearby, check their websites (see Resources for Trainers in the appendices). You can get significantly reduced prices on books from these companies. College or university bookstores and book websites (e.g., Amazon.com) are other great places to find books with marked down prices. They often have discontinued, overstocked, or out of print copies of books for as low as $1.00. These make valuable rewards for your learners.

Table 10-1. Tips for Motivating Learners

1. Listen!

2. Project optimism.

3. Communicate session objectives.

4. Be empathetic to needs.

5. Set a positive training environment.

6. Challenge.

7. Encourage involvement and creativity.

8. Promote questioning.

9. Recognize achievements and contributions.

10. Use incentives and rewards.

11. Show concern.

12. Review and reinforce regularly.

13. Build in camaraderie and teamwork.

14. Tie in learning to the real world.

15. Make learning FUN!

Like the national economy, human motivation is a topic that people know is important, continually discuss, and would like to predict.
    —Raymond J. Wlodkowski

Table 10-1 offers some ideas on how to develop a learning environment that can encourage learner motivation. These basic concepts of trainer behavior can drive the intrinsic values of learners that you read about earlier.

PUTTING YOUR BRAIN TO WORK: ACTIVITY

What value do you think external motivators can bring to training?_____

_____

What other types of rewards or incentives have you used or seen used in training sessions? _____

_____

What are some additional rewards that you can think of for use in your sessions? _____

_____

● MOTIVATION KILLERS

You have many chances to identify learning opportunities and apply them in your sessions. If done properly, you can establish an atmosphere in which learning is encouraged and individual intrinsic learner needs are met. Trainers, however, do things that turn learners off and stifle their desire to be in a session, to participate actively, or to learn. Take a look at the following list and use it as a checklist of things NOT to do in your sessions.

Ignoring the learning needs and preferences of your participants

Failing to focus on all three learning modalities

Addressing only one or so of the eight intelligences

Using negative communication and feedback skills

Incorporating threats, intimidation, or coercion into your session

Giving inappropriate rewards or recognition

Leaving participants out of the learning process

Limiting opportunities for creativity

Being unenthusiastic about the environment, learning, or your topic

Not connecting with learners on a personal level

Acting hesitant or resistant to learner input

Inadequately preparing or practicing for your session

Using outdated or inaccurate information in your session

PUTTING YOUR BRAIN TO WORK: ACTIVITY

From a personal standpoint, what types of actions or inactions do trainers make that demotivate you during training? _____

_____

_____

What can you do to help keep from demotivating your learners? _____

_____

_____

● **REINFORCING WHAT IS LEARNED**

In addition to reinforcing key elements of your material throughout a session, it is important to do a comprehensive review at the end. This is one of your last opportunities to emphasize the main points of the program and to clarify anything that you may need to. As you read earlier in the book about memory, learners are more likely to retain what is learned if the brain continues to experience the information or stimuli through different senses a number of times. Such reinforcement helps solidify images and data in various parts of the brain. This allows more opportunity and likelihood that recall can occur when the material is needed by the learner later.

As I do with activities throughout my sessions, I try to incorporate novelty, variety, and an element of FUN into end of session reviews. The following are some ideas for reviewing program material. The techniques can be adapted to virtually any program topic or format.

A Learning Wall

Depending on your group size, either hang a number of flip chart pages or unroll a length of newsprint onto a wall. Spray the paper with artist's adhesive (see The Trainer's Warehouse in Resources for Trainers in the appendices) before hanging to prevent getting it on the wall. Also, prepare these pages before participants arrive in case someone has a respiratory condition. Give learners a stack of various activity shapes (see Communicating with Graphic Images in the Tools for Trainers in the appendices) and tell them that they have 10 minutes to write briefly one major lesson or point learned in the session per shape. After 10 minutes, have each person, in turn, go to the paper and post their shapes. Have them read and explain the one idea that they think is most important. After everyone is finished, have them give a round of applause for what was learned during the day.

This activity reinforces what was covered as each person reviews notes and memory to create their shape responses. It also reinforces again when each person searches their memory for the best thing learned and then says and hears it again as they tell their peers what they thought was best. They also have material reinforced one more time as they listen to what others say was the best idea.

After participants leave, you can review what they wrote to discover if they got all the key points offered during the program. If something was missed or not listed, consider either strengthening your delivery of the point next time or dropping it because learners do not see it as important.

Allowing time for learners to recall creatively program elements in groups and make them visual is an excellent way to reinforce their learning. It also helps to ensure that points were not missed or misinterpreted because learners can discuss the issues as they develop mindmaps. To accomplish these goals, have learners form groups of three to five participants. Give each group a sheet of flip chart paper, randomly select leaders and scribes, and then have learners spend approximately 15 minutes creating mindmaps based on what they learned in the session. Encourage the use of color and graphic images to illustrate information. Once time has elapsed, have each group's leader post their chart. Have all learners walk around the room to view and discuss the creations. Follow their review with an instructor-led discussion on the key elements of the program. Have everyone give a round of applause for their creativity.

Circular Ball Toss

You can employ physical movement through a group review in which learners form either one large circle (if you have fewer than 15 participants) or several smaller ones. Brain research has shown that such activity can actually aid recall and memory through stimulation of chemicals in the brain.

Once you have formed a circle(s), give someone in the group a Koosh® or large foam rubber ball. Inform participants that they will gently toss the ball from one person to another, not giving it to any one person more than once. Starting with the original ball holder, before tossing to someone else, each person is to shout out a term, concept, or idea learned during the session. If someone cannot think of a term, he or she may say "pass" and toss to someone else. He or she is eligible to receive the ball again and may not pass a second time. Have participants keep the ball moving quickly by telling them they can hold it no more than 5 seconds.

After the review, have everyone move closer together, extend their right hands so that everyone touches, and on your count of three, as they pull their hands back from the group, yell Teamwork! Follow this by having everyone give a round of applause. Then, review any key points the group might have left out during their review.

Line Ball Toss

This is similar to the circular ball toss except that there is an element of team competition involved. To prepare, divide learners into two equal teams, have them form straight lines facing each other, and randomly select scribes from each team. Once scribes are selected, have them move over to the end of the opposite team's line, but tell them they remain part of their original team. Give each scribe a flip chart easel with paper and a marker. They will not participate in the review except to capture ideas from the team to which they are assigned.

Once all preparation is done, tell learners they will have 5 minutes for a competitive review. Give one person a ball (e.g., Koosh® or foam rubber) that they will randomly toss to someone on the opposing team while shouting out a term, concept, or key point received during the session. These can be something received from you or from each other. They may not repeat something that has been said by a member of either team. Participants can receive the ball only once and can hold it only 5 seconds. If they cannot think of anything to offer, they can say "pass" and toss it. They are then eligible to receive the ball again and cannot pass a second time. If everyone has received the ball one time and offered a term and time remains, have them start again until either time expires or it is obvious that all ideas are exhausted (a lot of people are passing). While the review is occurring, the scribes should capture the terms or concepts being offered by members of the team to which they are assigned on their flip chart. After 5 minutes, sound a whistle or other noisemaker, and have them stop and compare lists. Eliminate any term items appearing on a list that occurred earlier on the opposing team's list. Count the total and reward the team with the most accurate responses. You may want to give a small prize to the members of the other team also (e.g., candy bars or snack food packets) so that there are no losers. You can also reward your scribes, if desired.

Have each team form a circle, put their right hands in so that all hands touch, and agree on a team "yell" (e.g., Success) that they shout in unison on your count of three, while pulling their hands out of the center and returning to their seats.

Crossword, Word Search, Word Scramble, or Word Match

A fun, but less active way to review course content is through the computer-generated puzzles that you read about earlier in the book for use as interim reviews. You can create customized puzzles with clues and words from your program material to remind and review what was learned. Allow participants to use materials and notes when completing the puzzles, as this reinforces concepts as they reread information.

Award a prize to the first person accurately completing the puzzle, but have everyone else also complete the puzzle so they also review all concepts. You can give smaller prizes to the remaining learners.

Note to the Boss

Pass out either 3 × 5 index cards or strips of paper and a blank business envelope. Have each person write his or her name on the card or paper. Tell participants that they have 3 minutes to write the most important thing that they learned in the session and how they plan to apply it on the job. Once time is up, have each person, in turn, read what he or she wrote out loud. Next, have participants write the name, title, and department of their direct supervisors on the outside of the envelope. If you are conducting a session with people from different organizations, have them put the name, title, and mailing address for their supervisors on the envelope. Give each person a generic letter from you, addressed to "Dear Supervisor," which explains that the learner has just completed a course titled _____. That enclosed card also contains a description of what the learner feels is the most important thing learned and how he or she wants to apply it on the job. Also stress that you need the supervisor's assistance in supporting the learner in accomplishing the learner's implementation of the concept or idea. Have all participants include the letter along with that they wrote, then collect the envelopes and tell learners that you will see that supervisors get them.

You may encounter some people who for some reason do not want the items sent to their supervisors. Honor their request if you cannot convince them privately of the value of doing so.

Now Presenting!

Have learners form pairs and decide who will be No. 1 and who will be No. 2. Display a flip chart or project a transparency showing session learning objectives. Give each participant a blank piece of 8.5 × 11 inch paper. On a flip chart page write the following and display it:

INTRODUCTION

BODY

CLOSING

Tell participants to copy the words onto their papers, leaving a couple inches of space between each. Once they have done so, tell them they have 15 minutes to develop a short presentation that they will present to their partner.

To prepare for the presentation, tell them to select the learning objective for the session that they feel is most important to them personally and write it under "INTRODUCTION" on their paper. Partners cannot select the same objective. Next, have them go through session material and notes to find a number of points or items related to their chosen objective. These should be written under "BODY" on their paper. Finally, have them think of one or more reasons or ways that the objective selected will satisfy a workplace issue or help them improve performance. Stress that the purpose of their presentation is not only to review material but also to convince their partners that their chosen objective was the most important thing learned in the session. This is written in the CLOSING section.

After 15 minutes of preparation time, tell all No. 1s to make their presentation and try to convince their partners that they have selected the most important objective. Give participants 3–5 minutes for presentations, then have partners switch roles. After everyone has given a presentation, lead a discussion in which you go down the list of learning objectives asking all those who selected a particular one to comment on why they chose it. This gives you an idea of which objectives learners thought were most important and may cause you to modify your next delivery of the material. Summarize that all objectives are important and give examples of how they can be applied in the workplace if you have not already done so during the program. Award small prizes to learners, if desired.

Storytelling

Have participants form teams of six to eight people. Tell them that they have 30 minutes to develop a short story or tall tale about their workplace that is no longer than 5 minutes. Instruct them that they should not use the names of real people (I call this changing names to protect the ignorant!). They should incorporate as many of the session elements as possible into their story. Give each group 5 minutes to tell their story.

You may want to hold a vote and give prizes for the most creative story and the story including the most elements from the training session. Give all learners candy or other small prizes for their efforts and have a joint round of applause from participants.

Singing Along

Similar to storytelling, form teams and have each team develop a rap or other type of song using elements of session material. Give groups 30 minutes to develop their song and 5 minutes or less to sing it as a group. Vote on the most creative and the version including the most information from the session and award prizes. Give applause.

Bright Ideas Page

If you included a Bright Ideas (**Figure 10-1**) page at the end of your handouts, have learners turn to that page. Ask them to spend 5 minutes reviewing material and listing any ideas or concepts that they wish to think about further or try on the job. Once they finish, form groups of four to six participants and spend 15–20 minutes sharing what they have written with one another. Have them also discuss how the ideas can be applied to their workplace or other environments. Following their discussion, lead a group discussion on which points they thought were valuable. Add anything they forgot or omitted and explain how it is useful in a variety of situations.

Flash Card Review

Before your session begins, list key session concepts on poster board flash cards. Cards measuring 8 × 20 inches work well and allow large lettering (keep your words to a minimum without sacrificing comprehension). You can later hold these up for your group or you can put either Velcro or magnetic strips on the back, as described in Chapter 8. With such backings you can either display on cloth boards or magnetic backed easels or dry erase boards.

Form two equal teams of learners (e.g., left side of the room and right side). As you show the first term, designate one team to call out as many program-related terms or concepts as they can think of. Next, have members of the other team call out as many applications or uses in the workplace for the term or concept. For the second and subsequent terms keep reversing the roles of the two teams so that they call out terms one time and applications the next. Reward teams at the end.

Touting Benefits

A good way to generate future selling points for your programs, while having learners reflect and review, is to have them generate a list of benefits received. These benefits are

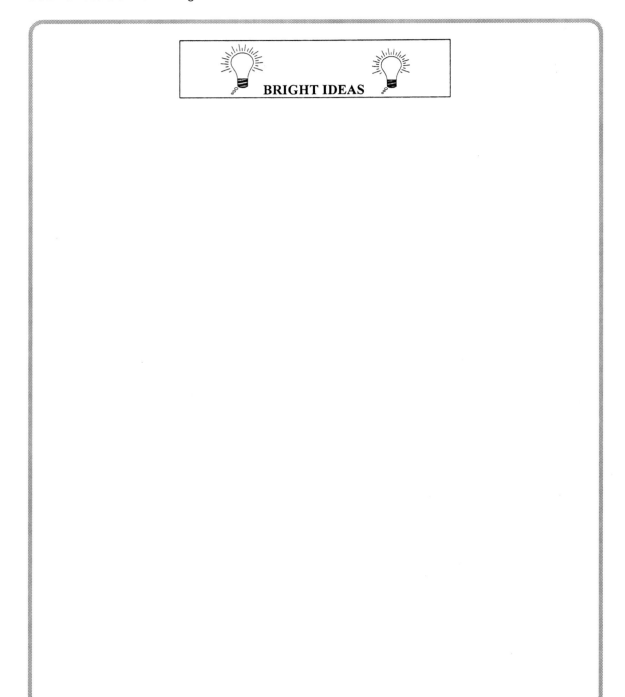

FIGURE 10-1. Sample Bright Ideas page

ways in which session concepts or material learned can help increase effectiveness and efficiency or reduce stress in the workplace or other environment.

To prepare, form teams of six to eight participants and provide flip chart paper to each team. Randomly select leaders and scribes for each group. Tell teams that they have 10 minutes to brainstorm as many benefits received from the session as they can think of and list them on their papers. After 10 minutes, have group leaders reveal and explain the list of benefits that they developed. Reward appropriately.

Play a Game

Use a TV game show format to review key concepts. There are software programs that model popular game show (e.g., "Jeopardy" and "Family Feud") that allow you to customize categories and answers to your material. You can also buy flashing lights and sounds (see The Trainer's Warehouse in Resources for Trainers in the appendices) and customized game show type theme music (see Creative Presentation Resources in Resources for Trainers in the appendices). Games can be played with individuals or teams.

Certificate Exchange

If you are giving course certificates, pass them out randomly making sure that no one gets his own. Have everyone stand and locate the owner of the certificate he holds. He can then share what he believes is the most important thing he learned in the program and explain why he believes it to be so.

PUTTING YOUR BRAIN TO WORK: ACTIVITY

What are other ways you can think of for individuals to review session content? _____

_____

What are other ways for groups to review session content? _____

_____

BRIGHT IDEA

Identifying Review Activities

Make a trip to your local bookstore, library, or Internet bookstores to search for books on games and activities that can be used for closing a session. Build a file of various activities so that you can use more variety in your reviews. Start using an end of session review in addition to interim reviews during you sessions to reinforce the learning.

I've never sought success in order to get fame and money;
it's the talent and the passion that count in success.
—Ingrid Bergman
Actress

BRINGING YOUR SESSIONS TO A CLOSE

If you introduce new information right up to the scheduled ending time for a session you are doing a disservice to your learners. Bringing your program to a formal end is important for two reasons. The first is that you appear more organized and professional if you pull together the program's activities and summarize learning points. Consider it the difference between wrapping a present for someone in nice paper and giving it to them like that, or wrapping it and then adding a pretty ribbon and a bow. The first option looks nice and the thought is probably appreciated; however, something likely seems to be missing. That is how a training session without a proper closing can appear. The closing becomes your ribbon and bow and brings together a nice image.

Think of how you have felt as a participant in sessions in which the trainer did not close effectively. Perhaps the person delivered information right up to the scheduled ending time for the program, then asked quickly, Are there any questions? There usually are not because people are ready to leave. As an afterthought the trainer may have said, "Oh, I almost forgot, please take a few minutes to complete the session evaluation that is being passed around now." You and others probably put little effort into giving evaluation feedback and left feeling less than fulfilled.

A more important reason for bringing formal closure to your session is that you provide a structured vehicle for reinforcement of learning. By scheduling in adequate time to review concepts, you assist participants to assimilate what they experienced. In doing so, you can aid memory, recall, and ultimately the likelihood of transfer of learning to the workplace or other environments.

Closures are so crucial to the learning process that you should consider allocating an average of 5–10 percent of session time for a review and closing rituals. For example, in a 1-hour program, give approximately 5–10 minutes; in an 8-hour workshop, allow 45–50 minutes for closure.

ELEMENTS OF AN EFFECTIVE CLOSE

Many things can enhance the effectiveness of your program closure. There have been volumes written on the topic by trainers and presenters over the years. By building the following elements into your closing, you increase the chance of successfully drawing all the learning pieces together and having participants actually use what they learned later.

Bridge the Learning

During your closing, incorporate a solid review of session objectives by specifically addressing how each was addressed. Instead of assuming that all learners "get it," help them to bridge or connect mentally the elements of the learning. Answer any questions they have and spend time reviewing how each learning objective is related.

Help Transfer Learning

Provide ways in which participants can apply what they have learned to their lives outside the classroom. Some people are not good at extracting information and applying it to other situations. Whereas a point or concept may seem simple to you, other people may be very linear in their thinking and do not recognize abstract or direct applications. This is similar to what I have discussed related to taking everyday items, such as toys, and using them as training aids.

Show Return on Investment (ROI)

Remind participants of what they have gained in terms of knowledge, skills, and/or attitude. By defining more value, you can enhance perceptions about you and the training experience. Value can be equated with such things as financial gain for them and the organization, personal goals and advancement, improved working conditions, and assistance to peers and customers.

Answer "What's Next?"

Provide a means for participants to determine what they should do to continue the learning begun during the session. It also identifies resources for their future use. This is similar to my providing you with dozens of tools and contact points for information and products in the appendices. Encourage learners to continue the learning process once they leave the room.

Provide a Roadmap to Success

This is related to the preceding paragraph. Help learners develop a strategy or action plan for implementing what they have learned. It is good that you give people the tools; however, some people need an extra push because of time constraints in the workplace or because of lack of planning skills. You can accomplish this by providing time for the creation of a personal action plan during your closing. Give the format for such a plan and have them complete it before leaving the room. Such a strategy should include specific next steps (e.g., contact XYZ Company to get a catalog of toys and incentives). Each of these steps should be measurable in terms of time (e.g., before November 15) or other criterion. Encourage learners to put the dates and action steps into their calendar or event planner or on a wall in their work area to make it visible.

Issue a Call to Action

Following development of an action plan, give learners a call to action. Stress that they now have implementation goals for what was learned; however, they should now take steps to put their plan in action. Encourage them to think of who they can get to help implement and support their action plan.

Allow Time for Feedback

Build in time to receive some sort of feedback (e.g., session evaluation form or activity shapes on the wall) from learners. Get their perceptions on specific things that worked and did not work during the session. Also, do not lose sight of the fact that your learners are customers and, were it not for them, you would not have a job.

If you did a good job communicating and holding interim reviews throughout the session, many questions will already have been answered. You may still want to allow one more opportunity for learner questions and clarification of misunderstandings.

Give "Thank You" Time

Take the time to say "thank you" to participants for their participation and attention. You can also include an opportunity for learners to thank one another for support and contributions. In some of my sessions, I use a series of seven transparencies with the following on them:

T

H

A

N

K

S

THANKS

I use these transparencies to get the participation of all learners. First I ask everyone to read along in unison in a loud voice as I project the images on the screen. Starting with the "T" I go through all seven transparencies. Once the last one is viewed and read, I reply, "Thank you for being a wonderful group and for your great ideas!" I then have all participants give a loud round of applause for themselves.

Complete an Evaluation Form

Many trainers do not like or use evaluation forms at the end of programs. They call these "smile face" sheets because some formats actually have scales for rating various elements of the session with small smile face graphics on them. As you read about interim reviews early in this book, I pass out evaluations at the beginning of a session. Then, as part of the interim reviews conducted during the program, I have participants write general comments about things they like and dislike about the session on the evaluations. At the very end of the day, I ask them to add final thoughts and rate the elements of the program by circling points on rating scales. This process typically gives me formal comments and the "smile face" ratings, which are usually the only thing received when you wait until the end of a session to pass out the forms.

Tell of Follow-Up Steps

In addition to the end of session evaluation that learners complete for you, explain that you will be doing follow-up with them (assuming that you will) in about 30 days to see how things are going. Part of this follow-up might be a feedback form sent to them and to their supervisor and customers(s) (see **Figures 10-2 and 10-3**). Getting on the job feedback reinforces the program content because it causes learners to review material covered in order to respond on the questionnaire. It also gets feedback from others as to how well the learner is applying what was learned.

Bring Closure to the Learning

Depending on the length of your session, hold some type of celebration of the learning. Make the event joyous, upbeat, and festive in order to end on a positive note. You can use music, videos, party favors, or whatever you like to accomplish such an atmosphere.

BRIGHT IDEA

Muppet Video

There is a series of wonderful short video vignettes with humorous short cartoon-type scenarios for use to introduce a break and at the end of a session. There is one with the Jim Henson Muppets, titled *The Sky's the Limit,* which I have used effectively for years. Participants love it and it says perfectly that they can use what they have learned to reach their goals (see Videos in the Resources for Trainers in the appendices).

(text continues on page 394)

SAMPLE POST-SESSION PARTICIPANT QUESTIONNAIRE

Program _____

Date of program _____

Now that you have had (<u>number of days</u>) to apply what was learned in the training program, please respond to the following questions related to the session. Your feedback will assist in improving the quality and content of future training sessions.

1. What do you believe was the primary objective of the training session? _____

_____

2. In what ways did the program accomplish its objectives and assist your on-the-job performance? (Please explain) _____

_____

3. In what ways do you feel that the program could be improved to add more value? (Please explain)

_____

_____

4. What other skills and knowledge do you wish the program had addressed? (Please explain)

_____

_____

Print name _____
         (Optional)

Signature _____

May we use your comments to promote this program in the future? Yes _____ No _____

If yes, give name and sign.

Thank you for taking the time to assist in making this program more valuable to you and the organization.

FIGURE 10-2. Sample post-session participant questionnaire

SAMPLE POST-SESSION SUPERVISOR/
CUSTOMER QUESTIONNAIRE

(<u>Name of Participant</u>) recently attended a workshop titled _____

in which the following objectives were addressed:

1.

2.

3.

To assist in future program improvements, it is important to have your perspective on how well new skills and knowledge gained in the session are being applied on the job. Please take a few minutes to rate the following based on the objectives listed above.

4. How often do you interact with (<u>Name of Participant</u>) during the week? (Please be specific)

5. The participant's ability to handle routine tasks prior to the program?

1	2	3	4	5	6	7
Low						High

Comments:

_____

_____

6. The participant's ability to handle routine tasks since attending the program?

1	2	3	4	5	6	7
Low						High

Comments:

_____

_____

7. In what performance or knowledge areas has the participant improved since the training? (Please be specific) _____

_____

continued

FIGURE 10-3. Sample post-session supervisor/customer questionnaire

8. In what performance or knowledge areas does the participant still need improvement? (Please be specific) _____

_____

9. General comments regarding the participant's knowledge or performance:

_____

_____

Print name _____
          (Optional)

May we contact you to clarify your comments? Yes _____ No _____

Thank you for taking the time to provide this valuable feedback.

FIGURE 10-3. *(Continued)*

● CLOSING ON A HIGH NOTE

As you read in the preceding, it is important to celebrate learning in your closure. People tend to remember the beginning and end of a program more than the details in the middle. That is why you should consider how you will end your sessions. Once you have conducted a solid review, you can send participants off in a memorable manner.

In planning your close, go back to review all the earlier chapters related to brain-based learning and creating and setting the right environment. If your session has been filled with interaction, fun, and experiential strategies, you certainly want the ending to be equally as memorable and effective.

Here are some strategies that I have used or witnessed over the years that you may want to consider incorporating into your session closing. I often use one or more of these combined.

Quote memorable sayings related to the program content.

Relate a silly story tied to the concepts presented.

Tell a session-related joke.

Use unique or inspirational music (get copyright licenses from BMI or ASCAP first). One of my favorites is Roy Rogers singing "Happy Trails" which I play as learners are exiting the room.

Do a little skit about the session with cloth hand puppets. You can sew buttons or cloth facial features onto socks for this.

Have a party with refreshments. Pass out party hats, favors, and noisemakers and decorate the room with streamers and balloons during the last break of the day.

Have an award ceremony by giving a sheet of paper listing the following categories:
Most creative

Most helpful

Most confident

Most carefree

Most knowledgeable

Most curious

Most fun

Have learners vote by putting the name of one peer per category (they can self-nominate). The name of a learner can be used in more than one category. After the voting, collect all the sheets and tally the responses. Reward winners and give small prizes to everyone else.

BRIGHT IDEA

Oh, the Places You Will Go!

One of my favorite ways to end a day-long program is to read from the Dr. Seuss book, *Oh, the Places You Will Go!* The message of the book has impact because it deals with hope, optimism, and reaching for goals. I follow the reading with a brief statement of encouragement for learners strive to achieve their action plans.

APPLYING WHAT YOU LEARNED
Strategies for Celebrating

1. What are some of the criteria that you will use to select rewards in the future?

_____

_____

2. How can you change your current training environments to meet the motivational needs of your learners better? _____

_____

3. List some of the common intrinsic rewards that you see in your learners on a regular basis.

_____

_____

4. What things are you currently doing in training that might be unknowingly stifling learner motivation?

_____

_____

5. What techniques do you plan to use to bring future training programs to a more formal close?

_____

_____

6. How can you add memorable endings to you sessions in the future? _____

_____

ENDNOTES

[38] Pierce, J.H., _The Owner's Manual for the Brain: Everyday Applications from Mind–Brain Research,_ Bard Press, Marietta, GA, 2000, pp. 597–598.

Glossary of Terms

Accelerated learning uses a wide variety of experiential learning activities, such as role-plays, games, metaphors, music, props, and images that appeal to all five learner senses.

Active learning describes training in which participants put forth much of the effort to make learning occur. It is brain based, energized, engaging, challenging, and fun.

Americans with Disabilities Act of 1990 is U.S. Federal legislation that guarantees people with actual or perceived disabilities, and those with a history of impairment, equal access to the workplace, including training and professional development opportunities.

Amygdala is one of the components of the midbrain or limbic area of the human brain. Among other things, it functions to help link emotions with memory and helps control blood circulation, breathing, and other automatic body functions.

Analogy is an inference relating one thing to something similar for the purpose of making a point or showing someone that he or she already has a base knowledge of a concept or idea.

Andragogy is a term used by Malcolm Knowles, sometimes known the "father of adult learning." This theory of learning suggests that adults learn and process information differently from children; therefore content and activities should be designed to address their specific needs. For example, children are viewed as blank slates to be written upon or taught from a level of no knowledge, whereas adults have previous learning, knowledge, and skills that can be tapped and incorporated into their learning experiences.

Baby boomers is a term that has been applied to people born between 1946 and 1964.

Behavior modification is a process used by trainers to help maximize learning. It involves setting measurable learning objectives, demonstrating or otherwise modeling desired behavior, having the learner attempt to exhibit desired behavior, and providing feedback throughout training on progress toward meeting the objectives.

Body language is a term applied to nonverbal communication cues involving gestures, facial expressions, and body movements.

Borders are boundaries used around page text, or the edge of flip charts, transparencies, or slides. They are either solid lines or can be made up of a series of graphic images (e.g., balloons or smiling faces) repeated in a border pattern.

Brain-based learning is a term applied to the theory incorporating research on the human brain; its implications on education and training; and creative strategies to enhance acquisition, retention, and recall of information.

BrainGym refers to a series of activities used in training and education to physically stimulate learners. Such movements causes enhanced mental activity and processing of information. The term derives from a book written by P.E. and G.E. Dennison.

Brain teasers are fun activities that challenge learners to use creative problem-solving strategies to come to solutions with different types of activities, such as puzzles, math, word, or geometric problems. They can be used to spark training, energize, add a novel approach to learning, or create a less formal, fun environment.

Brain writing is a technique of reducing ideas to writing. On either flip chart pages or a writing pad, each member of a small group writes his name and the topic or question to be addressed at the top of the sheet. He then writes an idea or response and either moves to the sheet of the person on the right (flip charts) or passes his pad to the right. That person then responds to the idea or response with comments before moving or passing to his right. Once everyone in the group has responded, ideas are reviewed by all participants.

Cerebellum is the large dorsal projection at the rear base of the brain adjacent to the brainstem. It coordinates muscle and equilibrium functions.

Cerebrum is made up of two large hemispheres and constitutes approximately 85 percent of the brain's weight. Most high-level brain functions take place in the cerebrum.

Clip art is ready-to-use graphic images that can be obtained from computer software programs or books and can be used in the development of training materials such as flip charts, handouts, job aids, transparencies, or slides.

Contextual refers to the interrelated conditions in which something occurs or exists, such as an environment or a setting.

Convergent thinking is the ability to examine logically and dissect a variety of ideas and ultimately choose the best option for a given situation. It also involves the ability to bring components of various parts together to form a single strategy or solution.

Cortex or neocortex is a thin layer of cells covering that protects the brain. It is approximately ⅛ inch thick and deciphers patterns by identifying relationships between objects and other stimuli.

Cross-lateral activities are energizing movements that involve using both hemispheres of the brain to conduct coordinated activity in which a learner uses opposite parts of the body. An example would be touching the right elbow to the left knee as it is raised off the floor, then alternating and touching the left elbow to the right knee.

Culture refers to the collective knowledge, beliefs, values, social norms, and behaviors exhibited by a group of people or within an organization.

Divergent thinking is the intellectual process of generating large numbers of original, diverse ideas.

Electroencephalogram (EEG) is a medical test in which brain waves are traced and recorded visually on graphs.

Experiential learning provides opportunities for learners to gain from doing through activities and practical application.

Face is a term used in many Asian and other societies to refer to a public self-image that people want to present to others in social interactions. Care should be given not to embarrass or cause someone to "lose face" when dealing with them.

Frontal lobe of the brain is located around the forehead and assists with problem-solving, creative thinking, planning and organizing, judgment, and will power.

Full-spectrum lighting is lighting designed to simulate natural light as closely as possible. It covers all parts of the visual spectrum although it does not exactly mimic daylight. Such lighting is often integrated with natural lighting through the use of sources such as windows and skylights.

Graphic organizers are visual representations of ideas and knowledge. They can be in a variety of forms, such as flow charts, Post-it® Notes organized on a wall, or mindmaps.

Hierarchy of needs theory was developed by Dr. Abraham Maslow. The five levels of needs that he believes people go through are basic or physiological, safety or security, social or belonging, esteem or status, and self-actualization.

Hippocampus is located in the midbrain and is the area of the human brain responsible for the formation and storage of memories.

Hypothalamus lies beneath the thalamus at the midline of the brain base. It is believed to control many vital bodily activities, such as drinking, temperature regulation, eating, sleep, sexual activity, and emotions.

Icebreakers are training activities used near the beginning of a training program to help with participant introductions and create a relaxed, less formal environment while often tying into the program theme.

Intangible rewards have perceived value and come in the form of recognition or feedback that can cause a person to want to change behavior.

Interim reviews are activities inserted throughout training programs for review of material covered during the session. These are typically fun, action-oriented activities designed to involve all participants. The purpose of the activities is to determine if participants are learning key content elements while providing a reinforcement of those elements as participants review points in many creative ways. The reviews often involve the use of toys, handouts, flip charts, games, and other experiential approaches.

Job aids are items that supplement the learning process following training or education. They come in a variety of forms that serve the purpose of providing a reference for future use, such as an operator's manual for a computer or a poster outlining the steps of a process such as cardiopulmonary resuscitation (CPR).

Keystone effect refers to the distortion of a projected transparency image on a projection screen. The image appears wider at the top of the screen than at the bottom. This distortion can be eliminated by tilting the top of the screen forward at about a 90° angle.

Kudos are praise, compliments, awards, honors, or prestige given for acts of achievement or accomplishment.

Lateral thinking is a technique for creative thinking that involves trying to find a solution or solve a problem by looking at things from a different perspective, challenging common assumptions, or considering different alternatives. The process was developed by Edward de Bono.

Learning is complex and involves conscious and unconscious processes, peripheral perceptions, and concentrated attention. It is the gathering, analyzing, storing, and reaction to stimuli received from the environment through all five human senses.

Learning styles refers to the three modalities in which people take in information through their senses of hearing (auditory), seeing (visual), and touch or feeling (kinesthetic).

Legally blind describes someone with sight impairment to the point that he or she has certain legal rights. The legally blind and totally blind have specific rights under the Americans With Disabilities Act of 1990 and state laws. They also are eligible for such benefits as higher Social Security payments, handicap signs and stickers, and free fishing rights on some state and city lakes.

Limbic system is the second oldest part of the brain to develop, according to researcher Dr. Paul MacLean, who proposed the classic triune brain theory. This section of the human brain acknowledges rewards and punishments. It also controls the autonomic nervous system and houses emotions.

Linear thinking involves looking at things from an analytical, structured perspective.

Lobes are the term given to the four sections of the human brain. Each has specific functions yet all are believed to interact and help process information as a single unit. The four lobes are frontal, temporal, parietal, and occipital. Some researchers also believe there is a fifth area called the midbrain.

Metaphor is a saying or figure of speech in which one concept or idea is used to refer to another, such as *quick as lightning*.

Mindmapping is a technique developed by Tony Buzan of England for visually capturing a large amount of ideas or information in a free-flowing format. This is accomplished by writing a key concept in the center of a piece of paper, drawing a circle around it, then branching out with key trigger words or concepts related to the central theme.

The end product looks much like the branches coming off the trunk of a tree.

Mnemonics are memory devices or tools to aid in the retention and recall of information. The word comes from the ancient Greek goddess Mnemosyne, meaning "mindful."

Neurolinguistic programming (NLP) was developed by John Grinder and Richard Bandler and comes from three terms—neuro (refers to the neurological system), linguistic (the way people use language), and programming (a coding system for experiences). It involves the study of conscious and unconscious human processes that enable people to do what they do.

Nonverbal cues or signals are communication messages sent through movements and gestures of body parts such as the head, face, shoulders, hands, arms, legs, and feet. Cues can also be sent through grooming, dress, and the types of accessories and possessions one has (e.g., clothes, jewelry, furniture, office space and location, and personal belongings).

Occipital Lobe of the brain is located in the rear middle section of the cerebrum and has primary responsibility for vision.

Operant conditioning is used by behavioral scientists who manipulate environmental and other factors to observe and measure the behavioral effects on a study subject. Ivan Pavlov with his studies on dog salivation is one of the noted proponents of the process.

Optical illusions are pictures or images that play tricks on the eyes and distort perception.

Osmanthus is a flower that is native to China. It is valued for its fruity-floral apricot aroma and is used in tea and other Far East beverages.

Paradigms are the way a person views the world. People have differing perspectives based on previous experiences, education, role models, personal environments, values, beliefs, and many other functions.

Pedagogy is the term derived from the Greek words *paid*, meaning "child" and *agogus* meaning

"leader." The word has come to refer to the art, science, and profession of educating children and serves as a model for many elementary through secondary schools in the United States and in other countries.

Parietal lobe of the brain is located on the top rear area of the cerebrum and works to receive and process language and higher sensory data.

Rapport building refers to actions, language, or behavior that is used to establish a psychological bond with others in an effort to gain cooperation or friendship.

Reality-oriented performance experiential system (ROPES) is a form of active training that can incorporate elements of individual as well as team activity. The goal of the training is to offer personal and team challenge that involves such skills as interpersonal communication, teamwork, time and resource management, creativity, strategic planning, goal setting, problem-solving, and decision-making. Activities typically include the use of various materials such as boards, cinder blocks, bricks, logs, rope, and toys. There are high as well as low elements (obstacles) that must be overcome during the activity.

Return on investment (ROI) is a phrase that relates to showing a valid gain from time, effort, money, energy, or other valuable commodity used in a given learning situation.

Revelation technique refers to the practice of revealing one point or line of text on a flip chart page, transparency, or slide at a time. This is done on flip charts by pulling the bottom of the page up toward the top and using a strip of tape to hold it in place so that participants see only a single point or line of text. When ready to go to the next point, the paper edge is detached, moved down one line, and reattached. On a transparency, coverage is done with a blank sheet of paper placed under the transparency and moved downwards as points are discussed. On a computer slide, one line of text at a time is brought into the image.

Rewards are anything viewed as valuable or predictable, and that are used to encourage behavior change.

Role-play is a learning technique in which learners assume roles based on realistic events or situations to practice and hone knowledge and skills that they can use outside the classroom.

Self-talk is the term given to the intrapersonal messages people give themselves as they think about an issue or situation. Such messages are influenced by memory, personality, values, beliefs, and how a person feels about himself or herself.

Spatial thinking occurs in the right posterior region of the brain and is where perceptions of ideas or objects and the ability to manipulate and rotate them occur.

Storyboarding involves developing an idea, concept, or theme by assembling a series of small images, words, or ideas on separate pieces of paper on a wall or other surface. The individual parts collectively form a larger image or solution, similar to the way comic strips form a complete message.

Subculture is a group within a culture that has its own distinct language, beliefs, behavior, or characteristic patterns that distinguish it from the parent group, for example, an American who is also Jewish or gay.

Subordinate clauses, also dependent clauses, are parts of speech in the English language that do not express a complete thought and cannot stand alone as a sentence.

Syntax refers to the structure of words, phrases, clauses, or sentences to form meaningful language or communication.

Tangible rewards are physical items that a person might receive to induce behavioral change, such as toys, stickers, candy, or other small prize.

Temporal lobes of the brain are located on the left and right side of the cerebrum and are tasked with such functions as processing sounds, language meaning, and some memory.

Thalamus lies beneath the cerebrum and connects it to the brain stem. It consists of two gray tissue masses in the middle of the brain. The main purpose of the thalamus is sensory signal relay to the cortex and for outgoing motor signals from it.

Theory X and theory Y were developed by Douglas McGregor and focus on what motivates people and human behavior. He suggested two assumptions about people in the workplace. Theory X assumes that people inherently dislike work and avoid it when they can. Theory Y assumes that people like work and believe that the mental and physical nature of work is fun and enjoyable.

Threats are intimidating actions or words that imply intent to cause harm, injury, or loss to someone.

Training agreement refers to either a handout or flip-charted list of roles that trainees and the trainer will assume during a training session. Such agreements aid in a smoother running training program because everyone knows and has agreed on basic role guidelines.

Two-factor theory was developed by Frederick Herzberg and was derived from Abraham Maslow's hierarchy of needs theory of motivation. In the theory Herzberg defines *hygiene factors* as being outside the job (e.g., pay or benefits). While the presence of these factors can cause unhappiness on the job, their presence does not necessarily motivate workers. Herzberg also defined *motivators* or intrinsic factors that can lead to job satisfaction (e.g., achievement, recognition, responsibility, or the possibility of growth).

Wall talk is a form of practicing for a group presentation by standing in front of a blank wall and making your comments along with gestures, just as you plan to do in class. Using a sterile background eliminates distractions while allowing you to hear the sound of your voice as it comes back to you.

White noise is a low-frequency sound or hissing that is intentionally pumped into large training rooms and cubicle-type work areas to deaden or mask noise and conversations.

Resources for Trainers

The items and vendors listed in this section are provided for your reference and possible use only. Accuracy of information was current at the time of publication, however, the author and publisher cannot be held responsible for changes, as organizations frequently revise their business strategies and operational processes.

The author and publisher do not endorse these organizations or their products and services. Creative Presentation Resources, Inc. is the exception, in that it is owned by the author, who stands behind its products and services.

Books

Activities and Games

Arch, D., *Tricks for Trainers: 57 Tricks and Teasers Guaranteed to Add Magic to Your Presentations*, Resources for Organizations, Minneapolis, MN, 1993.

Battaglia, P., *So You Think You're Smart: 150 Fun and Challenging Brain Teasers*, Tab Books, Blue Ridge Summit, PA, 1988.

Brandreft, G., *The Great Book of Optical Illusions*, Sterling Publishing, New York, 1985.

Jensen, E., *Trainer's Bonanza: Over 1000 Fabulous Tips & Tools*, The Brain Store, San Diego, CA, 1998.

Newstrom, J.W. and Scannell, E.E., *Games Trainers Play: Experiential Learning Exercises*, McGraw-Hill, New York, 1980.

Paraquin, C.H., *The World's Best Optical Illusions*, Sterling Publishing, New York, 1987.

Pike, B. and Solem, L., *50 Creative Training Openers and Energizers*, Jossey-Bass/Pfeiffer, San Francisco, CA, 2000.

Scannell, E.E. and Newstrom, J., *More Games Trainers Play: Experiential Learning Exercises*, McGraw-Hill, New York, 1983.

Scannell, E.E. and Newstrom, J., *Still More Games Trainers Play: Experiential Learning Exercises*, McGraw-Hill, New York, 1991.

Scannell, E.E. and Newstrom, J., *Even More Games Trainers Play: Experiential Learning Exercises*, McGraw-Hill, New York, 1994.

Scannell, E.E. and Newstrom, J., *The Big Book of Presentation Games*, McGraw-Hill, New York, 1998.

Scannell, E.E. and Newstrom, J., *The Big Book of Teambuilding Games*, McGraw-Hill, New York, 1998.

Snow, H., *Indoor/Outdoor Team-Building Games for Trainers: Powerful Activities from the World of Adventure-Based Team-Building and ROPES Courses*, McGraw-Hill, New York, 1997.

Solem, L. and Pike, B., *50 Creative Training Closers*, Jossey-Bass/Pfeiffer, San Francisco, CA, 1997.

Sugar, S. and Takacs, G., *Games That Teach Teams*, Jossey-Bass/Pfeiffer, San Francisco, CA, 2000.

Summers, G.J., *The Great Book of Mind Teasers & Mind Puzzles*, Sterling Publishing, New York, 1996.

Thiagarajan, S. and Parker, E., *Teamwork & Teamplay: Games and Activities for Building and Training Teams*, Jossey-Bass/Pfeiffer, San Francisco, CA, 1999.

Ukens, L.L., *Energize Your Audience: 75 Quick Activities That Get Them Started and Keep Them Going*, Jossey-Bass/Pfeiffer, San Francisco, CA, 2000.

Wujec, T., *Five Star Mind: Games & Puzzles to Stimulate Your Creativity & Imagination*, Doubleday, New York, 1995.

Adult Learning, Learning, and Intelligence

Bransford, J.D., Brown, A.L., and Cocking, R.R., *How People Learn: Brain, Mind, Experience and School*, National Academy Press, Washington, DC, 2000.

Caroselli, M., *Memory Tips for the Forgetful*, Richard Chang Associates, Irvine, CA, 1999.

Dryden, G. and Vos, J., *The Learning Revolution: To Change the Way the World Learns*, The Learning Web, Torrance, CA, 1999.

Gardner, H., *Multiple Intelligences: The Theory in Practice*, Basic Books, New York, 1993.

Hayes, E. and Flannery, D.D., *Women as Learners: The Significance of Gender in Adult Learning*, Jossey-Bass, San Francisco, CA, 2000.

Knowles, M., *The Adult Learner: A Neglected Species*, Gulf Publishing, Houston, TX, 1984.

Knowles, M.S., Holten III, E.F., and Swanson, R.A., *The Adult Learner*, 5th ed., Butterworth-Heinemann, Woburn, MA, 1998.

Merriam, S.B. and Caffarella, R.S., *Learning in Adulthood: A Comprehensive Guide*, Jossey Bass, San Francisco, CA, 1999.

Appearance and Image

Bixler, S. and Nix-Rice, N., *The New Professional Image: From Business to the Ultimate Power Look*, Adams Media, Avon, MA, 1997.

Malloy, J.T., *New Woman's Dress for Success*, Warner Books, New York, 1996.

Maysonave, S., *Casual Power: How to Power Up Your Nonverbal Communication and Dress for Success*, Bright Books, Austin, TX, 1999.

Weber, M., *Dress Casually for Success . . . for Men*, McGraw-Hill, New York, 1996.

Wetzel, K. and Harmeyer, K., *Mind Games: The Aging Mind and How to Keep It Healthy*, Thomson Learning, Albany, NY, 2000.

Brain-based and Active Learning

Dennison, P.E. and Dennison, G.E., *Brain Gym*, Edu-Kinesthetics, Ventura, CA, 1994.

Hall, D., *Jump Start Your Brain*, Warner Books, New York, 1995.

Hannaford, C., *Smart Moves: Why Learning is NOT All in Your Head*, Great Ocean Publishers, Arlington, VA, 1995.

Hannaford, C., *The Dominance Factor: How Knowing Your Dominant Eye, Ear, Brain, Hand & Foot Can Improve Your Learning*, Great Ocean Publishers, Arlington, VA, 1997.

Herrmann, N., *The Creative Brain*, The Ned Herrmann Group, lake Lure, NC, 1995.

Ivy, D.K. and Backland, P., *Exploring Gender Speak: Personal Effectiveness in Gender Learning*, McGraw-Hill, New York, 1994.

Jensen, E., *Super Teaching*, The Brain Store, San Diego, CA, 1995.

Jensen, E., *Brain-Based Learning*, Turning Point, Delmar, CA, 1996.

Jensen, E., *Sizzle and Substance: Presenting with the Brain in Mind*, The Brain Store, San Diego, CA, 1998.

Pierce, H.J., *The Owner's Manual for the Brain: Everyday Applications from Mind-Brain Research*, 2nd ed., Bard Press, Marietta, GA, 2000.

Race, P. and Smith, B., *500 Tips for Trainers*, Gulf Publishing, Houston, TX., 1996.

Rose, C. and Nicholl, M.J., *Accelerated Learning for the 21st Century: The Six-Step Plan to Unlock Your Master-Mind*, Dell, New York, 1997.

Silverman, M., *101 Ways to Make Training Active*, Pfeiffer & Co., San Diego, CA, 1995.

Sylwester, R., *A Celebration of Neurons: An Educator's Guide to the Brain*, ASCD, Alexandria, VA, 1995.

Environment

Wolverton, B.C., *How to Grow Fresh Air: 50 Houseplants That Purify Your Home and Office*, Penguin Books, New York, 1997.

Graphics and Design

Backer, L. and Deck, M., *The Presenter's EZ Graphics Kit: A Guide for the Artistically Challenged*, Mosby, St. Louis, MO, 1996.

Bromley, K., Irwin-DeVitis, L., and Modlo, M., *Graphic Organizers: Visual Strategies for Active Learning*, Scholastic, New York, 1995.

Frank, D., *Terrific Training Materials: High Impact Graphic Designs for Workbooks, Handouts, Instructor Guides and Job Aids*, HRDPress, Amherst, MA, 1996.

Griffin, G. and Walker, K., *How to Draw Funny Faces*, Kidsbooks, Chicago, IL, 1999.

Kearny, L., *Graphics for Presenters: Getting Your Ideas Across*, Crisp Publications, Menlo Park, CA, 1996.

Lucas, R.W., *The Big Book of Flip Charts*, McGraw-Hill, New York, 1999.

Rabb, M.Y., *The Presentation Design Book: Projecting a Good Image With Your Desktop Computer*, Ventura Press, Chapel Hill, NC, 1990.

Raines, C., *Visual Aids in Business: A Guide for Effective Presentations*, Crisp Publications, Los Altos, CA, 1989.

Robertson, B., *How to Draw Charts and Diagrams*, North Light Books, Cincinnati, OH, 1988.

Rosen, M. and Kurzban, S., *Puzzle Makers Handbook: How to Create and Market Your Own Crosswords and Other Word Puzzles*, Random House, New York, 1995.

Sonneman, M.R., *Beyond Words: A Guide to Drawing Out Ideas*, Ten Speed Press, Berkeley, CA, 1997.

Tollison, H., *Cartooning*, Walter Foster, Tustin, CA, 1989.

Wescott, J. and Hammond Landau, J., *A Picture's Worth 1000 Words: A Workbook for Visual Communication*, Jossey-Bass/Pfeiffer, San Francisco, CA, 1997.

Zelazny, G., *Say It With Charts: The Executive's Guide to Visual Communication*, 3rd Ed., McGraw-Hill, New York, 1996.

Training and Communicating with Diverse Audiences

Axtell, R.A., *Gestures: The DO's and TABOOs of Body Language Around the World*, John Wiley & Sons, New York, 1991.

Axtell, R.A., *Gestures: The DO's and TABOOs of Using English Around the World*, John Wiley & Sons, New York, 1995.

Dresser, N., *Multicultural Manners: New Rules of Etiquette for a Changing World*, John Wiley & Sons, New York, 1996.

Foster, J., *How to Get Ideas*, Berrett-Koehler, San Francisco, CA, 1996.

Gray, J., *Men Are from Mars, Women Are from Venus: A Practical Guide for Improving Communication and Getting What You Want in Relationships*, HarperCollins, New York, 1992.

Maloff, C., and Wood, S.M., *Business and Social Etiquette with Disabled People: A Guide to Getting Along with Persons Who Have Impairments of Mobility, Vision, Hearing, or Speech*, Charles C Thomas, Springfield, IL, 1988.

Morris, D., *Bodytalk: The Meaning of Human Gestures*, Crown, New York, 1994.

Morrison, T., Conaway, W.A., and Boren, G.A., *Kiss, Bow, or Shake Hands*, Adams Media, Holbrook, MA, 1994.

Reardon, K.K., *They Don't Get It, Do They? Communication in the Workplace—Closing the Gap Between Women and Men*, Little, Brown and Company, Boston, MA, 1995.

Tannen, D., *You Just Don't Understand: Women and Men in Conversation*, Ballantine Books, New York, 1990.

Tannen, D., *Talking from 9 to 5—Women and Men in the Workplace: Language, Sex and Power*, Avon Books, New York, 1994.

Tracey, W.R., *Training Employees with Disabilities: Strategies to Enhance Learning and Development for an Expanding Part of Your Workforce*, AMACOM, New York, 1995.

Van Gundy, A.B., *Brain Boosters for Business Advantage: Ticklers, Grab Bags, Blue Skies, and Other Bionic Ideas*, Pfeiffer & Company, San Diego, CA, 1995.

Wolfgang, A., *Everybody's Guide to People Watching*, Intercultural Press, Yarmouth, MA, 1995.

Creativity and Creative Problem-Solving

Ayan, J., *Aha!:10 Ways to Free Your Creative Spirit and Find Great Ideas*, Three Rivers Press, New York, 1997.

Buzan, T., *The Mind Map Book—Radiant Thinking*, BBC, London, 1993.

Forbes, R., *The Creative Problem Solvers Toolbox: A Complete Course in the Art of Getting Solutions to Problems of Any Kind*, Solutions Through Innovation, Portland, OR, 1993.

Higgins, J.M., *101 Creative Problem Solving Techniques: The Handbook of New Ideas for Business*, The New Management Publishing Company, Winter Park, FL, 1994.

Leonard, D. and Swap, W., *When Sparks Fly: Igniting Creativity with Groups*, Harvard Business School Press, Boston, MA, 1999.

Mattimore, B.W., *99% Inspiration: Tips, Tales & Techniques for Liberating Your Business Creativity*, AMACOM, New York, 1994.

Michalko, M., *Thinkertoys: A Handbook of Business Creativity for the 90s*, Ten Speed Press, Berkeley, CA, 1991.

von Oech, R., *A Whack on the Side of the Head*, Warner, New York, 1990.

Motivation

Kohn, A., *Punished by Rewards: The Trouble with Gold Stars, Incentive Plans, As, Praise and Other Bribes,* Houghton Mifflin, Boston, MA, 1993.

Music

Campbell, D., *The Mozart Effect,* Avon Books, New York, 1997.

Jensen, E., *Music with the Brain in Mind,* The Brain Store, San Diego, CA, 2000.

Millbower, L., *Training with a Beat,* Stylus, Sterling, VA, 2000.

Vos, J., *The Music Revolution,* Learning Web, Auckland, New Zealand, 1999.

Products/Seminars

Brain and Creative Thinking Products/Books

MindWare
121 Fifth Avenue, N.W.
New Brighton, MN 55112
(800)274-6123
www.mindwareonline.com

Creative games, books, and materials

The BrainStore
4202 Sorrento Valley Blvd., Ste B
San Diego, CA 92121
(858)546-7555/(800)325-4769
www.thebrainstore.com

Books, reference materials, and props related to brain-based learning and teaching

Button/Badge Makers

Badge a Minit
345 North Lewis Avenue
Oglesby, IL 61348
(815)883-9696
(800)223-4103
www.badgeaminit.com

Button/badge making equipment and supplies

Clip Art

ClickArt
Broderbund
88 Rowland Way
Novato, CA 94945
(415)895-2000
www.broderbund.com

Key Mega ClipArt 7000
The Learning Company
One Athenaeum Street
Cambridge, MA 02142
(800)845-8692
www.learningco.com

Key Click Art 5,001
The Learning Company
One Athenaeum Street

Cambridge, MA 02142
(800)845-8692
www.learningco.com

3000 Customatic Clip Art
COSMI
2600 Homestead Place
Rancho Dominguez, CA 90220
(310)886-3510
www.cosmi.com

1500 Clip Art Images
COSMI
2600 Homestead Place
Rancho Dominguez, CA 90220
(310)886-3510
www.cosmi.com

3500 Clip Art Images
Expert Software
P.O. Box 144506
Coral Gables, FL 33114-4506
(800)759-2562

Print House
Corel Corporation
1600 Carling Avenue
Ottawa, Ontario, Canada K1Z 8R7
(613)728-3733

PrintMaster
88 Rowland Way
Novato, CA 94945
(415)897-9900
www.printmaster.com

Print Shop
Broderbund
88 Rowland Way
Novato, CA 94945
(415)895-2000
www.broderbund.com

Creative Training Products/Sessions

Creative Presentation Resources, Inc.
P.O. Box 180487
Casselberry, FL 32718-0487
(407)695-5535/(800)308-0399
www.presentationresources.net

Toys, games, ribbons, Koosh® balls, chicken pointers, pencils, erasers, videos, books, copyright free music, overhead projector pointers, and props. Also creative training, train-the-trainer, and other workplace skills workshops

The Trainer's Warehouse
89 Washington Avenue
Natick, MA 01760
(508)653-3770/(800)299-3770
www.trainerswarehouse.com

Toys, electrical props, team games, books, artist's photo adhesive, overhead projector pointers and supplies, flip chart supplies

The Bob Pike Group
7620 West 78th Street
Minneapolis, MN 55439-2518
(800)383-9210
www.bobpikegroup.com

Seminars, toys, books, and props

Lakeshore Learning Materials
2695 E. Dominguez Street
Carson, CA 90810
(310)537-8600/(800)421-5354
www.lakeshorelearning.com

Toys and teacher supplies

Crossword Puzzle Software

Crosswords & Word Games/Crosswords and More
Creative Presentation Resources, Inc.
P.O. Box 180487
Casselberry, FL 32718-0487
(407)695-5535/(800)308-0399
www.presentationresources.net

Create customized word search, word match, crossword puzzles, and other word games

Fancy Paper/Presentation Supplies

Paper Direct
P.O. Box 2970
Colorado Springs, CO 80901-2970
(800)272-7377
www.paperdirect.com

Fancy paper and presentation equipment

Game Software/HRD Books

American Society for Training and Development
1640 King Street, Box 1443
Alexandria, VA 22314-2043
(800)628-2783
www.astd.org

Training books, reference materials, conferences, memberships, Gameshow Pro Software

Graphic Art Materials

Chartpak
(800)788-5572
www.chartpak.com

Graphic art materials, flexible curves

Staedtler, Inc.
P.O. Box 2196
Chatsworth, CA 91311
www.staedtler-USA.com
(800)776-5544

Graphic art supplies, flexible curves

Graphics Software

PowerPoint®
Microsoft®
One Microsoft Way
Redmond, WA 98052-6399
(425)882-8080
www.microsoft.com

Computer-generated slide program

Freelance Plus
Lotus Software
IBM Software Group
One Rogers Street
Cambridge, MA 02142
(617) 577-8500
www.lotus.com

Graphics and slide software

Harvard Graphics
Serif, Inc.
The Software Center
13 Hampshire Drive, Suite 12
Hudson, NH 03051-4948
(603) 889-8650
www.serif.com

Graphics and slide software for creation of charts, text, and graphs

Motivational Posters/Products

Successories
2520 Diehl Road
Aurora, IL 60504
(630)820-7200
www.successories.com

Motivational posters, plaques, books, and incentives

Music Licensing

BMI
10 Music Square East
Nashville, TN 32703
(800)925-8451
www.bmi.com

License agreements for use of copyrighted songs and music

ASCAP
One Lincoln Plaza
New York, NY 10023
(800)952-7227
www.ascap.com

License agreements for use of copyrighted songs and music

Office Supplies

Staples
500 Staples Drive
P.O. Box 9256
Framingham, MA 01701
(800)333-3330
www.staples.com

Office supplies and equipment

Office Depot 2200 Old Germantown Road Delray Beach, FL 33445 (888)463-3768 www.officedepot.com	Office supplies and equipment
Quill 100 Schelter Road Lincolnshire, IL 60069-3621 (800)789-8965 www.quill.com	Office supplies and equipment
Viking Office Products 950 West 190th Street Torrance, CA 90502-1001 (800)421-1222 www.vikingop.com	Office supplies and equipment

Party Supplies & Decorations

M&N International P.O. Box 64784 St. Paul, MN 55164-0784 (800)479-2043 www.mninternational.com	Party decorations, hats, and favors for various holiday celebrations

Presentation Equipment and Accessories

Graphic Products P.O. Box 4030 Beaverton, OR 97076-4030 (800)788-5572 www.graphicproducts.com	Electronic writing board and presentation equipment
Clearanswer Limited 11604 Carlsbad Road Reno, NV 89506 (775)845-7626 www.clearanswer.com	Static cling writing surfaces

Training Organizations

National ASTD
1640 King Street
Box 1443
Alexandria, VA
(800)628-2783
www.astd.org

International Alliance for Learning (IAL)
Box 26175
Colorado Springs, CO 80936
(800)426-2989/(719)596-6827
www.ialearn.org

International Federation of Training &
  Development Organizations (IFTDO)
www.iftdo.org

International Society for Performance
  Improvement (ISPI)
1400 Spring Street, Ste 260
Silver Spring, MD 20910
(301)587-8570
www.isp.org

National Speaker's Association
1500 S. Priest Drive
Tempe, AZ 85281
(480)968-2552
www.usaspeaker.org

Toastmasters International
P.O. Box 9052
Mission Viejo, CA 92690
(949)858-8255
www.toastmasters.org

Videos

Enterprise Media
91 Harvey Street
Cambridge, MA 02140
(800)423-6021
www.enterprisemedia.com

Creative Presentation Resources, Inc.
P.O. Box 180487
Casselberry, FL 32718-0487
(800)308-0399/(409)695-5535
Fax (407)695-7447
www.presentationresources.net

Contact information changes

Muppet video—*The Sky's the Limit*

Training videos on various topics

Tools for Trainers

Solution to How Many Squares? (from page 49)

No. of Squares	Location
1	Entire square
16	Squares 1–16
1	1,2,3,5,6,7,9,10,11
1	2,3,4,6,7,8,10,11,12
1	5,6,7,9,10,11,13,14,15
1	6,7,8,10,11,12,14,15,16
1	1,2,5,6
1	2,3,6,7,
1	3,4,7,8,
1	5,6,9,10
1	6,7,10,11
1	7,8,11,12
1	9,10,13,14
1	10,11,14,15
1	11,12,15,16
1	17,18,19,20
1	21,22,23,24
1	25,26,27,28
1	29,30,31,32
16	Squares 17–32

50 Total squares

Sample Brainstorming Guidelines

No criticism of ideas is allowed

Quantity, not quality, is encouraged

Anything goes; all ideas are valid

"Piggy-backing" of ideas is fine

No discussion of issues (do this later)

Everyone participates; no observers

One person speaks at a time

Use inclusive language (consider diversity)

LIGHTING THE CREATIVITY LAMP

Analogy ___S___   A. To dissect ideas logically

Brainstorming ___K___   B. Stage 1 of Creativity Process

Convergent ___A___   C. Stage 2 of Creativity Process

Divergent ___R___   D. Creator of Mind Mapping process

Enablers ___Q___   E. Use string, scarves, cards and money

Illumination ___G___   F. Reality Oriented Performance Experiential System

Illusions ___L___   G. Stage 4 of Creativity Process

Incubation ___C___   H. Conversations held with oneself

Inhibitors ___O___   I. Figure of speech referring one concept to another

Magic Tricks ___E___   J. The way a person views the world

Metaphor ___I___   K. Process for structured idea gathering

Mindmap ___N___   L. Pictures that distort perception

Paradigm ___J___   M. Allows acting out real-life issues

Preparation ___B___   N. Technique for making ideas visual

Role Play ___M___   O. Factors blocking creativity

ROPES ___F___   P. Stage 3 of Creativity Process

Self-talk ___H___   Q. Strategies to assist thinking outside the box

Tony Buzan ___D___   R. Generating large numbers of ideas

Verification ___P___   S. Relating one thing to something similar

FIGURE 2-4. Word Match Puzzle Answer Key (from page 57)

TRAINING AGREEMENT

Please consider this program a "*safe*" environment --- What we say here, stays here.

It's alright to...

- *Express your ideas.*
- *Challenge the facilitator's ideas.*
- *Offer examples (please keep them generic with no names used).*
- *Question.*
- *Relax.*

Your Role...

- *Be on time (from breaks and lunch).*
- *Participate.*
- *Learn in your own way.*
- *Provide honest, open feedback on evaluations.*
- *Enjoy yourself!*

Facilitator's Role...

- *Start and end on time.*
- *Professionally facilitate the exchange of information and knowledge.*
- *Allow time for and encourage your input.*
- *Listen nondefensively.*
- *Help you grow personally and professionally.*

PRESENTATION PREPLANNING CHECKLIST

Program _____

ACTION TAKEN
Facilities

_____ Who to call for help and phone number

_____ Emergency alarm procedure

_____ Location of copy machine

_____ Smoking/eating/drinking/cell phone policy verified

_____ Restroom location

_____ Phone location

_____ Stairs/elevators location

_____ Parking accommodations

_____ Snack/refreshment location

_____ Signs for direction to class

Room

_____ ADA compliance assessment (e.g., doors 32 inches wide, tabletops 30–54 feet high)

_____ Check light controls and set level

_____ Check temperature and set level

_____ Disconnect phone in room (if permissible)

_____ Chairs/tables—number and arrangement

_____ Extension cord (at least 25 feet with multiple three-prong outlets)

_____ Electrical cords taped down

_____ Location of electrical outlets

_____ Three-prong to two-prong plug adapter

_____ Pencil sharpener, if needed

_____ Coat rack, if applicable

_____ Lectern, if desired

_____ Water pitcher and glasses on tables

_____ Blinds drawn to avoid distractions

Overhead Projector

_____ Operational

_____ Spare bulb (test bulb in projector)

_____ Focused and positioned

_____ Glass, lens, and mirror cleaned of fingerprints and lint

_____ Focus adjusted

_____ First transparency in place

Computer/Projection Unit

_____ Operational

_____ Slide presentation installed on PC and a diskette backup copy present

_____ Compatible with projection system

_____ Connector cables work

_____ PowerPoint or other program presentation tested

_____ Remote available and working

_____ Laser pointer (if using)

Video/VCR/DVD Player

_____ Operational

_____ Location/visibility checked

_____ Sound level adjusted

_____ Video cued up to title frame or opening scenario

_____ Monitor screen clean, if using

_____ Projection screen set up, if using

_____ Heads cleaned, if using a VCR

Slide Projector

_____ Spare bulb (test bulb in projector)

_____ Focused and positioned

_____ Tray cued to slot no. 1

_____ Remote control

_____ Opaque slide in slot no. 1 and after last slide

Music

_____ CD/cassette present

_____ Cued to music start

_____ Volume adjusted

_____ Power source

_____ Extension cord, if needed

Screen

_____ Location/adjusted to prevent key stoning (90°)

_____ Size

Flip chart

_____ Location (light shining onto paper rather than from behind easel)

_____ Visibility checked

_____ Paper supply

_____ Pages tabbed

_____ Assorted markers—black, dark blue, dark green, red (check for dry ink)

_____ Rubber band across top

_____ Masking tape (1-inch width)

_____ Pointer (e.g., dowel rod, plucked chicken, cardboard arrow)

Microphone

_____ Lavaliere

_____ Extra cord length for movement

_____ Sound level checked

_____ Backup mike

Board

_____ Dry erase markers/chalk

_____ Eraser

_____ Clean

_____ White board cleaner, if appropriate

_____ Rags/towel

Refreshments

_____ Regular coffee

_____ Decaffeinated coffee

_____ Tea/hot water

_____ Juice

_____ Soft drinks

_____ Ice

_____ Water

_____ Sugar/cream

_____ Spoons

_____ Napkins

_____ Cups/glasses

_____ Other (e.g., food)

Participant/Instructor Materials

_____ Note pads

_____ Pencils/pens

_____ Handouts

_____ Nametags

_____ Roster

_____ Agenda, if needed

_____ Incentive rewards, if used

_____ Toys/props

_____ Program evaluations

Final Mini-Rehearsal

_____ Opening

_____ Sequence/time check

_____ Closing

IMPORTANT PROGRAM INFORMATION

Please follow these guidelines to assist in the facilitation of this workshop. Thank you.

Bob Lucas—Your Facilitator

- Find a seat where you are most comfortable, yet can fully participate in the program.

- Sit next to someone whom you do not know (Networking is so much FUN!!!).

- Switch your brain to the creative training mode before entering the room.

- Be prepared to share and gain new ideas with your peers.

- Upon entry into the room, go around and respond to each flip-charted question by placing a single vertical mark, where applicable (e.g., "I").

- On the 3 × 5 card given as you entered the room, please write something you expect from the workshop (i.e., one thing I expect from this workshop is . . .). Deposit the card in the box on the chair by the entrance as you enter the room.

WARNING ◈◈◈ WARNING ◈◈◈ WARNING ◈◈◈ WARNING

Entry into this program could change your views on how to conduct training and give presentations.

People who are. . .

- ✓ Set in their ways

- ✓ Unwilling to share their knowledge

- ✓ Of the belief that learning must always be serious

- ✓ Reluctant to have FUN

. . . may want to grab some coffee and go for a walk!! ☺☺☺

FIGURE 3-1. Entry handout

OPENING WITH A BANG

```
G N I M R O T S N I A R B S U
X D S N O I T C U D O R T N I
H H E B T J U F B A L L O O N
C S R R B E V L O V N I L I R
R N U U E E R E H P S O M T A
A E T R G N O I T N E T T A P
E T A C I N U M M O C L C T P
S W C H N J S P O R P W E C O
D O I A N I C E B R E A K E R
R R R L I G F A C T S V T P T
O K A L N S K J E E U A I X L
W I C E G A V C R Z L R I E I
D N S N S W W S O E A F U G W
S G O G N I B F R H U M O R F
I C S E T O U Q F I S L A Y K
```

AMAZE	COMMUNICATE	PROPS
ATMOSPHERE	EXPECTATIONS	QUOTES
ATTENTION	FACTS	RAPPORT
AVARFM	HUMOR	RELATE
BALLOON	ICEBREAKER	SHOCK
BEGINNINGS	INTERIMREVIEW	TEASERS
BINGO	INTRODUCTIONS	WORDSEARCH
BRAINSTORMING	INVOLVE	
CARICATURES	JIGSAW	
CHALLENGE	NETWORKING	

FIGURE 4-8. Sample Word Search: Opening With a Bang Answer Key (from page 154)

Tic, Tac, Toe Board

1	2	3
4	5	
6	7	8

PRESENTATION PIZZAZZ:
Adding Impact to Learning

by

BOB LUCAS
President, **Creative Presentation Resources, Inc.**

© Copyright 1993, 2001
Creative Presentation Resources, Inc.
P.O. Box 180487
Casselberry, Florida 32718-0487.
(800)308-0399/(407)695-5535.
E-Mail: blucas@presentationresources.net
All Rights Reserved.

FIGURE 8-1. Sample workbook cover sheets

PRESENTATION PIZZAZZ:
Adding Impact to Learning

A Special Presentation

by

BOB LUCAS
President, Creative Presentation Resources, Inc.

FIGURE 8-1. *(Continued)*

VIDEO EVALUATION FORM

1. Overall, what were the key points presented in the video? _____

_____

_____

2. How does what you saw apply to your own workplace or situation?

_____

_____

3. How does what you saw differ from your own workplace or situation?

_____

_____

4. What specific techniques did you see used that were effective in the situation(s) you viewed?

_____

_____

5. What specific techniques did you see used that were ineffective in the situation(s) you viewed?

_____

_____

6. What suggested changes can you offer to improve the outcome of the situation(s) viewed?

_____

_____

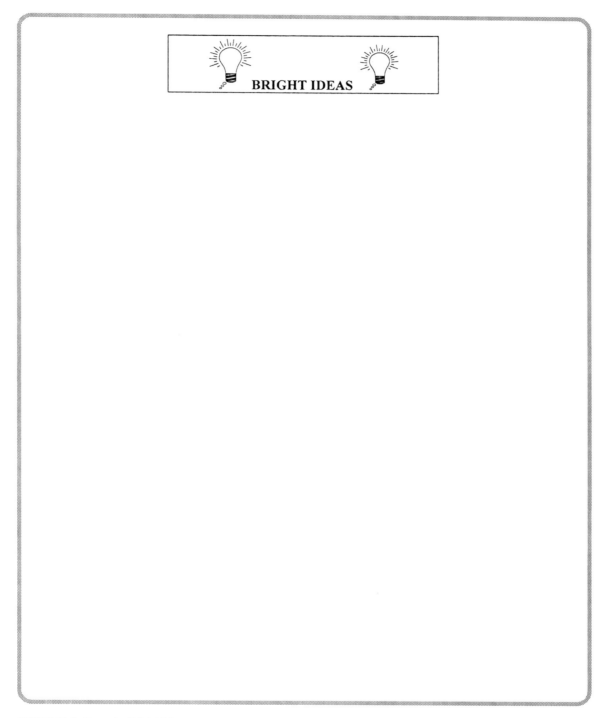

FIGURE 10-1. Sample Bright Ideas page

SAMPLE POST-SESSION PARTICIPANT QUESTIONNAIRE

Program _____

Date of program _____

Now that you have had (<u>number of days</u>) to apply what was learned in the training program, please respond to the following questions related to the session. Your feedback will assist in improving the quality and content of future training sessions.

1. What do you believe was the primary objective of the training session? _____

   _____

2. In what ways did the program accomplish its objectives and assist your on-the-job performance? (Please explain) _____

   _____

3. In what ways do you feel that the program could be improved to add more value? (Please explain)

   _____

   _____

4. What other skills and knowledge do you wish the program had addressed? (Please explain)

   _____

   _____

Print name _____
                    (Optional)

Signature _____

May we use your comments to promote this program in the future? Yes _____ No _____

If yes, give name and sign.

Thank you for taking the time to assist in making this program more valuable to you and the organization.

FIGURE 10-2. Sample post-session participant questionnaire

SAMPLE POST-SESSION SUPERVISOR/
CUSTOMER QUESTIONNAIRE

(<u>Name of Participant</u>) recently attended a workshop titled _____

in which the following objectives were addressed:

1.

2.

3.

To assist in future program improvements, it is important to have your perspective on how well new skills and knowledge gained in the session are being applied on the job. Please take a few minutes to rate the following based on the objectives listed above.

4. How often do you interact with (<u>Name of Participant</u>) during the week? (Please be specific)

5. The participant's ability to handle routine tasks prior to the program?

1	2	3	4	5	6	7
Low						High

Comments:

_____

_____

6. The participant's ability to handle routine tasks since attending the program?

1	2	3	4	5	6	7
Low						High

Comments:

_____

_____

7. In what performance or knowledge areas has the participant improved since the training?
   (Please be specific) _____

_____

continued

FIGURE 10-3. Sample post-session supervisor/customer questionnaire

8. In what performance or knowledge areas does the participant still need improvement? (Please be specific) _____

_____

9. General comments regarding the participant's knowledge or performance:

_____

_____

Print name _____
            (Optional)

May we contact you to clarify your comments? Yes _____ No _____

Thank you for taking the time to provide this valuable feedback.

FIGURE 10-3. *(Continued)*

Graphics for Trainers

ACTIVITY SHAPES

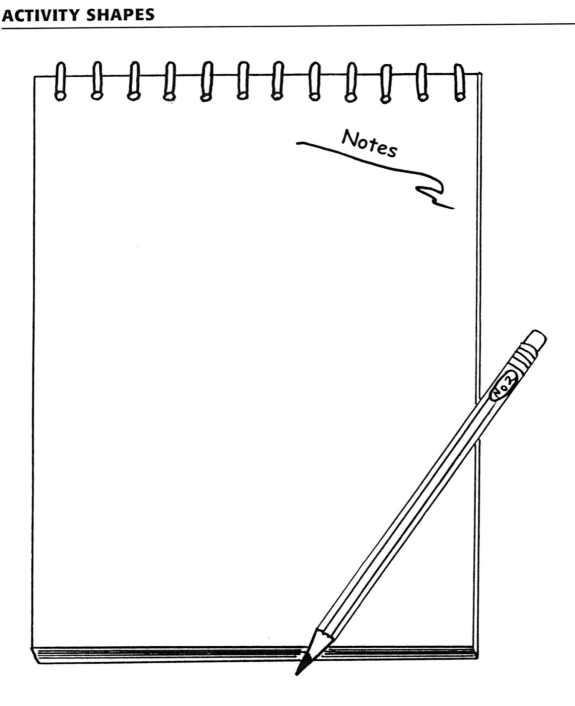

Communicating with Graphic Images

ACTIVITY SHAPES

Communicating with Graphic Images

ACTIVITY SHAPES

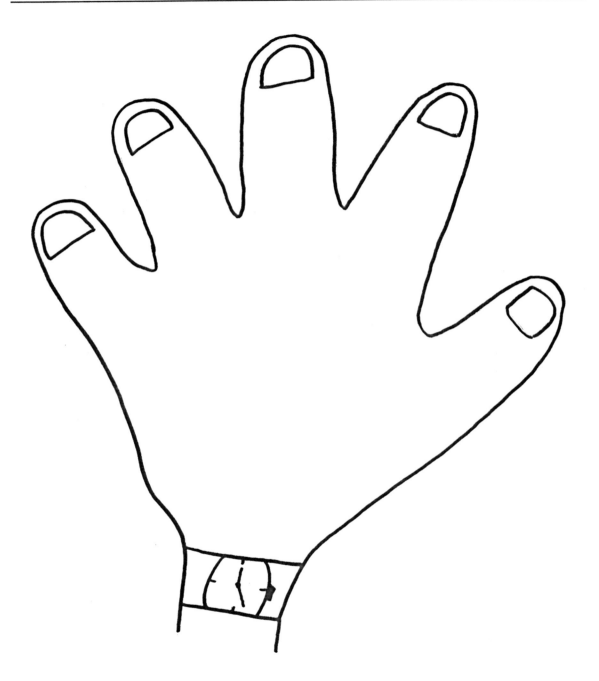

Communicating with Graphic Images

ACTIVITY SHAPES

Communicating with Graphic Images

ACTIVITY SHAPES

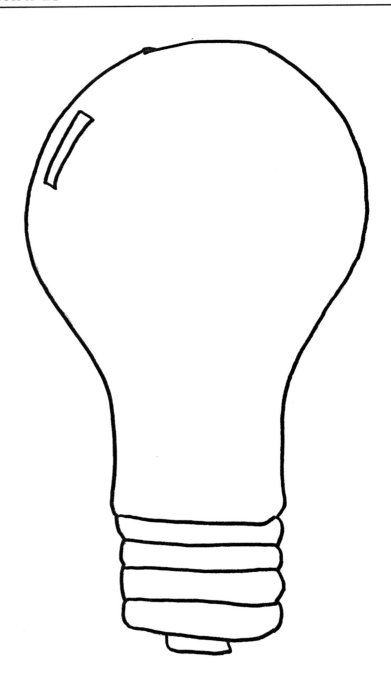

Communicating with Graphic Images

ACTIVITY SHAPES

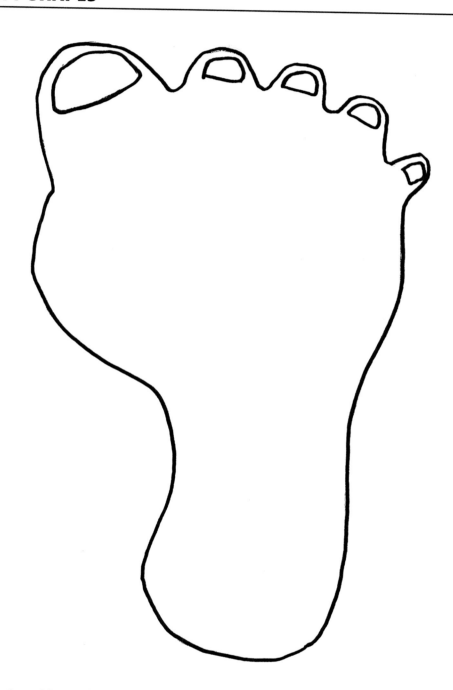

Communicating with Graphic Images

ACTIVITY SHAPES

Communicating with Graphic Images

ACTIVITY SHAPES

Communicating with Graphic Images

ACTIVITY SHAPES

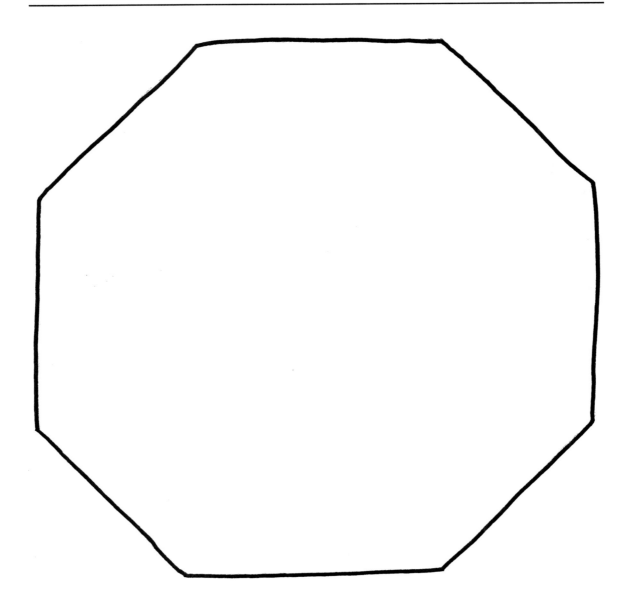

Communicating with Graphic Images

ACTIVITY SHAPES

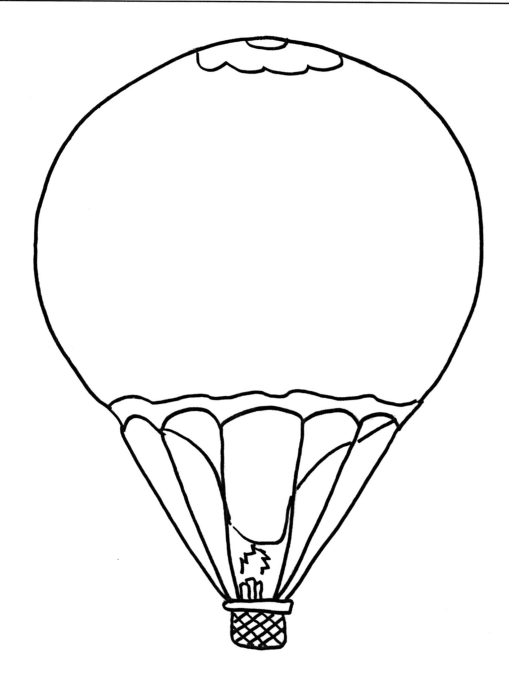

Communicating with Graphic Images

ACTIVITY SHAPES

Communicating with Graphic Images

ACTIVITY SHAPES

Communicating with Graphic Images

ACTIVITY SHAPES

Communicating with Graphic Images

ACTIVITY SHAPES

Communicating with Graphic Images

BASIC ART SHAPES

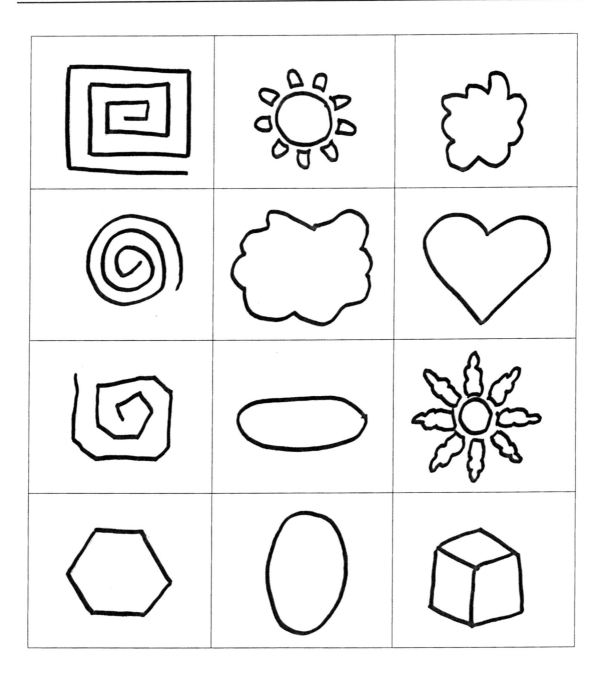

Communicating with Graphic Images

BASIC ART SHAPES

Communicating with Graphic Images

BASIC ART SHAPES—THINGS

Archery Target	Football Goal	Mountains
Open Mind	Storm Cloud	Brick Wall
Sun	Finger Reminder	Magic Hat
Overhead Projector	Flying Time	Flip Chart

Communicating with Graphic Images

BASIC ART SHAPES—THINGS

Building	School	Church
House	Cityscape	Idea Bulb
Flip Chart	Overhead Projector	Computer
Flower	Pencil	Telephone

Communicating with Graphic Images

BASIC ART SHAPES—THINGS

Money	Clock	Stoplight
Book	Book	Truck
Justice Scale	Building Blocks	Lock and Key
Sailboat	Hot Air Balloon	Cruise Ship

Communicating with Graphic Images

BASIC ART SHAPES—THINGS

Lightning Bolt	Mailbox	Artist's Pallet
Balloons	Rabbit	Giraffe
Palm Tree	Tent	Flowers
Lady Bug	Elephant	Bird

Communicating with Graphic Images

BASIC ART SHAPES—STICK FIGURES

Communicating with Graphic Images

BASIC ART SHAPES—STAR PEOPLE

Communicating with Graphic Images

BASIC ART SHAPES—FACIAL FEATURES (EYES)

Communicating with Graphic Images

BASIC ART SHAPES—FACIAL FEATURES (NOSES)

Communicating with Graphic Images

BASIC ART SHAPES—FACIAL FEATURES (MOUTHS)

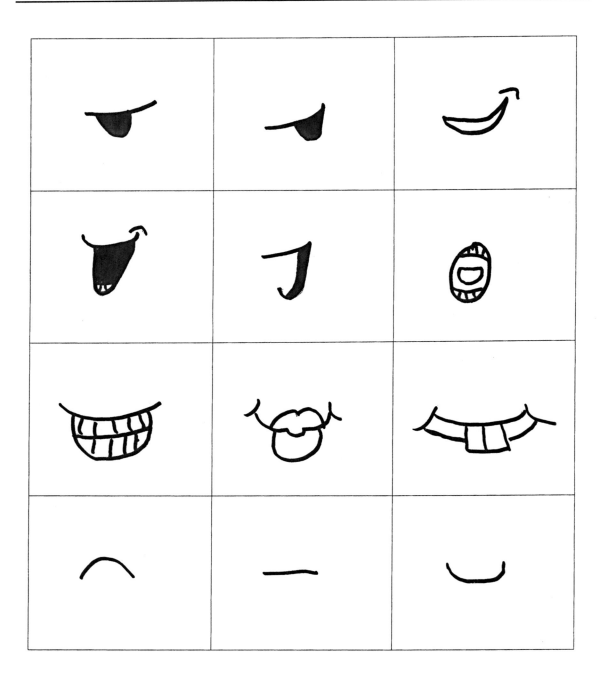

Communicating with Graphic Images

BASIC ART SHAPES—FACIAL FEATURES (EARS)

Communicating with Graphic Images

BASIC ART SHAPES—FACIAL FEATURES (FACES)

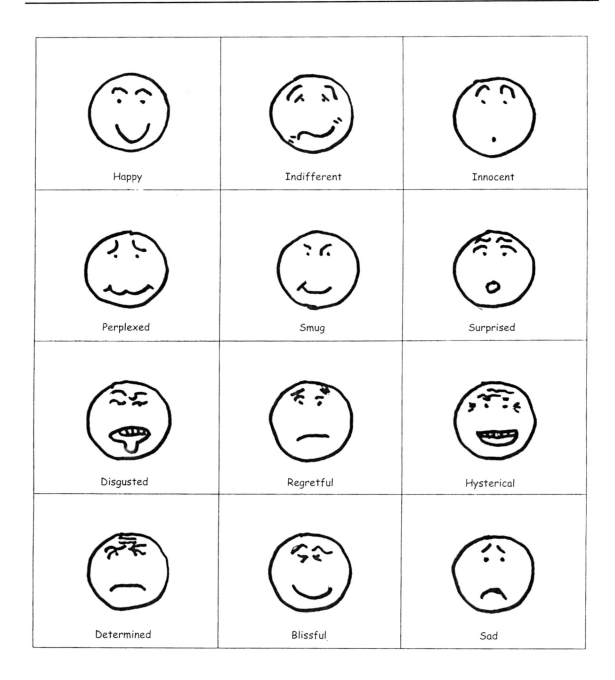

Communicating with Graphic Images

BASIC ART SHAPES–ICON BULLETS

Using symbols, icons or bullets helps direct participant attention to the beginning of a new idea or point. They also allow you to add a bit of pizazz and color to your flipcharts. Here are some possible considerations:

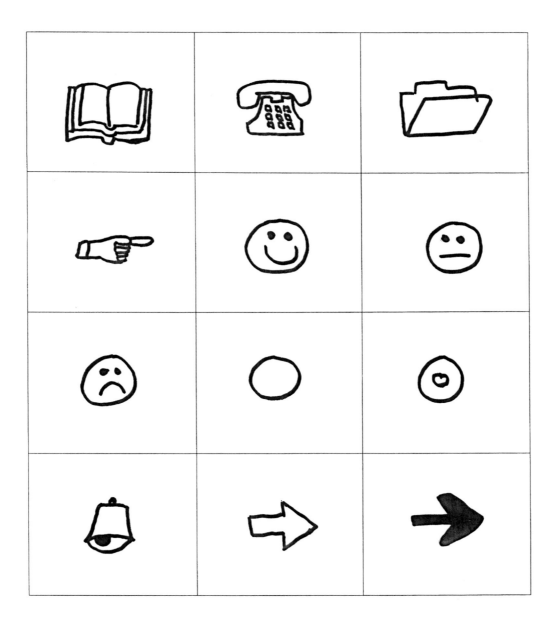

Communicating with Graphic Images

BASIC ART SHAPES—ICON BULLETS

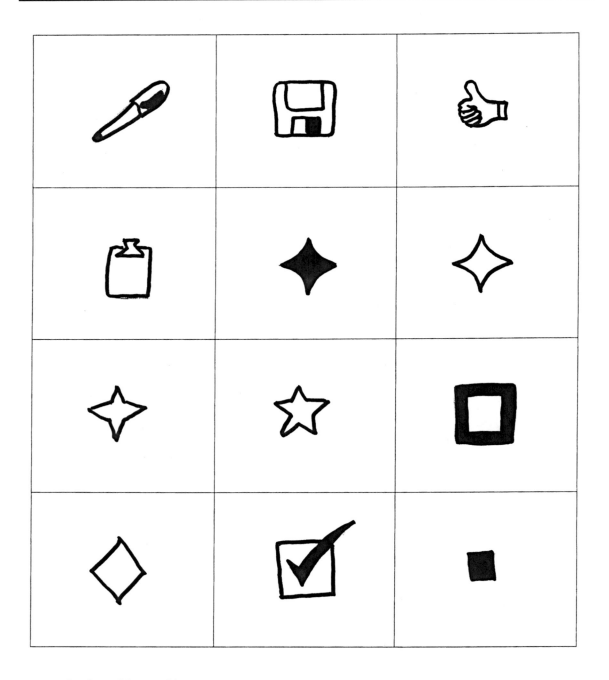

Communicating with Graphic Images

Index

Printed in the United States
149331LV00003B/2/A